In This Academy

In This Academy

THE PENNSYLVANIA ACADEMY OF THE FINE ARTS, 1805-1976

A SPECIAL
BICENTENNIAL EXHIBITION

ORGANIZED BY THE
PENNSYLVANIA ACADEMY OF THE FINE ARTS

1976

Library of Congress Catalog Number 76-2131

DESIGNED BY KURT WIENER
PRINTED IN THE UNITED STATES OF AMERICA
BY MUSEUM PRESS, INC., WASHINGTON, D.C.

THIS EXHIBITION AND CATALOGUE ARE SUPPORTED BY GRANTS FROM THE NATIONAL ENDOWMENT FOR THE ARTS IN WASHINGTON, D.C., A FEDERAL AGENCY, AND THE COMMONWEALTH OF PENNSYLVANIA COUNCIL ON THE ARTS.

Cover Illustration
Taken from William Sidney Mount, *The Painter's Triumph,* (cat. no. 72)

Frontispiece
Richard Diebenkorn, *Interior with Doorway,* (cat. no. 316)

CONTENTS

The Pennsylvania Academy of the Fine Arts represents a kind of heart line in the history of American art. It stretches from the tentative beginnings of a serious regard for art in America in the late eighteenth century, through the various vicissitudes that marked its course in the century that followed, to the self-consciously anti-academic attitudes of more recent times. Through it all the Academy has been an eager teacher, a discerning patron, and at times an understandably alarmed—but forgiving—parent. Its existence as a center for artists and a home for art has lent strength and stability to a mobile scene, not only in Philadelphia but for American art in general. Over the years it has built up one of the major collections of American art, and no proper research in the field can be carried on without consulting its archives and the records of its exhibitions.

JOSHUA C. TAYLOR
Director
National Collection of Fine Arts

What I admire most about the Pennsylvania Academy is its integrity. If the chief job of the museum is to preserve, as I believe it is, then the Academy has done its job well. The great Furness building remains intact while most of our other nineteenth-century museums have been "improved" beyond recognition. The collection itself is a fine one, greater by far as a preserved whole than as a gathering of undeniable masterworks. In an age when museums seek to dazzle, the Academy is one of a handful of institutions which seeks to preserve its heritage, keeping faith with the past while planning for the future.

THEODORE E. STEBBINS, JR.
Curator of American
Painting and Sculpture
Yale University Art Gallery

The Pennsylvania Academy of the Fine Arts is the oldest art institution in the United States. Important for almost two centuries, it is still vital today. It stands for the long tradition of fine arts in America that can look to the past with pride and the future with confidence.

JAMES THOMAS FLEXNER

PREFACE

Walking north from City Hall along Broad Street, the visitor to Philadelphia will unexpectedly discover one of the city's most remarkable architectural landmarks. Although it is almost obscured by modern office towers, the instant this building comes into view it reveals a structure of uncommon design and exceptional strength. Completed in 1876, restored in 1976, and conceived in a style variously called "High Victorian," "Venetian Gothic," or "Polychrome Picturesque," this extraordinary building is the home of an extraordinary organization — the Pennsylvania Academy of the Fine Arts.

The Pennsylvania Academy of the Fine Arts is unique among American art institutions, and its formation gave America its first true art museum. The Academy was founded in 1805, just six years after the death of George Washington and during Thomas Jefferson's second administration; the application for its charter was signed in Independence Hall, and its first president, George Clymer, was a signer of the Declaration of Independence. Thereafter, in a manner of speaking, the Academy grew with the country. By 1905, at its hundredth anniversary celebration, William Merritt Chase could call it "the most important art institution in America." And indeed it was. It was also the oldest.

With one or two exceptions, the great boom in American museum construction in the nineteenth century began in the seventies, when plans for the Academy's third and present building were already well underway. The Wadsworth Atheneum in Hartford was founded in 1842, the Corcoran Gallery of Art in Washington, D.C. in 1869, the Metropolitan Museum of Art in New York and the Boston Museum of Fine Arts in 1870, and the Philadelphia Museum of Art in 1876.

While other museums were forming their collections and erecting their buildings, the Pennsylvania Academy continued its leading role in the training and support of the American artist. Its annual exhibitions were internationally known and included the best American art of the day, much of which was acquired for the Academy's collection. William Merritt Chase was just one painter in a long list of American artists who were associated with the Academy as exhibitors and who, as students and teachers in its school, helped to build its tradition and shape its direction.

The Academy's age and tradition, its long service in the support of American art, the significance of its school and collection, and its continuing vitality make it one of the most important art institutions in this country and certainly the most historically important in Philadelphia. Yet history is only a part of what makes it unique. To those who come to know it, it is a very special place, and for those who know it well, it is a very special place indeed. The word institution does not adequately describe its easy informality, its accessibility, or the very personal quality that pervades its atmosphere and gives the Academy its particular charm. Although it cannot be called a neighborhood museum, it nevertheless has a strong community feeling; its traditions are intensely local as well as national. Local architects designed each of its buildings, and the competition for the design of the present building was actually limited to Philadelphia architects. Its school is heir to the tradition of Charles Willson Peale, Thomas Eakins, Robert Henri, and Arthur Carles, and its collection was formed primarily by Philadelphia taste. When Academy tradition parted with national tradition, it did so because of local preference.

Too much emphasis on local tradition can be a weakness. It leads to parochialism, of which the Academy had been guilty in the past. However, it is also a source of strength; it does give the Academy a strong sense of continuity, and as indicated by the exhibition *In This Academy,* it is the combination of national and local tradition which gives this institution its character. When the charter for the Pennsylvania Academy was written, the two traditions were synonymous. "The Object of this Association," it states, "is to promote the cultivation of the fine arts in the United States of America." That was in 1805. Today, 171 years later, that purpose is still the same.

And it is to this purpose that the exhibition is addressed. The ten essays in the catalogue, each in its own way, examine the Academy's historic role in the development of American art and consider the American tradition side by side with that of the Pennsylvania Academy.

RICHARD J. BOYLE
Director

ACKNOWLEDGMENTS

With the resurgence of interest in American arts during the past twenty years has come a deeper and broader understanding of American painting. The state of scholarship in American painting has improved dramatically over the past two decades, but, nonetheless, it is still in its infancy. Scholarly monographs, catalogues raisonnés, and catalogues of important public collections of American art are scarce. Serious voids in the literature on American painting exist. One such lacuna has been the recognition of the historic role of America's oldest existing art institution, the Pennsylvania Academy of the Fine Arts, in the development of an American tradition in painting. One purpose of this catalogue is to bridge the gap between traditional assumptions about the Pennsylvania Academy and heretofore obscured or unknown facts. This catalogue is the initial effort to evaluate the Pennsylvania Academy's 170-year history.

The catalogue and exhibition reflect the collaborative thinking and work of many dedicated professionals. I am particularly grateful to Louise Lippincott, who has performed the endless tasks of this exhibition with diligence, responsibility, and wit. Her daily assistance has been incalculable. Each of the guest curators — Doreen Bolger, Carolyn Diskant, Joan Marter, and Mark Thistlethwaite — has made valuable contributions to the exhibition. Their careful scholarship has added to a greater understanding of the Academy, and each has our sincerest thanks.

I am also grateful to Caryl Horty and Margaret Pyle Hassert for editing the entire manuscript of the catalogue. Their insistence on excellence has greatly improved the substance and form of the catalogue.

In This Academy is more than an exhibition of the Academy's great American collection. The Academy wishes to acknowledge the generosity of museums and private collectors for making works of art available to the exhibition, and wishes especially to thank Richard Brown Baker, Sydney and Frances Lewis, Mr. and Mrs. Harrison S. Wright, Mrs. Percy Madiera, Mr. and Mrs. Henry S. McNeil, Sewell Biggs, Dr. and Mrs. Elliot Vesell, Cecily Langdale, Roy Davis, Mr. and Mrs. Francis Walters, Mrs. John C. LeClair, Ruth Martin, Helen Farr Sloan, Antoinette Kraushaar, Mrs. John Wintersteen, Meyer and Vivian Potamkin, the Sidney Janis Gallery, Ann Freedman of the André Emmerich Gallery, and Mr. Lawrence Rubin of Knoedler Contemporary Art.

The authors wish to acknowledge the following scholars, curators, registrars, teachers, and friends for their assistance: Evan Turner, Darrel Sewell, Anne d'Harnoncourt, and Barbara Chandler of the Philadelphia Museum of Art; Laura Luckey of the Museum of Fine Arts, Boston; William P. Campbell of the National Gallery of Art; Elizabeth Culler of the Virginia Museum of Fine Arts; Frances M. Gupton of the Amon Carter Museum of Western Art; Peter Marlow of the Wadsworth Atheneum; Professor John W. McCoubrey of the University of Pennsylvania; Professor William H. Gerdts, Beth Treadway, Ronald Pisano; Sarah Faunce and Linda Ferber of the Brooklyn Museum; Percy North, Lois and Harvey Dinnerstein, Lily Harmon, Robert Philipp, Alice Melrose of the National Academy of Design; John K. Howat, Natalie Spassky, Lewis I. Sharp, and Margaret Lawson of the Metropolitan Museum of Art; Carolyn Milligan and Jerry Hand of the American Philosophical Society; Roberta K. Tarbell, Deborah B. Thomas, Joseph Fraser, Morris Blackburn, Teri Edelstein, and Randi Thistlethwaite.

For their thoughtful commentaries on the Pennsylvania Academy, our thanks to Professor Theodore E. Stebbins, Jr. of Yale University, Joshua C. Taylor, Director, National Collection of Fine Arts, and James Thomas Flexner.

Robert Venturi, Steven Izenour, Tony Atkins, Stanford Hughes, and Stanley Taraila of Venturi and Rauch have brought their own creative flair and deep appreciation of architecture and art to the design of the exhibition. They have the Academy's sincerest thanks.

Hy Myers has aided tremendously in anticipating many of the installation problems of the exhibition. His dedicated enthusiasm for the Academy is a source of great inspiration.

For their quality work in the design and publication of the exhibition catalogue, the Academy thanks Kurt Wiener and Sheldon Caplan of Museum Press, Inc.

Finally, I personally want to thank every member of the Academy's staff, each of whom has in some way aided in the preparation of this exhibition. Their assistance has been immeasurable. I am particularly indebted to Richard J. Boyle, Joseph Amarotico, Elizabeth Bailey, Susan Leidy, Louise Schutz, Kathy Zickler, Jay MacLaughlin, Pam Carunchio, and Phebe Cooke and Barbara Greenfield of the Women's Committee of the Pennsylvania Academy. For the past year Marcela de Keyser has shouldered the brunt of daily correspondence and the preparation of the catalogue manuscripts with dedication and willingness. Grateful acknowledgement is made to Edward I. Bernstein, Harvey Steinberg, Charles S. Steinberg, and Joel Cohen of Quaker Moving and Storage Company.

FRANK H. GOODYEAR, JR.
Curator

LENDERS TO THE EXHIBITION

American Philosophical Society
Anonymous Lenders
Art Institute of Chicago
Mr. Richard Brown Baker
Mr. Sewell Biggs
The Brooklyn Museum
Mr. and Mrs. Ralph Carron
Amon Carter Museum of Western Art
The Colorado Springs Fine Arts Center
The Columbus Gallery of Fine Arts
Commerce Bancshares, Inc.
Davis and Long Company
The Detroit Institute of Arts
Andre Emmerich Gallery
Fort Worth Art Museum
The Forum Gallery
Mr. Frederick Fraley
Indianapolis Museum of Art
Sidney Janis Gallery
Joslyn Art Museum
Mrs. Alberta Allen Kelly
Kraushaar Galleries
Mrs. John C. LeClair
Mr. and Mrs. Sydney Lewis
The Library of Congress
Marian Locks Gallery
Mrs. Percy C. Madiera, Jr.
Mr. R. Lee Mastin
The Metropolitan Museum of Art
Mrs. J. Maxwell Moran
Munson-Williams-Proctor Institute
Museum of Fine Arts, Boston
The Museum of Modern Art
National Collection of Fine Arts, Smithsonian Institution
National Gallery of Art
William Rockhill Nelson Gallery of Art
Pennsylvania Horticultural Society
Philadelphia Museum of Art
Mr. and Mrs. Meyer Potamkin
Mr. Richard J. Ranck
Mrs. Herbert P. Reed
Lawrence Rubin, Knoedler Contemporary Art
Dr. and Mrs. Ira Leo Schamberg
Mr. Charles Coleman Sellers
Mrs. John Sloan
Mr. and Mrs. James Titelman
Dr. Elliot Vesell
Virginia Museum of Fine Arts
Wadsworth Atheneum
Mary MacDowell Walters
Mrs. William H. S. Wells
Mr. Nelson White
Whitney Museum of American Art
Mrs. John Wintersteen
Mr. and Mrs. Harrison S. Wright

Unless otherwise indicated, the works of art illustrated in this catalogue are owned by The Pennsylvania Academy of the Fine Arts.

Frank H. Goodyear, Jr.

A HISTORY OF THE PENNSYLVANIA ACADEMY OF THE FINE ARTS, 1805-1976

THE OBJECT of this association is to promote the cultivation of the FINE ARTS in the United States of America, by introducing correct and elegant copies from works of the first masters in sculpture and painting and by thus facilitating the access to such standards, and also by occasionally conferring moderate but honorable premiums and otherwise assisting the studies and exciting the efforts of the artist gradually to unfold, enlighten and invigorate the talents of our countrymen.

Application for Charter
Pennsylvania Academy of the Fine Arts
December 26, 1805 PAFA Archives

The 170-year history of the Pennsylvania Academy of the Fine Arts has been distinguished by growth and indifference, by stunning successes and discouraging failures. Each generation has contributed its own deeds to the association that has become the Pennsylvania Academy of the Fine Arts, building on the public-spirited vision of its seventy-one founders.

The Pennsylvania Academy has been the long-time guardian of the arts in America. In its studios an extraordinary number of America's most illustrious artists and sculptors have been trained. Throughout its history, the Academy school has been both a point of pride and challenge. On the gallery walls the masterpieces of American art have hung. Many of these exhibitions have been the most avant-garde for their times; many have not. All have been in the service of good art. Over the years, the Academy has acquired for its permanent collection many of the masterpieces of American painting and sculpture. The Pennsylvania Academy has performed its guardianship with abiding humanity and integrity.

The guardianship has not been without serious difficulty. At times the very existence of the Academy has been threatened. Almost always there has been a shortage of finances and adequate facilities. The question of *Who is to run the Academy?* has periodically raised acrimonious feelings between artists and directors. Factions have divided its resolution.

Who is to run the Academy?, c. 1870s, PAFA archives.

There have been many missed opportunities, and, worst of all, there has been apathy. Yet, out of these difficulties there has always emerged a new resolve that the Pennsylvania Academy must meet the changing demands of the times. It is to that resolve that this catalogue is dedicated. Remarkably, the Pennsylvania Academy has survived.

The new American republic had neither an art academy nor a museum in 1783, when independence was finally wrested from the British. Between the end of the Revolutionary War and the founding of the Pennsylvania Academy in 1805, attempts to establish art societies were made in Philadelphia and New York City. Peale's Museum, founded in 1786 by Charles Willson Peale in Philadelphia, was one of the earliest. By the early 1790s Peale was proceeding with plans for an art academy modeled after the Royal Academy in London.

Peal's Museum 1786

cat. no. 32.
Charles Willson Peale.
Self-Portrait "in the character of a painter," 1824.

cat. no. 33. Rembrandt Peale.
Self-Portrait, ca.1845.

These efforts resulted in the founding of the Columbianum in 1794. The short-lived Columbianum, an association of thirty professional and amateur artists, factious from the outset, sponsored a single exhibition, which was held in Independence Hall, and hastily organized an academy for art instruction. Much to the disappointment of Charles Willson Peale and other artists, the Columbianum never had a chance to succeed. Rembrandt Peale, one of its members, recorded that it "died a natural death, by schisms" in 1795.[1]

The Columbianum had been founded by a group of artists who had as their purpose the protection and encouragement of the "infant" fine arts in America. Its demise temporarily left Philadelphia without a fine arts institution. When the new Academy was founded, its principal organizers were, unlike those of the Columbianum, non-artists.

The direct inspiration for the Pennsylvania Academy's formation came from New York. There in 1802 a body of prominent merchants, led by Robert and Edward Livingston, had founded the New-York Academy of the Fine Arts. It was the example of the New-York Academy, rather than the Columbianum, that inspired the Philadelphians to establish their own academy. The elder Peale (cat. no. 32), his son Rembrandt (cat. no. 33), and the sculptor William Rush (cat. no. 34) were the only artists among the seventy-one founders. The principal organizers came from the legal and business community. Peale recognized that this Academy was a far cry from what he had envisioned.

only 3 artists in the 71 founders

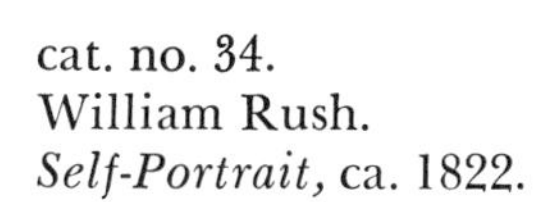

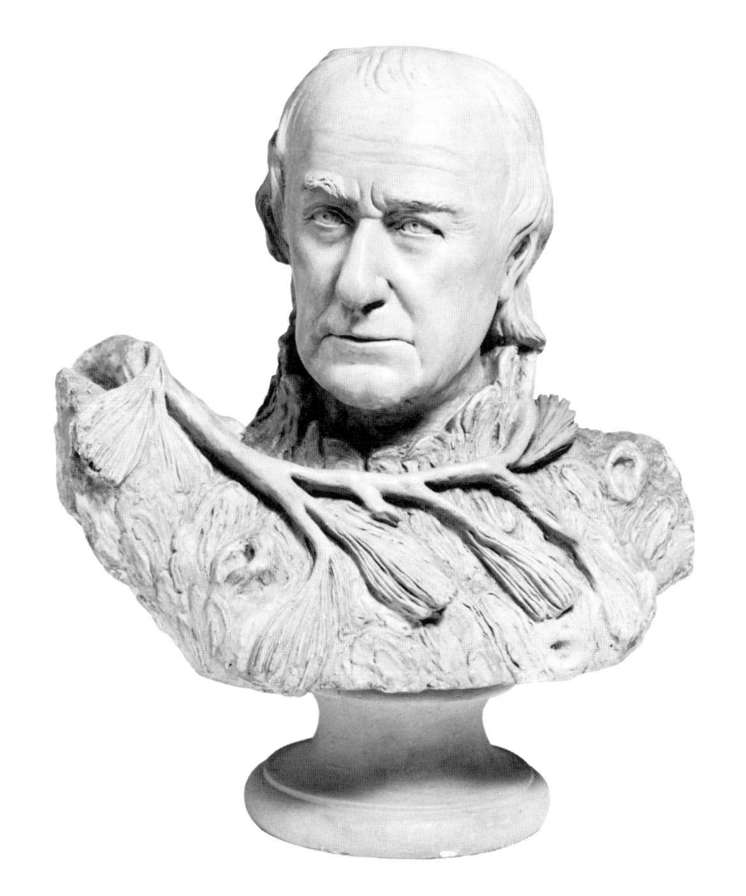

cat. no. 34.
William Rush.
Self-Portrait, ca. 1822.

The Formative Years:
1805-1845

The Revolutionary generation, once hostilities had ceased, actively promoted a national consciousness and style in the arts and letters. At the same time, it recognized the need for associations devoted to the cultivation of the fine arts in America if such goals were ever to be realized. An early devotee of the arts in America summarized these popular feelings when he remarked that academies would help to

> improve artists, to correct public taste, to call forth talents from obscurity, to promote a laudable emulation and finally, to give a character to the fine arts in America and, prevent the emigration of young artists to foreign countries.[2]

It was in this self-conscious spirit of nationalism that the Pennsylvania Academy was founded.

Plans for the new Academy were well along by December 26, 1805, when its founders met in Independence Hall to sign an application for an act of incorporation. Charles Willson Peale had written his friend Thomas Jefferson in the early summer that

> we hope soon to begin a building for the reception of casts of statues, also for a display of paintings, by the exhibition of which a revenue may be had to defray the expense of a keeper who shall be capable to give instruction to the Pupils.[3]

A week later Peale wrote Benjamin Latrobe informing him that upwards of $2400 had been

cat. no. 31.
Charles Willson Peale.
George Clymer, ca. 1807-09.

cat. no. 39. Benjamin Tanner. *The Pennsylvania Academy of the Fine Arts—First Building,* 1809.

subscribed for the Academy.[4] That same day, at a meeting of subscribers, George Clymer (cat. no. 31) was elected the Academy's first president, and a board of twelve directors was chosen.[5]

The new board carried out its initial duties with dispatch. At its first meeting, on July 1, 1805, it unanimously elected Benjamin West, president of the Royal Academy in London, its first honorary member. This was an obvious move to enlist West's support, for it was hoped that he would endow his native city with several of his own "designs" which would become the foundation of the Academy's collection. The board also authorized the expenditure of $1000 to purchase antique casts in Paris for the anticipated drawing classes,[6] and it commissioned John Dorsey, an amateur architect and member of the board, to design a building (cat. no. 9) in the proper neoclassical style for the exhibition of paintings and sculpture.

By May 1806, when a charter was finally obtained, the infant Academy had already made giant strides. The new building on the north side of Chestnut Street between Tenth and Eleventh streets, reminiscent of Benjamin Latrobe's Pumping Station of 1800 at Center Square, opened to the public in the spring with an exhibition of European paintings. An admission fee of twenty-five cents was

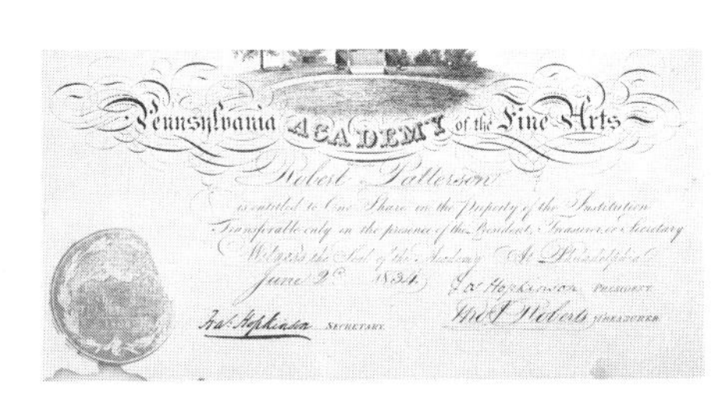
Pennsylvania ACADEMY of the Fine Arts
Robert Patterson

charged; stockholders and their families were admitted free. Mondays were set aside exclusively for ladies, and the plaster casts of nudes that lined the walls were removed from sight.

The fact that the Pennsylvania Academy was a stockholder corporation raised serious problems among professional artists, who normally could not afford to pay fifty dollars to become a shareholding member. Who was the Academy for, after all, if not for the artists? Why couldn't it be made more accessible to them? Charles Willson Peale labored to make the Academy's facilities more accessible to artists, but he had limited success. Peale was somewhat of a dissenter on the board. He saw the Academy's school as the first priority; the board's primary objective was to collect and exhibit works of art.

In 1810 the Society of Artists of the United States was organized as a protest against the Academy's failure to organize exhibitions of contemporary works and to operate a school. Almost immediately, the Society, in need of the Academy's facilities, proposed a merger. The merger was never effected.[7] Out of the negotiations, however, must have come the resolution on the part of the Academy to do more for the professional artist in Philadelphia. In 1811 the Academy turned over its galleries to the Society of Artists for an exhibition of contemporary American art, which also included European works. It resolved the same year that

> Master Charles Leslie be an élève of this academy, and that we will afford all the faculties in our power . . . in giving him an education calculated to call forth the powers of his mind.[8]

The Academy sent Leslie to study in London with Washington Allston and Benjamin West; the Leslie family repaid its debt to the Academy in 1831, the year Charles Leslie was elected an Academician, with the gift of his *Murder of Rutland by Lord Clifford* (cat. no. 25). In 1812 the Academy joined the Society of Artists in sponsoring the Second Annual Exhibition. The same year, the board elected the first body of Pennsylvania Academicians, twenty-four "distinguished" painters, sculptors, engravers, and architects. The Pennsylvania Academicians, who enjoyed the privileges of stockholders, would serve the Academy in the administration of the annual exhibitions and the school until the association's dissolution in the 1870s.[9]

Even though the Academicians increased and regularized instruction at the Academy, instituting a "Life Academy" for the study of the human figure and a course of lectures on anatomy, dissatisfaction over the Academy's lack of commitment to student art education persisted among professional artists. The problem finally came to a head in 1828. In a "Memorial of the Resident Artists of Philadelphia," a group of artists outlined their grievances.[10] The board answered strongly, but with respect for the dissident artists. Most importantly, it dismissed its "keeper," James Thackara, whose offensive treatment of artists trying to use the Academy facilities had been the real cause of the dissension. With Thackara gone, John Neagle noted in a letter of 1829 to President Joseph Hopkinson that "we will return with increased energy and affection to the support of your academy."[11] The dissidence had been temporarily curtailed.

There were other problems. Minutes of the Board of Directors contained, especially in the years 1808 to 1810, the simple inscription "No Quorum." Apparently, assembling the directors was a difficult task. Joseph Hopkinson, in the annual discourse delivered before the Pennsylvania Academy in 1810, noted lengthy periods of despondency. But Hopkinson also felt that the Academy by 1810 "may now be considered as completely formed and established" and that the threat of disbandment was over.[12] If any individual deserved distinction for having sustained the Academy through its infancy, it was Joseph Hopkinson.

While the infant Academy struggled to survive, it also realized significant gains. The years of George Clymer's presidency produced important exhibitions and acquisitions. Sixteen paintings from the Robert Fulton collection, including Benjamin West's *King Lear* and

cat. no. 25. Charles Robert Leslie. *Murder of Rutland by Lord Clifford,* 1815.

Ophelia, were exhibited at the Academy in 1807. It was Fulton who unsuccessfully argued that the Academy should purchase twenty-five canvases by West for $32,888! Additions to the collection included a collection of "impressions of Gems and Medals, some valuable Books of Engravings and several casts from Ancient Statues"[13] given by Joseph Allen Smith. Of far greater consequence, in the years 1811 and 1812, were the Emperor Napoleon's gift of twenty-four volumes of engravings by Piranesi, William Bingham's bequest of Gilbert Stuart's "Lansdowne" portrait of George Washington (cat. no. 152), and the purchase for the Academy of Thomas Sully's *George Frederick Cooke as Richard III* by friends of the artist.

After George Clymer's death in 1813, Joseph Hopkinson became the Academy's second president. For the succeeding twenty-nine years Hopkinson guided the Academy with a deft, affectionate hand, and by 1842, the year of his death, the Pennsylvania Academy had become the most prestigious and complete art association in America. Under Hopkinson's leadership, the Academy's facilities and collections increased significantly, its annual exhibitions grew in importance and popularity, and its finances became less precarious.

The small, Greek-style building designed by John Dorsey in 1805 for the Academy allowed little room for internal expansion. In 1810 a north gallery had been appended to the rear of the Dorsey building. Under Hopkinson three building programs were initiated. By 1820 a statue gallery on the east flank was under construction. Three years later a director's room and a library were added south of the statue gallery. These two additions in 1823 were probably designed by William Strickland.[14] Finally, in 1835 two small buildings were erected in front of the Academy. These were immediately leased as exhibition space for the newly incorporated Artists' Fund Society. In twenty-five years the physical facilities of the Academy had practically doubled.

cat. no. 8. Shobal Vail Clevenger.
Joseph Hopkinson.

cat. no. 1. Washington Allston. *The Dead Man Restored to Life by Touching the Bones of the Prophet Elisha,* 1811-13.

Benjamin West. *Death on a Pale Horse,* 1817.

During these years important additions were made to the permanent collection. In one of its most pioneering and courageous moves, the board negotiated the purchase in 1816 of Washington Allston's *The Dead Man Restored to Life by Touching the Bones of the Prophet Elisha* (cat. no. 1). The painting had attracted the Academy's attention three years earlier when it had been exhibited at the Royal Academy, where it was awarded a prize of two hundred guineas. The board agreed to pay Allston $3500 for the large Biblical canvas. Through subscription—forty-six subscribers at $20 each—it raised over $900. The balance was paid to Allston with money raised in 1817, when the Academy borrowed $4500 at 5 percent for four years, mortgaging its building as security. When the painting was first shown at the Academy in 1816 in a special exhibition along with Allston's *Donna Mencia in the Robber's Cavern* (Museum of Fine Arts, Boston), its popularity and the recognition of its importance must have gratified the board. Certainly, Washington Allston was gratified, for he wrote to his agent in Philadelphia, James McMurtrie, of "the honor conferred by the Academy" in purchasing his work.[15]

A preference for monumental history and religious painting, in the manner of the Renaissance and Baroque traditions of Europe, prevailed among the Academy's directors responsible for special exhibitions and acquisitions. Clearly, the Academy directors, as gentlemen of taste, were acting out the aesthetic principles of their English peers. Special exhibitions, such as the 1833 exhibition of the masters of the Venetian, Spanish, Flemish, Dutch, French, and English schools, were thought to be ideal. Moreover, the annuals always contained a section of traditional European art. The work of American artists like Allston and West was also popular at the Academy because it reflected the stylistic traditions of European history painting.

The Academy had purchased Allston's *Dead Man* in 1816, but the early schemes for acquiring an important canvas by Benjamin West had all failed. By West's death in 1820, the Academy *still* did not own an example of his work. It was not until 1836 that it realized this objective, acquiring West's *Death on a Pale Horse* from his son Raphael for $7000. Again, the Academy had to mortgage its building to meet the expense.

cat. no. 24. John Lewis Krimmel. *Fourth of July in Centre Square,* ca.1810-12.

The Academy's commitment to American painting was shared by the directors, even though individual taste seemed to prefer European works. A specific appreciation for contemporary American painting existed among a small group of Academy directors who were active collectors. Of them, Edward L. Carey and Henry D. Gilpin were the most active and vocal in their support of American art. Carey was a generous supporter of American artists, many of whom were his close friends. Gilpin argued for the support of native genius, especially the Philadelphia school, on the basis that every great civilization spawned and profited from an important tradition in the arts.[16]

In Philadelphia, the most significant artistic events in the early nineteenth century were the Academy's annual exhibitions. These were normally held in the spring and were open to all serious professional artists and sculptors, American and European. The annuals provided a public forum for young American artists to expose their work and an opportunity to evaluate it within the context of the entire exhibition. The cumulative effect of these exhibitions on American arts, artists, and public taste was colossal.

The Academy was dependent on raising sizeable sums of money through door receipts from the annuals to defray its yearly operating costs. Through sales of stock, subscriptions, gifts, and admissions, it raised the remainder of its annual budget. Money was almost always in short supply. However, the directors who managed the Academy's affairs in these formative years were both generous and wise in their expenditures.

Joseph Hopkinson died in 1842. He left the Academy in particularly good order, with increased support and major improvements to its facilities. The 1845 annual report to stockholders noted that "the pecuniary affairs of the institution are in a more flourishing condition than during any singular period for the last twelve years."[17] Nine days after this report was issued, fire caused extensive damage to the Academy building and its contents.

The fire was described in a Philadelphia newspaper as "disastrous in the extreme,"[18] and it was featured in *The Illustrated London News* with an engraved view of the building on fire.[19] Fortunately, the fire was extinguished before it destroyed the entire building and its contents. The most serious damage occurred in the antique statue gallery, where the entire collection of casts was destroyed, and in the north gallery and the director's room. Important European paintings were lost. Remarkably, West's *Death on a Pale Horse* was cut from its stretchers by volunteer firemen as fire burned its edges.

The fire, set by a deranged "incendiary," was a cruel blow to the prospering Academy. It came at just the time when the young institution was realizing some financial solvency. However, it was only a temporary setback. From the disaster, the Academy emerged with a renewed sense of dedication and purpose. The Academy, through its struggles to survive, had served too many needs to be allowed to fail.

cat. no. 43. Claude Joseph Vernet. *Shipwreck,* 1782.

Claude Joseph Vernet. *The Royal Family of Naples at Portici,* 1746.

America's Most Conspicuous Art Institution: 1845-1876

At mid-century, with the popularity of American art rising, the Pennsylvania Academy was recognized, along with the National Academy of Design and the Boston Athenaeum, as a leader in its support of American art. Asher B. Durand, in acknowledging his election as an Honorary Professional Member of the Academy in 1854, noted his "full appreciation of this connection with the oldest Institution of its kind in the country, and which has been so long prominent for the service it has rendered to the great cause of art."[20] Even more flattering was the reception that greeted the Academy's president, Henry Gilpin, throughout his European travels in the summer of 1854. Gilpin proudly remarked:

> I assure you, it has been a source of constant gratification to me to find that my connection with the Academy is a passport to the good feeling and attention everywhere of artists and friends of art.[21]

Further on in the same letter, Gilpin reconstructed his encounter with Baron von Humboldt, who was well acquainted with the Pennsylvania Academy, regarding it as "an honourable pioneer in one of the many roads of usefullness that are considered as characteristic of the American spirit."[22] An anonymous writer for *The Crayon,* on the fiftieth anniversary of the Academy's incorporation, concluded that "the institution itself is the noblest monument to Art we have in this country."[23]

In 1845 the immediate task was to repair the damage inflicted in the galleries by the fire and to replace the cast collection. The directors offered an architectural competition for the reconstruction; designs were submitted by John Notman, John Haviland, and Richard Gilpin. Gilpin, whose brother Henry was later to serve as president of the Academy, was selected for the job. Reconstruction commenced in July 1846, over a year after the fire. The new galleries were opened to the public in May of 1847. From the proceeds of benefits, the Ladies' Committee contributed $9550.95 toward the cost of reconstruction! The remainder of the cost was raised by subscription. New plaster casts for the collection were secured with the aid of Count de Nieuwerkerke, principal director of the Louvre, and at the same time the facilities of the school in the basement were improved.

It was impossible to replace the European paintings lost in the fire. However, in a move to strengthen the European collection, the directors authorized the purchase of four paintings from the collection of Joseph Bonaparte, Napoleon's older brother, the ex-king of Spain, who had a summer estate in Bordentown, New Jersey. The Academy was able to acquire from the Bonaparte collection two important canvases by the French painter Joseph Vernet: *Shipwreck* (cat. no. 43) and *The Royal Family of Naples at Portici.* It also moved to acquire European works by offering substantial cash prizes for historical, scriptural, and dramatic canvases, as well as landscapes judged by a jury of outside experts to be superior works in the annuals. The jury selections were almost exclusively European canvases; one of the popular works acquired in this way was the *Rouget De Lisle Singing the "Marseillaise",* painted by the Belgian Godfried Guffens in 1849.

James R. Lambdin, a portrait painter and a director of the Academy, endeavored to amend the concept of this yearly awarding of prizes by proposing that the paintings chosen "must be by an American artist and executed within the United States or by American artists residing temporarily abroad."[24] Lambdin, whose resolution was defeated, represented a faction that urged the Academy to extend its support exclusively to American artists. Outside voices, like *The Crayon,* expressed the same concern:

> The Pennsylvania Academy is nobly persevering in the purchase of works of Art. . . . Three pictures were procured last year: a landscape by Weber, "The Dying Brigand," by May, and "Datheen Preaching in the Neighborhood of

Godfried Guffens. *Rouget de Lisle Singing the "Marseillaise,"* 1849.

> Ghent," by Wittkamp; the first two were appropriate additions to the Academy's collection, and, under the circumstances, so was the picture by Wittkamp. The latter acquisition however, is a bad precedent, if likely to be followed by similar successors. We presume the Academy desirous of favoring the growth of Art in America . . . let it judiciously buy, therefore, all works by native artists who need the encouragement and appreciation of home patronage, particularly that of an institution; *they have a right to it through their genius without regard to any national considerations whatever.*[25]

It was not until the 1870s that a taste for American art predominated at the Academy. Collections like those formed by Edward L. Carey (cat. no. 38), which came to the Academy in 1879 as a bequest from his brother Henry, stimulated an interest in modern American painting.

Traditionally, academies have taken a stern view toward contemporary art. Through the latter half of the nineteenth century the Pennsylvania Academy stood in the vanguard of artistic taste. The annuals were a forum for contemporary American painting. Every major American nineteenth-century artist, at one time or another, exhibited his work at the Pennsylvania Academy. Even in the school, where one might expect a more conservative bent, the instruction was innovative.

Special exhibitions dealt with contemporary work. Both of Thomas Cole's allegorical landscape series—*The Voyage of Life* and *The Course of Empire*—were shown at the Academy, in 1844 and 1852 respectively. Over the anguished cries of ladies whose sensibilities were offended by the nude female figure, Hiram Powers's *Greek Slave* was unveiled in 1848. Paintings by German artists of the Düsseldorf School attracted attention in 1850. Eight years later the now famous "American Exhibition of British Art," organized by William Rossetti, which consisted exclusively of English Pre-Raphaelite works, was opened at the Academy. The exhibition consisted of 105 oils and 127 watercolors, including, among others, the work of William Holman Hunt, Daniel Maclise, Ford Maddox Brown, John Brett, Frederick Leighton, and John Ruskin. In 1860 Frederic Church's cosmic landscape, *Heart of the Andes,* after a triumphal success in London, was hailed in Philadelphia at the Academy.

In addition to exhibiting modern works, the Academy bestowed professional honors on contemporary American and European painters, sculptors, and architects. It is not surprising that Asher B. Durand and Daniel Huntington were elected Honorary Professional Members of the Academy in 1854, but in recognizing the talents of Frederic Church, John F. Kensett, Jasper Cropsey, and Thomas Crawford, the Academy was well ahead of critical and popular recognition. Remarkably, the Academy during the previous year had gone so far as to recognize a group of renegade English artists and architects, like William Dyce and William Butterfield, who were out of favor in English academic circles.

The Academy also recognized its own artists for distinguished services. From 1867 to 1872, the year Thomas Sully died, the Sully Fund, raised from the board, paid a yearly stipend of $1000 to the aging artist in recognition of his "steadfast labors amongst us, and as a tribute to his upright character and his social virtues."[26] In the same spirit, in 1868 the board offered Christian Schussele a $1000 gift as a testimonial for his services as an instructor. When Schussele declined the gesture, the board subscribed to purchase a painting from him for $2000. The board also recognized its social obligations; twice during the Civil War it turned over its door receipts for the benefit of the United States Sanitary Commission to aid wounded Union soldiers. In 1864 it made its galleries available to the organizers of the Great Central Fair.

During the middle years of the nineteenth century, the Academy was blessed with energetic, resourceful leadership. On its board were distinguished lawyers and businessmen, influential artists, scholars, and collectors. In Henry D. Gilpin (cat. no. 20), president of the Academy from 1852 to 1859, and his successor Caleb Cope, president from 1859 to 1872, the

cat. no. 38.
Thomas Sully.
Edward L. Carey, 1859.

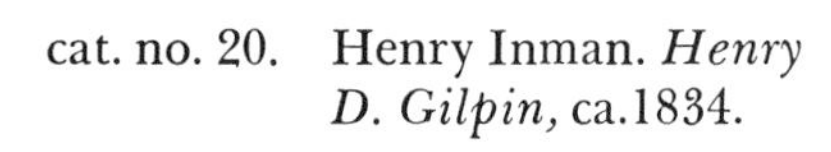

cat. no. 20. Henry Inman. *Henry D. Gilpin,* ca.1834.

Academy had two able leaders. Under their leadership, the Academy prospered. In his stockholders' address of 1851, Gilpin noted with satisfaction the improved position of the Academy in many respects.[27] In 1845 there had been 304 Academy stockholders. In six years the number had more than doubled to 614. By 1857, 721 stockholders were recorded, and in 1859, 813. From an average of 5000 visitors to the Academy in the 1840s, an average of 13,000 was recorded in the mid-1850s.[28]

Not only was the patronage of the Academy on the rise, but the size of its school enrollment and annual exhibitions was rapidly growing. As early as 1856, at the celebration of its fiftieth anniversary, murmurings of the need for additional space were heard. In 1860 a committee of the board was formed to ascertain the terms of a possible sale of the Chestnut Street property. The same committee noted the poor condition of the Chestnut Street building. For the next five years, no affirmative action was taken to find new headquarters. In 1865 a special committee, composed of John Sartain, James Claghorn, and George Whitney, reported to the board that the Chestnut Street building "in its present condition, not only impedes the operation of the Academy, but is rapidly hastening to distruction [*sic*] the works of art contained in it."[29] After hearing the committee's plans for enlarging the existing structure, the decision was reached to erect an entirely new building. The board authorized the disposal of the Chestnut Street property for not less than $90,000.

The board did not reach a decision to erect a new building until late in 1869. In December 1869, Joseph Harrison, James Claghorn, and William Struthers were appointed as a committee to select a new site. In May 1870, President Caleb Cope reported that the Chestnut Street building had been sold for $135,000. A decision was being forced on the Academy.

Serious disagreement developed in the Harrison Committee over the choice of a new site. Harrison favored a site in Fairmount Park, hoping the Academy would ally itself with the Park Commissioners. He proposed a comprehensive scheme of public educational improvement, whereby the collections of other institutions would be brought together at the same site, with free admission for nine months of the year; the other three months, during the annuals, admission would be charged. President Cope argued the impractibility of conducting a school in such a remote locality. After heated debate, the decision to purchase the "Steele" lot at Broad and Cherry streets was approved in November 1870. Harrison, dismayed by the selection, resigned from the board after fifteen years of service. Fortunately, Harrison bore no animosity to the Academy; in 1878 part of his princely collection of American painting came to the Academy. His place on the board was filled by Fairman Rogers.

In June 1871, John Sartain, James Claghorn, Henry Gibson, Henry Morris, and Fairman Rogers were appointed as a committee to select a design for a new building. The committee instituted a competition, preparing a program of instructions for the guidance of the architects. They specified that the new structure was not to cost more than $250,000. Not surprisingly, the facilities and design of the new building represented an enlarged concept of Peter B. Wight's 1866 National Academy of Design in New York. John Sartain had a crucial voice in outlining the requirements of the new school facilities.

The firm of Frank Furness and George Hewitt was awarded the commission. For Furness, a student in the New York firm of Richard Morris Hunt, the Academy commission represented his first major job. It is generally agreed that Furness was responsible for the work. To the task, he brought his own personal flamboyance and creative energies.

In 1872, after thirty years of service to the Academy, Caleb Cope resigned as president. His successor, James Claghorn, presided at the laying of the cornerstone of the new building on December 7, 1872. On that occasion, a letter from Horace Binney, aged ninety-two and the only surviving original founder, was read; other addresses followed. The capstone was lifted into position, and the invited guests repaired to the Union League to inspect the architects' drawings. It was a joyous, optimistic occasion.

cat. no. 36a. John Sartain. *The Pennsylvania Academy of the Fine Arts—Second Building.*

Illustration from Frank Leslie's Illustrated Newspaper, June 3, 1876.

America's Oldest Art Institution: 1876-1905

At 11:30 A.M. on Saturday, April 22, 1876, amidst a clamor of festive excitement, the Academy opened the doors of its new building (cat. nos. 13, 14, 15). Throngs of dignitaries and art lovers packed into the galleries to marvel for the first time at the bold exuberance of the architecture. They listened attentively as the speakers declaimed on the liberality of the Academy's patrons, on the wisdom of its founders, and on the limitless prospects for the future. The principal speaker, the Reverend William H. Furness, father of the architect, proudly hailed "the Rejuvenescence of our venerable Academy" and "the new day that now dawns upon the Beautiful Arts, that help so powerfully to gladden and refine and elevate the life of man."[30] At the conclusion of the address, marble statues of *Jerusalem* (Philadelphia Memorial Park, Inc.) by William Wetmore Story and *Deborah* by G. B. Lombardi were unveiled. President Claghorn then pronounced the building open. In the centennial year of the nation, the new Academy building created a sensation among visitors to Philadelphia; an American masterpiece in architecture had been erected.

The opening of the new Furness building represented a milestone in the history of the seventy-one-year-old Academy. President Claghorn called the year 1876 "the *most* important in the history of the Institution since its first organization in 1806."[31] While museums like the Metropolitan in New York and the Museum of Fine Arts in Boston, both founded in 1870, and art schools like the Art Students League, founded in 1875, were but fledglings, the Pennsylvania Academy, with its new facility, was literally reborn to maturity. The Academy directors recognized their institution's historic preeminence; on the motion of Charles Henry Hart, it was ordered that the words "Founded 1805" always be printed after the name of the Academy.[32]

With the recognition of this historic preeminence and with more adequate facilities came a new commitment to growth and professionalism. Moreover, the board at that time was composed of many of Philadelphia's wealthiest, most ambitious leaders—Fairman Rogers, Edward H. Coates, Henry C. Gibson, James Claghorn, Edward T. Stotesbury, and Joseph E. Temple—and these men imparted their personal ambition to the Academy, making the last quarter of the nineteenth century one of the most spectacular and innovative periods in the Academy's history.

The most spectacular growth came with additions to the permanent collections. In April 1876, the John S. Phillips bequest of European prints and drawings was announced. One of the largest print collections in America, it contained more than sixty thousand items, and the bequest included $12,000 to maintain and increase the collection. In 1878, four years after Joseph Harrison's death, eleven paintings from the Joseph and Sarah Harrison Collection were given to the Academy. Among these were Benjamin West's *Christ Rejected* (cat. no. 45) and *Penn's Treaty with the Indians,* John Vanderlyn's *Ariadne Asleep on the Island of Naxos* (cat. no. 85), and Charles Willson Peale's *Artist in His Museum* (cat. no. 100).[33] The latter painting, along with Peale's portraits of George Washington and Benjamin Franklin (cat. nos. 95 and 94), had been purchased in 1854 at the Peale Museum Gallery sale for $175. As an expression of the board's gratitude for this princely gift, Sarah Harrison was unanimously elected the Academy's first honorary lady member.

Shortly after the Harrison gift came the bequest of paintings from Edward Carey's collection by his brother Henry Carey. In 1886 a small collection of miniatures, with examples by Edward Greene Malbone and James Peale (cat. nos. 103 and 104), came to the Academy from Frank Marx Etting. The following year, the John W. and Eliza Field Collection, which included a double portrait of the donors (cat. no. 36) painted by John Singer Sargent in Paris in 1882, became part of the Academy's collection. In 1891, with the death of Henry C. Gibson (cat. no. 42), the largest and most valuable bequest ever made to the

cat. no. 5. Alexander Cabanel. *The Birth of Venus,* 1863.

Academy was announced. The Gibson Collection contained more than one hundred European paintings, including works by Eugène Boudin, Alexander Cabanel (cat. no. 5), Gustave Courbet, Thomas Couture, Jean Baptiste Camille Corot, Henri Fantin-Latour (cat. no. 12), Jean-Léon Gérôme (cat. no. 233), Jean-François Millet, and James Jacques Tissot (cat. no. 40). The collection also included four monumental pieces of American sculpture: Joseph Bailly's *The Expulsion* and *First Prayer,* William Henry Reinhart's *Hero,* and Howard Roberts's *Eleanor.*

At the same time that the Academy was receiving major additions to the collection, it was also the recipient of two funds for the purchase of contemporary American art. The first of these, bequeathed in 1860 but not received until 1878, came from Henry D. Gilpin. The other, given in 1880 by Joseph E. Temple (cat. no. 41), specified that one-half its income be applied to keep the museum open at least one free day a week and the other half be used for the purchase of contemporary American art. The Gilpin Fund has made possible the purchase of 155 American works; the Temple Fund, 138. It was noted in 1901 that the Temple Collection was "one of the fullest groups of contemporary American art in the country."[34]

The initial Temple Fund purchases reflected a curious eclectic taste: in 1881 the Academy acquired William Picknell's *On the Borders of the Marsh;* in 1884 Frank Kirkpatrick's *In the Museum* and Charles Sprague Pearce's *Fantasie;* in 1885 Thomas Craig's *Evening;*[35] in 1889 William Mason Brown's *Fruit and Art Objects* and George Maynard's *Sappho;* in 1891 Alexander Harrison's *The Wave* (cat. no. 191), Charles Davis's *The Brook,*

cat. no. 42.
Albert Bernhard Uhle.
Henry C. Gibson, 1891.

cat. no. 41.
Albert Bernhard Uhle.
Joseph E. Temple, ca. 1885.

cat. no. 19. Winslow Homer. *The Fox Hunt,* 1893.

Robert Vonnoh's *Companion of the Studio,* and William T. Richard's *Bell Buoy, Newport, R.I.* If anything, the acquisitions indicate a preference for the work of expatriate American artists.

In June 1892, the Academy hired Harrison S. Morris (cat. no. 10) as managing director. In Morris it acquired the services of a man with impeccable taste and extensive knowledge of modern American art. During Morris's tenure, which ended with his stormy resignation in 1905, the Academy engaged in some of the most enlightened collecting in its history. In 1894 Morris purchased Winslow Homer's *Fox Hunt* ($1200; cat. no. 19) from the annual, as well as Frank Duveneck's *Turkish Page* ($500; cat. no. 61), William Merritt Chase's *Lady with the White Shawl* ($500; cat. no. 215), and Robert Vonnoh's *November* (cat. no. 208). In 1896 Cecilia Beaux's *New England Woman* was purchased; in 1897 Thomas Eakins's *The Cello Player* ($500; cat. no. 228). In 1898 George de Forest Brush's *Mother and Child* ($5000) became part of the collection, along with William Morris Hunt's *The Flight of Night* ($1200) and *Girl with White Cap* ($200). In 1899 Edmund Tarbell's *The Golden Screen* ($700) and two paintings from the Thomas B. Clarke collection—Charles Curran's *A Breezy Day* and Dwight Tryon's *Evening* (cat. no. 181)—were acquired. In 1900 Henry Tanner's *Nicodemus* (cat. no. 246) and in 1902 Childe Hassam's *Cat Boats: Newport* ($500; cat. no. 192) were accessioned. Not only was the Academy acquiring masterpieces of American painting, it was also recognizing America's greatest talent well ahead of the times. Morris's buying was daring.

cat. no. 10. Thomas Eakins. *Harrison S. Morris,* 1896. COLLECTION OF MR. AND MRS. HARRISON WRIGHT.

Photograph of the Sixty Ninth Annual Exhibition, Gallery F, The Pennsylvania Academy of the Fine Arts, 1900. On the far right Winslow Homer's *The Gulf Stream* is visible along with paintings by Chase, Sargent, Whistler, Hassam and Vonnoh. PAFA archives.

Members of the Academy's Board of Directors were also purchasing contemporary American works from the annuals. Edward Stotesbury acquired a choice collection of paintings by Winslow Homer, including *Eight Bells* (Addison Museum of American Art). Edward Coates, part of whose collection came to the Academy in 1923, owned several works by Thomas Eakins, including *A Pathetic Song* (The Corcoran Gallery of Art). John Converse purchased Daniel Ridgway Knight's immensely popular *Hailing the Ferry* (cat. no. 194) and Clement Newbold bought Edmund Tarbell's *Breakfast in the Studio* (cat. no. 205), both of which are now in the permanent collection. In addition to purchasing works, the board encouraged artists with the establishment of valuable cash prizes awarded during the annuals.

The annuals continued to be immensely popular. While admission statistics are not consistently available, the recorded figures do suggest huge turnouts. In 1889 receipts, at 25¢ per head, totalled $6,657.25. In 1900 the annual attracted 45,000 visitors, or an average of over 1000 per day. In 1901 the attendance reached 53,257 for forty-one days; in 1903, 55,226, with the largest attendance for a single day 5034 visitors. One reason the annuals remained so popular was that they attracted not only the best American artists, but often their best work. The annuals were events that attracted a national audience.

Special loan exhibitions on topics as diverse as architectural drawings, photography, and art posters were also regularly offered at the Academy. Often, the Academy turned its spacious galleries over to other art associations for their use. In 1879 the first annual exhibition of the Philadelphia Society of Artists was held at the Academy; in 1883 the Academy opened its galleries to the Philadelphia Society of Etchers; between 1898 and 1901 the Philadelphia Photographic Salons were seen at the Academy; and in 1904 the first exhibition of the Watercolor Society was held.

The Academy also organized its own special exhibitions. In 1881, "Paintings by American Artists at Home and in Europe" provided a chance for Americans to see the work of an important group of expatriates working primarily in Paris, Munich, and London.

cat. no. 30. Maxfield Parrish. *Poster Show: Pennsylvania Academy of the Fine Arts,* 1896.

cat. no. 17. Charles Grafly.
Thomas Pollock Anshutz.

Included in the exhibition was James A. McNeill Whistler's *Arrangement in Grey and Black: Portrait of the Artist's Mother* (Louvre, Paris), which was offered for sale at $1500. Regrettably, the Academy declined this opportunity to purchase one of Whistler's greatest works. In 1887-88 the first great loan exhibition of American colonial historical portraiture was held at the Academy. Subsequently, concerted efforts to build the collection of historic American portraits were made. In 1891 the Thomas B. Clarke Collection of modern American painting was shown. The following year, the second great English Pre-Raphaelite exhibition at the Academy was held. The exhibition comprised works from the collections of several distinguished patrons of Pre-Raphaelite painting, including Samuel Bancroft, Jr., and Professor Charles Eliot Norton of Harvard University; among the Bancroft collection were Dante Gabriel Rosetti's *Lady Lilith* (Delaware Art Museum) and *Found* (Delaware Art Museum). In 1893, a selection of works later shown at the Chicago World's Fair was first exhibited in Philadelphia. In 1896 the Academy organized a fine arts poster show, the announcement for which was designed by Maxfield Parrish (cat. no. 30); works by American artists such as Edwin Austin Abbey, Will Bradley, Edward Penfield, and John Sloan were exhibited along with posters by Pierre Bonnard, Toulouse-Lautrec, Aubrey Beardsley, and Walter Crane.

While the Academy's collections were taking on increased significance and its exhibitions were recognizing new styles and media, its finances were being placed on a surer footing. In 1885 the idea of instituting an endowment fund was first proposed. Previously, the Academy had operated on receipts and donations. By 1887 the treasurer was able to report gifts totaling $112,500.[36] By the end of 1905 the endowment fund was in excess of $300,000.[37] By 1895 the city was appropriating $5000 annually for the Academy's use in return for scholarships in the school and free days in the museum. By 1905 the city appropriation had doubled.

When the Academy school reopened in September of 1876, its directors noted with pride that, in their opinion, the school had "no superior in any country."[38] Under the directorship of Christian Schussele, and with Thomas Eakins, the sculptor Joseph Bailly, and

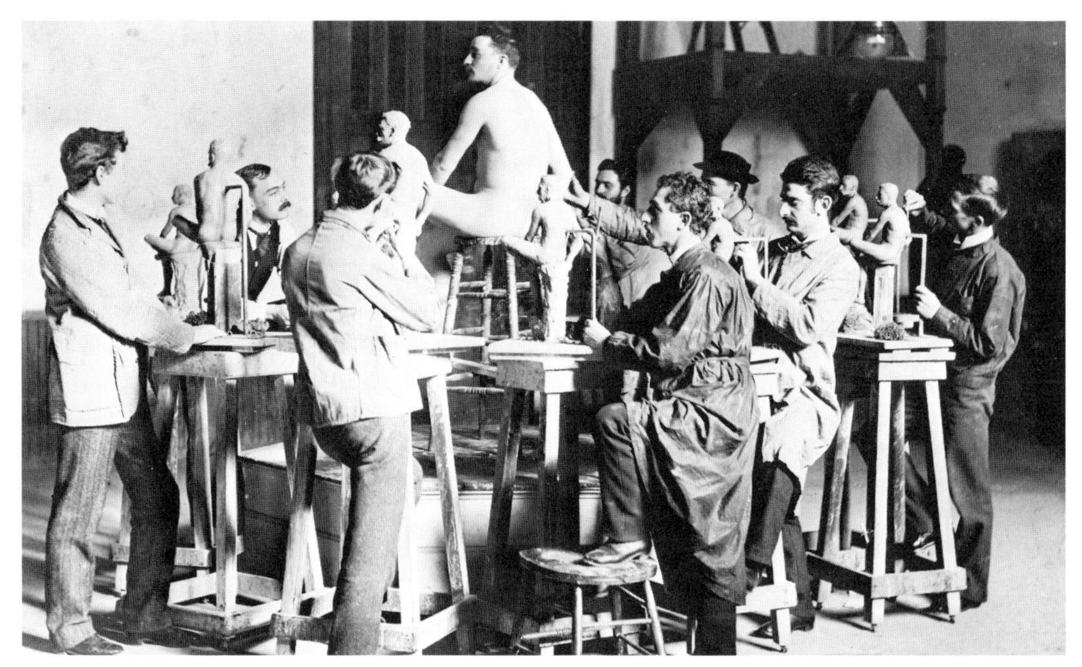

Photograph of the men's sculpture class at the Pennsylvania Academy, 1890s. PAFA archives.

Photograph by J. Liberty Tadd of a cast drawing class at the Pennsylvania Academy, 1901. The seated figure at the far right is John Marin. PAFA archives.

Dr. W. W. Keen on the staff, the Academy school was singled out for its well-organized, progressive system of instruction.[39] In 1876, there was no student tuition. By 1879 the board noted "the rapidly decreasing available funds of the Institution"[40] and considered releasing Christian Schussele. In 1882 the board was forced to initiate a modest tuition. In the first year, the tuition brought in $1140. In 1895 the average tuition was still less than ten dollars.

Prior to the opening of the new facilities, the ill-equipped, cramped quarters at Tenth and Chestnut streets had been the initial training ground of many future important American artists: Mary Cassatt, Thomas Eakins, Edwin Austin Abbey, and William Michael Harnett. There were many other students who came and went in anonymity. Reminiscences abound. Abbey remembered the Academy as

> a fusty, fudgy place. . . . The trail of Rembrandt Peale and of Charles Leslie, of Benjamin West, and all the dismal persons who thought themselves "Old Masters," was over the place, and the worthy young men who caught colds in that dark basement with me, and who slumbered peacefully by my side during long anatomical lectures all thought the only thing worth doing was the grand business, the "High Art."[41]

Among the earlier students at Chestnut Street, such impressions as Abbey's seem not to be the exception.

The new school and its small teaching staff attracted a throng of aspiring artists. They came first to study with Christian Schussele, who died in 1879, and then with Thomas

cat. no. 3.
Joseph A. Bailly.
William E. Cresson,
1866.

Eakins, who resigned from his position in 1886, and later with Thomas Hovenden and Thomas Anshutz (cat. no. 17). Subsequently, students had the opportunity to study with William Merritt Chase, Cecilia Beaux, Emil Carlsen, Robert Vonnoh, Charles Grafly, Joseph DeCamp, and Henry Thouron. The Academy's faculty was one of the most prestigious in American art schools.

Robert Henri, William Glackens, George Luks, John Sloan, and A. Stirling Calder remembered their student days at the Academy with gratitude. Others, like John Marin, Everett Shinn, Charles Sheeler, Morton Schamberg, and Arthur B. Carles, found their student training at the Academy of limited value. It was especially Thomas Anshutz's inspired teaching and great humanity that so many artists later acknowledged with deep respect. A. Stirling Calder summarized his feeling about the Academy:

> There I received ineffaceable impressions that have colored my life. There I formed habits of thought that have persisted. There I received a broad generous opportunity that has left me poor, but free.[42]

It was out of such experiences as Calder's that the Academy Fellowship was formed in 1897 to foster a spirit of fraternity and to benefit the Academy in other ways. During its history, the Fellowship has sponsored exhibitions, awarded premiums in the annuals, conducted important lectures, and supported artists in times of need.

Not until the beginning of the twentieth century did the opportunity exist at the Academy for students to study abroad on traveling scholarships. In 1891, with a contribution from the board, an Academy student, John R. Connor, was able to spend a year abroad on a traveling scholarship. Each year through the 1890s similiar scholarships were offered. In 1902 Emlen and Priscilla Cresson bequeathed an endowed fund to the Academy in memory of William E. Cresson (cat. no. 3), a promising Academy student who had died at a tragically young age. The income from the fund was specified for foreign scholarships. Then the largest bequest ever received by the Academy, the fund provided, and still provides, the opportunity for student travel abroad.

The Academy did not move headlong toward its centennial without serious problems, even setbacks. In April 1886, a fire greatly damaged the largest exhibition gallery in the Furness building, destroying forty-nine paintings and damaging seven.[43] In addition, only twenty years after the building's completion, the board, constantly reminded of the lack of space, appointed a committee to investigate the possibility of acquiring adjacent property for the school; the architect Frank Miles Day was requested to submit alteration plans for the adaption of studio spaces to galleries.[44] And there was always the frustration of having insufficient funds to purchase the countless major American works which were available. Certain missed opportunities are documented—the chance of purchasing Whistler's *Portrait of the Artist's Mother* for $1500 or Copley's portrait of Mr. and Mrs. Ralph Izard (Museum of Fine Arts, Boston) for $6000. Moreover, attribution mistakes were made; the Academy purchased the portrait of Elizabeth Willing Powel as a work by Copley, later to discover it was painted by Matthew Pratt. The number of unrecorded missed opportunities must be countless. The Academy did well, but it might have done much better.

The one hundredth anniversary banquet, held on the evening of February 23, 1905, marked a milestone in the Academy's history. It was a gala affair, presided over by President Coates, with the attorney general of Pennsylvania, Hampton Carson, and Howard Horace Furness, the Shakespeare scholar, addressing the assemblage. The ever popular, dapper William Merritt Chase, an instructor at the Academy since 1896, spoke on behalf of the assembled artists and students. Chase called the Pennsylvania Academy the most important art institution in America. Even an unbiased outsider probably would have agreed with Chase's appraisal. The Academy had served its purposes well. In the twentieth century, would it be able to meet the changing demands of the time?

A Healthy Stake in the Twentieth Century: 1905-1930

In 1905 the Pennsylvania Academy, in its one hundredth year, stood at the pinnacle of its history. It had a solid international reputation, it attracted the most prestigious instructors and talented students, its collections were exemplary, it met the demands of its public, and it grew increasingly popular. For the next quarter century the Academy would continue its position of leadership. During this time, however, forces in the art world were beginning to undermine the authority of all art academies. By the 1930s the Pennsylvania Academy began its slide into anonymity as its leadership became overly conservative.

Between 1905 and 1906 both Harrison Morris and Edward Coates resigned from the Academy. Their successors, John Trask and John Frederick Lewis, were keenly interested in American art. President Lewis was especially interested in historical portraiture, which he bought extensively and sometimes indiscriminately; Trask was an acknowledged authority on contemporary art. Through these two, the acquisition program remained active. Between 1908 and 1912 important works by George Bellows (cat. no. 271), John Twachtman (cat. no. 206), Willard Metcalf (cat. no. 196), Philip Hale (cat. no. 190), and Robert Henri were added to the collection. In 1911 the Academy's funds were supplemented with the bequest by John Lambert of a third fund for contemporary purchases.

The most consistently impressive events at the Academy between 1905 and 1930 were the loan exhibitions. These exhibitions indicated a genuine interest in avant-garde American art as well as more traditional styles. The fact that the Academy sponsored modern art exhibitions contradicts the traditional belief that the Pennsylvania Academy was an exclusive bastion of conservative taste. Certainly, the annuals included fewer examples of modernistic work, but intermixed into the season were modern exhibitions. The combination of these events proved extremely popular; between 1908 and 1916, yearly attendance exceeded 170,000 visitors. In 1908, 214,594 visitors went through the Academy.

The earliest avant-garde exhibition at the Academy comprised a selection of photographs from the newly founded Photo-Secession gallery in New York; included were examples by Edward Steichen and Alfred Stieglitz. Stieglitz, who earlier had served on juries for the Philadelphia Photographic Salons seen at the Academy from 1898 to 1901, represented the center of American involvement in modernism. Again, it was Stieglitz who served on the selection committee for the important "Exhibition of Paintings and Drawings Showing the Later Tendencies in Art," held at the Academy in 1921. The exhibition was the most complete survey of American modernism shown in Philadelphia up to that time. "Later Tendencies," along with the 1920 exhibition, "Representative Modern Masters," which included major European moderns like Matisse, Picasso, Redon, Severini, and the Neo-Impressionists, and "Contemporary European Paintings and Sculpture," with a catalogue introduction by Albert C. Barnes, were solid expressions of the Academy's involvement in modernism.

The Academy also featured more traditional styles of contemporary painting; it especially favored the new brand of realism associated with the Ashcan School and American Impressionism. There were early exhibitions of the work of Robert Henri, Everett Shinn, and Ernest Lawson, and in 1908 the Academy sponsored the now famous exhibition of "The Eight," which had first been seen at the Macbeth Galleries in New York. In Philadelphia the show attracted large crowds, but there were no sales. Immediately after its closing, the Academy held the tenth anniversary exhibition of the Ten American Painters, two of whom, William Merritt Chase and Joseph DeCamp, were Academy instructors. In the winter of 1917-18 the Academy paid tribute to the late Thomas Eakins, with an exhibition of 139 works.

In the 1920s the Academy organized a series of landmark retrospectives of eighteenth- and nineteenth-century American painters. The first, held in 1922, commemorated the fiftieth anniversary of Thomas Sully's death. The Sully retrospective was followed in 1923 with the first modern exhibition of the work of Charles Willson, James, and Rembrandt Peale. In 1925 the Academy organized the only major exhibition of John Neagle's work ever held. In saluting these five artists, the Academy recognized not only their eminent abilities but also their service to the Academy in its formative years.

In the late nineteenth and early twentieth centuries, the Academy school trained many of the future leading American modernists: Charles Demuth, Charles Sheeler, A. Stirling Calder, John Marin, H. Lyman Saÿen, Morton Schamberg, Arthur B. Carles, and Carl Newman. Their training came from men like William Merritt Chase, Charles Grafly, and Thomas Anshutz—unlikely fonts of modernism. However, at least with Anshutz, whose teaching philosophy strongly opposed giving a student "a formula that will cramp him to its own limits,"[45] the Academy student was encouraged to develop his own strengths and interests. With the presence of modernist painters like Arthur B. Carles, Hugh Breckenridge, and Henry McCarter on the faculty, a greater sympathy for modernistic painting existed at the Academy.

In 1914 President Lewis remarked that the school was in a "more flourishing condition" than at any time in its history. Its enrollment, which was to exceed 300 students in 1925, averaged between 200 and 250 students. Student scholarships had been liberally provided in memory of William L. Elkins and George D. Widener, a board member lost on the Titanic in 1912. In 1917, ninety students enrolled in the first summer school session at Chester Springs, Pennsylvania. The summer school provided a valuable opportunity for students to paint out-of-doors.

During the early years of the twentieth century the Academy was a vital organization. The assessment by Milton Brown that academies never played any significant role on the American artistic stage after 1913 is, of course, simply not true.[46] The Pennsylvania Academy continued to keep step with the changing times. It remained the most important focus for the American arts in Philadelphia.

Survival in the Twentieth Century: 1930-1976

An assessment of the Academy's recent history reveals several problems that have impeded the growth of the Academy during the past four decades. The general feeling that the art world eclipsed the Academy is probably fair; certainly the Academy failed to respond to the new movements in the art world. No single factor contributed to this condition. Internally, acute financial problems developed; the board, with limited aspirations for the Academy, failed to provide adequate financial support. Professional museum help was limited. Externally, academies came in for increased criticism for their conservative attitudes to art. Serious outside competition developed at the Philadelphia Museum of Art, and in New York at the Whitney Museum of American Art and the Museum of Modern Art. Contemporary, avant-garde American artists gravitated to these latter institutions for the support they once had realized from the Academy.

John Frederick Lewis, the Academy's twelfth president, died in 1932. Lewis bequeathed the Academy a notable collection of portraits and self-portraits of artists like George Healy (cat. no. 18), Emanuel Leutze (cat. no. 27), Sanford Gifford (cat. no. 23), William Sidney Mount (cat. no. 28), and Henry Inman. Before his death, Lewis had hired Joseph Fraser (cat. no. 44), a young architecture student from the University of Pennsylvania, to run the summer school at Chester Springs. Fraser ran the school from 1932 to 1936, and in 1936 he became director of the Academy. He retained this position until his retirement in 1969. In 1944 Fraser was awarded the Academy's Gold Medal of Honor for distinguished service to the Academy. Fraser's years, under six presidents, provided continuity, but comparatively little growth. The Academy had become a "slumbering giant," a reference to the widely held recognition of its tremendous assets.

cat. no. 44. Franklin C. Watkins.
Joseph T. Fraser, 1970.

Augustus Saint-Gaudens. *Mr. and Mrs. Wayne Macveagh,* 1902.

Fraser's thirty-three-year term as director is perhaps best characterized by his personal friendship with, loyalty to, and interested support of local artists. Fraser's support helped cement the ties of artists like Walter Stuempfig, Franklin Watkins, Francis Speight, and Hobson Pittman to the Academy. During Fraser's tenure the Academy school flourished, increasing its student body and support. The summer school at Chester Springs prospered until its closing in 1950. Additional awards, prizes, and traveling scholarships recognized student work.

Important additions were made to the collection. In 1941 Augustus Saint-Gaudens's marble bas-relief portrait of Mr. and Mrs. Wayne Macveagh came to the collection. In 1950 Henry S. Drinker gave a large study collection of the work of his aunt, Cecilia Beaux. Stuart Davis's *Ultra-Marine* (cat. no. 279) was purchased through the Temple Fund in 1952. In 1954 landscapes by Jasper Cropsey (cat. no. 163), George Inness (cat. no. 172), and John F. Kensett (cat. no. 173) were given to the Academy by John Frederick Lewis, Jr. In 1961 ten portraits, including three self-portraits by Jacob Eichholtz, were presented to the Academy by Mrs. James Beal. The following year the Academy purchased Alexander Calder's *Route Barrée* (cat. no. 313). Four highly important portraits were acquired between 1964 and 1969: an 1806 self-portrait by Benjamin West (cat. no. 89), portraits of Joseph Pemberton and Ann Galloway Pemberton by James Claypoole, Jr., and Charles Willson Peale's double portrait of Gouverneur and Robert Morris (cat. no. 93), painted in 1783.

Coincidentally, an indiscriminate amount of deaccessioning of European works in the collection was approved by the board. Works that were sold were considered either insignificant or irrelevant to the collection. Even worse was the dispersal of monumental sculptured marbles and casts deemed "not suitable" and "valueless" for the collection. One such piece, William Wetmore Story's *Jerusalem* had been prominently featured in the Academy's 1876 opening. One of Story's most important works, it now sits, defaced by the weather, in Philadelphia Memorial Park, Frazer, Pennsylvania. Other pieces were even less fortunate; partially damaged casts were destroyed on the recommendation of the Committee on Collections.

Each generation at the Academy has responded in a meaningful way to the important anniversaries of the institution. On the occasion of its 150th anniversary in 1955 two significant events were sponsored: the publication by Anna Wells Rutledge of a *Cumulative Record of Exhibition Catalogues. The Pennsylvania Academy of the Fine Arts, 1807-1870,* an invaluable research tool for American arts scholars, and a catalogued exhibition of the work of twenty-five deceased American artists and sculptors who had been associated with the Academy. In recognition of the need for a current history of the Academy, a chronology of important events in the Academy's history was included in the catalogue. The exhibition, after opening in Philadelphia, was seen in Madrid, Florence, Innsbruck, Ghent, and Stockholm.

Recently the Academy has endeavored to identify and celebrate its own history through catalogued exhibitions. There have been highly successful, popular exhibitions of the work of Andrew Wyeth (1966) and scholarly exhibitions like the 1967 Gilbert Stuart show and the 1971 "Philadelphia Painting and Printing to 1776," in conjunction with Winterthur Museum. The majority of the recent exhibitions organized by the Academy have dealt with the Academy's own artists or collections. In 1970-71 the exhibition "To Save A Heritage" brought national attention to the Academy's collection. Recently, exhibitions such as "Held in Trust," "Pennsylvania Academicians," "The Beneficent Connoisseurs," "John Sloan in Philadelphia," "Susan Macdowell Eakins," "Cecilia Beaux; Portrait of an Artist," and "The Pennsylvania Academy and Its Women, 1850-1920" have focused on specific topics directly connected with the Academy. These exhibitions have developed a deeper understanding of important aspects of the Academy.

Along with this self-education has come a heightened sense of obligation and responsibility to an increasingly aware public. This has taken numerous directions. In 1970, the Academy instituted an active conservation program with expanded conservation facilities. At the same time, it undertook the renovation of painting storage vaults. In 1972 it started a docent program as a public educative vehicle. Most recently, the restoration and modernization of its main building at Broad and Cherry streets has been underway. These endeavors are all designed to safeguard the Academy's nationally important artistic heritage, to provide meaningful interpretation and enjoyment, and to make the Academy more accessible to the public.

The restoration of the great Furness building is analogous in many ways to its construction one hundred years ago. As it then signaled a rebirth of the Pennsylvania Academy, so today does it signal a belief in the past and a new stake in the future. One hundred years ago the Academy was primed for a quarter century of success. One hundred years later its future as a guardian of the American arts appears optimistic.

William Wetmore Story. *Jerusalem,* 1876. PHILADELPHIA MEMORIAL PARK, INC.

cat. no. 89. Benjamin West. *Self-Portrait,* 1806.

Doreen Bolger

THE EDUCATION OF THE AMERICAN ARTIST

Let a student enter the school with this advice:
No matter how good the school is, his education is in his own hands. All education must be self-education.
. . . The school is a thing of the period. It has the faults and virtues of the period.
It is up to the student whether he becomes a school-made man or whether he uses the school as a place of experience where there are both good and bad advices, where there are strengths and weaknesses, where there are facilities, and much information to be had from the instructors, and much to be gained by association with the other students.
. . . A school should be an offering of opportunity, not a direction, and the student should know that the school will be good for him only to the degree that he makes it good.

Robert Henri, *The Art Spirit*
(1923; rev. ed. 1960), pp. 120-21.

The development of a creative talent always depends largely upon self-education, but this self-education is in turn conditioned by the limitations and potentialities of the individual's environment. Since the colonial period, the American artist has trained himself visually by studying the works of old masters and contemporary artists, intellectually by reading instructional manuals and theoretical treatises, and technically by repeated observation and practice in drawing, painting, and composition. During the nineteenth century, the American art academy emerged and developed as "a place of experience" where the artist could pursue his self-education. The growth of the American art academy was evolutionary rather than revolutionary. Although innovations were frequently made in the academic program, their ultimate acceptance and assimilation took place through a gradual process of growth and expansion. The art academy adhered persistently to tradition and responded cautiously to the new ideas imposed upon it by contemporary educational developments in London, Düsseldorf, and Paris, the three European art centers which had the greatest impact on the evolution of our academic program during the course of the nineteenth century. By the end of the century, the art academy had thoroughly institutionalized training in antique and life drawing, the study of anatomy and perspective, practice in painting, modeling, and composition, as well as the more practical pursuits of illustration and decorative painting. More importantly, it had institutionalized the student-teacher relationship, replacing the age-old master-apprentice relationship with a complete and structured academic program. Each art school and academy participated in this process of institutionalization; each was more or less "a thing of the period," reflecting the interests and concerns of the art world around it. Each art academy was uniquely organized and administered and made an individual contribution to the history of art education in America, a contribution which must be measured not in the extent of its facilities or the number of its students, but by its particular role in the evolution of the academic program.

By the end of the eighteenth century, American artists had the opportunity to acquire the elementary skills of their craft in drawing schools such as Alexander and Archibald Robertson's Columbian Academy in New York and the school opened by Matthew Pratt and John Drinker in Philadelphia. For example, when John Vanderlyn attended the Columbian Academy during the 1790s, he received instruction in painting portraits and miniatures, in drawing from nature and engravings, and in design.[1] Drawing schools like the Columbian Academy proliferated throughout the late eighteenth and nineteenth centuries, providing elementary training for professional artists and art amateurs.

This period also saw the development of art academies, which not only offered facilities for exhibitions and educational programs but also provided their members with artistic theories and aesthetic standards. The first institution of this kind was the Columbianum, founded in 1794 by Charles Willson Peale and other Philadelphia artists. Modeled after London's Royal Academy, the short-lived Columbianum established an academic program for students to draw from the antique (a few broken statues donated by Peale) and, to a limited degree, from life; it scheduled a series of lectures on such art topics as anatomy, perspective, chemistry, sculpture, painting, and architecture; and in 1795 it sponsored the first American group exhibition. Unfortunately, factional interests and lack of public support brought an end to this ambitious undertaking within a year of its inception.[2]

It was another decade before art academies were established in New York and Philadelphia: the New-York Academy of the Fine Arts (later known as the American Academy of the Fine Arts) was founded in 1802,[3] and the Pennsylvania Academy of the Fine Arts in 1805. Both were founded and administered by businessmen and amateurs rather than by artists. Like the Columbianum, these academies chose the Royal Academy as their model, hiring keepers to supervise their buildings and collections of casts and promising broad educational programs, which, regrettably, they failed to implement. Frustrated by the lack of educational opportunities, artists organized their own programs: in 1810, a group of Philadelphia artists formed the Society of Artists, which partially compensated for the educational inadequacies of the Pennsylvania Academy; in 1825, New York artists, outraged by the American Academy's mistreatment of students, established an independent drawing association which soon became the National Academy of Design, one of the two most prestigious and powerful American art institutions throughout the nineteenth century.[4] However, even academies run by artists were unable to maintain a satisfactory educational program. Throughout the century, students submitted demands for changes in and additions to the curriculum. In 1875, this increasingly assertive spirit culminated in the formation of the Art Students League, a school founded and run by students.[5] While art enthusiasts, artists, teachers, and students vied for control of American art schools and academies, the academic program expanded from antique and life drawing, supplemented by occasional lectures, to encompass anatomy, practical training in painting and modeling, and classes in sketching and composition, innovations which were increasingly drawn from German and French models.

cat. no. 85. John Vanderlyn. *Ariadne Asleep on the Island of Naxos,* ca.1809-14.

cat. no. 80. John Smith. *Her Royal Highness Princess Ann of Denmark,* 1692.
THE LIBRARY OF CONGRESS, WASHINGTON, D.C.

cat. no. 88. Benjamin West. *Elizabeth Peel,* ca. 1757-58.

Antique casts were imported by the American Academy and the Pennsylvania Academy of the Fine Arts during the first decade of the nineteenth century. Early in the century the study of the antique cast was the core of the academic program. As the curriculum expanded and life classes were scheduled with more regularity, the antique class diminished in importance, although it remained the most elementary training provided for the American art student. The antique class held certain advantages for the beginner. According to Christian Schussele, an instructor at the Pennsylvania Academy from 1868 to 1879, the merits of the antique cast were "its immobility, never changing place nor light" and "the uniform color showing form more clearly and truly than in life where the various tints of the flesh often bewilder the young and inexperienced student."[6] The regulations for the antique class at the Pennsylvania Academy were typical of the period: throughout the school year, casts were available for study during the daylight hours and sometimes at night by gaslight; the professor visited the classes several times a week to guide the students in selecting casts suitable for their varying abilities; only the professor was permitted to move the casts; and "singing, whistling, smoking, loud conversation, or other indecorous conduct were prohibited."[7]

By the 1860s, art schools divided their antique classes into groups of beginning and advanced students; the junior group was limited to drawing from casts of heads, hands, and feet, while the senior group executed drawings from casts of antique statues. The successful completion of these cast drawings gained the student admission to the life class.[8] The *trompe l'oeil* still-life painter William Michael Harnett may have completed his charcoal drawing after the cast of the *Borghese Gladiator* (cat. no. 68) as just such an entrance requirement at either the Pennsylvania Academy or the National Academy of Design. Painters of all specializations studied the antique. For example, the landscapist William Trost Richards recorded the original *Venus de Milo* at the Louvre in 1855 (cat. no. 76) . Perhaps it was this firsthand contact with such classical statues which inspired him to enroll in the Pennsylvania Academy's antique class upon his return to Philadelphia in 1856.

During the early years of the nineteenth century, art students had been compelled to produce innumerable drawings from the antique cast. These accurate reportorial drawings were usually executed in crayon and later in pencil and were generally as lifeless as the casts they depicted. As the century progressed, the National Academy continued to require an antique drawing each year as a prerequisite for readmittance to its life class, but elsewhere progressive teachers began to reassess this aspect of the academic program. "The object of the system of instruction [in the antique] . . . [is now] mainly to train the pupil's sense of action and proportion, and to make the department a place of study rather than, as is too often the case, a mere manufactory of drawings," wrote Joseph R. DeCamp, instructor of the antique class at the school of the Museum of Fine Arts in Boston during the 1880s.[9] Thomas Anshutz's charcoal drawing *Milo of Crotan* (cat. no. 47), with its boldly blocked areas of light and dark, its concentration on mass rather than detail, and its concern for compositional interest, typifies this more vital approach toward antique drawing during the late nineteenth century.

Drawing from the human figure had been an essential part of European academic practice since the end of the sixteenth century, and it remained the core of academic art education throughout the nineteenth century.[10] The first sustained effort to furnish the American art student with an opportunity to study from the living model was a series of life classes sponsored by the Society of Artists and the Pennsylvania Academy in 1812-13.[11] The National Academy did not organize a life class until 1834, when its students cooperatively hired their own model; in 1836 the National Academy assumed some financial responsibility for this endeavor. The following year, it opened a life school for its advanced students, although it was nearly two decades before this institution scheduled life classes with any regularity.[12] Initially, the model was usually male and often clothed; he assumed a pose which resembled that of the classical statues studied in the antique class. During the

cat. no. 47. Thomas Pollock Anshutz. *Milo of Crotan.*

cat. no. 72. William Sidney Mount. *The Painter's Triumph,* 1838.

late 1850s, both the Pennsylvania Academy and the National Academy began to provide life classes more frequently, and, thereafter, the life class received more attention in the American academic program.[13] By this date, drawing from the nude model was the norm, although it is impossible to document with any certainty when this practice began. Models assumed more relaxed poses and the use of the female was more common.[14] However, Victorian proprieties were upheld throughout the century: no conversation was permitted between the model and any member of the class, and there were separate classes for male and female students. During the final quarter of the century, there was a new concern for astute observation and realistic depiction of the model, an attitude which Thomas Eakins encouraged in his students at the Pennsylvania Academy. Maxfield Parrish's drawing of a male nude, which may date from his student years at the Academy during the early 1890s, is typical of such late nineteenth-century studies in its discerning individualization and casual pose, although the artist's use of pencil rather than the paintbrush or the charcoal and stump is unusual for the academic practice of this period.

"To draw the human figure," asserted Thomas Eakins, "it is necessary to know as much as possible about it, about its structure and its movement, its bones and muscles, how they are made, and how they act."[15] Artists had studied the musculature and skeleton of the human figure since the Renaissance. In America, anatomical study was incorporated into the academic curriculum quite early through lectures and drawings from anatomical casts such as Jean Antoine Houdon's *L'Ecorché* (cat. no. 70). As early as 1812 lectures were offered in Philadelphia by both the Pennsylvania Academy and the Society of Artists,[16] and in 1826, only one year after the foundation of the National Academy of Design, Dr. F. G. King lectured there on anatomy.[17] Of course, artists also had opportunities to study anatomy outside of the art academies, both with doctors and from the many treatises which were available at an early date.

During the 1840s and 1850s, the study of anatomy became increasingly scientific with the introduction of the "subject" or cadaver to supplement the usual casts and the living model. In 1845 Dr. Robert Watts, professor of anatomy at the National Academy, invited his students to study with him at the Medical College; by 1857 Dr. A. R. Thomas had moved his lectures from the life class at the Pennsylvania Academy to a local medical school to facilitate "illustration from the subject," thereby beginning the Pennsylvania Academy's tradition of scientific anatomy.[18] Within three years, the Pennsylvania Academy considered replacing the cadaver with a manikin since female students found it "too repugnant," but the manikin was too expensive and the study of the subject continued.[19] Dr. A. R. Thomas's "Programme of anatomical studies" included demonstrations from casts, engraved plates, manikins, and dissections. It began with a discussion of the anatomical knowledge of the ancients—a concession to the antique drawing which was still a prerequisite for the life class—and went on to cover human skin, tissues, muscles, bones, joints, comparative anatomy, sexual and national characteristics, and finally, the "Passions and Emotions" and their impact on the "Anatomy and Expression of the Face."[20]

By the 1870s anatomy had become part of the curriculum in most art schools, but nowhere did it receive the attention it was accorded at the Pennsylvania Academy, where dissection remained an important aspect of the curriculum during the 1870s and 1880s. The National Academy hired William Rimmer to lecture on anatomy in 1865,[21] but in 1872 it was equally satisfied to have its artist-instructor Lemuel E. Wilmarth direct the study of "artistic anatomy" by assigning his students the task of drawing an entire skeleton to scale.[22] Even Rimmer, who distinguished himself by the publication of his *Art Anatomy* (Boston, 1877), was not so demanding as anatomists at the Pennsylvania Academy, since he simply lectured, drew diagrams on the blackboard, and occasionally had students model anatomical studies in clay.[23] The Art Students League of New York actually took pride in the fact that its anatomy classes were artistic rather than scientific. "The difference between the analysis of a surgeon who thinks only of the detail and the analysis of an artist who considers the organic structure of man in relation to Art must be apparent with a single moment's thought," wrote Frank Waller, the League's historian, in 1879, and he recommended that students simply "be compelled to draw, from time to time, and hand in to the professor, the several bones of the size of nature."[24]

During the 1870s and 1880s, the Pennsylvania Academy continued with the scientific approach it had developed at mid-century. In 1876, Thomas Eakins began to assist Dr. William W. Keen with his dissections. His decision to appoint some students to help prepare the dissections for Keen's lectures was an innovation which pleased his superior, Professor Schussele, since the students could thereby "gain a clearer and more distinct idea of Anatomy, also recieving [*sic*] instruction in dissecting at the same time."[25] Thomas Anshutz, who was assistant demonstrator in 1878 and 1879, depicted the various aspects of anatomical study pursued by Academy students in his *Dissecting Room* (cat. no. 46) : two students are engrossed in dissecting a cadaver; behind them a classmate leafs through a book, presumably one of the anatomical treatises of the period; another group gathers around a skeleton; one student examines a specimen under a microscope, while another is "finishing" a plaster anatomical cast. During the early 1880s, Eakins supervised the preparation of a series of casts from the human body, an example of which is *Male Ventral Torso* (cat. no. 63). His students also studied live animals, and they dissected sheep, dogs, and horses.[26] *Academy Students Dissecting a Horse* (cat. no. 65) by Charles L. Fussell shows a group absorbed in dissecting and examining an enormous equine corpse in a bone-boiling establishment. Studies of this sort later resulted in casts such as Eakins's bas-relief *Ecorché Horse and Detail of Neck* (cat. no. 62).[27] The Philadelphia tradition of intense anatomical study was spread by Eakins, who taught at the New York Art Students League for seven years and at the National Academy of Design beginning in 1888 (although he did no dissections there), and by Thomas Anshutz, who presented a series of six lectures on anatomy to Robert Henri's class at the New York School of Art in 1906, an event illustrated by John Sloan's etching *Anshutz on Anatomy* (cat. no. 79).[28]

During the first half of the nineteenth century, the American art academy had focused on drawing, first from the antique cast, then from the live model; anatomy had also become an integral part of the academic program. However, formal instruction in these rudimentary subjects had been minimal. There had been little attempt to procure the services of artists committed to teaching students. Instead, art academies had relied upon temporary instructors and lecturers, whose efforts were supplemented by occasional visits from interested Academicians and other practicing artists. This system, which was derived from the practice of the Royal Academy, inevitably fostered neglect[29] since the student had limited and irregular contact with his instructors. Consequently, he had to study many of the technical aspects of his craft outside of the academy with an established master in an apprenticeship situation. Early in the century such artists as Gilbert Stuart in Boston, John Trumbull in New York, and Thomas Sully in Philadelphia offered practical instruction and professional encouragement to the young artists who frequented their studios. This apprenticeship system had its limitations, since after the student found a willing master, he had no guarantee that his instruction would be complete or continuous. Perhaps, then, the single most significant development in the American art academy during the third quarter of the nineteenth century was the institutionalization of the student-teacher relationship. When the academy began to hire full-time, salaried instructors, this relationship was transferred from the private studio to the art academy. This innovation permitted a concurrent expansion of the academic curriculum to include practical training in painting, sketching, and composition. Among the first academic teachers were Thomas S. Cummings and Robert Wylie,[30] who held administrative posts at the National Academy of Design and the Pennsylvania Academy of the Fine Arts. They began to assume more teaching responsibilities and worked far more closely with the students than had their predecessors. They organized a more formal curriculum of drawing, as well as lectures on anatomy and perspective, and published rules and regulations for their students.[31]

cat. no. 79. John Sloan. *Anshutz on Anatomy,* 1912.

This awareness of the need for a stronger, more intimate student-teacher relationship paralleled contemporary developments in the academic system in Europe. There the master class, which had been inaugurated in Düsseldorf,[32] provided an opportunity for advanced students to work more closely with their teacher, learning the practical aspects of their craft, assisting the master with his projects, and doing some original work of their own. This type of instruction did not become widespread in the American academic system until the late 1860s, since a series of national crises—including the Panic of 1859 and the Civil War—had diverted attention and financial support from our art schools, thwarting their development and expansion. When the American art academies were ready to begin a system of full-time, salaried instructors in the late 1860s, Düsseldorf had been replaced by Munich and Paris as the major European centers for artistic study, so that these cities determined both the content and format of the American program. The French atelier system, with its emphasis on the study of the nude, its diversified curriculum, its concern for technique, and its emphasis on competition and prizes, was adapted by such progressive schools as the Art Students League, the school of the Museum of Fine Arts in Boston, and the Pennsylvania Academy of the Fine Arts. These schools expanded their academic program to include painting and modeling, as well as a program of training in sketching and composition. This expansion was facilitated by the European-trained artists who began to exert a greater influence on art academies around 1870. Christian Schussele, who was hired by the Pennsylvania Academy in 1868, and Lemuel E. Wilmarth, who was hired by the National Academy two years later, had received extensive training abroad.[33] These teachers attempted to make reforms in the academic program, but their initial efforts were inhibited by the financial and organizational problems confronting their institutions.

As America faced her first centennial, her two oldest and most prestigious art schools were either closed or faltering. The Pennsylvania Academy suspended its classes between 1871 and 1876,[34] pending completion of a new building, and the National Academy, faced with severe financial difficulties, did not rehire Wilmarth after the spring term in 1875. Both Schussele and Wilmarth continued to instruct their pupils outside the art academy, a testimony to the relationship which had already developed between these teachers and their students. Schussele conducted a small class at his home,[35] while Wilmarth taught at the Art Students League, a new art school founded in 1875 by frustrated National Academy students who wanted to continue their study of the live model. Although Schussele resumed his teaching activities at the Pennsylvania Academy when it reopened in 1876 and Wilmarth returned to the National Academy the following year, the lack of opportunities for academic training at this juncture in the history of American art had an important effect on the development of the academic program. In a sense, the void created by the five-year hiatus in educational activities at the Pennsylvania Academy and the brief closing of the National Academy school had set the stage for a new and more vital era of art education.

The progressive young artists who began to assume teaching posts during the late 1870s—like Thomas Eakins, William Merritt Chase, and J. Carroll Beckwith—had been trained in Paris or Munich, and they espoused new styles of painting unacceptable to the American academics. Many of these younger men joined together to found a new liberal exhibition organization, the Society of American Artists, whose liberal policies constituted a rebellion against the conservative National Academy. Their presence as teachers in art academies triggered a parallel revolution in the academic program, which was amplified and brought into line with more sophisticated contemporary artistic needs. The revolutionary ideas which they borrowed from European academic models were more easily assimilated because the American academic system had suffered an interruption in its educational continuity and because a number of totally new art institutions opened their doors during the late 1870s: in 1875, the Art Students League of New York and the St. Louis School and Museum of Fine Arts; in 1876, the School of Drawing and Painting at the Museum of Fine Arts in Boston; in 1877, the Rhode Island School of Design in Providence; and in 1879, the Chicago Art Institute. This numerical and geographic expansion of art schools continued throughout the 1880s and 1890s, as did the growth of the academic program.

For most of the nineteenth century, drawing—whether from the antique or from life—was the mainstay of the American academic system; the only painting which the art student was permitted to do within the academy was copying, an artistic practice common in America since colonial times. The copy was intended to develop the technical and compositional abilities of the pupil, but its marketability also provided him with a potential source of income. Students and professional copyists crowded the galleries at home and abroad.[36] Jane Cooper Sully Darley's copy (cat. no. 58) after Raphael's *Madonna della Sedia* illustrates the extreme to which this practice was carried: in 1826, she copied the copy made in 1809 by her father, Thomas Sully, from the "original" (itself probably a spurious copy) in the collection of Benjamin West.[37] Unfortunately, copies glutted the picture market, discouraging the patronage of original works by contemporary artists. The abuses of copyists

cat. no. 61. Frank Duveneck, *Turkish Page,* 1876.

were so severe that in 1868 the Pennsylvania Academy was forced to issue a long list of rules which emphasized that "permission to copy from pictures belonging to the Institution is granted under the presumption that it is purely for the purpose of study and improvement in skill, and not in the spirit of trade to supply the picture market with copies."[38] Even after artists had more opportunities to paint in the art academy, they continued to make copies. Around 1873, the Impressionist Mary Cassatt copied Frans Hals's *Officers and Sergeants of the St. Hadrian Civic Guard Company* (cat. no. 53), capturing the fresh vitality of the Dutch original in broad fluid strokes.

While art students made copies independently, American art academies did not offer extensive training in the technical aspects of painting until the 1870s.[39] This seems less *retardataire* when considered in the context of European developments. The French Ecole des Beaux-Arts, for example, did not institute this reform until 1863.[40] Within two years, members of the National Academy, led by Emanuel Leutze, were discussing the possibility of organizing a painting class, although apparently no action was taken on this proposal.[41] In 1869, only six years after the French reforms, the Pennsylvania Academy permitted its students to paint. This innovation was prompted by students who expressed their desire to paint from the model and by the recently-hired Christian Schussele, who "considered this method highly conducive to the advancement of the students in painting; while copying from the pictures in the gallery is of little service to them."[42] The National Academy was reluctant to accept this innovation. In 1869 William Page called for a painting class at the Academy in order to make the institution, "as its name implies, a higher School of Instruction in the Arts of Painting and Sculpture."[43] In 1870, a special committee proposed a class for painting still lifes and the nude and draped model, but there is no record that this recommendation was acted upon. However, early in 1873, several artists renewed efforts to establish a painting class, and by February 3, 1873, a group of sixteen men and women were painting in a still-life class taught by Thomas Le Clear.[44] This was an improvement over the previous program offered by the National Academy, but it was not as progressive as the Pennsylvania Academy's move to paint from the living model nearly four years earlier. Unfortunately, the closing of the National Academy and the Pennsylvania Academy during the mid-1870s called a temporary halt to these important classes.

In April 1877, only half a year after the reopening of the Pennsylvania Academy, students submitted a petition requesting a model for a painting class three mornings a week for April, May, and September of that year.[45] When William C. Brownell visited the school in 1879, both Schussele and Eakins were teaching, and he reported that the students in the life class "almost without exception . . . use the brush—which would excite wonder and perhaps reprehension from the pupils of the National Academy." Under Eakins's direction, painting took precedence over drawing, for he believed that

> the brush is a more powerful and rapid tool than the point or stump . . . the main thing that the brush secures is the instant grasp of the grand construction of a figure. There are no lines in nature . . .; there are only form and color . . . I don't at all share the old fear that the beauties of color will intoxicate the pupil, and cause him to neglect the form.[46]

Alice Barber's *Female Life Class* (cat. no. 49) and Walter M. Dunk's *Male Life Class* (cat. no. 217) show Eakins and his pupils painting the human figure, while only a few students utilize the more conventional charcoal and stump. *Study of a Model* by Thomas Anshutz (cat. no. 48) may have been painted in such a class. In this color study, Anshutz emphasized form and contour rather than facial or anatomical detail, and he surrounded the figure with an atmospheric envelope of light and air.

By the mid-1880s, instruction in painting was offered in all major American art schools, and native art education had made a significant step toward equalizing the art student's opportunities for study at home and abroad. When the Art Students League opened

cat. no. 54. Jefferson D. Chalfant. *Study for "Bouguereau's Atelier at the Julian Academy, Paris,"* 1891. PRIVATE COLLECTION.

cat. no. 55. Jefferson D. Chalfant. *Bouguereau's Atelier at the Julian Academy, Paris,* 1891. PRIVATE COLLECTION.

in 1875, the life class worked almost exclusively in crayon and charcoal; only a few of the students were using either oils or watercolors. By 1885 the League offered classes in painting from the nude and draped model, the head, or the still life.[47] In 1879 the Boston Museum School allowed its students to paint; six students worked independently, painting both figures and still lifes, while less advanced students were permitted to paint from casts.[48] The Boston Museum School reversed its decision the following year, and once again restricted painting to its most advanced students,[49] a decision directly opposed to Eakins's approach at the Pennsylvania Academy. "Color is so interesting and so difficult, and for both reasons is so engrossing a study, that if students do not learn to draw before they begin to paint, they generally never learn to draw at all," noted the Boston school's annual report for 1881.[50] The National Academy of Design was equally conservative. After discussing the possibility of establishing a painting class in 1882, this institution hired William H. Lippincott as professor of painting in 1883, but only seven pupils were considered sufficiently advanced to enroll in his classes.[51] Once this type of technical instruction was introduced into the curriculum—even on a limited scale as at the Boston Museum School and the National Academy—it quickly became an integral part of the academic program. During the 1880s, the painting class spread to most art schools, and painting was permitted in a wider variety of classes, including the still-life and portrait classes.

Still-life objects were appropriate models for the novice painter, since they were readily available, immobile, and easily placed in compositional arrangements, and they effectively demonstrated problems of form and color. Under Schussele, the Pennsylvania Academy's drapery class was essentially a still-life class, since it involved the study of "grouped objects of art" and "various objects of still life" as well as work from the draped manikin.[52] His successor, Eakins, organized a makeshift still-life class in the dissecting room at the Academy in 1882, primarily to provide exercises in color, and he informed the Board of Directors the following year that he was "very anxious to have a still-life painting class resumed where color and tone experiments might be made on a greater scale than the gray tones of flesh afford in the life class room."[53] R. Swain Gifford of the Woman's Art School of the Cooper Union and William Henry Lippincott at the National Academy also used still-life arrangements to demonstrate problems of form and color.[54] Despite the widespread use of still-life objects by individual teachers, the still-life class was not institutionalized until the 1890s, when such artists as William Merritt Chase and Francis C. Jones offered still-life classes at the Art Students League and the National Academy of Design.[55] Chase's crudely painted *Still Life* (cat. no. 57) was completed in a few hours as a classroom demonstration, illustrating the facile technique which he encouraged in his students.

For the American artist, portraiture had consistently been one of the most reliable and financially lucrative fields of specialization. However, until the late 1870s, extensive training in portraiture was not offered in American academies, although lectures on the subject were occasionally presented. Early in 1876, the Art Students League initiated a small portrait class which soon became an important part of its curriculum.[56] By 1877, the Pennsylvania Academy also offered a portrait class, initially with little professional criticism or instruction, although Eakins and later Anshutz and Bernhard Uhle served as teachers in this class.[57] In 1878, students at the National Academy petitioned for a portrait class; they repeated the request two years later, specifying John George Brown as the instructor to be hired at their own expense.[58] The spread of the portrait class was facilitated by the influx of sophisticated Munich- and Paris-trained portraitists who could serve as instructors. Also, unlike the life class, the portrait class could provide its own models by having students pose in turn, and a large membership could be sustained since both male and female students were permitted to attend simultaneously. By the 1890s the portrait class was an accepted part of the academic program; in 1899, the Pennsylvania Academy even added an "advanced" portrait class taught by William Merritt Chase.[59]

Although sketching and practice in composition liberated the imagination of the art student and developed his ability for invention, these exercises were not emphasized in the American academic program until the late 1870s. Earlier in the century, artists had organized social clubs where they could sketch informally from imagination and from the model in order to supplement the cast and life drawing then available as a part of the academic curriculum.[60] The interest in sketching and composition classes seems to have stemmed from the confluence of several factors, such as the widespread acceptance of sketch-like qualities in the "finished" work of art and the increased significance of figure painting as an American subject matter. Furthermore, French art had a growing influence on American art during the 1870s and 1880s, and painted sketches had become an important part of the French academic program as early as 1816, when the Ecole des Beaux-Arts instituted the *concours de composition*.[61]

Although the sketch class and the composition class were related in purpose and activity, the sketch class appeared as a part of the academic curriculum earlier than the composition class and was scheduled with greater frequency. In 1875 the New York Art Students League inaugurated what may have been the first American sketch class; it was scheduled between four and five o'clock each afternoon—"after the serious business of the day was over"—and each student took his turn at posing in costume for his fellow students.[62] This informal and inexpensive class was later adopted by other institutions: by 1878, both the Pennsylvania and National academies had added sketch classes to their curriculums; in 1879, students at the Boston Museum School organized a Friday afternoon sketch class, and within a year, advanced students at the school were being encouraged to spend much of their time making sketches on an assigned theme.[63] In 1878, Daniel Huntington, president of the National Academy, pointed out the merits of the sketch class, noting that there were "occasional trials of skill in sketching rather rapidly and in making drawings of a figure in a given short time. . . . These two methods, of extreme care and perfectness on the one hand, alternating with rapid and resolute dash at the result should be praticed side by side in every School of Art as it must be in every artist's private studies."[64] The sketch had received the ultimate academic endorsement! The growing fascination with the sketch may have inspired the publication of student-produced periodicals such as *The Art Student* (Boston, 1882-84), *Palette Scrapings* (St. Louis, 1882), and *The Sketch Book* (Cleveland, 1883), which were generously illustrated with student sketches. It certainly encouraged the formation of artists' clubs dedicated primarily to sketching: in 1860, the Philadelphia Sketch Club; in 1871, the New York Salmagundi Club; in 1877, the Tile Club; in 1879, the Boston Paint and Clay Club; in 1881, the New York Kit Kat Club. Such clubs became a characteristic feature of urban artistic life during this period.[65]

Figure painting—whether realistic or arcadian, historical or contemporary—achieved unprecedented popularity during the 1880s, and the more sophisticated level of compositional ability which it demanded of the artist precipitated a heightened interest in formal academic training in composition. Art academies were quick to respond to this artistic need. An experimental monthly composition class was organized in 1882-83 at the Boston Museum School.[66] By 1884, the Art Students League offered a similar class, which met monthly with Edwin H. Blashfield as instructor, and weekly "talks on composition and cognate subjects" were presented by other instructors.[67] By 1882 the Pennsylvania Academy offered a series of six lectures on perspective and composition, and in 1889 the Academy scheduled a composition class which met once each month for a lecture and a criticism of drawings which were prepared on a previously assigned theme.[68] Wilmarth gave a similar class at the National Academy during the 1880s; after his resignation, the composition class was continued by George W. Maynard, and it became the school's most heavily attended class.[69] Composition also received increased attention in student competitions. In 1885 the National Academy voted to offer a prize for composition from the Hallgarten Fund.[70] By the 1890s the Pennsylvania Academy had adopted the French *concours* procedure for awarding competition

cat. no. 49. Alice Barber. *Female Life Class,* 1879.

prizes and traveling scholarships; students were assigned themes such as "Rest," "Sympathy," "Motherhood," "Adversity," and "Prosperity" and were judged on the basis of their compositions.[71]

Figure painting and the introduction of sketch and composition classes generated another addition to the academic program—the costume class, which received increased attention during the late 1870s partially as a result of the popularity of historic genre painting and the artistic interest in exotic costumes and bric-a-brac. Of course, historical costumes and decorative objects were always of interest to the painter and were an important part of his training, no matter what field of specialization he chose. As early as 1840, the National Academy of Design began its costume department with a contribution of a "suit of olden times" donated by the painter Charles C. Ingham.[72] Between 1856 and 1869, the Pennsylvania Academy appropriated one hundred dollars annually "towards the formation of a Cabinet or Collection of such objects as artists frequently have occasion to paint from."[73] Initially, costumes and drapery—sometimes simply unbleached muslin—were arranged on manikins or lay figures, which made inexpensive and immobile models, suitable for extended study, much like a still life.[74] As figure painting grew in importance, however, students became interested in the action, expression, and gesture of the costumed figure, and the live model replaced the manikin, precipitating scheduled costume classes in most art schools. "The human model should . . . be always employed in preference to a manikin," asserted *The Art Amateur* in 1885, "for it conveys a lesson in vitality as well as in drapery and color."[75] The students executed their costume studies in black and white, in oils, and in watercolor and supplemented their classroom work by attending lectures on the subject. During the early 1880s, Frank D. Millet lectured at the National Academy of Design and at the Boston Museum School, where he had models pose in Greek and Roman costumes while he discussed their attire and the students sketched or took notes.[76] By the 1890s there was less interest in costume painting, and this subject began to receive less attention in American art academies.

In America, the practical study of sculpture remained tied to the apprenticeship system throughout the nineteenth century. Until well after mid-century, serious sculptors pursued their study abroad, usually in Italy, where the neoclassic sculptor had the advantage of a large community of fellow artists, a wealth of sculptural inspiration from all periods, and a readily available source of marble and marble-carvers. American art academies provided the sculptor with the same elementary training as the painter, but this was hardly sufficient for a thorough understanding of three-dimensional form. As early as 1856, the Pennsylvania Academy accepted a model in lieu of a drawing for entrance into the life class; by 1859, it had a group of twenty students modeling from life.[77] However, these were isolated incidents; generally modeling did not become a part of the academic curriculum until the 1870s, when the sculptors Joseph A. Bailly and Francis X. Dengler taught at the Pennsylvania Academy and the Boston Museum School respectively.[78] Even at this late date, modeling was considered as a supplement to the education of the painter, rather than an independent discipline.

In his plan for the reorganization of the Pennsylvania Academy in 1877, Christian Schussele proposed two modeling classes—one from the antique (for both male and female pupils) and a second from life (for male pupils only)—a proposal which reflected his insistence on students drawing from the antique before drawing from life. The antique modeling class began in October 1877 and was terminated in 1884-85,[79] probably because Eakins, who was then director, favored the model to the antique cast in all branches of artistic study. Eakins had studied sculpture in Paris and under his direction, modeling was given greater attention through the establishment of a separate modeling class of twelve to fourteen students who worked in clay and wax from the human figure and from animals.[80] *The Modeling Class* (cat. no. 71) by James P. Kelly shows a group of male students working from a male model in a classroom crowded with workstands surmounted by small figures and Houdon's *L'Ecorché* (cat. no. 70) in the background. "Eakins advocated an inclusive training, urging the painters to model and the sculptors to paint, and all to dissect the dead body to learn anatomy," recalled A. Stirling Calder.[81]

Modeling was not universally accepted as a part of the academic program during the 1880s. During the late 1870s, Dr. William Rimmer had used modeling to teach anatomy to his students at the Boston Museum School. In 1878 he offered a weekly criticism to a class of eight or nine pupils who modeled daily, spending six to eight weeks on each of a series of three-dimensional anatomical studies, including an arm and a hand, a chest and a back, and finally, a head. After Rimmer's death in 1879, his pupil Edward R. Smith continued this anatomy-modeling program, but by 1882 it had been deleted from the school's curriculum.[82] The National Academy apparently did not offer modeling until the late 1880s, but its choice of instructors—Edwin Elwell and Olin L. Warner—signaled a new direction in American sculpture, as well as a new direction in American art education.[83] These sculptors were among the many Americans who studied in Paris during the 1880s, and their bronze statues and monuments in the French Beaux-Arts style brought a new level of sophistication to American sculpture. Sculptors began to teach more extensively in art schools: Bela Pratt began teaching at the Boston Museum School in 1893; by 1891 Augustus Saint-Gaudens was instructor of modeling at the Art Students League; during the early 1890s, Herbert Adams joined the faculty at Pratt Institute in Brooklyn; in 1892 Charles Grafly returned from Paris to teach at the Pennsylvania Academy.[84] Grafly's portrait of Hugh Breckenridge (cat. no.

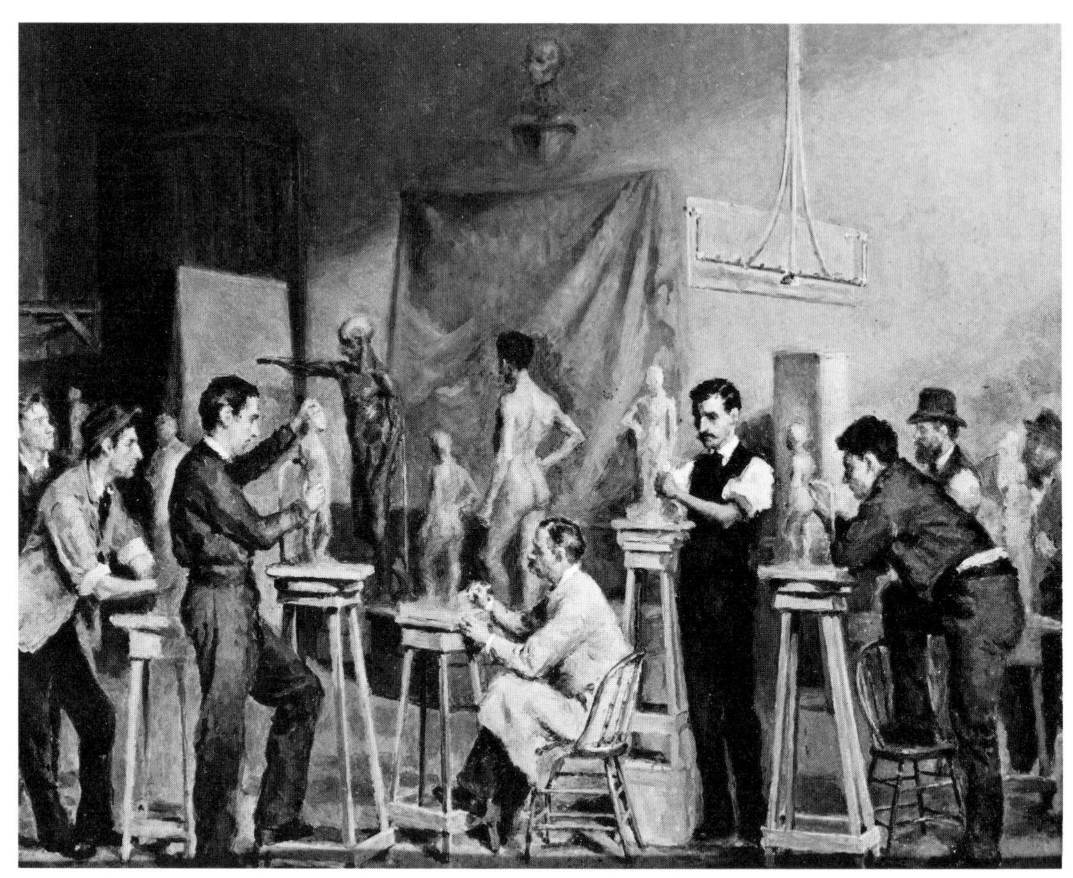

cat. no. 71. James P. Kelly. *The Modeling Class,* 1879.

67) was modeled in 1898, and it shows the influence of his Parisian study in the quick, lively treatment of its bronze surfaces, which capture light and create an energetic, irregular contour. Under Grafly's influence, the Academy altered the modeling class schedule, ordered two tons of French clay, had the evening modeling class reopened, and reorganized a "preparatory modeling class."[85] In spite of this new, more professional instruction for the sculptor in the art academy, art schools were still unable to offer him technical training in such problems as casting. Consequently, the sculpture student still needed to supplement his academic training by serving an apprenticeship or studying abroad.

When art academies closed for the summer months, students and professional artists gathered in rural areas and outdoor art schools to continue their work. In Europe, Americans sought artistic instruction and encouragement as well as friendship and inexpensive communal living arrangements in such scenic locales as the Bavarian village of Pölling, the Brittany villages of Concarneau and Pont Aven, or Fontainebleau, the well-known haunt of the French Barbizon artists.[86] Cecilia Beaux spent the summer of 1888 in Concarneau, working with the Americans Alexander Harrison and Charles Lasar. In the oil sketch *A Country Woman* (cat. no. 51), Beaux has rendered an informal genre subject with fluid brushwork and a lightened palette to achieve a fresh, plein-air effect.

Landscape painting must have been taught at least informally in many American art institutions, but it was Impressionism which brought the art school outdoors and made plein-air landscape painting an important feature of the academic program. By the 1880s, American artists were painting directly in oil outdoors in an effort to capture the more transient effects of light, atmosphere, and color—an innovation made possible by such technological advances as the collapsible paint tube. During the late 1870s and early 1880s, students at such academic institutions as the Syracuse University of the Fine Arts and the Boston Museum School began to sketch outdoors occasionally, inaugurating a major innovation in American art education.[87]

Plein-air painting was not easily incorporated into the curriculums of established art academies, most of which were located in urban areas, and was not thoroughly institutionalized until the 1890s, when the Impressionists popularized summer study in their classes and schools. Most of the older and more influential art schools did not organize their own summer classes until after the turn of the century. Given the universal success of outdoor summer schools, it is surprising that established art academies were so reluctant to conduct their own summer schools, although financial limitations and the existence of independent summer schools, often run by members of their own faculties, may have precluded the necessity for art schools to extend their programs in this direction. The Art Students League of New York did not found its summer school at Woodstock until 1907, five years after William Merritt Chase stopped teaching at Shinnecock.[88] The Pennsylvania Academy did not open its Chester Springs summer school until 1917; but as early as 1899, it had begun to exhibit the plein-air paintings of the students working under Chase at Shinnecock.[89]

If Chase's Shinnecock Summer School of Art was not the first American school of plein-air landscape painting, it was certainly one of the most important, for it established the outdoor summer school as a legitimate form of art education and served as a model for the myriad of similar schools which opened before the turn of the century.[90] When the exuberant Chase opened his school in 1891, he offered a weekly criticism and supervised his students' landscape and figurative work with the help of assistant instructors; he also made virtuoso demonstrations and presented monthly lectures. Ella Hergesheimer, a student at the Pennsylvania Academy, painted *In Competition, Shinnecock Hills* (cat. no. 69) in Chase's summer class in 1900. This work depicts a student painting an oil sketch or study outdoors as the model poses in the sunlight. Hergesheimer's style, composition, and subject matter are clearly derived from her teacher.

By the mid-1890s the vogue for summer art schools and plein-air painting had spread: Theodore Robinson taught a summer course at Princeton, New Jersey; John Henry Twachtman at Cos Cob, Connecticut; William Baer at Chautauqua, New York; Lemuel Wiles at Silver Lake, New York; and Robert Henri at Darby, Pennsylvania, and Avalon, New Jersey.[91] As early as 1895, the National Academy of Design admitted that "things may be taught in open air that cannot be taught under a skylight," but it did not offer a summer class until a group of its students organized the Country Sketch Club, whose summer headquarters were located in Hackensack, New Jersey, and whose stated purpose was "to paint and study, unrestrained from the drudgery of the class-room."[92] In 1899, Charles W. Hawthorne opened the Cape Cod School of Art in Provincetown; during the early 1900s, Frank Vincent DuMond, a popular teacher at the Art Students League, began a summer school which had settled in Old Lyme, Connecticut, by 1901.[93] This rapid expansion of schools dedicated to plein-air painting also inspired individual students and interested amateurs to work outdoors independently. "If it so happens that you, my student-reader, cannot attend a summer art school," noted Rosalind A. Pratt in 1894, "just serenely plant your white umbrella somewhere, anywhere, and go to work. . . . Can it not be said . . . that a white umbrella and an art student under it, a will to do in his head and a love in his heart, creates a summer school?"[94]

cat. no. 66. Daniel Garber. *Students of Painting,* 1923.

At the close of the nineteenth century, American art education was thriving. There were more schools and a richer academic program. Opportunities to study art at museums, exhibitions, expositions, and schools spread nationwide.[95] Nonetheless, art schools faced a crucial problem: how to prepare their graduates to earn a living as practicing artists, given the relatively limited demand for work by painters and sculptors. The solution seemed to be to train the artist in such marketable skills as decorative design, etching, mural painting, and illustration. The Arts and Crafts movement helped to gain artistic acceptance for craft and industrial design, and more and more painters and sculptors ventured into these fields of artistic expression. Mrs. T. M. Wheeler addressed the Gotham Art Students in New York in 1889, voicing the aesthetic sentiment which offered a philosophical justification for the practical need for training in design:

> Too many young people, beginning the study of art . . . have nothing in view beyond a general desire to become artists of some sort. . . . But there are many of the industrial arts in which a lesser degree of skill and knowledge may be turned to account; and it is to these that most of our art students must look for employment. . . . As a people, we have reached that point that we want beautiful things around us. We are no longer satisfied with a few pictures on our walls; we require that the dish out of which we eat, the bed in which we sleep, the carpet on which we tread, shall have some share of beauty.[96]

Schools of design in America and in Europe had offered such training in the "minor arts" since mid-century. The best known of the American schools was the Cooper Union for the Advancement of Sciences and Art, which opened in 1857 "to be devoted forever to the union of Art and Science in their application to the useful purposes of life."[97] Its curriculum included not only the usual academic cast and life drawing, painting, modeling in clay, and perspective, but also mechanical, architectural, and ornamental scroll drawing, wood-engraving, and the design of stained glass, tessellated flowers, ceilings, tiles, and wall paper.[98] Similar trade schools were developed in other cities: in Philadelphia, the Drexel Institute of Art, Science, and Industry, the Philadelphia School of Design for Women, founded in 1844, and the School of Industrial Art at the Pennsylvania Museum, which opened its classes in 1877; in Boston, the Lowell School of Practical Drawing.[99]

Although these trade schools offered practical training to designers and craftsmen, the art academy remained convinced that these students should follow the customary theoretical training offered to painters and sculptors and then gain the practical knowledge of their craft in the workshop. In 1889 the Pennsylvania Academy emphasized in a statement of its purpose that it intended to train men and women as professional painters and sculptors and to offer "no advantages but those of pure art education."[100] The Academy had struggled to separate the artist from the craftsman and to attain a superior status for the artist; until the late nineteenth century, even the practical aspects of painting and sculpture had been excluded from the academic program. Thus there was a conflict between the desire to maintain the integrity and superiority of the academic program and the need to equip the art student as a professional.

Until the 1890s, illustrators generally learned their craft by serving as staff artists for newspapers and such magazines as *Century* and *Harper's;* Edwin Austin Abbey and Arthur B. Frost were among the many artist-illustrators who began their careers in this manner. Illustration gained academic acceptance during the final decades of the nineteenth century: well-known critics such as Joseph Pennell, William Anderson Coffin, and Francis Hopkinson Smith wrote about its history in America; magazines such as *The Art Student* and *The Quarterly Illustrator* reviewed contemporary illustrators and their techniques; several art schools began their own illustrated periodicals; newspaper, book, and magazine illustrators began to make their presence felt in art academies, precipitating an increased interest in caricature and the cartoon, which quickly became a favorite diversion from more serious work and an informal preparation for commercial employment.[101]

During the early 1890s, the prominent illustrator Howard Pyle recognized the need for a thorough training in illustration, and he offered his services as an instructor to the Pennsylvania Academy, which declined his offer. In 1894 he began to teach black and white illustration at the Drexel Institute in Philadelphia, a post he held until 1900.[102] By 1895, when he established his own school, his lectures and criticisms were so successful that the Academy invited him to teach a course there, an offer which he refused.[103]

The study of illustration was introduced in the art academy as a series of lectures given by art directors rather than by artists, a fact which testifies to the commercial motivation behind its introduction. In the spring of 1893, W. Lewis Fraser, formerly art director for *Century* magazine, lectured to students at the National Academy of Design on the history and technique of illustration, although it was not until 1902 that this school inaugurated an actual illustration class.[104] Between 1894 and 1900, both Fraser and Walter Appleton Clark, then art director for *Century,* lectured on illustration at the Pennsylvania Academy, which had tried unsuccessfully to hire a number of artist-illustrators to teach this course. Maxfield Parrish, Alice Barber Stephens, and Arthur B. Frost had all declined the post, which was assumed in 1900 by the artist-illustrator Henry McCarter, an Academy graduate.[105]

The Boston Museum School was perhaps the first major art academy to encourage its pupils to study decorative painting, a fact which is not surprising since the great muralist

John La Farge played an active role in its administration. As early as 1881, Frederic Crowninshield offered a voluntary "decorative class," where he lectured to students on the mural paintings of such masters as Michelangelo and Raphael, encouraged students to draw from illustrative objects in the museum collection, and had them decorate the school lunch room "in the Egyptian style." By 1884 the school planned an "experimental" decorative class, which was instituted the following year under C. Howard Walker; this course was so successful that a regular three-year program in decoration was established in 1890.[106] Although the Pennsylvania Academy did not offer courses in decoration, it too was influenced by the success of mural painting during the 1890s. After the Academy's lecture room was electrified and renovated in 1896-97, Henry Thouron, the instructor of composition, directed a group of students in the execution of a series of mural decorations, which were unveiled in April 1897 and praised for their "artistic harmony . . ., a typical result of the courses offered by the Academy Schools."[107] Instruction in mural painting was not institutionalized until two decades later. In 1915 Edwin H. Blashfield initiated a class in mural painting at the National Academy and the architect James Monroe Hewlett offered a series of lectures on architectural decoration, assigning the students subjects appropriate for mural work.[108]

During the early twentieth century, the academy's role as an educator was threatened. Just as it was no longer the primary exhibitor of contemporary art, it was no longer the solitary educator. Other institutions such as colleges and universities added studio art to their curriculums, and new schools offered more progressive art programs. Moreover, between 1900 and 1930 American painters and sculptors absorbed developments in modern European art, which had developed as a revolution against European academic systems. The American academic program, which had modeled itself on these Old World precedents, had little to offer the avant-garde modernists. Indeed, its concept of modernity remained tied to the artistic endeavors of the previous century, to "innovations" like mural painting, etching, and illustration. During the late nineteenth century, the human figure was not only the central focus of art education but also the primary subject of painting and sculpture. This correlation explains the success of the art academies of this period. Stylistic and thematic innovations in the twentieth century presented new challenges to the artist, and the art academy, a great proponent of tradition, could not fully prepare him to meet these challenges. Once again the art student was forced to supplement his training in the art academy, to learn his craftsmanship within its framework but to receive his inspiration in the galleries, museums, and periodicals which would bring him in closer contact with the important aesthetic developments of his age. After the Armory Show of 1913, major art events occurred more often outside the academy; independent exhibition organizations became more common, as did private and governmental support of the arts. The academic program still offered the art student continuity: the timeless study of the human figure, the mastery of craftsmanship, and a tradition which, at schools like the Pennsylvania Academy, stretched from student to teacher, from today's students to Morris Blackburn, from Franklin Watkins to Arthur B. Carles, from Thomas Anshutz to Thomas Eakins, to Christian Schussele and beyond, across nearly two hundred years of American art.

Louise Lippincott

CHARLES WILLSON PEALE AND HIS FAMILY OF PAINTERS

In my view of the Academy of fine arts, its objects are to bring forth the dormant Genius of the Pencil; and give the public a true taste of the merits of Painting.

A Genius in obscurity by exhibiting a good Picture is brought into Notice, and thus meets with Incouragement.

A Painter viewing his pictures in his painting-Room, may think his work faultless, but putting them into a Picture Gallery, the Artist then see's his faults, consequently he will improve in some parts of his labors.

Charles Willson Peale to the
Managers of the Pennsylvania Academy
May 20, 1821 PAFA Archives

Although members of the Peale family were painting through the nineteenth century, their aesthetic was rooted firmly in the eighteenth. The remarkable continuity of the family style, uninfluenced by the developments in nineteenth-century painting, the invention and improvement of the camera, and the beginnings of modern art, can be ascribed to the work and to the character of the dynasty's founder, Charles Willson Peale (1741-1827). The theories which Peale developed during his career as a painter in the eighteenth century shaped his family's approach to art and life, which endured through four generations. Blessed with an optimistic nature, a hand skilled for every task, and a keen interest in contemporary issues, regardless of importance, Peale led a happy, busy, and extremely long life. His hopes of sharing his happiness and success were evident in his efforts to teach most of his family to paint and in his constant interest in their careers. His perseverance was only partially rewarded, however; if most of his family applied his theories of art and life to their work and careers, few of them were successful. Nevertheless, the Peale tradition persisted to the twentieth century, although its adherents lacked the talents and energies which characterized its founder.

Throughout his career as a portrait painter Charles Willson Peale was concerned with two problems which shaped his painting style and determined his advice to his family. The first was how to paint an acceptable likeness, and the second, how to find adequate patronage. The importance of these prosaic concerns in his career distinguishes Peale from his teachers Benjamin West and John Singleton Copley, who transcended such minor considerations to make important contributions to the development of English art theory. In contrast to the attitudes of these two masters, Peale's manner of thinking was closer to that of the early eighteenth-century itinerant artist or craftsman.

The foundations for Peale's approach to the art of portraiture were laid very early in his career. A saddle-maker's apprentice until he was twenty, Peale married his first of three wives in 1762 and established his own saddlery business in Annapolis, Maryland. He soon accepted his younger brother James (1749-1831) as an apprentice. His responsibility for his family, coupled with debts incurred in beginning his business, led him to experiment with other trades including watch repair and sign and portrait painting. He mastered portraiture in the same way he learned to fix watches—by trying. Seeing the work of a local painter in 1763, he determined to do better, and, equipped with a few home-made brushes and paints, he executed a self-portrait. From the beginning, Peale viewed painting as a craft rather than as an art, and as a means of support for his family rather than as an intellectual endeavor. This pragmatic attitude insulated him later from the elevated theories of Benjamin West and Joshua Reynolds in the eighteenth century and from the romantic visions and impractical experiments of his son Rembrandt in the nineteenth.

In 1763 Peale traveled to Philadelphia, where he purchased a book on painting, *Handmaid to the Arts,* and proper brushes and colors. The improvement these aids produced encouraged him to take painting lessons from John Hesselius and to consider painting seriously as a viable alternative to saddlery.

Like Hesselius and most other contemporary portraitists, Peale found he had to travel to find commissions. In 1765 travel became an absolute necessity when his Annapolis creditors took steps to have him imprisoned for debt. That year he stopped briefly in Boston, and, after seeing examples of John Smibert's work exhibited in a paint shop, he was directed to the painting room of John Singleton Copley. For the two weeks of his visit, Peale visited Copley regularly and was profoundly influenced by his work. Copley gave Peale a portrait painted by lamplight to copy, initiating the Peale tradition of the lamplight portrait as a trial of skill. Peale may also have seen Copley's portrait of John Hancock (1765; Museum of Fine Arts, Boston) for he adopted the three-quarter-length seated pose soon afterward in his portrait of James Arbuckle (1766; Collection of Mrs. Walter B. Guy). From Hesselius and Copley, Peale learned to respect a good likeness and to think of painting as an imitation of reality.

Peale worked as an itinerant portrait painter until 1767, never earning enough to pay off his debts, but impressing his Philadelphia patrons with his talent and with his desire to improve. In 1766-67 several of them raised a subscription that enabled Peale to study with Benjamin West in London. Peale was quickly disappointed with his English training, perhaps because it had little practical relevance to the problems and limitations of painting in America. West had all but abandoned portraiture in favor of the grander art of history painting and probably had little patience with Peale's less elevated aspirations. He was unable to dissuade Peale from the basic tenet of his painting—that a scrupulous likeness of the sitter guaranteed a pleasing portrait.

This hard-edged realism had characterized Copley's American work as well. It was a style consistent with American pragmatism. English portraiture, on the other hand, had been moving away from the exact imitation of reality. Joshua Reynolds was beginning to develop his theories[1] of generalized form and erudite allusion in portraiture, as illustrated by *Lady Sarah Bunbury Sacrificing to the Graces* (1765; Art Institute of Chicago), which Peale may have seen in London. Peale's attempts in a similar vein were distressingly awkward. *William Pitt* (1768; Westmoreland County Museum), which Peale reproduced in mezzotint (cat. no. 91), shows the statesman in Roman armor in a setting of symbolic statuary, inscribed scrolls, and patriotic mottoes. Peale's obvious discomfort with such an elaborate format was no doubt increased by the necessity of copying the head from another portrait, as the minister was too busy to sit.

Any pretensions to the grand style of portraiture Peale may have entertained were discouraged after his return to Annapolis in 1769. His American audience was less sophisticated than the English patrons *Pitt* was designed to please. Since Americans had little patience with the philosophical trappings of English neoclassical portraiture, the mezzotint failed to sell in the colonies, even when a lengthy explanation of its symbolism was included. Consequently in his full-length portraits painted in America between 1770 and 1776, Peale discarded the use of classical garb in favor of contemporary dress but continued to employ symbolic devices such as flowers, scrolls, and sculptures. During the Revolution, Peale replaced symbolic objects with straightforward narrative details describing the sitter and his situation in life. Such details form the background of *George Washington at Princeton* (cat. no. 140) and illustrate the stages of Peale's career in his later self-portrait, *The Artist in His Museum* (cat. no. 100). Most of Peale's commissions during the 1770s were for simple head-and-bust or half-length portraits. With these, he developed his skill and his speed at taking likenesses.

As he abandoned English portrait conventions and returned to American realism, Peale's admiration of Copley revived. Hearing that Copley was in New York in 1772, Peale journeyed north to see him. He found Copley preparing to move to England to try his hand at history painting. Peale was surprised by Copley's sudden interest in Reynolds's "generalities." He had struggled to imitate the hard-edged realism of Copley's American portraits only to find Copley advocating English styles. But Peale accepted the limitations of his own abilities and of his patrons' tastes. He wrote from New York:

> What I do is by mier [*sic*] imitation of what is before me, perhaps I have a good Eye, that is all; . . . a good painter of either portrait or History must be well acquainted with the Grecian and Roman statues to be able to draw them at pleasure by memory, and account for every beauty in all he sees—These are some of the requisites of a good painter. These are more than I shall ever have time or opportunity to know, but as I have variety of Characters to paint I must [do as] Rembrandt did make them my Anticks [Antiques] and improve myself as well as I can while I am painting for my support.[2]

Although Peale continued to regard English history painting and portraiture as an aesthetic ideal, he gradually ceased to emulate it in his own work.

Peale supported his growing family and paid off his debts by resuming his career as an itinerant painter, centered in Annapolis, although his search for patronage took him more and more often to Philadelphia, the leading city in the colonies. Its large, prosperous population promised him plenty of business without the necessity of travel. In 1776, on the eve of the Revolution, Peale and his family moved to Philadelphia. He was just getting into business when the war began, and he joined Washington's army as a member of the Philadelphia militia. His brother James, still resident in Annapolis, enlisted in a Maryland regiment.

The war halted Peale's portrait work temporarily but ensured a flourishing miniature business. Miniatures, small and intimate, were popular presents which soldiers sent to their families back home. Peale required only three short sittings to complete a likeness, and his equipment was small and easy to carry. Thus, while Charles Willson Peale participated in the battles of Princeton and Trenton, the years 1776 and 1777 are notable for his output of miniatures, over one hundred fifty each year. Another benefit which Peale derived from his

cat. no. 100. Charles Willson Peale. *The Artist in His Museum,* 1822.

career as a soldier was a collection of portraits of the heroes of the Revolution. He had two sittings from General George Washington, one in 1776 and another in 1779. He also painted a number of officers, including Generals Rochambeau, de Kalb, Lafayette, and von Steuben (cat. no. 92). Their portraits, which Peale exhibited in his exhibition room in Philadelphia, attracted public attention and additional sitters.

After the war, Peale continued his portrait work. The years 1781 to 1794 were the most successful and productive of his career. The foremost painter in Philadelphia, he was busy enough to support his growing family, which comprised seven children by 1794. His patrons included the wealthiest and most important men in the United States. In 1783 Peale received a commission from Robert Morris for a number of portraits of himself, his family, and his friend Gouverneur Morris. Peale painted *Gouverneur and Robert Morris* (cat. no. 93) to commemorate their partnership in the Office of Finance during the Revolution. As in *George Washington at Princeton,* the composition of *Gouverneur and Robert Morris* contains details which describe the subjects' roles in the Revolution. In this case, their financial support of the young nation is suggested in the inscription to which Robert Morris points, "A plan of Finance to restore public credit & for establishing a national Bank." The restrained color and simple forms of the composition reflect the conservative tastes of both sitters.

By the year of the constitutional convention, Charles Willson Peale's portrait painting had led him into a new venture, a museum of natural history and American portraiture. The idea for the museum grew out of the success of his exhibition room, to which he had begun charging admission in 1781. The success of his portrait exhibitions, which included *von Steuben* and the portraits of other military heroes, induced him to add more portraits and other attractions, including moving picture shows and specimens of natural history. By 1786 his gallery had developed into a museum of American portraiture and natural history and had become his chief obsession.

As Peale's interest in natural history grew, the portraits he painted for his museum began to take on new meanings for him. To him the purpose of the museum portrait was to represent man as "the head of the Linnean order" of nature. For his museum, therefore, he wanted to collect the best human as well as the best animal specimens. Peale considered the best human specimens to be "the persons who have been highly distinguished in their exertions in the late glorious revolution,"[3] with George Washington heading the list. The portrait of Washington which Peale painted in 1787 (cat. no. 95) was his effort to preserve the features of the great man. In Peale's mind, the *Washington,* the *Franklin* (cat. no. 94), and the rest of the museum portraits were like the preserved birds and animals which stood below them in the gallery in that they illustrated the perfection of the order of nature.

To preserve his human specimens in portraits, Peale felt he had to achieve as close a likeness as possible. Therefore, he began to render even the smallest details of his sitter's features with great fidelity. He also devised a special format for the museum portraits, which set off the likeness and minimized distracting details. The portraits show the sitter's head and shoulders only, usually against a plain background, enclosed in a gilt oval mat and rectangular frame. The entire interest is focused on the likeness to the exclusion of all detail but military insignia.

The emphasis on the details of a sitter's appearance which characterized Peale's museum portraits is also evident in his later commissioned work. Such is the case with his portraits of James Latimer (cat. no. 96) and Sarah Geddes Latimer (cat. no. 97), painted in 1789-90. James Latimer's presidency of Delaware's constitutional ratification convention may have led Peale to take a special interest in his appearance. Both portraits, however, are excellent characterizations of the Latimers because of the attention Peale paid to the minute details of their features and expressions. The simplicity and careful realism of the Wash-

cat. no. 93. Charles Willson Peale. *Gouverneur and Robert Morris,* 1783.

ington, the Franklin, and the Latimer portraits contrast with the style of contemporary English historical portraiture. Peale had developed a portrait style which suited his talents and the tastes of a middle class republic.

Charles Willson Peale's success in Philadelphia had encouraged his brother James to move north after resigning his commission in 1781. A developing painter, James soon found plenty of practice assisting his brother with reproductions of his full-length portraits of Washington. James also made the frames, usually simple black moldings, for his brother's portraits, receiving between one and two pounds for each. The black frames edged with gold leaf on the Latimer portraits may be his work. In this manner, with the addition of a few portrait commissions of his own, he began his career as a painter in Philadelphia. By 1786 Charles Willson Peale had more business than he could accommodate, and he began sharing his patronage with James. James painted miniatures, while Charles Willson painted oil portraits. James's miniature painting was a mixed success; his patronage was unsteady, and there were several other competent miniaturists in Philadelphia. James Peale's miniatures painted before 1790 show how much he relied on the work of Charles Willson Peale. Painted

cat. no. 94. Charles Willson Peale. *Benjamin Franklin,* ca.1785.

with wiry, short brushstrokes on very small ivories, they are entirely in his brother's manner.[4] His oil portraits of this period, some commissions for which are recorded in Charles Willson Peale's letter books, were even more dependent on his brother's work. It is likely that some of the portraits attributed to Charles Willson's early Philadelphia period are actually the work of James, who had yet to develop an independent style.

After 1790 portrait painting in Philadelphia became a highly competitive business. As other portraitists moved to Philadelphia, patronage became an increasingly difficult problem for Charles Willson Peale. Not only did he have to encourage his own patrons, but he had to find buyers for James's miniatures. In addition, his two older sons were promising painters and were on the verge of launching their careers. Peale's response to the problem was characteristically businesslike and optimistic. In his own portrait business, he lowered his prices to encourage patrons, kept his painting room full of portraits of eminent men and handsome women, and learned how to paint a likeness quickly while carrying on an animated conversation with his sitter. His reputation as a pleasant, competent, and undemanding portraitist stood him in good stead throughout his career.

Peale planned to retire from portrait painting when his sons were ready to take over his business. In 1790 he began exploring other possible sources of income. His museum was becoming an extremely profitable business, and it offered outlets for his manual skills in the preservation of specimens and the portrayal of great men. Peale also tried his hand at printing, inventing, pamphlet writing, and a variety of other interesting occupations.

After 1790 Peale devoted himself to two projects—promoting his museum and teaching his children how to paint. He instructed all of his children in drawing. Of the three eldest children, Raphaelle (1774-1825), Rembrandt (1778-1860), and Angelica Kauffman (1775-1853), Angelica displayed the most promise as an artist. Rembrandt labored over his drawings for hours, while Raphaelle was frequently unwilling to practice at all. Rembrandt was the most diligent of the children, appropriating Angelica's drawing book for his own use and helping his father and uncle make picture frames.[5] In the face of such competition, Angelica soon stopped drawing, and she never painted. Rembrandt, however, began to paint in oils in 1791, at the age of thirteen, and his precocity may have inspired his father to plan an art academy for Philadelphia that year. Charles Willson Peale's effort to promote his son's education failed when other Philadelphia artists and patrons did not respond to his proposal. A European education for Rembrandt was also considered. However, the uncertain political relationships between England, France, and the United States made travel abroad difficult. Therefore, the Peale children remained in Philadelphia and received their education in art from their father.

As Peale soon realized, he could not offer his children the kind of training he had received in London. He had no examples of the old masters to show them, no history painting, no genre, no landscape paintings, nor did he have facilities for life study or for drawing from the antique. Consequently, Rembrandt and Raphaelle received very limited educations, which were founded chiefly on Charles Willson's portrait and miniature work. They practiced painting still lifes, self-portraits, and portraits of members of the family. After a while Charles Willson Peale set them to copying the portraits in the museum. In spite of his sons' amateurish training, Peale had great plans for their success. In 1794 he announced his retirement from portrait painting and recommended his sons to the public in his stead. Sharing their patronage as Charles Willson and James had, Raphaelle painted miniatures while Rembrandt devoted himself to portraiture.

The establishment of Philadelphia as the capital city of the United States in 1794 carried with it the promise of increased patronage for the city's artists. Unfortunately for Raphaelle and Rembrandt, however, along with the nation's diplomats, statesmen, and intellectuals, came Gilbert Stuart. The younger Peales suddenly had to compete with an older artist of international reputation, whose fluid, elegant style of portraiture was well beyond their capabilities.

Charles Willson Peale offered all the aid to his sons that he could. In an effort to improve their training, he organized an art academy called the Columbianum. To Peale, the most important aspect of the organization was its school. He donated some casts so that students could draw from the antique. However, the only regular member of the antique class was Rembrandt Peale. Rembrandt was also a member of the ill-fated life class, which met only once.

The Peales also hoped that the Columbianum exhibition would attract patrons for their work. As might be expected, the family made a strong showing at the 1795 exhibition. Charles Willson Peale exhibited *The Staircase Group* (1795; Philadelphia Museum of Art), and James sent a small conversation piece, probably *The Artist and His Family* (cat. no. 105). Both works were intended to be virtuoso displays of their talents—Charles Willson's in the area of *trompe l'oeil* realism and James's in miniature portraiture. Raphaelle sent several portraits but expressed his own preferences by including *trompe l'oeil* paintings as well. Rembrandt was represented by portraits.

cat. no. 105. James Peale. *The Artist and His Family,* 1795.

The Columbianum did not last long enough to establish Rembrandt and Raphaelle with Philadelphia patrons. Unable to compete with the brilliant Stuart, their next alternative was flight from the city. Just before they left, Charles Willson Peale was able to persuade President Washington to give his sons some sittings. A life portrait of Washington hanging in Rembrandt's painting room might attract some patrons. Rembrandt's portrait of the President (1795; Historical Society of Pennsylvania), showing him as a gloomy, tired old man, was not the happiest of images, especially when compared to the "Lansdowne" and the "Athenaeum" portraits which Gilbert Stuart was painting that year. Almost before the portrait was dry, Rembrandt and Raphaelle packed it and about twenty-five replicas of museum portraits and moved to Charleston, South Carolina. Exhibited in the town hall, their gallery of national heroes enjoyed great success. Rembrandt sold ten replicas of his *Washington.* A year later the brothers moved on to Baltimore, where Rembrandt was commissioned in 1798 to paint a portrait of William Raborg (cat. no. 74), a local merchant. The Raborg portrait shows Rembrandt employing the S-shaped pose favored by his father. He was, however, beginning to develop his own approach to the depiction of skin tones and flesh, painting them with a softness not found in Charles Willson's work.

The brothers' partnership broke up in 1797, when Raphaelle returned to Philadelphia to marry and to work in his father's museum. Rembrandt returned to Philadelphia in 1799, perhaps emboldened by some success in Baltimore, only to meet with the same disappointing "lack of encouragement for his art." Although his painting had improved, it still lacked the grace and sophistication which made Stuart's work so popular. Rembrandt made some tentative attempts at imitating his rival's style, but the results were stiff and awkward.

Charles Willson Peale was the only member of the family unaffected by Stuart's success. More or less retired from commissioned portrait painting, he derived his income from his immensely profitable museum. He painted only to please a friend, to add another hero to his gallery, or to experiment with a new technique. As he did not have to seek patronage, he was not compelled to alter his style or to travel. As much of his work as possible was diverted to James, Rembrandt, or Raphaelle. James Peale does seem to have absorbed some of Stuart's influence early in the nineteenth century. Securely established in the miniature business, James was also painting some portraits in oil and the latter demonstrate his familiarity with Stuart's work. His undated *Self-Portrait* (cat. no. 106), probably painted between 1800 and 1805, adopts the head-and-bust three-quarter view of Stuart's *Dr. William Shippen, Jr.* (c.1798; Collection of the Philadelphia College of Physicians), which James copied for Peale's Museum.[6] James's portrait of his wife *Mary Claypoole Peale* (c.1800-1805; Pennsylvania Academy of the Fine Arts) seems to be a humbler version of *Mrs. George Plumstead* (Pennsylvania Academy of the Fine Arts), painted by Stuart in 1800. James's adoption of the red curtain and marble column for the background of this and several other portraits of the period suggests that he was imitating Stuart, who used the device frequently.

After 1800 the Peales responded to the competition from other artists by diversifying their occupations and their painting. Every member of the family from Charles Willson Peale to his youngest son, Titian Ramsay II, explored different sources of income or different kinds of painting after 1800. Various members of the family became museum entrepreneurs, natural historians, soldiers, businessmen, writers, inventors, and explorers, as well as painters. They were frequently employed in several kinds of work simultaneously. While Charles Willson and James Peale had painted oil portraits and miniatures almost exclusively before 1800, after 1800 the Peale family artists were producing history paintings, allegories, still-life paintings, *trompe l'oeil* paintings, landscapes, lithographs, and book illustrations.

Another Peale family project was the exhumation and exhibition of the bones of a mastodon. The prospect of an entire skeleton of an extinct elephant for the museum drew

Charles Willson and Rembrandt to New York in 1801. After buying the rights to excavate and designing a pump to empty water from the site, Charles Willson Peale supervised the operation with the aid of his son. As the skeleton of the beast emerged from the ground, Rembrandt suggested that once it had been assembled, he would take it to London and Paris for exhibition. He argued that not only would he make a great deal of money for the museum, but he would also be able to study with the masters of portraiture of both cities. The family agreed, and Rembrandt and Rubens sailed for England in 1802 on what proved to be an abortive expedition.

The skeleton was received without enthusiasm in London. Moreover, Benjamin West had just been expelled from the Royal Academy and was unable to help Rembrandt enter the school. Rembrandt and several other students hired their own models and did some drawing from life, but his study was neither long enough nor intense enough to have any effect on his work. The prospects of war with France made a trip to Paris impossible. In the fall of 1803 the two brothers and the giant skeleton returned to Philadelphia.

Back in Philadelphia, Raphaelle made money for the first time in his life by taking silhouettes at the museum with a new machine called the physiognotrace. In 1803 he toured the South with this machine, cutting thousands of silhouettes and painting a few miniatures as well. But, when Raphaelle returned to Philadelphia, he found that several competitive silhouette cutters had taken all of his business. He was forced to return to portrait and miniature painting, which he disliked, and to find consolation in drink.

In 1800 the national capital was moved from Philadelphia to Washington, D.C., and in 1803 Gilbert Stuart followed his patrons south to the new city. The next two years showed a slow but progressive rise in the family's fortunes, although the preceding frustrating decade had left its mark on Rembrandt and Raphaelle. Charles Willson Peale's interest in painting revived enough for him to plan a trip to Washington to update his collection of portraits of the great men. He took Rembrandt along to help, hoping that new examples of his work would attract patronage:

> Especially as the very small degree of attention bestowed on painting in this City has rather discouraged him, and almost induced him to relinquish his profession if from anything else he could obtain competency.[7]

Rembrandt painted several portraits in Washington and seems to have collaborated with his father on others, including a portrait of Gilbert Stuart (1805; New York Historical Society). Both Peales visited Gilbert Stuart's painting room; Rembrandt, who had not seen it before, was impressed. In a letter to Stuart of 1806 Rembrandt said that he was studying by lamplight as Sir Joshua Reynolds recommended in the *Discourses,* and he added:

> It seems to favor the manner which I have heard you say principally distinguishes you from Mr. West, in producing the effects of projection, instead of depending, merely, on the accuracy of the outline.[8]

If the letter shows that Rembrandt was attempting to develop his own portrait style in emulation of Reynolds and Stuart rather than of West and Charles Willson Peale, he was also beginning to follow the practical advice of the latter artists by building a painting room and charging low prices for his work. He was beginning to get commissions, and his confidence rose rapidly, although he did not yet have enough business to charge full prices.

The founding of the Pennsylvania Academy of the Fine Arts in 1805 seemed to promise more opportunities for recognition for the Peales. Charles Willson and Rembrandt had followed the development of a similar institution in New York City in 1802 and were instrumental in the organization of its Philadelphia counterpart. During the first six years of its existence, however, the Academy did little for the city's artists. The Peales' requests for life schools and frequent exhibitions were ignored. Still, the artists associated with the

cat. no. 115. Rembrandt Peale. *George Washington* (Patriae Pater), ca.1824.

Academy were allowed to select objects for the Academy to purchase and to arrange infrequent exhibitions. In 1807, Charles Willson Peale hung the Academy's first exhibition,[9] which consisted of paintings from the collection of Robert Fulton.

The biggest disappointment for the Peales was the Academy's failure to establish a life school. Charles Willson Peale wished both Rembrandt and Raphaelle to study from the model, as they were deficient in knowledge of the human figure. Their ignorance was so great that a performance of a war dance by a tribe of scantily dressed Osage Indians at Philadelphia's only theatre was a revelation to Rembrandt. He later wrote for *The Crayon:*

> I was much struck by their manly proportions—each chief being above six feet high, realizing an aggregate of the most celebrated examples of Greek sculpture. I observed many beautiful articulations which I had imagined were licenses taken by the old sculptors, especially the hips, the firm pectoral and uninflated abdominal muscles.[10]

The fundamental ignorance of human anatomy and of the nude human figure shared by every member of the Peale family except Charles Willson probably explains why he was the only member of the family ever to paint original full-length portraits.

As Rembrandt began to succeed with Philadelphia patrons, his growing ambition encouraged him to try his luck abroad once again. In 1808 he sailed for Paris to paint ten museum portraits of the leading men of France. He had been able to raise his prices from thirty to fifty dollars a head, and he planned to live in France for a year on the five hundred dollars he would earn. He proposed to study portraiture with France's most eminent painters, only to find to his surprise that in France the great artists were not portrait painters.[11] However, he was welcomed by Napoleon's minister of culture, Dominique Vivant Denon, who took him to visit the studios of David and Gérard. Rembrandt was not nearly so impressed with these French neoclassicists as he was with the work of Peter Paul Rubens, which he saw in the Luxembourg Palace.

Rembrandt's work was well received in France. He reported to his father that his portrait had been praised as being in the manner of Van Dyke, although that style does not seem particularly evident in the portraits of David (Pennsylvania Academy of the Fine Arts), Houdon (cat. no. 114), Denon (cat. no. 113), and other luminaries, which he completed in Paris. What Rembrandt obviously did learn in France was high finishing for portraits. After his return from Paris, Rembrandt gave all of his portraits an extremely high finish.

Even with this new technique, however, Rembrandt was not successful. His declining popularity as a portrait painter after 1815 can be blamed on his slowness. The grimly resolute expressions of his male sitters and the wilting poses of his females can be ascribed to the long sittings he required to complete his work. In addition, Rembrandt had developed a bizarre concept of ideal portraiture while abroad. On the voyage home he wrote to his father:

> I have studied their [the old masters'] beauties, noticed their defects, methodized their systems & have formed an Union of their various excellencies in the *Picture of My Brain,* which is still to be my model, assisted by Nature—which I believe is sufficiently beautiful in America.[12]

Entirely different from his father's, which was based on likeness and the minute depiction of reality, Rembrandt's ideal was a generalized image which he could alter to create a resemblance to his sitter. This "Picture of My Brain" influenced all of Rembrandt's work after 1808, but it is nowhere more evident than in his *National Portrait and Standard Likeness of George Washington* (1823) also known as "The Porthole Portrait." Conceived in Rembrandt's active imagination, it is a composite of the Stuart, Peale, and Trumbull portraits of Washington. The final result was intended to portray Rembrandt's concept, rather than memory, of Washington's appearance. The Pennsylvania Academy's replica of this portrait (cat. no. 115), six feet high and four and one-half feet wide, also demonstrates that for Rembrandt a monumental painting was basically a very large museum portrait.

Rembrandt's constant experiments with coloring systems and new media arose from his interest in portraying imaginary ideals. With encaustic painting, a technique he learned in France, he thought that he had found the perfect solution for the problem of depicting skin tones and textures. He described the discovery to his father with his usual enthusiasm:

> My tints surpass the fairest complection and equal what the imagination can conceive—Beauty shall come to me for immortality, for its texture flows from my Pencil as I trace its forms—to create flesh is no longer difficult—to modify it with color, light or shadow no longer tedious—consequently my principal attention may be to character and beauty, etc.[13]

Rembrandt's interest in flesh tints, "beauty," and "character" sometimes interfered with his ability to take likenesses. Even Charles Willson Peale could not defend his son's systems when a Mrs. Bottner rejected her portrait because it did not look like her, because it added twenty years to her age, and because the tints around her mouth looked more like a beard than like shadows.[14]

For a while, Rembrandt influenced his father's painting style. Charles Willson Peale, who resumed portrait painting in 1808, experimented with several of Rembrandt's coloring systems. However, he was much more cautious and frequently was the first to notice defects in the systems. Never did he abandon imitation of nature for a system, although a system would doubtless have made his late work, hampered by weak eyesight, much easier. Charles Willson Peale's later work combines Rembrandt's warmer coloring and high finish with his own careful study of appearances and with his superior knowledge of the human figure and of composition. His *Lamplight Portrait* (cat. no. 101) of his brother James and his monumental self-portrait *The Artist in His Museum* (cat. no. 100) show that Charles Willson Peale was still the most capable and versatile artist in the family. In 1823 he painted a self-portrait[15] as ambitious as *The Artist in His Museum,* combining the *trompe l'oeil* effect of *The Staircase Group* with the narrative detail of the former. The success of the painting, done in his old manner, finally led him to repudiate Rembrandt's advice altogether. In 1823 he wrote to his son:

> Truth is better than a high finish. The Italians say give me a true outline & you may fill it up with turd. . . . I am of the opinion that the portrait painter must dispatch his work as quick as possible, by aiming at good character, truth in drawing & coloring—effect at a proper distance if not so highly finished may be acceptable with the multitude.[16]

Throughout his career Charles Willson Peale supplied a viable high standard of achievement for the other painters in his family. Under his influence, the works of James, Raphaelle, and Rembrandt exhibited the formal characteristics which defined the family style. Attention to physical details, persistent use of static neoclassical poses, restrained brushwork, and lack of interest in surface textures establish their portraits in the Peale tradition and differentiate them from the work of other portraitists in Philadelphia during the ninteenth century. In spite of their adherence to a family tradition, however, James, Raphaelle, and Rembrandt shared one stylistic trait not characteristic of Charles Willson Peale's work. They painted a portrait by applying the sitter's features to a schematic or generalized shape in order to achieve a likeness. In Rembrandt's case the basic form was "The Picture of My Brain," and later, in his instruction manual *Graphics,* he suggested an oval for primary shape. Both James and Raphaelle constructed heads from simple geometric forms. This construction technique was less sophisticated than Charles Willson Peale's, which was based on his knowledge of the human form and anatomy. Although Rembrandt's

cat. no. 101. Charles Willson Peale. *James Peale* ("The Lamplight Portrait"), 1822. THE DETROIT INSTITUTE OF ARTS.

techniques were complicated, his labors extreme, and his results highly finished, he, like James and Raphaelle, was working in a stylistic tradition harking back to that of the eighteenth-century limners.

After 1810 neither Charles Willson nor Rembrandt received good prices for their portraits, and their subsequent experiments with history painting should be seen as efforts to raise money and to attract patrons. The Peales did not regard history painting as the highest level of artistic achievement, but rather as a public spectacle. During the 1780s the rise of the museum portrait to the position history painting usually occupied in Sir Joshua Reynolds's hierarchy of artistic genres had relegated history painting to the status of the five-legged cow Peale's Museum had acquired in its early years. Both could be enjoyed for the multiplicity and complexity of their forms and for their moral and philosophical connotations. Both attracted the admission-paying public.

Rembrandt was inspired to begin history painting after Adolph Ulrich Wertmuller's popular and financial success with the exhibition of his *Danae* (1787; Nationalmuseum, Stockholm) in Philadelphia in 1811. That year Rembrandt painted a nude subject of his own, *The Dream of Love* (location unknown), and also *The Roman Daughter* (Private Collection).[17] Both became major attractions in the museum he opened in Baltimore in 1814. His major effort, *The Court of Death* (1820; Detroit Institute of Arts), was inspired by the monumental Biblical canvases by West, exhibited at the Academy. *The Court of Death* earned nine thousand dollars for its creator in 1821.

Charles Willson Peale's efforts in the genre were less spectacular and less pretentious, but often more interesting. He selected his subjects as much for their appropriateness to his interests as for their potential as exhibition pieces. *Noah and His Ark* (cat. no. 99), painted for the museum, was copied from a work by the immigrant painter of animals and landscapes, Charles Catton, Jr. Peale copied the painting because it embodied all of his ideas about the harmony of art, religion, and nature in one charming, minutely detailed whole.

James and Raphaelle also developed proficiency in other artistic genres in order to augment their incomes from portrait and miniature painting. Unlike Charles Willson and Rembrandt, they painted still lifes. There were several sources for their compositions, including the still lifes which John Singleton Copley used in his American portraits and which Charles Willson Peale imitated. However, the most important prototypes for the Peale still lifes were the seventeenth-century Dutch paintings then popular with Philadelphia collectors. Rembrandt Peale claimed the credit for introducing Raphaelle to the genre, having bought some Dutch still lifes in 1803.[18]

James and Raphaelle were painting still lifes by 1805, but they produced most of their work in this genre after 1811, the year of the Pennsylvania Academy's first annual exhibition. That exhibition seems to have introduced Raphaelle and his father to the aesthetic and financial possibilities of still-life painting. Of the three hundred paintings displayed, over sixty were by Dutch or Flemish artists; most were still lifes and all were owned by private collectors. Charles Willson Peale was soon urging Raphaelle to apply himself to still-life painting. Raphaelle sent three still lifes to the annual exhibition in 1812, twelve in 1813, and seventeen in 1814. He offered still lifes for sale every year at the Academy until he died in 1825.

For Raphaelle at least, a still-life painting was more than another source of income. Alcoholic, unhappily married, and burdened with debts, he created in his still-life painting the order and calm which he could not find in his life. Unlike the rest of his family, he was interested in the formal problems of composition and spatial organization. Even his simplest compositions are rigorously ordered and carefully executed. Raphaelle was perhaps the only Peale who did not feel that the best painting was the one most elaborately composed or cluttered with detail. He preferred to limit his subject matter and to work and rework his compositions on a series of small wooden panels. *Apples and Fox Grapes* (cat. no. 111) and *Fox Grapes and Peaches* (cat. no. 112) seem to have been part of such a series. Such careful preparations on a small scale undoubtedly contributed to the precise mastery of space and composition which Raphaelle displayed in his larger still lifes.

James Peale did not begin to paint still lifes seriously until about 1820, and he did not exhibit them at the Academy until 1824. James did not share Raphaelle's rigorously formal approach to still-life painting. Preferring to heap a variety of fruits or vegetables on a table or in a basket, he achieved a rich rather than restrained composition. He was also not above duplicating successful works; two versions of *Still Life No. 2* (cat. no. 108) exist, of which the Pennsylvania Academy's is probably the original.[19] In their warm coloring and abundance of objects, James's still lifes reflect his happier, less austere outlook on life. Like Raphaelle, he suffered from gout, but he had a happy family life. As his health failed, his daughters helped him with his work and later contributed to his support with the proceeds from their own painting.

Titian Peale II (1799-1885), Charles Willson Peale's youngest son, developed another facet of his family's artistic interests. A natural historian, explorer, and collector, he became a skilled draughtsman and scientific illustrator. He accompanied several important exploring expeditions as an artist and illustrator, going with Long's Expedition up the Missouri River in 1819 and with the Wilkes Expedition to the South Seas from 1839 to 1842. The Long Expedition supplied Titian with much of the material for his later work. He brought skins of specimens back to Philadelphia and mounted them for the museum with his father's help.

cat. no. 99. Charles Willson Peale. *Noah and His Ark,* 1819.

cat. no. 119.
Titian Ramsay Peale II.
Missouri Bears, ca. 1820.
THE AMERICAN PHILOSOPHICAL SOCIETY, PHILADELPHIA.

cat. no. 111. Raphaelle Peale. *Apples and Fox Grapes,* 1815.

Charles Willson Peale painted one of Titian's specimens, a turkey, in the foreground of *The Artist in His Museum.* After it was mounted and installed in the museum, the turkey served as the model for Titian's illustration of the species in Charles L. Bonaparte's *American Ornithology* (cat. no. 122).[20] There is a similar history behind the animals in the drawings which Titian exhibited at the Pennsylvania Academy in 1822. *Missouri Bears* (cat. no. 119) shows specimens from the Long Expedition mounted in a museum habitat group.

Illustration was an art form which exactly suited Titian's training and tastes. He had received all of his artistic training from his father and was, therefore, a careful observer and a good copyist. These were the skills which a good scientific illustrator needed; fortunately for Titian, problems of coloring and composition were irrelevant. His limitations became readily apparent in the more ambitious oil paintings he created between 1850 and 1875. Nostalgic representation of his memories of his western expeditions, they are crudely composed and executed.

After 1811, all of the Peale painters—Charles Willson, James, Raphaelle, Rembrandt, and Titian—relied on the Pennsylvania Academy's annual exhibitions for exposure of their

cat. no. 108. James Peale. *Still Life No. 2,* 1821.

cat. no. 103. James Peale.
Frances Gratz Etting, 1794.

cat. no. 104. James Peale.
Reuben Etting, 1794.

work to prospective patrons. Charles Willson Peale also used the exhibitions to evaluate his own work as well. He would carry a recently completed portrait to the Academy, stand it next to a painting he admired, and compare the two for several minutes. Then he would return home with his painting and improve it. James and Raphaelle used the annuals as indicators of public tastes and as a market place for their pictures. Their still-life paintings and James's interest in romantic landscape painting after 1820 reflect the public tastes expressed in the exhibitions. Titian probably sent his drawings to the 1822 annual in order to enhance his reputation as an illustrator.

The Pennsylvania Academy of the Fine Arts proved most useful to two of James's daughters, who followed in his footsteps and became portrait and miniature painters. Anna Claypoole Peale (1791-1878), a miniature and still-life painter, exhibited at the Academy every year from 1811 to 1842. Her sister, Sarah Miriam Peale (1800-1885), sent portraits to the exhibitions from 1817 to 1831. In 1824 both were elected Pennsylvania Academicians, the first women to receive that honor. Anna Claypoole (cat. no. 107) was a miniaturist, working in her father's style (cat. no. 90). Sarah Miriam painted portraits, learning the craft by assisting her father with the details of his occasional commissions. Later, she studied with her cousin Rembrandt in Baltimore, acquiring some of his methods of coloring and finish. Another daughter of James, Margaretta Angelica Peale (1795-1882), was also a painter, although she shared none of the professional ambitions of her sisters. Margaretta's still lifes (cat. no. 109), imitations or copies of James's and Raphaelle's work, are painted in a relatively primitive style.

cat. no. 90. Anna Claypoole Peale.
Madame L' Allemand, ca. 1818.

Not all of Charles Willson Peale's family became professional artists, although most of them painted at some point in their lives. Rubens Peale (1784-1865), one of Charles Willson's sons, was a museum manager and businessman until his retirement, when he devoted his time to copying or imitating still lifes by his uncle James and his brother Raphaelle. Rubens's daughter, Mary Jane Peale (1827-1902), was a follower of Rembrandt Peale. The subjects of her portraits have the wooden expressions characteristic of Rembrandt's later work. Mary Jane lacked Rembrandt's technical skills, however, and her original portraits verge on the primitive. She was the only Peale ever to enroll at the Pennsylvania Academy as a student, studying there in 1879 as a student of Christian Schussele and Thomas Eakins.[21]

After the death of Charles Willson Peale in 1827 his family gradually withdrew from the increasingly competitive world of contemporary American art, while involving themselves somewhat more actively in the running of the nation's developing art academies. Rembrandt Peale was both a Pennsylvania Academician and an Academy director. He was especially influential in that institution's belated founding of an art school in 1856. In addition, he briefly served as the president of the American Academy of Arts and as a member of the National Academy of Design. His brother Franklin (1795-1870) also served as director of the Pennsylvania Academy, although he was one of the few members of the Peale family who did not paint.

The shift in the Peale family style, from original and stylish portraiture to simplistic imitation, resulted from a number of factors. Due to the failure of early Philadelphia art

cat. no. 107. James Peale. *Anna and Margaretta Peale,* ca.1805.

cat. no. 109. Margaretta Angelica Peale. *Strawberries and Cherries.*

schools and the political disputes which made travel abroad difficult, the young Peales never received a thorough grounding in the basic principles of academic art, which might have enabled them to equal or surpass Charles Willson Peale. Competition from other artists forestalled their establishment as independent painters and also impeded their stylistic development beyond the limit of Charles Willson's achievements. The very closeness of the family and the reliance of its members on each other, and on Charles Willson especially, also tended to discourage development outside of the family traditions. After Charles Willson Peale's death, the important characteristics of his tradition changed. Instead of emulating the hard work, ingenuity, and persistence which characterized Charles Willson Peale's involvement in every venture, his family continued the superficial aspects of his tradition, painting museum-type portraits, running museums, and joining art academies. Most importantly, many of them worked in his style or copied his paintings without trying to improve their skills or to surpass his achievements. But, regardless of questions of aesthetic merit or technical ability, the work of the Peale family represents one of the young nation's most interesting and expressive artistic traditions.

cat. no. 152. Gilbert Stuart. *George Washington,* 1796. ("The Lansdowne Portrait").

Mark Thistlethwaite

THE ARTIST AS INTERPRETER OF AMERICAN HISTORY

It is extremely gratifying to the lovers of the fine arts in this country, to see a taste and disposition to encourage historical painting and engravings, by introducing among us a taste for subjects from our own history. It is certainly the most proper method to establish schools of art in America.

G[eorge]. M[urray].
"Review of the Second Annual Exhibition,"
The Port Folio, 8 (July 1812), 22.

Between the War of Independence and the Civil War, generations of Americans were filled with a sense of destiny as well as with concern for the future of their new nation. A major interest then was the inventing and sustaining of a sense of national identity and uniqueness. The assertive nationalism of the age, evident in George Murray's remarks of 1812, provided the motivating spirit for the founding of the Pennsylvania Academy of the Fine Arts. Art, particularly images of American historical events and personages, furnished visual concretization of the emerging American identity. Moreover, history painting, through the late eighteenth and most of the nineteenth centuries, was idealized as the highest branch of art, "the *epic* of the art," [1] an early nineteenth-century journal declared. From its inception, the Pennsylvania Academy manifested respect for and encouragement of the art of history painting.

In a letter of 1805, setting forth the plans and organization of the new Pennsylvania Academy, founder Charles Willson Peale informed Thomas Jefferson that "Mr. West is very anxious to have all his designs, the originals of historic paintings placed here." [2] Benjamin West, a native of Pennsylvania, historical painter to George III, and, in the words of Robert Fulton, "an artist of the most transcendental merit," [3] personified the high standard of art to which the founders of the Pennsylvania Academy aspired. In 1807 the Academy exhibited four paintings by West from the collection of Robert Fulton and also eleven paintings by Robert Smirke, illustrating scenes from Joel Barlow's epic patriotic poem

Columbiad. Related primarily to the history of America, Smirke's works were considered "gems in the art of history painting."[4] In 1850 the high status accorded history painting by the Pennsylvania Academy was evidenced by a competition in which the category of Historical, Scriptural, and Dramatic carried a substantially greater monetary award than that of the other class, Landscape or Marine.[5] A specific interest in American historical subjects was shown by the Temple Historical Painting Competition of 1883, which was restricted to entries depicting the War of Independence and its antecedent events. Special exhibitions such as "Revolutionary Pictures" of 1898 and "A Gallery of National Portraiture and Historical Scenes" in 1926 further attest to the Academy's interest in American history painting. The Academy's collection now includes major monuments of history painting, notably Benjamin West's *Penn's Treaty with the Indians* and *Perry's Victory on Lake Erie* by Thomas Birch. A particular strength of the Academy's collection lies in historical portraiture, as exemplified by Charles Willson Peale's *George Washington at Princeton* and Gilbert Stuart's famous "Lansdowne" portrait of George Washington.

While the Pennsylvania Academy did collect and exhibit American history painting, it actually favored other forms of American art, especially portraiture. Although critic Henry Edwin Brown claimed in 1900 that the "Academy seems to have had a surfeit of historical paintings since the days of Benjamin West,"[6] an examination of the Academy's annual exhibition catalogues reveals that American historical works rarely constituted even five percent of the total objects of any given exhibition. In fact, paintings treating European historical events were as, if not more, popular; of the sixteen paintings judged in the competition of 1850, fourteen were by foreign artists and none depicted American history. The Pennsylvania Academy's most ambitious attempt to support American history painting was the Temple Historical Painting Competition of 1883. Limited to depictions of events of the Revolutionary War, the competition offered a first prize of $3000 and various medals. However, the competition proved unsuccessful when only four artists submitted entries. The lack of artist participation not only indicated the low status of history painting in the late nineteenth century but also symbolized history painting's inability to succeed throughout most of American history.

Except in the mid-nineteenth century, during a flourishing of nationalism before the devastating blows of sectionalism and civil war, American history painting never really took root in this country. Early artists with grand ambitions as history painters—men like Benjamin West, John Singleton Copley, John Trumbull, John Vanderlyn, Washington Allston, and Samuel F. B. Morse, all of whom were Pennsylvania Academicians—either left America or worked in frustration and disappointment. With insight, Charles Carroll, the patron of Charles Willson Peale, warned Peale as early as 1769 of the prospects of history painting in America:

> Few arrive at a High Point in the Perfection of it and indeed in this Part of the World few have a taste for it and very few can thro' the Expense of Giving that Encouragement that such an artist would desire.[7]

Insufficient large-scale and consistent patronage (in Europe the traditional role of church and state), the rise of landscape and genre painting as expressions of American nationalism, and the impact of the camera adversely affected the development of history painting in America. To some artists, notably Washington Allston, the painting of battle scenes, a major staple of historical art, seemed essentially immoral in nature. A few, finding "the want of a picturesque past," demanded: "After taking out the Indians and the Puritans, what is there left besides the contentions of deliberative assemblies and the mathematical evolutions of the wars of Great Britain and Mexico?"[8] Even the nature of history painting was questioned; Fairman Rogers, a director of the Pennsylvania Academy, noted in regard to the Temple Competition: "Some care will have to be exercised in defining what historical painting is, which it strikes me is not an easy thing to do."[9] Rogers's concern was, in large part, prompted by the breakdown in distinctions between history and genre painting. While these factors restricted the growth of history painting in America, such painting was more prevalent than is generally realized today. Furthermore, history painting was repeatedly encouraged, at least in principle, during the late eighteenth and much of the nineteenth centuries.

In their encouragement of history painting, American artists and writers continually extolled the lofty characteristics traditionally associated with the art. For example, *The Crayon* of January 1855 described history painting as an art that should be "the embodiment of grand and noble emotions, of heroic exploits, and, as far as possible, should uphold and depict the dignity, and not the weakness of human nature." [10] In an address delivered at the Pennsylvania Academy before the Artists' Fund Society in 1836, John Neagle defined history painting, especially paintings of American history, as

> those Arts, which, without fanning the flame of political disquietude, exert a moral and religious influence over the mind, elevate the character of the people, and by their pictorial commemoration of national events inculcate or confirm that love of country which is the safeguard of our liberties.[11]

The faculties necessary in achieving success as a history painter were discussed in an article on Benjamin West in *The Port Folio* of October 1809:

> To attain eminence in this style is the most difficult effort, while it is the highest ambition of a painter of true genius, for it requires great diversity of talent, as it unites in itself all the varieties of painting. An historical painter must possess in a peculiar degree, a quick invention, correctness of design, bold expression, and finished execution, aided by all the other arts of the profession.[12]

West had indeed achieved "eminence in this style," exemplified by *Penn's Treaty with the Indians,* now in the collection of the Pennsylvania Academy. Furthermore, his *Death of Wolfe* of 1770, rendering a scene from the French and Indian War, became mythologized as a "revolution" in history painting. Although he rejected the convention of classical garments demanded even in paintings of contemporary history, West nevertheless maintained the sense of dignity and grandeur expected of history painting. In so doing, he effectively declared modern action as heroic as that of the antique past, a point emphasized by John Sartain in an 1862 article accompanying his engraving of West's painting (cat. no. 146).[13] The heroic mode and "revolutionary" character of *Death of Wolfe* offered nineteenth-century American artists history painting in its august form. George Peter Alexander Healy's *Franklin Urging the Claims of the American Colonies Before Louis XVI* of about 1874 (cat. no. 132) continued this grand style. However, the nineteenth century also saw the emergence of a "genre-ization" or domestication of history painting, in which exalted historical figures became secularized and events of minor importance were portrayed. The two sides of history painting, the heroic and the domesticated, are exemplified by Junius Brutus Stearns's *Washington as Statesman, at the Constitutional Convention* (cat. no. 151) and his *Washington as Farmer, at Mount Vernon* (cat. no. 150). The former apotheosizes Washington as a hero; the latter humanizes him as farmer. In both, however, the size and scale are that of genre rather than history painting. Winslow Homer's *Prisoners from the Front* (cat. no. 134) and William Ranney's *Return of Revolutionary Veterans* (cat. no. 143) further typify this popular mode of historical genre.

By their selection and treatment of subject matter, artists serve not only as history's recorders but also as its interpreters. The artist may choose to reconstruct the past, as in Healy's *Franklin Before Louis XVI,* or to render a contemporary event, like *Perry's Victory on Lake Erie* by Thomas Birch (cat. no. 125). In representing history, the artist may strive for historical accuracy, as in William Trego's *Battery of Light Artillery en Route* (cat. no.

154), for an imaginative re-creation, like *The First Landing of Christopher Columbus* by Frederick Kemmelmeyer (cat. no. 138), or for more obviously mythical aspects, as in *Parson Weems' Fable* (cat. no. 155), a painting by Grant Wood. Artists may also derive their subjects from literature, as seen in James Hamilton's *Old Ironsides* (cat. no. 131) and *Last Moments of John Brown* (cat. no. 136) by Thomas Hovenden. And with each generation interpreting the past in the light of its own experience and expectations, artists may elect to employ past events to express meaning for their present, as Peter Rothermel did in *State House, Day of the Battle of Germantown,* painted in 1862 (cat. no. 144). However the artist renders American history, his art not only reflects and defines that history but also contributes to it.

While a complete survey of American history painting is beyond the scope of this exhibition, the selection of art objects does offer varying conceptions of history painting and visual interpretations of American events from the moment of discovery to the tragedy of the Civil War.

The discovery and settlement of America have been favorite subjects for history painters. Frederick Kemmelmeyer's fanciful representation of *The First Landing of Christopher Columbus* (cat. no. 138), painted between 1800 and 1805, anticipated the numerous works which were to be inspired by Washington Irving's 1827 *Life of Columbus.* Kemmelmeyer interpreted the event as an amiable, though tentative, confrontation between Europe and the New World. Columbus and his group, appearing sophisticated and elegant, scrutinize the natives across a small, symbolic gulf of water. Approaching in the middle-ground, one of Columbus's men holds out jewelry to a crouching Indian, who, in return, offers the fruits of the New World.

Joseph Andrews's 1869 engraving *The Landing of the Pilgrims* (cat. no. 124), after a painting by Peter Rothermel exhibited in the 1854 Pennsylvania Academy annual, depicts another popular American scene. But, like the Kemmelmeyer, this dramatic composition is not merely a record of historical fact; rather it seems to be a visualization of the following poem by Felicia Hemans:

> The breaking waves dash'd high
>   On a stern and rock-bound coast,
> And the woods against a stormy sky
>   Their giant branches toss'd;
> And the heavy night hung dark,
>   The hills and water o'er,
> When a band of exiles moor'd their bark
>   On the wild New England shore . . .
> What sought they thus afar?
>   Bright jewels of the mine?
> The wealth of seas, the spoils of war?
>   They sought a faith's pure shrine!
> Ay, call it holy ground,
>   The soil where first they trode:
> They have left unstain'd what there they found—
>   Freedom to worship God.[14]

Although not documented, it is probable that Rothermel was directly inspired by this popular poem for his painting. Nineteenth-century history painters, Rothermel in particular, commonly drew from literary sources, for the idea of literature and the visual arts as kindred spirits was prevalent among artists and men of letters. Rothermel, who was a major Philadelphia painter of historical canvases, had a distinguished career with the Pennsylvania Academy, serving on its Board of Directors and as an instructor in its school. In 1852 the Pennsylvania Academy formally petitioned Congress to commission Rothermel

cat. no. 138. Frederick Kemmelmeyer. *First Landing of Columbus,* ca.1800-05. THE NATIONAL GALLERY OF ART, GIFT OF EDGAR WILLIAM AND BERNICE CHRYSLER GARBISCH, 1966.

to execute a painting for the enlarged Capitol at Washington.[15] Shortly afterward, the Congressional Committee on the Library resolved to "inquire into the expediency of employing . . . Mr. Rothermel . . . to execute two paintings, the subjects . . . to be drawn from the Revolutionary history."[16] Although the matter was considered again in 1853, the artist never received the commission.

Edward Hicks's *Peaceable Kingdom* (cat. no. 133), a mid-1830s variation of a recurrent theme in his work, contrasts in form and content with Rothermel's *The Landing of the Pilgrims.* Hicks, a Bucks County carriage painter and Quaker leader, was self-taught, and his primitive style differs greatly from the European-derived academicism of Rothermel. While Rothermel depicted man's struggle against nature, Hicks conveyed man in harmony with the world. Inspired by the prophecy of Isaiah (11:6), the Quaker artist depicted in the foreground:

> The wolf shall dwell with the lamb,
> and the leopard shall lie down
> with the kid,
> and the calf and the lion and the
> fatling together
> and a little child shall lead them.

cat. no. 144. Peter Frederick Rothermel. *State House, Day of the Battle of Germantown,* 1862.

By coupling this foreground arrangement with a middleground group based on an engraving of West's *Penn's Treaty with the Indians,* Hicks created a "Quaker icon" glorifying the peaceable kingdom of Penn's Holy Experiment.[17]

The Revolutionary War has proved to be the source for many of the most important and popular American history paintings. As a subject, it was immediately adopted by such dissimilar artists as Amos Doolittle and John Trumbull, who executed the most famous series of paintings related to the event. Another contemporary work is *The Battle of Lexington,* a 1798 engraving by Cornelius Tiebout (cat. no. 153) after a design by Elkanah Tisdale. With its obvious theatrical gestures and poses, the composition assumes a tableau-like quality. By such means, the artist created a stirring, patriotic, and historically inaccurate scene. For Americans, the achievements of the Revolution were vast and, with the reinforcement of such dramatizations as *The Battle of Lexington,* assumed mythic proportions. "It is doubtful if any other event in this history of nations called forth so many heroic deeds, so many noble virtues, and so many sublime sentiments," [18] asserted an early nineteenth-century journal. The Revolution provided an instant history, a "usable past." [19] As Albert G. Remington, writing at mid-century, claimed: "Though we have no Marathon or Thermopylae, Agincourt or Cressy, we have Saratoga, Bunker Hill, and Monmouth." [20]

While Tiebout's engraving renders the heat of battle, Peter Rothermel's *State House, Day of the Battle of Germantown* (cat. no. 144) delineates the results of conflict—not the glory of war but rather its inevitable human wreckage. Outside the State House, which served as a hospital and prisoner-of-war jail during the British occupation of Philadelphia, American prisoners wounded in this 1777 battle are tended by American women.

Rothermel's unusual "battle" scene can be interpreted as portraying the important contributions made by women during the Revolutionary War. Furthermore, the work, painted in 1862, may have been designed to pay homage to contemporary women as well. Like their Revolutionary forebears, women during the Civil War heroically nursed and cared for the suffering. In fact, women initiated and figured prominently in the United States Sanitary Commission, an organization founded in 1861 to provide medical relief to soldiers. It was highly appropriate that Rothermel's painting was exhibited at the Great Central Fair held in Philadelphia in 1864 for the benefit of the Sanitary Commission.

A more traditional battle representation is Thomas Eakins's bronze relief panel on the Trenton Battle Monument, *The Opening of the Battle* (cat. no. 129). This panel, with its companion-piece, *The Army of Washington Crossing the Delaware* (cat. no. 127), was placed on the monument in 1895. Both panels are included here as photographs of the plaster models taken and inscribed by the artist. Eakins's *Washington Crossing the Delaware* offers an alternative composition to what is today probably the best-known American historical work, Emanuel Leutze's painting of the same subject. Rather than rendering Washington as a Moses-figure leading his people, Eakins depicted, with convincing historical correctness, a seated, pensive general contemplating the battle ahead.

Of all Revolutionary subjects—indeed of all American historical subjects—the most consistently popular has been George Washington. Early in the nineteenth century the visiting Russian diplomatic official and artist Pavel Svinin observed the American preoccupation with this hero: "It is noteworthy that every American considers it his sacred duty to have a likeness of Washington in his house, just as we have images of God's Saints." [21] A selection of works in this exhibition demonstrates the range of interpretations brought to bear on the "Father of Our Country."

In 1779 Charles Willson Peale, who had painted Washington as early as 1772 when he was a colonel in the Virginia militia, was commissioned by the Supreme Executive Council of Pennsylvania to render a full-length portrait of the General for its Council Chamber. The council desired the portrait "not only as a mark of the great respect which

cat. no. 140. Charles Willson Peale. *George Washington at Princeton,* 1779.

they bear to His Excellency, but that the contemplation of it may excite others to tread in the same glorious and disinterested steps which lead to public happiness and private honor." [22] The aims expressed are those of history painting, and the work is indeed historical portraiture. The composition (cat. no. 140) depicts a relaxed and confident Washington after the victory at Princeton. At the feet of the General lie, symbolically, the captured enemy flags. Visible in the background are Nassau Hall and Hessian prisoners being led off. The artist, who served in the Revolutionary army, created a scene correct in its detail. With its combination of portraiture and history, Peale's *George Washington at Princeton* was very successful; in all, Peale painted nineteen replicas from the original.

In contrast to the informal assuredness displayed by Peale's *Washington at Princeton* is the more idealized and formal characterization of Gilbert Stuart's "Lansdowne" portrait of Washington (cat. no. 152). Stuart finished this portrait in his Germantown studio in 1796. Painted for the prominent Philadelphian William Bingham, the work fulfilled the purpose of a state portrait: "not the portrayal of an individual as such, but the evocation through his image of those abstract principles for which he stands." [23] Even more than Peale, Stuart rendered Washington as the personification of an ideal, as an icon.

The mythic image that Stuart achieved in the "Lansdowne" and in his other portraits of Washington is honored in Carl Heinrich Schmolze's *George Washington Sitting for His Portrait to Gilbert Stuart,* painted in 1858 (cat. no. 147). Schmolze, a German who settled in Philadelphia in 1856, exhibited this work at the 1858 Pennsylvania Academy annual. In this painting, he employed a common nineteenth-century motif: the depiction of a notable incident in the history of art. Examples of this genre which Schmolze may have seen in the Academy annual exhibitions of 1856 and 1857 included *Guido Reni Painting Beatrice Cenci* by A. Ratti and *Rembrandt in His Studio* by H. F. Tenkate. Schmolze's painting honors not only Washington but also Stuart as the interpreter and perpetuator of the hero's fame; ultimately, such a work pays homage to the art profession. In the composition, Washington appears dignified and nobly aloof. The elderly woman, to whom Stuart turns somewhat condescendingly, is undoubtedly Martha Washington. It was she who commissioned the "Athenaeum" portrait of Washington, a sketch of which is discernible on Stuart's canvas.

Junius Brutus Stearns illustrated the life of Washington in a series of paintings executed in the mid-nineteenth century. One of those works depicts Washington as a statesman; another shows him as a farmer. Stearns aimed for an accurate portrayal of the event and its participants in his *Washington as Statesman, at the Constitutional Convention* of 1856 (cat. no. 151). The very presence of Washington at the convention, acting as its president, served to assure its success, and Stearns portrayed the climactic moment, just prior to the voting, when Washington was about to address the delegates after four months of self-imposed, official silence. Washington appears as a hero, a symbol of stability and leadership in a time of chaos. In contrast to this work is Stearns's *Washington as Farmer, At Mount Vernon,* painted in 1851 (cat. no. 150) and exhibited at the Pennsylvania Academy in 1854. The hero, still a leader, now becomes humanized and domestic; his pose is a "domesticated Lansdowne." This romantic scene shows the dignified gentleman-farmer—the role Washington most preferred—supervising heroic slaves in the harvesting of wheat, while his two adopted grandchildren play nearby. The sentimental and patriotic spirit of Stearns's work undoubtedly reflects the great interest during the 1850s in the restoration of Mount Vernon.

Both the humanization of Stearns's *Washington As Farmer* and the mythic nature of Schmolze's painting of Washington sitting for Stuart had been presaged in literature by the writing of Mason Locke Weems. Weems's *The Life of Washington,* first published in 1800, enjoyed phenomenal success and, although fundamentally fictive, became the source of popular notions regarding Washington. The extent to which Weems the myth-maker has influenced American thought is demonstrated by Grant Wood's *Parson Weems' Fable,*

cat. no. 147. Carl H. Schmolze. *Washington Sitting for His Portrait to Gilbert Stuart,* 1858.

cat. no. 151. Junius Brutus Stearns. *Washington as Statesman, at the Constitutional Convention,* 1856. Virginia Museum of Fine Arts.

cat. no. 150. Junius Brutus Stearns. *Washington as Farmer, at Mount Vernon,* 1851. Virginia Museum of Fine Arts.

painted in 1939 (cat. no. 155). In this canvas, which is strikingly similar to Charles Willson Peale's *The Artist in His Museum* of 1822, the Parson draws back a cherry-tassled curtain and points to an enactment of his famous, or infamous, cherry tree incident. The fictional episode appeared in the fifth edition of the *Life of Washington,* published in 1806:

> *George,* said his father, *do you know who killed that beautiful little cherry-tree yonder in the garden?* This was a *tough question;* and George staggered under it for a moment; but quickly recovered himself; and looking at his father, with the sweet face of youth brightened with the inexpressible charm of all-conquering truth, he bravely cried out, *"I can't tell a lie, Pa; you know I can't tell a lie. I did cut it with my hatchet."* [24]

Wood, feeling the need to make the "sweet face of youth" immediately recognizable, transplanted Gilbert Stuart's portrait of Washington to the body of the child. The artist's use of this clever device recalls John Neal's remark of 1823: "If George Washington should appear on earth, just as he sat to Stuart, I am sure that he would be treated as an imposter, when compared with Stuart's likeness of him, unless he produced credentials." [25] The Stuart iconic Washington is thus wedded to the mythic Washington of Weems. Although his painting was critized by some irate citizens, Wood maintained that he liked the cherry tree story and hoped it would continue to be taught as a fable.[26]

Weems's influence on art is further evidenced by the print *General Marion in His Swamp Encampment Inviting a British Officer to Dinner* by John Sartain (cat. no. 145). A passage in Weems's 1809 biography of Francis Marion, the "Swamp Fox" of the Revolution, served as the inspiration for John Blake White's painting after which this mezzotint was taken. The scene portrays the hardships that Marion's men endured in the name of liberty.

Graphic works such as Sartain's were vehicles which provided the public with the instructive, elevating, and patriotic qualities of history painting. Published in quantity, prints had the advantage of being relatively inexpensive, making art available to the masses usually unable to purchase works of art. Lacking patronage, history painters could have their work engraved in the hopes of increasing their income and reputation. Both artists and the public benefited from the distribution of prints as premiums and prizes offered by art unions and organizations, such as the Apollo Association (later the American Art-Union). By achieving fairly wide circulation, prints of history paintings aided in the securing of an American identity.

Like Sartain's print of Marion, another popular print portraying a Revolutionary military hero was David Edwin's engraving of 1814, *Peter Francisco's Gallant Action, with Nine of Tarleton's Cavalry, in Sight of the Whole Troop of 400 Men* (cat. no. 130). The original painting by J. Warrell was listed in the catalogue of the Pennsylvania Academy's 1812 exhibition, with a lengthy passage describing the efforts of the superhuman Virginia patriot Francisco in overcoming tremendous adversity. Surely this print had special significance for Americans then engaged in the War of 1812. Although criticizing the painting from which the engraving was taken as "rude" in drawing, George Murray commended the artist Warrell, stating:

> We have every reason to hope that with proper application this young painter will soon be able to produce in this high and important branch of the arts, [historical painting] something that may prove of consequence in forming, what appears yet wanting, a *national gallery* of the works of American artists consisting of subjects from our own history.[27]

The crude, yet powerful, style of *Peter Francisco's Gallant Action* differs greatly from the sophisticated handling of form in George Peter Alexander Healy's *Franklin Urging the Claims of the American Colonies Before Louis XVI,* painted about 1847 (cat. no. 132). The

cat. so. 155. Grant Wood. *Parson Weems' Fable,* 1939. The Amon Carter Museum of Western Art, Fort Worth, Texas.

cat. no. 132. George P. A. Healy. *Franklin Urging the Claims of the American Colonies Before Louis XVI,* ca.1847. American Philosophical Society, Philadelphia.

work is the original study for the large painting commissioned by King Louis Philippe and lost in the Chicago fire of 1871. The painting focuses on the plainly attired Benjamin Franklin, a symbol to the French of Rousseauian New World primitivism, standing amid the splendor of Versailles. Healy, a renowned portraitist, not only rendered recognizable likenesses of the main figures in the composition but also, after extensive research, attained historical authenticity throughout in details of the setting and the costumes.

Quite unlike Healy's awe-inspiring scene is William Ranney's humorous *Return of Revolutionary Veterans,* painted in 1848 (cat. no. 143). Last seen publicly in an 1866 Pennsylvania Academy exhibition, the painting was once described in the following terms: "a merry picture. The old soldiers are going home in a dilapidated condition. Their equipage is a rude cart drawn by a ruder steed." [28] Inscribed on the cart are the names of major Revolutionary battles; it is believed that the two soldiers in the wagon are Generals Henry Knox and Anthony Wayne. Through historical genre, the artist humanized and poked fun at great men. Ranney's interpretation of history in this manner parallels contemporary ideas expressed by Washington Irving:

> I have availed myself the license of biography to step down occasionally from the elevated walk of history, and relate familiar things in a familiar way; seeking to show the prevalent passions and feelings, and humors of the day, and even to depict the heroes of Seventy-six as they really were—men in cocked hats, regimental coats, and breeches; and not classic warriors, in shining armor and flowing mantles, with brows bound with laurel, and truncheons in their hands.[29]

The War of 1812, like the Revolution, provided artists with heroes and heroics to immortalize. During the war years numerous battle scenes hung in the Pennsylvania Academy's annual exhibitions, visually supporting the war's importance as an aggressive assertion of American nationalism. Thomas Birch, Keeper of the Pennsylvania Academy from 1812 to 1816, executed numerous depictions of naval engagements. His *Perry's Victory on Lake Erie* (cat. no. 125), an unusually large composition in his *oeuvre,* was exhibited at the Pennsylvania Academy's 1814 annual, and a descriptive key identifying the nautical combatants was published in the catalogue. Rendering an incident which was well known to his contemporaries, Birch sought to combine the reportorial with a sense of the heroic.[30] Striving for verity, the artist had "naval commanders . . . describe to him incidents, and from their descriptions he produced the scenes on canvas." [31]

Birch's literal interpretation of an actual event contrasts with James Hamilton's romantic seascape *Old Ironsides* (cat. no. 131), inspired by Oliver Wendell Holmes's famous poem of the same title. The canvas, typical of the artist's work with, as John Sartain noted, its "appearance of having been dusted off at a heat," [32] has inscribed on its reverse a stanza from the Holmes poem. Completed in 1863 and exhibited the same year at the Pennsylvania Academy, Hamilton's dramatic image of the famous War of 1812 frigate had symbolic meaning for the Civil War: the *Constitution* floundering on a sea of turmoil.[33]

cat. no. 143. William T. Ranney. *Return of Revolutionary Veterans,* 1848. Collection of Mrs. William H. S. Wells.

cat. no. 125. Thomas Birch. *Perry's Victory on Lake Erie,* 1814.

cat. no. 148. Christian Schussele. *General Andrew Jackson Before Judge Hall,* 1815.

Christian Schussele's *General Andrew Jackson Before Judge Hall, 1815* (cat. no. 148) represents an unfamiliar incident of the War of 1812. Schussele, the first professor of drawing and painting at the Pennsylvania Academy, specialized in historical, Biblical, and genre painting. The date of this compositional study is unknown; it may relate either to a larger painting of the same subject executed by Schussele in 1858-60 (now in the Gilcrease Institute of American History and Art) and shown in the Pennsylvania Academy annual exhibitions of 1860 and 1866, or to his woodcut designs prepared for a serial biography of Jackson published in *Sartain's Magazine* in 1852.

The subject of the study is the trial of Jackson on charges of illegally declaring martial law and defying civil authority in New Orleans at the close of the War of 1812. Desiring historical fidelity in his work, Schussele based his composition on eyewitness accounts. He rendered the dramatic moment when, following a wild outburst of defiance by the pro-Jackson crowd:

> Jackson looked around with an expression of calm and august majesty, which was long remembered by those who saw his commanding features on that occasion; he only waved his hand in rebuke and instantly order and silence were restored. Then turning to the judge, he slightly lowered his head, as if he meant to say: I am here in obedience to your command. The Judge looked as serene and impassible as if nothing had happened. There was a grandeur in the scene which struck all the bystanders.[34]

After paying a fine and being cheered and carried aloft through the streets by his supporters, the hero of New Orleans harangued the crowd: "I have shown you how to repel invasion, and I have shown you how to defend the liberties of your country, and I now set you an example of obedience to its constituted authorities, which I hope may be profitable to you."[35] Schussele's content—the obedience to union and authority—undoubtedly relates to the political upheavals of the 1850s and 1860s.

The taming of the West was another subject often treated by painters of American history. During America's westward course, the zealous spirit of Manifest Destiny was often tempered by the harsh realities of the frontier. Two paintings in this exhibition—one rendering contemporary history, the other looking back to a romantic past—offer visual interpretations of the all-too-real tragedies and dangers inherent in the populating of the continent.

William Ranney's *Prairie Burial* of 1848 (cat. no. 142) shows a melancholy scene on the frontier. Although not a record of a specific occurrence, the work illustrates the hardships and losses endured by the bands of anonymous pioneers. Ranney's historical genre paintings of the West were praised not only for their artistic merit but also for their value as interpretive records of an American era.[36]

The quietism of Ranney's *Prairie Burial* is countered by Walt Kuhn's image of frontier violence in *Wild West No. 1* (cat. no. 139). In a loose, abstract manner, the artist represented a single standing white man battling several Indians on horseback. Although not specifically documented as such, the scene recalls Custer's Last Stand. The work is part of a series of nostalgic paintings by Kuhn entitled *An Imaginary History of the West.* The artist, stimulated by his reading of books on the West, executed the series from 1918 to 1920.

The depiction of the hero and his exploits has always been a major aspect of history painting. A popular but controversial hero is the subject of Thomas Hovenden's *Last Moments of John Brown.* Hovenden's painting received wide recognition through his 1885 etching, the original plate of which is owned by the Pennsylvania Academy (cat. no. 136). Hovenden, who taught painting at the Academy, played upon the sentimental chord of his society with this work. Lauded as "the best American historical picture yet produced,"[37] the work, the public was informed, "should be hung on the walls of every lover of freedom."[38] The artist tapped two sources in creating this painting: the general inspiration came from John Greenleaf Whittier's poem "Brown of Ossawattomie," two stanzas of which are inscribed at the bottom of the copper plate; and the features of the hero were copied from a photograph owned by "that sturdy Abolitionist Dr. Furniss [sic]."[39]

John Brown is the subject of another work in the Pennsylvania Academy's collection —Horace Pippin's *John Brown Going to His Hanging,* painted in 1942 (cat. no. 141). The blunt, primitive quality of Pippin's work varies sharply from the technical naturalism of Hovenden's. Pippin, a self-taught black artist, rejected art schools and the sort of academic standards Hovenden embraced, for he believed that "it seems impossible for another to teach one of art."[40] The artist based this painting (one of three he did of John Brown) on his mother's eyewitness account.[41] Pippin's hard-edged style conveys the crystalline nature of that December day. Stark, leafless trees not only indicate the season but also reinforce the sense of impending death. Seated on his own coffin, John Brown rides to his execution in a wagon drawn by two white horses; he passes before a crowd of solemn bystanders. The only black person in the scene, a tensely grim woman who turns her back to the episode, may be the artist's mother. Action within the composition is minimal, creating a feeling of grave stillness.

Like the Revolution and the War of 1812, the Civil War offered the artist a wealth of subjects to render. Examples presented here range from Xanthus Smith's monumental battle scene *Final Assault on Fort Fisher, N.C.* to the small, intimate view of *A Trooper Meditating Beside a Grave* by Winslow Homer.

cat. no. 141. Horace Pippin. *John Brown Going to His Hanging,* 1942.

cat. no. 149. Xanthus Smith. *Final Assault Upon Fort Fisher, N.C.,* 1873.

Like Thomas Birch's *Perry's Victory on Lake Erie,* Smith's *Final Assault on Fort Fisher, N.C.* of 1873 (cat. no. 149) presents a panorama of a naval battle. Like Birch, Smith rendered his scene with a great deal of historical accuracy; however, whereas Birch had little nautical experience and relied on the information of others, Smith had witnessed such action, having served on the staff of the Union admiral S. F. Du Pont and with Admiral David Farragut at the Battle of Mobile Bay. In his composition, Smith chronicles the final Union attack on Fort Fisher, the large fortification erected by the Confederacy to protect a favorite harbor of blockade runners at the mouth of the Cape Fear River in North Carolina. The artist's scene surveys the thunderous shelling inflicted by ironclads and other Union vessels. Smith, who studied at the Pennsylvania Academy and contributed to the annual exhibitions from 1856 to 1887, painted this work, as well as three other Civil War scenes, for Joseph Harrison. Harrison's collection, strong in historical paintings and portraiture, came to the Pennsylvania Academy as two gifts—one in 1878, the other in 1912.

William Trego's *Battery of Light Artillery en Route* (cat. no. 154), winner of the first Toppan Prize, awarded by the Pennsylvania Academy in 1882, exemplifies the academic style which characterized the artist's more than two hundred battle paintings. Trego, who became an authority on military uniforms, valued fidelity to fact and attention to detail. The high degree of realism he achieved is astonishing since he was crippled from infancy and had to work painfully with paralyzed hands. Throughout his career Trego stressed draughtsmanship and academic correctness. "Why should not the Academy be Academic?" he asked Edward H. Coates, president of the Pennsylvania Academy.[42] Prior to studying in Paris with Adolphe W. Bouguereau and Tony Robert Fleury, Trego spent three years at the Pennsylvania Academy under Thomas Eakins. But his relationship with Eakins was not pleasant; he later remarked: "Fortunately for myself I was drilled in the principles of drawing in my father's studio before I went to the Academy, so that I was able to some extent to brave the sarcasm and neglect of Eakens [*sic*]."[43] Ironically, it was Fairman Rogers, a staunch supporter of Eakins's teachings, who purchased Trego's painting and presented it to the Pennsylvania Academy.

Winslow Homer's well-known *Prisoners from the Front* of 1866 (cat. no. 134) portrays, as does Smith's *Final Assault on Fort Fisher,* the conflict between North and South. Now, however, the confrontation is personal and psychological, rather than anonymous and physical. Homer created a scene of tense contemplation rather than bombastic violence. As the three captured Rebels eye him, an assured Union officer coolly appraises his prisoners. A disparity exists between the disheveled appearance of the captives and the orderliness of their captor. In this scene of historical genre, the Rebels display not only three different ages, but also three dissimilar attitudes toward their common enemy: the boy seems anxious, the old man humble, and the young soldier proud, possibly defiant. The depiction of the psychological gulf between this last Confederate and the Union soldier in large part accounted for the work's immediate success as an expression of the unbridgeable difference between North and South.[44]

Another painting by Homer, *A Trooper Meditating Beside a Grave* (cat. no. 135), also portrays a contemplative moment, now intimate rather than tense. As in *Prisoners from the Front,* the artist's emphasis is on the human element of war. In this small painting, Homer offers a poigant interpretation of the Civil War. Even more, the introspective soldier effectively becomes a universal figure contemplating the consequences of man's inhumanity to man.

cat. no. 134. Winslow Homer. *Prisoners from the Front,* 1866. THE METROPOLITAN MUSEUM OF ART, GIFT OF MRS. FRANK B. PORTER, 1922.

Also interpreting the tragedy of combat, contemporary artist Edwin Dickinson created a specter of the Civil War in *Shiloh* of 1940 (cat. no. 126). The title, evocative rather than narrative, refers to the bloody battle waged in Tennessee in 1862. Eerie lighting and the crumpling of the drapery and the body (a self-portrait) create a haunting image of death.

William H. Johnson's *Lincoln at Gettysburg III,* painted about 1939-42 (cat. no. 137), treats an episode of national significance: Lincoln at the dedication of the Gettysburg National Cemetery. In rendering the gaunt figure of Lincoln, Johnson employed a primitive style similar to that of another black artist, Horace Pippin. However, unlike Pippin, Johnson had a solid academic training and consciously moved to a more "naive" style in the late 1930s and early 1940s. His aim was "to give, in simple and stark form, the story of the Negro as he has existed."[45] Certainly, a work treating a famous event in the life of the Great Emancipator had special meaning for a black artist. *Lincoln at Gettysburg III* is one of three sketches which may have been preparatory drawings for a mural which was never completed.[46] Johnson's imaginative interpretation of the event derives its appeal and power from the artist's ability to create a viable mythic scene with the simplest of forms.

The Civil War, in effect, served as the last great subject of American history painting. During the war Matthew Brady and his crews demonstrated the camera's effectiveness and established photography as the medium for recording contemporary history. While paintings of historical events after the Civil War do exist, American history painting was largely eclipsed by the utilization of the camera.

As recorders and interpreters, American artists have rendered American history in a variety of ways. Compositions range from the heroic and monumental to those more sentimental, anecdotal, and even humorous in nature. Regardless of their form, visual interpretations of American history have served numerous significant and vital purposes: honoring and glorifying the United States and its patriots; conveying ideals to posterity; and providing elevating examples of virtue. Most importantly, however, historical art has assisted in creating and sustaining a sense of national identity and uniqueness.

cat. no. 137. William H. Johnson. *Lincoln at Gettysburg III,* ca.1939-42. National Collection of Fine Arts, Smithsonian Institution.

Frank H. Goodyear, Jr.

AMERICAN LANDSCAPE PAINTING, 1795-1875

It strikes the European traveller, at the first burst of the scenery of America on his eye, that the New World of Columbus is also a new world from the hand of the Creator. In comparison with the old countries of Europe, the vegetation is so wondrously lavish, the outlines and minor features struck out with so bold a freshness, and the lakes and rivers so even in their fulness and flow, yet so vast and powerful, that he may well imagine it an Eden new sprung from the ocean.

Nathaniel P. Willis,
American Scenery (London, 1840),
intro.

Traditionally, academies have shown little involvement with landscape painting.[1] The Pennsylvania Academy was no exception. The curriculum of the Academy school centered on the study of the human figure; it was not until the 1880s, after the tremendous popularity of American landscape painting had subsided, that the study of landscape was instituted at the Academy school. Moreover, until the 1880s, landscape painting as a genre was not granted the status of history painting and portraiture at the Academy.

As early as the 1830s, prizes for drawing and modeling life figures and casts were awarded by the Pennsylvania Academy. In the 1850s premiums awarded to historical, scriptural, or dramatic paintings in the annuals were more than double those awarded to landscapes. In 1881 a special prize of $200 was established for the best landscape painting exhibited in an annual,[2] but it is unclear from existing documentation whether this award was regularly offered. It was not until 1902, with the establishment of the Jennie Sesnan Gold Medal, given to the best landscape in an annual, that landscape painting was regularly awarded a premium.

Most serious collectors in Philadelphia were more inclined to acquire portraiture or historical canvases than landscape painting. Philadelphians generously patronized their own school of portrait painters, especially Rembrandt Peale and Thomas Sully, that dominated the artistic milieu in Philadelphia through the first half of the nineteenth century. Every important Philadelphia collection in the nineteenth century owned at least one canvas by the popular American history painter, Peter F. Rothermel. Serious collections of French Barbizon landscape painting were formed in Philadelphia from the mid-1860s through the nineteenth century,[3] but no comparable collections of American landscape painting existed. Edward Carey did own landscapes by Thomas Doughty and Joshua Shaw, but even Carey preferred contemporary English landscapes. Joseph Harrison, Jr., owned important canvases by Sanford Gifford, Thomas Cole, William Trost Richards, and Jasper Cropsey, but Harrison's collection favored historical portraiture and history painting.[4] On the other hand, a few collectors did seem to prefer landscape painting. George Whitney and Harrison Earl were two of the most important patrons of the Philadelphia landscape and marine painter William Trost Richards. Whitney also owned works by Asher B. Durand, John Kensett, and Jervis McEntee.

Local landscape painters were the most popular with Philadelphia's collectors. Thomas Birch and Thomas Doughty were regarded by Philadelphia connoisseurs as the most important landscapists of the early nineteenth century. Later in the century, such artists as Russell and Xanthus Smith, Paul Weber, Edmund Darch Lewis, James Hamilton, and William Trost Richards were held in the highest esteem. They were popular, it seems, simply because they represented the best local work. Generally, landscape painters from New York and elsewhere received minimal patronage from Philadelphians. Frederic Church, Albert Bierstadt, and Martin Johnson Heade were ignored by Philadelphia collectors.

Considering the status of landscape painting at the Pennsylvania Academy and the limited taste for it among Philadelphia collectors, it is perhaps surprising to find that it constituted an important portion of the annuals. Although not nearly so important in the Pennsylvania Academy's annuals as in comparable exhibitions at the National Academy of Design or the Apollo Association and American Art-Union in New York, nonetheless, the most avant-garde work by the most highly regarded American landscapists was exhibited regularly at the Academy. Through the nineteenth century, every major American landscapist exhibited in the Pennsylvania Academy's annuals.

The Academy also sponsored special loan exhibitions of landscape painting.[5] Both of Thomas Cole's allegorical landscape series—*The Voyage of Life* and *The Course of Empire*—were shown at the Pennsylvania Academy, in 1844 and 1852 respectively. Cole was recognized as America's greatest landscapist. In 1860 Frederic Church's cosmic landscape, *Heart of the Andes,* which had previously been hailed by the English artist-critic John Ruskin as a work equal in quality to that of Joseph Turner, was on special exhibition at the Academy.

The Academy had a unique opportunity in the nineteenth century to purchase many of the masterpieces of American landscape painting; in 1844, for instance, the second series of Thomas Cole's *The Voyage of Life* was available for sale at three hundred dollars per canvas. Unfortunately, the board decided not to purchase this important series of paintings, even with the knowledge that Cole considered it his most successful work. The number of similar, but unrecorded, lost opportunities must be prodigious. They constitute a failure on the part of the Pennsylvania Academy to recognize and support important American schools of painting. The Academy's permanent collection has no works by Thomas Cole, Frederic Church, Albert Bierstadt, and Martin Johnson Heade.

Landscape painting in America grew out of the revolutionary generation's desire to identify American images. It had been a minor art in the eighteenth century, primarily linked with portraiture and history painting. Some pure landscape painting, derived from both topographical and classical sources, did exist, but mostly in the form of overmantel paintings, often painted by semi-professional itinerants.

At the beginning of the nineteenth century, landscape painting in America was still in a fledgling condition, with few practitioners and even fewer patrons. Over the next fifty years it became the most popular, most quintessentially American genre of painting—an expression of the American psyche and a symbol of Manifest Destiny. Its proponents were considered heroes whose canvases, eagerly competed for, commanded huge prices.

cat. no. 170. William Groombridge. *View on the Schuylkill River,* 1800. Private Collection.

However, no single landscape style predominated throughout its years of popularity. In the early nineteenth century, the landscape tradition in America was strongly influenced by English and Dutch traditions. Gradually, an indigenous style of romantic-realism supplanted the earlier European influences, but by the mid-1870s it had begun to lose currency. The stylistic influences of the Barbizon School and French Impressionism became dominant in the last quarter of the century.

Philadelphia and Baltimore were the earliest centers of landscape painting in America. The immediate impetus for such activity came from English landscapists who immigrated to America in the mid-1790s,[6] bringing with them a diversity of styles rooted in English landscape traditions. They found in Americans an emerging patronage, proud and conscious of the look of America. It was not the unexplored, dark-forested wilderness which lay beyond the mountains that these Americans sought to have painted on canvas, but rather the gentility of their own country seats and bustling cities. Americans wanted to show off America's "improvements" with a directness that would serve as a record of the nation's growth. It was the reality of specific places, depicted by artists in their works, that struck a respondent note among American patronage. Akin to the reality of appearance characteristic of eighteenth-century colonial portraiture, this consciousness of the look of America remained a vital ingredient in the emerging American landscape tradition.

cat. no. 158. Thomas Birch. *Fairmount Water Works,* 1821.

English-style landscapes of American scenes predominated in the period from about 1795 to 1825. In style, they varied from a meticulous, topographical realism in which architecture was prominent, to a more "picturesque" treatment in which the qualities of William Gilpin's aesthetic prevailed, to classical compositions in the manner of Claude and Poussin. Within these diverse styles, the desire to identify a specific place remained a constant. In landscapes like *View on the Schuylkill River* (cat. no. 170) by William Groombridge, a native of Kent, England, the rural quality of the scene along the Schuylkill River outside Philadelphia is developed in a loose, Gainsboroughesque style. The style of this painting, which was exhibited at the 1812 Academy annual, is in marked contrast to the meticulous, draftsmanlike detail found in landscapes of the period by Francis Guy, John James Barralet, and William and Thomas Birch. Such a precise style is observable in Thomas Birch's *Fairmount Water Works* (cat. no. 158) of 1821. Birch's painting is reminiscent of the engraved *Views of Philadelphia* which he and his father, William Birch, published in 1800. Not only is Birch's eye that of an engraver in *Fairmount Water Works,* but his ideas about landscape painting are based on aesthetic criteria and not on nature.

The desire to identify a specific place continued to be a strong determinant throughout nineteenth-century American landscape painting. In later works, like Russell Smith's *Chew House, Germantown* (cat. no. 180) of 1843 or William Trost Richards's *Paschall*

cat. no. 167. Jacob Eichholtz. *Conestoga Creek and Lancaster,* 1833.

Homestead at Gibson's Point, Philadelphia (cat. no. 175) of 1857, the identification of a site was the painter's chief concern. The public demand for such paintings increasingly was met by itinerant, semi-professional artists who worked outside the mainstream of an American landscape aesthetic. These artists, who saw things not in terms of style but rather of physicality, met the requirements for reportorial art. Jacob Eichholtz's work falls between this naive tradition and the high style work of his teacher, Thomas Sully. *Conestoga Creek and Lancaster* (cat. no. 167), a unique landscape in Eichholtz's *oeuvre,* reveals his dependence on Thomas Doughty's *Landscape with Curving River* (Pennsylvania Academy of the Fine Arts), but unlike Doughty's painting, it is a specific reference to a specific place.

In the 1820s the early emphasis on depicting merely man's "improvements" to nature was opposed by a group of writers who urged that the American experience be somehow embodied in a distinctly new national idiom. What better way was there to express the American uniqueness than through a glorification of the *natural* beauties of America? How distinct American scenery was from its European counterpart! Joshua Shaw, the English landscapist who came to America in 1817, remarked in his *Picturesque Views of American Scenery* on the "majesty and loveliness of nature [nowhere] more strikingly conspicuous than in America."[7] James Fenimore Cooper, William Cullen Bryant, Nathaniel Parker Willis, Thomas Cole, all extolled the manifest natural wonders of America, always preferring the freshness and radiance of the American wilderness to the "stiffness and formality"[8] of European scenery. In Europe there was the taint of civilization in nature; in America there was primeval wilderness. Wilderness, once feared in America,[9] became symbolic of purity and godliness.

The popular conception of nature was linked to the deistic belief that nature was a manifestation of a divine spirit. If one wanted to be near God and to benefit from His presence, one must commune with nature. Nature was believed to have therapeutic value; Bryant's poem *Inscription For the Entrance to a Wood* urged the woeful man who had seen enough of the world's sorrows

> To tire thee of it, enter this wild wood
> and view the haunts of Nature. The calm shade
> Shall bring a kindred calm, and the sweet breeze.
> That makes the green leaves dance, shall waft a balm
> To thy sick heart.[10]

Thus, around 1825 the emphasis in American landscape painting shifted from painting "improvements" to painting nature when New York City replaced Philadelphia as the center of landscape painting in America.

Thomas Doughty, one of the first American landscape painters to be elected a Pennsylvania Academician, was a pioneer in the development of this native landscape tradition. Although he painted topographical views of popular sites throughout the 1820s, the direction of his work steadily moved toward realistic landscape. *View Near Hartford, Connecticut* (cat. no. 164), painted in 1828, expresses Doughty's own perception of nature. Doughty preferred the intimate, pastoral look of rural America to its more grandiose, sublime scenery. An avid sketcher, he viewed nature as a storehouse where the details for his canvases could be found, to be selected and combined into a personal formula at a later time in his studio. This method of drawing plein-air sketches, often inscribed with color notations, became essential to the American perception of landscape painting. Asher B. Durand systematized the method in his widely read "Letters on Landscape Painting," published in *The Crayon* in 1855.

Just as public taste had favored topographical views earlier, so did it prefer realistic landscapes after 1825. Robert Gilmor, the important Baltimore patron, summarized the prevailing feeling:

> I prefer real American scenes to compositions, leaving the distribution of light, choice of atmosphere and clouds, and in short all that is to render its natural effect as pleasing and spirited as the artist can feel permitted to do, without violation of its truth.[11]

What public taste demanded, American landscape painters were inclined to provide. Thus, the force of economic necessities was a determinant on the style of American landscape painting.[12]

Realistic landscapes like those painted by Asher B. Durand (cat. no. 166) were the most popular in mid-nineteenth century America. Durand's attention to natural details, combined with a strong eye for compositional effects, produced works that appealed to the pragmatic American mind. The Durand landscape tradition continued well into the nineteenth century; Charles Lewis Fussell's *Landscape* (cat. no. 168), while painted in 1897, is typical of the style of Durand's work of the 1850s and 1860s.

Thomas Cole lamented the narrowness of public taste in America, which he felt impeded the progress of his work. Cole strove to unite artistic excellence with moral and religious subjects. He recognized that a great landscape painter's duty went well beyond "servile" imitation of nature. As early as 1825 he wrote his patron Robert Gilmor:

> If the imagination is shackled, and nothing is described but what we see, seldom will anything truly great be produced in either Painting or Poetry.[13]

cat. no. 164. Thomas Doughty. *View Near Hartford, Connecticut,* 1828.

cat. no. 162. Thomas Cole. *On the Arno,* 1837. COLLECTION OF DR. ELLIOT S. VESELL.

While he was a prodigious sketcher, Cole felt that before painting an observed scene, an artist should allow time to draw a veil over the details and unessential parts of nature. He often remarked bitterly that he had higher conceptions of art than a "mere leaf painter," and he evolved a broad, bold style of brushwork that defined only the essential masses and color of natural forms.

As an artist in America, Cole was well ahead of his time. By failing to elect him a Pennsylvania Academician, the Pennsylvania Academy implicitly voiced its disapproval of his "higher taste" in landscape painting. Frustrated by public taste and by his own lack of development, Cole went abroad in 1829. After sojourns in London and Paris, he settled in Florence in 1831. Cole thrived in Italy, calling it a "land of poetry and beauty,"[14] but he missed the rugged scenery of America. He wrote:

> I have found, though, no natural scenery yet which has affected me so powerfully as that which I have seen in the wilderness places of America.[15]

In Italy, Cole concentrated on developing panoramic views of Italian cities and ruins of Roman architecture. *On the Arno* (cat. no. 162), although not painted until 1837 in America, was inspired by his first visit to Florence. It is one of at least four versions Cole did of the subject and was painted in the same year that he completed his most ambitious panorama of Florence, *View of Florence from San Miniato* (The Cleveland Museum of Art).

Italy was a painter's paradise, and American landscapists sought out its salutory influences whenever possible.[16] They did not go to Italy to learn a painting technique, as they did later to Düsseldorf, but rather to be steeped in Italian traditions and the atmospheric light of the Italian countryside. From 1847 to 1849 Jasper Cropsey lived in Italy with his wife and his friends, Thomas Hicks and Christopher Cranch. One of his first major canvases was *Landscape with Figures, Near Rome* (cat. no. 163), signed "Roma/1847." In later years Cropsey became known for his loosely painted autumnal landscapes, but his early Italian landscapes show the strong influence of Thomas Cole. Like Cole, Cropsey was interested in both the vestiges of past civilizations and the observable peasant life on the Italian campagna.

Some American landscapists found the lure of Italian life so strong that they settled there for long periods. One such artist was George Loring Brown, a native of Boston who lived in Italy from 1840 to 1857, after which he returned to America. Brown's style, though consistently lacking the force of Cole's, reveals the eclecticism characteristic of Cole's. Moreover, like Cole, Brown was never content to limit his production to pure landscape painting, also finding inspiration in literary and Biblical subjects and painting allegories of high moral content. His *St. John the Baptist in the Wilderness* (cat. no. 160), painted in Florence in 1845-46 and first exhibited at the Pennsylvania Academy in 1848, reads as a landscape but transcends the idea of landscape in its Biblical reference. The imaginary setting, dominated by gnarled trees and a rocky river bed, with steep cliffs and soaring mountains in the background, suggests the influence of Italian Mannerist landscapes of the seventeenth century. However, even though the landscape reinforces the painting's subject, it lacks the sublime wildness present in Cole's *John the Baptist in the Wilderness* (Wadsworth Atheneum) of 1827.

During the 1850s and 1860s landscape painters were the titans of the American art world. Artists like Frederic Church, Albert Bierstadt, and John F. Kensett attracted constant public attention, and they achieved financial security and social prestige. They led adventurous lives: their worldwide expeditions in search of cosmic revelations took them into remote, uncharted territory—throughout the American West, into the jungles of South America and the icefields of the Arctic, along the Nile River, and through Greece, Turkey, and the Holy Land. The spectacular, often exotic subject matter which resulted from these trips gripped the imagination of the American public; at the same time, paintings of the American West evoked a feeling of patriotism.

cat. no. 163. Jasper F. Cropsey. *Landscape with Figures, Near Rome,* 1847.

cat. no. 160. George Loring Brown. *St. John the Baptist in the Wilderness,* 1845-46.

cat. no. 161. Frederic Church. *Mountains of Ecuador,* 1855. THE WADSWORTH ATHENEUM, HARTFORD, CONN., BEQUEST OF MRS. CLARA HINTON GOULD.

The style of artists like Church and Bierstadt was inherently American; it was also strongly influenced by the widely circulated writings of the English critic John Ruskin. It combined a closeness of observation, at times based on near scientific scrutiny, often aided by the camera,[17] and a romantic conception of nature and the role of the landscape painter. Church's *Mountains of Ecuador* (cat. no. 161) reflects the kaleidoscopic vision of the romantic-realist painter. Painted in 1855, after his first trip to Ecuador, where he had gone to sketch the sacred mountains of Cotopaxi and Chimborazo, the painting develops the theme of the relationship between man and nature. In this preoccupation Church continued the earlier tradition of his teacher, Thomas Cole, although he had even greater respect than Cole for both the destructive and regenerative powers of nature. In Church's mind, mankind was but a pawn in the presence of nature's timeless forces.

Church's great South American landscapes were rivaled in popularity only by Albert Bierstadt's equally monumental paintings of the American West. Although Bierstadt had been trained in the meticulous style of the Academy at Düsseldorf, he shared Church's obsession with nature's theatricality. Bierstadt's *Storm in the Mountains* (cat. no. 157) is a powerful statement of nature's impending fury. While more precise in style, it is reminiscent of Joseph Turner's *Snow Storm, Avalanche and Inundation in the Val d'Aosta* (Art Institute of Chicago) of 1837. Indeed, to Church and Bierstadt, Turner was the exemplary artist of the nineteenth century.

cat. no. 157. Albert Bierstadt. *Storm in the Mountains,* ca. 1870-80. Museum of Fine Arts, Boston, M. and M. Karolik Collection.

Church and Bierstadt painted nature as a cosmic force. Other American landscape painters focused on less philosophical considerations. From the mid-1850s to the mid-1870s two distinct styles of landscape painting developed in America: an American version of Pre-Raphaelitism, and Luminism. Pre-Raphaelitism, a style transplanted from England, but inherently American, had as one objective of its microscopic vision the conceptualization of the essential quality or qualities of natural phenomena. Luminism, an indigenous American style, dealt with phenomena seen through a saturating light that united compositional elements into a spatial whole.

The earlier of the two styles was an American expression of the Pre-Raphaelite aesthetic of John Ruskin. America's Pre-Raphaelite brotherhood, associated in the early 1860s with the Society for the Advancement of Truth in Art and with the publication of *The Crayon* (1855-1861) and *The New Path* (1863-1865), never attracted a large following among landscape painters. Except for such artists as Thomas Charles Farrer and Charles Herbert Moore, American followers of Ruskin's "Truth to Nature" aesthetic painted in the Pre-Raphaelite style only for short periods in their careers.[18] In Ruskin's opinion, his American disciples never developed beyond the "apprenticeship" state of rendering precise studies of nature.

cat. no. 176. William Trost Richards. *Plant Study,* 1860. The Brooklyn Museum, Gift of Edith Ballinger Price.

cat. no. 171. Martin Johnson Heade. *Salt Marshes, Newport, Rhode Island,* ca.1865-70.
MUSEUM OF FINE ARTS, BOSTON, M. AND M. KAROLIK COLLECTION.

The most accomplished of the American Pre-Raphaelite landscapists was the Philadelphia painter William Trost Richards.[19] A student at the Düsseldorf Academy and later at the Pennsylvania Academy, Richards's training at Düsseldorf in the steely, mechanical style of drawing aided his microscopic vision, enabling him in the 1860s to make close, accurate studies of bits of nature. *Plant Study* (cat. no. 176) of 1860 is characteristic of the small, scientific observations of nature of the American Pre-Raphaelite landscapists.

It was only natural that a style that emphasized careful draftsmanship would appeal to an academy. The Pennsylvania Academy sponsored two important English Pre-Raphaelite exhibitions in the nineteenth century. On the other hand, the American Luminists, other than periodically exhibiting their works in the annuals, had no specific involvement with the Academy. The principal Luminist artists, Martin Johnson Heade and Sanford Gifford, lived in New York City. Heade and Gifford preferred to work in a horizontal format and experimented with the effects of sunlight and weather on space and the objects in it. Heade's *Salt Marshes, Newport, Rhode Island* (cat. no. 171), painted about 1865-70, is typical of the Luminist style. While a greater sense of direct sunlight is apparent in this painting than in other haystack compositions by Heade, the scene is nonetheless cast in a vaporous, almost spongy, atmosphere that unites the multiplicity of observed forms. By reducing the size of his brushstrokes and limiting his palette to subtle tonal variations, Heade reinforces the unity of the composition.

Sanford Gifford's Luminist landscapes stand in contrast to Heade's, although both reveal that saturated quality of light that characterizes American Luminism. However, Gifford's landscapes are more ebulliently brushed and higher keyed than Heade's. In his small *The Falls of Tivoli* (cat. no. 169) of 1869 both these differences are apparent. Gifford labored to achieve a landscape composition united by atmospheric light. He recorded in his "Journal" the problems in realizing this effect:

cat. no. 169. Sanford Robinson Gifford. *The Falls of Tivoli,* 1869. PRIVATE COLLECTION.

> I find, however, on reviewing it that my mind had cherished only the broad and simple splendor of the scene, and had quite eliminated all that interfered with that breadth and simplicity. I have made many sketches, but they seem only to show me the difficulties instead of the beauties of the scene. They make me see how the broad flank of the mt. is broken up in petty lights and shadows, and how the flashing "cascatelle" and the windings of the Anio, make awkward lights which refuse to be subjugated.[20]

It is instructive to notice that Thomas Cole's 1832 *Cascatelli of Tivoli* (Collection of Mr. and Mrs. Walter Knight Sturges) reveals the very awkwardnesses that Gifford tried to overcome, but which Cole sought to emphasize. Cole's articulated forms stand in opposition to Gifford's broader conception, achieved through the use of atmospheric light.

By the mid-1870s the Luminist painters had taken their experiments as far as they could. The immediate influence for the succeeding generation of landscape painting in America came from the French Barbizon school.[21] The most important of the Barbizon style painters in America was George Inness. Inness's early work came out of the realist landscape tradition; he was almost an exact contemporary of Frederic Church and Jasper Cropsey. He had studied briefly in 1845 with Regis Gignoux in New York, but by the 1860s his work showed the Barbizon influence. *Woodland* (cat. no. 172) of 1891 reveals how far the mainstream of American landscape painting in the 1890s was from the realist tradition of preceding generations. Inness's interest lay in suggesting natural forms through the use of resonant colors and summary brushwork. The solidity of forms was replaced by a misty, poetic quality that one associates with the work of French artists like Corot or Daubigny. It was precisely this Barbizon influence that came to be so important to American landscapists; in the case

cat. no. 172. George Inness. *Woodland,* 1891.

of most American painters in the Barbizon style the influence came from direct contact in France with French Barbizon painters. Dwight William Tryon's *Evening* (cat. no. 181) of 1886 certainly shows the influence of his teacher Charles Daubigny. Even the realist painter William Trost Richards in his *February* (cat. no. 177) of 1887 approached the more somber, reflective moods of the Barbizon tradition.

By the mid-1870s the depiction of American and foreign scenery was no longer the *sine qua non* of American landscape painters. The influences of French Barbizon and Impressionist painting became dominant in the last quarter of the nineteenth century. These avant-garde styles were based on entirely different principles, which eventually fused American landscape painting with "art for art's sake" attitudes. These attitudes had their origins abroad and surprisingly easily supplanted older American attitudes about landscape. By the last quarter of the nineteenth century a passion for things European prevailed among Americans. This passion found expression in styles of painting; never again would American landscape painting be so American.

Richard J. Boyle

AMERICAN IMPRESSIONISM

My God, I would rather go to Europe than to Heaven.

William Merritt Chase, 1872

Miss Baker is trying "to see blue and purple" and is progressing.

Theodore Robinson, 1892

American Impressionism, more than any other style created in this country, was largely inspired by European precedents. From the time that Benjamin West first crossed the Atlantic in the mid-eighteenth century, he was followed by a procession of American artists who went to Europe for study and for inspiration. However, never had so many made the journey abroad as in the last quarter of the nineteenth century, when the dominant artistic thinking in America was directed toward Europe and when this trend of thought was woven into the American social fabric as well as in its aesthetic concepts. Over the years American artists had studied and worked in London, Florence, Rome, Düsseldorf, Munich, and Venice. But, in the 1870s and 1880s Paris was the preeminent international art center; the reputation of its art schools and academies attracted artists from all over the world. Yet these academies were primarily conservative, and the vital movements of European art were not to be found inside their walls. Impressionism did not come out of the academies or the established schools of art. Instead, it flowered outside these institutions, and its development was largely in reaction to the accepted official approach to art that was taught there.

Impressionism revolutionized the art of painting by its concern with the very act of painting, which in turn came about as the Impressionists found an innovative aesthetic framework for the expression of new ideas. Their primary innovation was a fresh approach to the use of color. The Impressionists reveled in a freedom of color made possible through the discovery of new pigments by the chemical industry.[1] Their pictures became brighter as hue replaced tone as the principal means of representing light and atmosphere on canvas. They supplanted theoretical knowledge with optical experience, thereby implying an expansion of sensuous perception. They broke with the older conception of a picture as a classically ordered unit in time and space and substituted that "fleeting moment" in time and fragments of continuous space, signifying movement. Hence, the changing elements, the representation of an overall light and atmosphere became their common concern.

cat. no. 194. Daniel Ridgway Knight. *Hailing The Ferry,* 1888.

Impressionism became an international style not long after its first public exposure in Paris in 1874. The American version, adopted in the 1880s, although markedly similar to its French prototype, was a compound of this Gallic-international mode and the American tradition of realism. Because the American artist sought to combine these two basically antithetical styles, American Impressionism evolved gradually; its acceptance by artists and the public was not assured until the 1890s. However, the ground was broken for public acceptance by the number of American collectors who acquired the work of French Impressionists; by exhibitions of French Impressionist painting in the mid-eighties, notably Durand-Ruel's massive and historic exhibition in New York in 1886, in which over three hundred paintings by masters of the Impressionist style were shown; and by the sheer number of talented American painters who practiced the style and who taught it as well.

In the mid-nineties the American Impressionists J. Alden Weir, Theodore Robinson, Robert Vonnoh, Joseph DeCamp, and William Merritt Chase all taught in the school of the Pennsylvania Academy. Although the Academy recognized their talents relatively early, it recognized their abilities as artists, not necessarily *Impressionist* artists. The Academy was not a driving force in the promotion of the style in America. Rather, the widespread acceptance of American Impressionism in the mid-nineties was a triumph of French influence and the climax of a period of dependence upon European culture.

The thrust toward a cultural dependence upon Europe became strong after the American Civil War. Prior to that conflict, there appeared to be a cohesiveness in American art, and a serenity. The War changed all that. It was the first modern war, and the growth of industrialism and economic change during and after the conflict turned the United States into the first modern industrial state, with all the attendant problems that transformation implied. American life became fragmented; the serenity of art was disrupted, not to reappear until later in the century through the delicate and genteel painting of the American Impressionists, for whom harmony in life and art was an espoused aim. As artistic directions became uncertain, American artists once again looked toward Europe, not only for training, as they had always done, but also for style.

A significant example of the shift in taste toward European art, particularly evident in the area of private collecting, is the comparison of three notable collections bequeathed to the Pennsylvania Academy—the Carey, Harrison, and Gibson collections. Edward Carey, scion of the famous Philadelphia publishing company founded by his father Mathew, was an ardent patron of American art in the 1830s and 1840s and was personally acquainted with many of the artists he supported. In the 1850s and 1860s, Joseph Harrison pursued an interest in American art as history. Henry C. Gibson, on the other hand, collected the leading *European* artists of his day, and his collection is heavy in the area of French painting, much of which he acquired abroad between 1879 and 1880. Many of the artists represented, such as Gérôme, Couture, Millet, and Courbet, either taught or influenced numbers of Americans who went abroad to study.[2]

Although Gibson acquired much of his collection abroad in 1879, he could have seen work by some of the same artists three years earlier in his hometown in the art section of the Philadelphia Centennial Exposition of 1876. This famous exposition can be used as a convenient, if not entirely precise, point of departure for a discussion of those American artists who flocked to Europe to study.

The Exposition was organized to celebrate one hundred years of American Independence, but its chief impact was not the emphasis on a century of past achievements or on the future of a successful democratic society and its culture; rather, it gave Americans a glimpse into the future age of machinery and their first large-scale look at the arts, artifacts, and luxuries of the Old World. The art exhibitions, shown in Memorial Hall, which afterwards became the foundation of the Philadelphia Museum of Art, gave many American artists a chance to see the work of their European colleagues at first hand. The French section was one of the strongest in the exhibition and was undoubtedly an important factor in inspiring the migration of American artists to Parisian studios.[3]

One of the most popular attractions in Philadelphia, the new building of the Pennsylvania Academy of the Fine Arts, was outside the fairgrounds. Designed by Furness and Hewitt and completed in April of 1876, the Academy building is imbued with a sense of Victorian optimism and exuberance. Yet, despite the European sources of its style, in its very eclecticism it retains—as did the work of the artists who confronted foreign styles—certain features which make it characteristically American. For one thing, there is clarity of structural form despite the profusion of decorative elements. In a way, it is an architectural statement comparable to George Inness's ideas about painting. Inness talked of "generalizing without losing that logical connection of parts to the whole which satisfies the mind" and concluded that "the elements of this, therefore, are solidity of objects and a transparency of atmosphere through which we are conscious of spaces and distances."[4] Inness was speaking for himself, but his statement reflects an aesthetic which was implicit in the attitude and work of most of the American artists who went abroad to study, and in particular those artists who went to Europe in the 1870s and 1880s. Many of them either studied at the Pennsylvania Academy or subsequently taught there, and they took with them the emotional and intellectual freight of American thought and experience. An important part of that experience was a preference for the factual, the real. This preference manifested itself early in the work of Benjamin West, of Charles Willson Peale, and of John Singleton Copley. And it was a strong part of Gilbert Stuart's thinking when he said, "For my own part, I will not follow any master. I wish to find out what nature is for myself, and see her with my own eyes."[5]

It is significant that when the Americans arrived in Paris in the 1870s and 1880s, they did not seek out the avant-garde or even follow their own independent paths. Basically conservative, they enrolled in the official art schools and studied with the masters of the French academic tradition. Even the Americans who subsequently became the stalwarts of American Impressionism and who, at least after 1874, could have sought out the French Impressionists were apparently not inclined or ready to do so; in fact, J. Alden Weir was quite shocked when he viewed his first French Impressionist exhibition. At the time, Weir, like many other American artists, was strongly influenced by the more conservative teaching of Jules Bastien-Lepage.

In the late 1870s, Lepage invented a style of picture-making which combined rigorous studio draftsmanship with the light and atmosphere of painting out-of-doors. It was a style both daring and safe—daring in its re-creation of outdoor atmosphere and safe in its careful drawing of the figures that always populated his landscapes. It was a compromise method, and it led the way toward the eventual public acceptance of Impressionism.

Lepage's plein-airism became his particular contribution to art. It was especially of interest to American painters because of the background of their own landscape tradition and their respect for the integrity of the object. In fact, plein-airism does bear a superficial resemblance to American Luminism of the 1860s. In both there is a concern for light and atmosphere, and in both there is a dependence upon careful draftsmanship for the final realization of the picture. However, there are major differences. Luminism tends to be more philosophical, more contemplative; through clarity of form and dramatic handling of light, it seeks to express a higher spiritual meaning in the rendering of the natural world. The quiet lyricism of this style creates a feeling of stillness and tranquility, and the smooth finish of its execution creates an air of detachment as though the presence of the artist's hand should not in any way detract from the evocation of nature's moods. Plein-airism, on the other hand, is more aesthetic than philosophical; it is concerned with style rather than meaning. And with its emphasis on a *method* of representing nature, it lacks the intensity of Luminist painting. Plein-airism is also a more painterly style than Luminism; there is a greater degree of impasto on the canvas, and the artist's hand is very much in evidence.

cat. no. 191. Thomas Alexander Harrison. *The Wave*.

Hailing the Ferry (cat. no. 194) by Daniel Ridgway Knight is a superb example of the Lepage plein-air method. The figures of the two girls, carefully drawn in an academic style, were obviously posed in the studio. The landscape, on the other hand, has a quality of immediacy and closely observed naturalism. Muted in color but evocative of light and atmosphere, it is representative of the kind of painting that made plein-airism a powerful and attractive movement.

A more important plein-airist than Knight was the expatriate Philadelphian, Thomas Alexander Harrison. Harrison was a student at the Pennsylvania Academy from 1880 to 1881, after which he made his way to France. Although he kept a studio in Paris, Harrison spent a great deal of time painting on the Brittany coast, in Concarneau, and in Beg-Meil. The seascapes he painted there were a sensation in his day and made this now obscure artist known the world over. *The Wave* (cat. no. 191) received a place of honor in the Paris Salon of 1884 and was subsequently exhibited throughout Europe. This picture was bought by the Pennsylvania Academy in 1891 for $5400, one of the largest sums paid by the Academy up to that time. Harrison S. Morris, the managing director of the Pennsylvania Academy, who saw the artist last in 1910, characterized him as "tall and distinguished, and polished in dress and manner" and described his pictures as "brilliant canvases of the sea, rare experiments in color and atmosphere, sure in drawing and in beauty."[6] Indeed, *The Wave* is an astonishing painting. "Sure in drawing," it nevertheless has all the atmosphere of plein-airism. Despite its size, it has the detached quality of American Luminist painting of the 1850s and 1860s. With its softly modulated tones and subtlely of color, its combination of French technique and aspects of American tradition, *The Wave* exhibits a pervasive poetic realism.[7]

Just as Bastien-Lepage commanded a middle ground between the academic approach and Impressionist practice, there were those American painters who occupied that ground midway between the Hudson River School and American Impressionism. They went beyond the tenets of earlier American landscape painting, yet they stopped short of the full Impressionist method. This group of "Pre-Impressionists," which included Homer Dodge Martin,

Dwight Tryon, Alexander and Birge Harrison, and Henry Ward Ranger, was noted for a particular quality which E. P. Richardson has called "quietism." Quietism describes a tranquil mood and an element of "quiet lyricism" which, side by side with realism, had emerged in the Hudson River School. These elements became more important in the Luminist style and later were among those characteristics which made the American version of Impressionism different from that of the French. The influences on the Pre-Impressionist painters were diverse; Alexander Harrison's painting, of course, was affected by Bastien-Lepage, while Henry Ward Ranger was at first influenced by The Hague School and later more strongly by Monticelli and Diaz. Like George Inness, Ranger represents "American art in the Barbizon mood."[8]

Ranger was particularly drawn to the work of the Dutch painters, especially to the masters of The Hague School, whose landscapes, seascapes, and genre pictures of life in Holland were extremely popular in America at the time. However, he always had a strong feeling for Barbizon painting, and he became known for the rich texture of his paint surfaces and for the glimmering shafts of light in his pictures of forest interiors. Although Ranger adhered to the tonalism of The Hague and the Barbizon schools, his palette in the work of the late nineties appears to be lighter and brighter, and his brushwork in such later works as *Sheep Pasture* (cat. no. 199) is more open, freer, and closer to Impressionist practice than that in his earlier pictures. This freedom of handling and brighter color is perhaps an indication of the fact that by the late nineties Impressionism had become thoroughly accepted by the American art world and no artist was wholly untouched by its influence.

If, in the overall view of American Impressionism, the "Pre-Impressionists" seem to be a link between "stability" and "dynamism," between Bastien-Lepage and Monet, or Henry Ward Ranger and John Twachtman, Winslow Homer stands out because his work in the 1860s shows interesting affinities to that of the contemporary French Impressionists. Like them, Homer became interested in the atmospheric properties of light as well as its effect upon objects, and he, too, began to paint certain pictures during a specific time of day because he wanted a particular kind of light. During this period, he painted a series of beach scenes in which the handling of light is not unlike that of Monet in his *Terrace at Sainte-Adresse,* painted about 1866-67 (Metropolitan Museum of Art). At the same time, Homer abandoned the dry, illustrative approach and the fussy details of his earlier painting and adopted instead a more freely brushed technique similar to that of Manet or of early Monet. Moreover, like them, Homer developed in his work a new feeling for texture and a stronger sense of immediacy. Although he later pursued a solitary path and became one of the most American of American artists in the late nineteenth century, Homer did anticipate some of the problems that would occupy such American Impressionist painters as Hassam, Weir, and Twachtman some twenty years later.

Homer spent the year 1867-68 in France. When he returned to this country, he brought with him aspects of French technique, but he continued to paint scenes of daily life in America. He drew his subjects, such as *Morning Call* (cat. no. 193) from the farms of New England and New York State, from the Adirondacks and the White Mountains, and from the popular and fashionable beach resorts on the Atlantic seaboard—all of them bathed in a pervasive and strong sunlight. However, the light in America is different than the light in France; American light is harder and more sharply focused. And Homer's painting was different from the French in a similar way. It also was harder, more sharply focused, and less ambient. As Lloyd Goodrich has pointed out, "To the true Impressionist, light and atmosphere were as important as nature's solid substance. . . . But Homer's chief interest remained the object, the thing-in-itself."[9]

In *Morning Call,* painted in 1870, the figure of the woman silhouetted against the landscape, although reminiscent of Monet, owes more to Homer's experience as an illustrator for *Harper's Weekly* in which, on June 11, 1870, the exact prototype of the girl blowing the horn was first published. The Detroit Institute of Arts owns a later and slightly different version of this picture, painted in 1873. E. P. Richardson calls it "one of the most cheerful of his pictures." Yet, he continues, "it has in small scale the monumental force of his style."[10] In addition to a concern for light, the "cheerfulness" of the picture also relates it to Impressionist painting. It was this element which American Impressionist painters would make much of and for which they would be called "painters of a holiday atmosphere."

This same "atmosphere" pervades *Honfleur* (cat. no. 210) by James Abbott McNeill Whistler. Small in size but great in charm, like the Homer it is a cheerful picture and much closer to an Impressionist conception. In its high-keyed color, it appears to be atypical of Whistler, particularly in comparison with his great nocturnes and the elegant portraits, carefully "arranged" and painted in the lovely muted color of a "quietism" taken to its ultimate conclusion. Whistler painted a number of such small seascapes during the sixties, but *Honfleur* is closer in style to *Coast Scene: Bathers* (Art Institute of Chicago), *Coast Scene with Boats* (Private Collection, London), *Bathing Posts, Brittany* (University of Glasgow), or *The Sea, Pourville* (Private Collection, London) —all of which were painted in the late eighties or nineties.

When Harrison Morris first visited Whistler in Paris in 1895, Whistler had practically achieved the status of an "old master," at least in the eyes of English-speaking artists. Morris later recalled that, when he was introduced as the director of the Pennsylvania Academy, "Whistler took on much animation and showed me special warmth, because, he said, the Pennsylvania Academy had awarded him a gold medal—which it had in 1893."[11]

The first picture by Whistler to be exhibited at the Academy was the celebrated portrait of his mother. It was shown in a special exhibition entitled "American Artists at Home and in Europe," organized in 1881. For this show, juries in London, Paris, and Munich selected paintings by Americans living abroad and, in addition to Whistler, the participants included John Singer Sargent and Theodore Robinson; John Twachtman, Childe Hassam, J. Alden Weir and Thomas Dewing, Frank Benson, Edmund Tarbell and Joseph DeCamp; Alexander Harrison, Robert Vonnoh, William Merritt Chase, Edward Redfield, William Picknell and Robert Reid. Most of these painters would become known as the best of the American Impressionists.

Whistler's portrait of his mother is one of the most famous American pictures ever painted. Unfortunately, the Academy missed the opportunity to purchase it, and there still is not an important example of his work in the collection. In his autobiography, *Confessions in Art,* Harrison Morris recalled his attempt in 1893 to buy one

> of those Whistler's, which I secured from The World's Fair in Chicago and brought to the Academy in Philadelphia. . . . The three large canvases, . . . Yellow Buskin, Princess of the Land of Porcelain, and Fur Jacket, were valued at $15,000 each. . . . I tried to raise the sum to buy one of them for the Academy; but the management that had failed . . . to take Whistler's "Mother" when exhibited at the Academy for $1,500, would have none of the extravagant canvases that cost so much more.[12]

Whistler shared an awareness of new ideas and current trends with Mary Cassatt, whose work he admired. Mary Cassatt was the first major American painter to adopt successfully the Impressionist style and to make of it a strong personal statement. She not only absorbed the style but also became a member of the French Impressionist group, which Degas invited her to join in 1877. She exhibited with the French Impressionists from 1879 until 1886. Yet her early schooling was quite conventional.

From 1861 to 1865 Mary Cassatt studied at the Pennsylvania Academy, where Thomas Eakins was a fellow student. Then, like Eakins, she left Philadelphia for Paris in 1866. The

cat. no. 193. Winslow Homer.
Morning Call, 1870.
PRIVATE COLLECTION.

outbreak of the Franco-Prussian War brought her back to the United States, and in 1872 she studied briefly in Italy and traveled in Spain, Holland, and Belgium.

Miss Cassatt's work in the late 1860s and early 1870s, inspired by her study of the old masters, was strongly modeled and dark in tone. The Academy owns one of her early pictures —*Bacchante,* painted at Parma in 1872, probably while she was studying with Carlo Raimondi. It is an interesting example of her academic work at that time. About 1875, influenced by Degas, she began to develop into an Impressionist painter.

In 1880 Mary Cassatt began her mother and child pictures, and she soon became known as *the* painter of the *maternité* theme. Her mother and child pictures were always somewhat detached, aloof, and so lacking in sentimentality that even Gauguin was moved to remark: "Mary Cassatt has charm, but she also has force."[13] In the late 1880s and 1890s she developed a large and luminous style with a feeling of permanence such as that evoked in *Young Thomas and His Mother* (cat. no. 184), done in 1893. Simple, direct, and strong, the picture is dominated by the two figures, which fill the picture plane and create a great sense of immediacy. Executed in pastel, it in no way reflects the inherent fragility of the medium.

But then Mary Cassatt was not a fragile person. Tough and independent, she went her own way, and she made the most complete statement of the *maternité* theme in her time.

cat. no. 184. Mary Cassatt. *Young Thomas and His Mother,* 1893.

Although her work was admired by her contemporaries, she never had an artistic following. However, she did have considerable influence as a tastemaker, as well as a deep interest in the struggles of art students and young artists. She was instrumental in introducing French Impressionist paintings into American collections, and her concern for young artists led her to refuse prizes and to decline jury memberships. In a letter to Harrison Morris, declining the Academy's Lippincott Prize, she expressed her feeling that awards should be money, a more practical thing for struggling students.[14] It is likely that she was also thinking of the students when she wrote to John Frederick Lewis, the president of the Academy, offering two portraits by Courbet, *The Mayor of Ornans* and *Madame Frond*.[15] The Academy accepted the pictures and two years later awarded her the Academy Gold Medal of Honor, not for any particular painting but for "eminent service in the cause of art."

Mary Cassatt was probably the only American Impressionist to be strongly influenced by Degas. In general, Edouard Manet's influence on the Americans was stronger, but the French Impressionist who exerted the greatest impact on American artists in the late eighties was Claude Oscar Monet. Monet's most famous American follower was Theodore Robinson. After Mary Cassatt, Robinson was the next major American painter to achieve successfully what John I. H. Baur has called the "wedding of French-born Impressionism to American art."[16] Robinson was a very quiet man, "a painter's painter," whose understated work was not well known in his lifetime. Harrison Morris spoke of Robinson's "gentle intelligence and something like genius" and recalled: "We engaged him to come over weekly from New York to teach his lovely landscape and figure art in the Academy Schools, and thus I came close to his simple qualities, his modest self-estimate."[17] Modest he may have been, but Robinson was one of the pioneers of American Impressionism and one of the most talented artists of the period.

Theodore Robinson painted in the realist tradition of Eastman Johnson and Winslow Homer before he visited Monet in Giverny in 1887. Yet, as often as the American visited the great French artist and sought his advice, he was never really a formal pupil. More of a follower, he was a delicate, individual painter, a master of the quiet, intimate *vue*. His work is lyrical, tender, and reticent. From 1890 on, Robinson painted some of his best "pure" Impressionist pictures. It was not easy. He was, for all his admiration of Monet, somewhat distrustful of the potential for total abstraction in the Impressionist approach. He believed sound draftsmanship to be the basis for good painting, and he once wrote:

> Altogether the possibilities are very great for the moderns, but they must draw without ceasing or they will "get left," and with the brilliancy and light of real out-doors combine the austerity, the sobriety, that has always characterized good painting.[18]

These elements are at work in *Port Ben, Delaware and Hudson Canal* (cat. no. 203) painted in 1893. Despite the variegated color, the loose brushwork, and the overall light, the subject is not dissolved in light and atmosphere. Moreover, the surface tension characteristic of Impressionist pictures is here violated by the diagonal thrust of the canal as it penetrates into deep space.

Port Ben came to the Academy by default. "Well, when he died," recalled Harrison Morris,

> some of his friends among the artists in New York . . . presented it, in his memory, to the Metropolitan Museum . . . the Metropolitan declined to accept the picture; and I thought it a tribute to Theodore Robinson and a liberal movement for the Pennsylvania Academy to indicate that it might find acceptance by the Academy. And it was offered and accepted.[19]

cat. no. 203. Theodore Robinson. *Port Ben, Delaware and Hudson Canal,* 1893.

cat. no. 198. William L. Picknell. *Road to Nice,* 1896.

Actually, the whole affair created quite a fuss and was the subject of several articles in the *New York Times* in January 1899. The picture was selected by John LaFarge, then president of the Society of American Artists, and bought by a group of artists, which included Will H. Low and J. Alden Weir. According to the newspaper accounts, the Metropolitan rejected the offer on the grounds that this was not the kind of art the trustees wanted to encourage. In later statements, they indicated that they did not think the painting was one of Robinson's best. They were mistaken. Not only is it one of his best, but also, as Morris pointed out, "when it makes its very seldom appearance on the walls of the galleries, all may see what a jewel of color and observation it is."[20]

"A jewel of color" is a more than apt description for *Summer Clouds* (cat. no. 183) by Soren Emil Carlsen. Carlsen, like William Lamb Picknell, practiced a very personal kind of Impressionism, and both deserve to be made better known to a wider segment of the public. Carlsen was born in Denmark and studied architecture at the Danish Royal Academy before immigrating to the United States in 1872. About 1891 he settled in New York. He taught intermittently at the Pennsylvania Academy until 1918, when he gave up teaching altogether. *Summer Clouds,* which was purchased by the Academy in 1913, was probably painted in Maine, but specificity of place gives way to the generalized poetry of beach, sea, and sky. *Summer Clouds,* like Carlsen's celebrated still-life pictures, is timeless, elegant, and still.

Timeless also is Picknell's *Road to Nice* (cat. no. 198). Picknell went to France in 1876 and soon made his way to the Breton village of Pont-Aven, which Paul Gauguin made famous a decade later. There Picknell worked with the Anglo-American artist Robert Wylie.

cat. no. 209. J. Alden Weir. *Midday Rest in New England,* 1897.

In 1880 he painted *Road to Concarneau* (Corcoran Gallery of Art, Washington, D.C.), which received a great deal of favorable comment when it was exhibited in the Salon of that year. Thereafter, Picknell painted a series of "Road to" landscapes, including the Academy's *Road to Nice,* dated 1896. *Road to Nice* is built up with a series of small brushstrokes in a tightly knit structure, filled with a vibrant and overall light.

Picknell died in 1897, the year the group which came to be called The Ten American Painters was organized. Late in December of 1897, Childe Hassam, J. Alden Weir, and John Henry Twachtman submitted their resignations to the Society of American Artists. They were joined in their new group by Thomas Dewing, Joseph DeCamp, Willard Metcalf, Edmund Tarbell, Frank Benson, Edward Simmons, and Robert Reid. Later, William Merritt Chase joined the group after Twachtman's death. They were all painters who, dissatisfied with the immense size and mediocrity of the Society's annual exhibitions, decided to form a loosely knit group of their own. Like the term "Impressionist" in France, the term "Ten Americans" was invented by the press; the name was derived from the title of the group's first exhibition, which was simply called "A Show of Ten American Painters," indicating the number of participants. The Ten American Painters constituted a kind of Academy of American Impressionism, and some of its members, notably Weir, DeCamp, and Chase, had close associations with the Pennsylvania Academy.

J. Alden Weir was a tireless worker on behalf of American art. He helped to organize the Society of American Artists in 1877 and served as secretary during 1879 and 1880. He also served as president of the National Academy from 1915 to 1917, and he was a visiting instructor at the Pennsylvania Academy from 1899 to 1905.

Weir painted without affectation and without mannerism. About 1889-90, Weir's palette began to brighten, at least in his landscape painting (he kept to a more low-key style in still life and portraiture). This change was perhaps due to the influence of Theodore Robinson and John Twachtman, with whom he painted in the late eighties and nineties. His special delight was painting out-of-doors—the fields, the woods, and, as in *Midday Rest in New England* (cat. no. 209), the farm. Weir painted *Midday Rest* in 1897 at his farm in Branchville, Connecticut, which the collector Irwin Davis had given him in exchange for a picture. In 1898 the Pennsylvania Academy bought this "beautiful landscape of his, fresh and green, and smelling of the countryside where he lived in the summer."[21] In March of that year the Academy lent the picture to the first exhibition of The Ten.

Another member of The Ten who had associations with the Academy was Joseph DeCamp. In 1895, Harrison Morris went up to Boston and hired DeCamp to run the Academy school; he replaced Robert W. Vonnoh, who had been conducting the school since 1891. Because of ill health, DeCamp had to resign in 1896.

DeCamp, Tarbell, and Benson were considered the "Boston men" of The Ten. DeCamp's work was not as spontaneous as Benson's nor as lively as Tarbell's. It was sober, solid, and based upon craftsmanship in the academic tradition. DeCamp was not as committed to the Impressionist style as were Weir, Twachtman, or Hassam; his Impressionism tended to be more conservative than theirs, his color more muted and tonal, as in *The Little Hotel* (cat. no. 185) of 1903.

> Harrison Morris recalled that when DeCamp had to leave the Academy School, there was one conspicuous artist and teacher whom it would be a crowning act to engage if he could be persuaded to come, this was William M. Chase. . . . Thus I went to see him . . . at his summer house and studio in the Shinnecock Hills, on Long Island; . . . Chase consented to come to the Academy schools on certain days of each week.[22]

William Merritt Chase taught at the Academy from 1896 to 1909. Chase was not only a vital member of The Ten, he was also, next to Whistler, one of the most important

cat. no. 192. Childe Hassam. *Cat Boats: Newport,* 1901.

cat. no. 206. John H. Twachtman. *Sailing in the Mist,* ca.1895.

cat. no. 205. Edmund C. Tarbell. *Breakfast in the Studio,* 1896.

personalities in American art in the late nineteenth century. Between the Philadelphia Centennial of 1876 and the World's Columbian Exposition of 1893, Chase absorbed and adapted nearly every artistic influence exerted on American painters in his time. He was obviously eclectic, but he was also a strong and brilliant virtuoso who painted in a broad, spirited style with a sense of elegance and éclat. After 1887, his most brilliant Impressionist work was done at Shinnecock, Long Island, where he conducted summer classes. It is unfortunate that the Academy does not own an Impressionist painting by Chase, for he painted some of his best pictures in that style, which was well suited to the verve and zest of his ebullient personality.

William Merritt Chase was the last member of The Ten to be "voted in," whereas Childe Hassam was one of the first. Hassam's early work was basically tonal, but his handling was broad and free, more in the manner of Manet than of Bastien-Lepage. By 1889 he had adopted the wiry brushwork and high-keyed palette for which he is best known. In the 1890s his style reached its maturity, and he was recognized as one of the leading artists of his day. He was popular in his time and he is popular still. Not, however, in Philadelphia. In 1894 Hassam complained to Morris that "Philadelphia is not the most encouraging place for the *painter* to send to . . . as I am sure all of us feel." [23] Nevertheless, he contributed extensively to Academy exhibitions, and in 1902 his picture *Cat Boats: Newport* (cat. no. 192) received a Temple Gold Medal and was purchased for the collection. *Cat Boats,* which Harrison Morris watched him paint in 1901, is one of his most cheerful and painterly pictures. Hassam had facility; his work is joyful and exuberant, but it has none of the intensity of some of Weir's pastoral scenes and certainly none of the profound introspection and the poetry of John H. Twachtman's.

Twachtman was the most unique, sensitive, and searching of all the American Impressionists. His "fragile dreams in color," as Morris called his paintings, were extremely personal. He understood abstraction better than most, and as a consequence, his work was not easily understood and he did not sell very much. "Do you know," he wrote to Morris the year before he died, "that I have exhibited eighty-five pictures this year and have not sold one?" [24] The Academy did not purchase *Sailing in the Mist* (cat. no. 206) until 1906, four years after the artist's death. *Sailing in the Mist* is one of his most beautiful pictures. Extremely subtle, it comes very near to Monet's paintings of the Thames. The subject provides Twachtman with an opportunity for a display of pure painting, an overall delicate relationship of hue against hue. Yet, unlike Monet, Twachtman was a romantic, and he liked painting from nature in all its isolation and silence.

It is interesting to compare Twachtman's work with that of Willard Metcalf, who was also sensitive to the moods of nature. Metcalf's *Twin Birches* (cat. no. 196) is a quiet, pleasing picture, but it has none of the profundity or the poetry of *Sailing in the Mist.* Yet Metcalf was known as "the poet laureate" of the New England hills; he received many honors and awards, including a gold medal from the Academy. And *Twin Birches* was bought for the collection during his lifetime.

While Hassam, Weir, and Twachtman were New York members of The Ten, Frank Benson and Edmund Tarbell, like Joseph DeCamp, were Boston-based. Benson was famous for his pictures of female figures in sunlit landscapes, painted with dash and with more than a little sentiment. They are good examples of that "holiday atmosphere" which permeated so much of American Impressionism. Benson also became very well known for his prints of birds in flight, which are similar to his painting *Great White Herons* (cat. no. 182). Painted in 1933, the picture has, in a tentative way, some of the flat patterns of Post-Impressionism. Although it has charm, it is not really Benson at his best.

On the other hand, *Breakfast in the Studio* (cat. no. 205) is one of Tarbell's best pictures. Painted in 1896, it is a classic example of a subject for which Tarbell became famous—an Impressionist version of the genre picture. His paintings of intimate family groups and figures in interiors are reminiscent of those of Degas, as well as evocative of the flavor of the seventeenth-century Dutch "Little Masters." The cut-off figure in the lower right is very Degas, and the handling of paint and the disposition of the elements in space are very modern. Yet the still life on the table and especially the figure of the maid servant seen through the open doorway recall the genre scenes of Pieter de Hooch. Tarbell exhibited frequently at the Academy, and, according to Morris, all three of the Boston members of The Ten, especially DeCamp, felt that their first recognition came from the Pennsylvania Academy.[25]

Edward Simmons and Robert Reid were rather minor Impressionists. Simmons was essentially a muralist, and he painted few easel pictures. Reid, too, was a muralist, but he also painted figure pieces and some landscapes in a rather sentimental and decorative manner. *The Mirror* (cat. no. 201), in its artiness and "mood," is very Whistlerian, but it lacks the austerity and sense of abstraction of Whistler's nocturnes and portraits.

The remaining member of The Ten, Thomas Wilmer Dewing, was, by no means, a minor artist. Next to Weir, Hassam, and Twachtman, Dewing was one of the group's most important members. Stylistically, however, he stood apart from the rest of the group, as Degas stood apart from his Impressionist colleagues. Like Degas, Dewing was a conceptual painter; drawing was his forte. His pictorial repertoire included portraits and figure pieces of women, painted with surpassing elegance and refinement. However, his women are detached, unapproachable, alone, and isolated from each other and from the viewer. *Spring* (cat. no. 186) is classic Dewing. There is the jewel-like color, the elegant surface, the mystery. There are the isolated figures that inhabit a refined and self-contained world, a world which exists solely on Dewing's canvases.

Although The Ten American Painters are considered to be a kind of academy of American Impressionism, there were other artists of merit who did not belong to that group but who deserve attention and recognition—Robert W. Vonnoh and William Ritschel, for example. Both were nationally known in their time; yet today their fame seems to be limited to certain geographical areas—Vonnoh to Philadelphia and Boston, and Ritschel to California.

Robert Vonnoh had strong associations with the Pennsylvania Academy. He ran the Academy school from 1891 to 1896, and, after his resignation from that post, he continued to substitute for various members of the Academy faculty through the 1920s. He was also involved in obtaining pictures for exhibitions and with their installation as well. He was active in recommending artists for faculty positions and seems to have had a voice in the selection of guest lists for special openings.

Vonnoh began his career in Boston. During his second trip abroad, in 1887, he adopted the Impressionist practice and palette, and in 1890 he was given a one-man show at the Academy consisting of the pictures he had painted in France. *November* (cat. no. 208) was in that exhibition; it became his best known work. Through his active association with the Academy, he soon made a name for himself in Philadelphia. "Nowhere, we think," wrote Morris, "have you a larger measure of consideration and regard than in Philadelphia." [26]

Californians had the same high regard for the work of William Ritschel, who emigrated from Germany in 1895. His *Rocks and Breakers* (cat. no. 202) exhibits a vigorous but conservative Impressionist style that was relatively rare on the West Coast. *Rocks and Breakers* appears to be a sober bridge between the Barbizon approach of William Keith and the more vibrant and experimental style of later California painters.[27]

By the time of the Chicago World's Fair of 1893, at which the best painters working in the Impressionist manner were represented, the generation of Americans who were born in the 1860s and 1870s could receive instruction from American artists who had already

cat. no. 208. Robert William Vonnoh. *November,* 1890.

cat. no. 200. Edward W. Redfield. *New Hope,* ca.1926.

assimilated the Impressionist style. Elmer Schofield and Edward Redfield, for example, studied under Robert Vonnoh at the Academy, and Philip L. Hale studied under J. Alden Weir before continuing on to Paris. Hale's painting tends to be decorative and somewhat sentimental, as in *The Crimson Rambler* (cat. no. 190), purchased by the Academy in 1909. In contrast, Schofield and Edward Redfield were exponents of "manly" American painting. Such terms as "virile and outstepping" were used to describe their work by the critics of their day. In his painting *Winter* (cat. no. 204), Schofield responded directly to that season. The strong dark verticals of the trees and the stark white of the snow are done with the strength and zest of a man who loved to paint out-of-doors in the winter. In 1903 Schofield settled in England, and thereafter, he traveled back and forth between England and America, but he always kept up his interest in the Academy, as did Edward Redfield.

Edward Redfield's painting bears striking similarities to that of Schofield. He too was known as a "painter of winter-locked nature," and his painting *New Hope* (cat. no. 200) is an example of his favorite theme. Redfield was an *alla prima* painter and was convinced that his paintings should be done on the spot with no later alterations in the studio. *New Hope,* probably done in just that manner, is a winter portrait of the town in Bucks County, Pennsylvania, where he settled when he returned from Paris in 1890. Redfield is credited with the founding of a lively art colony in New Hope, and he was also active in Pennsylvania Academy affairs; in 1907 he received the Academy Gold Medal for eminent service to art.

Redfield was a friend of Ernest Lawson and William Glackens, both of whom were members of The Eight. They both began their careers as Impressionist painters, and, although they held on to the style in some respects, they gradually developed in another direction. In *At the Beach* (cat. no. 189), Glackens owes a considerable debt to Renoir, and *Fort George Hill: Morning* (cat. no. 195) by Lawson has elements of the Impressionism of Twachtman, with whom he studied. Guy Pène du Bois said of Lawson that he "was an off-shoot which met new conditions, with eyes perhaps less blinded by the sun itself and more open, anyway, to its action upon matter."[28]

Du Bois wrote those words in 1916, and by that time "new conditions" were necessary indeed. Impressionism itself had run its course, and the American version, always less robust than its French counterpart, had become, in general, sentimentalized and decorative, as represented in the work of Frederick Frieseke and Richard Miller. Both were superficial artists but sound craftsmen; they were famous in their day, and they carried the style into the late 1930s. Frieseke had the benefits of the teaching of both Whistler and Monet, and *Seated Nude* (cat. no. 187) has the muted tones of Whistler and the brushwork of Monet, but these elements have been reduced to an easy formula. Frieseke lived most of his life in France, as did Richard Miller. The latter went to Paris from St. Louis in 1898 and stayed in France for twenty years. *The Boudoir* (cat. no. 197) is slick and pretty and represents the kind of painting done at the end of the Impressionist movement in the United States.

Although the Impressionist style did reach its high point in the 1890s in America, there were artists of merit who used it effectively even past the point of its decline. Daniel Garber was just such an artist. Garber's work has a strongly decorative, *designed* quality. He trained with Duveneck at Cincinnati in 1897 and with Anshutz and Weir at the Pennsylvania Academy from 1899 to 1905. His work is uneven, but in his good painting, such as *Battersea Bridge* of 1905 (cat. no. 188), and in his landscapes of Bucks County, where he lived for thirty years, there is a very personal sense of poetry and a lyricism of color which made him one of the more interesting of the late American Impressionists. Garber had a long association with the Pennsylvania Academy, serving on the faculty of the Academy school from 1909 to 1951, and through his painting and his teaching his personal brand of visual poetry was kept alive well into the twentieth century.

cat. no. 197. Richard E. Miller. *The Boudoir.*

cat. no. 188. Daniel Garber. *Battersea Bridge,* 1905.

Impressionism in America was developed by study abroad, of course. But the American landscape tradition was certainly a contributing factor to the American version, as was the influence of such key painters as Whistler, Bastien-Lepage, and Monet. Photography played an important role, as did the Japanese print. On the whole, although the American Impressionists were not innovators, there were still brilliant *individual and personal* achievements. Many of the best artists were associated with the Pennsylvania Academy as students, teachers, or exhibitors. Some of them, in the words of Harrison Morris, "held that their first recognition came from The Pennsylvania Academy in our time, in the way of medals," though not always, as he points out, "in the ways of the more necessary sales." [29] Nevertheless, that early recognition of talented artists who created many memorable images was an important contribution to the American tradition, which they and the Academy have served so well.

Louise Lippincott

THOMAS EAKINS AND THE ACADEMY

I taught at the Pennsylvania Academy from the opening of the schools until I was turned out, a period much longer than I should have permitted myself to remain there.
My honors are misunderstanding, persecution, and neglect, enhanced because unsought.

Thomas Eakins to Harrison Morris
April 23, 1894 PAFA Archives

Thomas Eakins's fame as a teacher at the Pennsylvania Academy rests on the circumstances of his resignation from the school's faculty in 1886. The public furor over his removal of the loincloth from a model in the women's life class made a small event into a controversial one. As a result, Eakins has been viewed as a martyr to Philadelphia conservatism rather than as a moderately successful teacher.

When Eakins's contributions to the Academy are considered, there seems to have been some justification for the directors' request for his resignation. By the time that Eakins joined the faculty in 1876, an academic curriculum based on the study of the nude and on the practice of painting from life had already been established; it included a modeling class and a small anatomy department. Eakins's contributions to the Academy curriculum consisted of modifying and expanding the courses already extant. Basically, Eakins taught a traditional academic curriculum distorted by his primary emphasis on painting, drawing, and modeling the nude human. figure at the expense of teaching composition and design. While his highly specialized interest in figure construction contributed to his uniqueness as an artist and theoretician, it narrowed the scope of his teaching until it was no longer appropriate for the majority of his students. Eakins's insistence on a specific course of study limited the flexibility of the curriculum and alienated many pupils. These problems were compounded by his deliberate disregard of conventional Victorian moral standards and by his uncompromising advocacy of intensive professional training for women.

Nevertheless, throughout his career at the Academy, Eakins endeavored to provide his students with the best art education possible. His conception of an ideal art education, opposed in many ways to the academic training he had received, was as unique and personal as his painting and as widely respected and misunderstood.

Eakins's association with the Pennsylvania Academy began early. He had displayed an unusual talent for drawing while still in grade school. He may have attended the Academy annual exhibitions, and he enrolled in the Academy's antique class after his graduation from Central High School in 1861.[1]

The Academy's school had been organized in 1856 to accommodate the needs of artists and art students in Philadelphia. While the antique class was designed to teach beginning students how to draw, the major purpose of the school was to provide facilities for the study of the live model. The life class was organized with the needs of the professional artist, rather than of the young art student, in mind. Those who wished to join the life class had to be over twenty-one years of age, and they had to submit a cast drawing to an artists' committee for approval.[2] Since there was no professor and the classes met only three times a week, supplemented by occasional lectures, they by no means provided, or were intended to provide, a complete education for a young student.

Eakins studied at the Academy for four years, but he found its curriculum frustratingly inadequate. Already a skilled draughtsman, he considered the emphasis on drawing from the antique dull and unrewarding. In 1864 he supplemented his studies in the antique class by attending lectures and anatomy classes at Jefferson Medical College. He was eventually admitted to the Academy life class,[3] but he continued to study anatomy at Jefferson as well. He also began to experiment with oil paints with his friend Charles Fussell, a member of the Academy life class in 1865. Fussell's portrait of the young Eakins (cat. no. 231), painted in 1865 or 1866, testifies to the inadequacy of his training, for his brushwork is labored and he painted Eakins's body with the simplified planes and monochromatic tones of a piece of antique sculpture. Eakins's own difficulties with painting probably convinced him that he could not receive a complete art education in Philadelphia. In the fall of 1866 he left for Paris to study at the Ecole des Beaux-Arts.

Eakins was admitted to the Ecole that year with the help of John Sartain, who knew a number of influential French academicians. Eakins elected to study with Jean-Léon Gérôme, one of the youngest teachers at the Ecole, perhaps because he had admired examples of Gérôme's work shown at Pennsylvania Academy annual exhibitions. In Gérôme's atelier, Eakins was introduced to a livelier and more demanding attitude toward art education than that which he had known in Philadelphia. Harry Niemeyer, who attended the atelier with Eakins in 1867, later recalled:

> Gérôme's method of instruction was purely academical, in the sense in which that word is understood, as leaving no room for the individuality of the student to assert itself . . . Gérôme's students were the only ones with the *cachet* of their master. On the other hand, as to conduct it was the most riotous atelier in the school, and was frequently closed for weeks at a time by the Administration in punishment for a disorder which became insufferable, and which seemed like a rebound from the constraint the students felt in their master's presence. This rebound spent itself in hazing, singing, smashing of easels, and other exhilerating exercises when that presence was withdrawn. However, in spite of this, a great deal of good work was done there, for when a chorus of *"assez"* rang through the room it was a foolish fellow who dared to interrupt the silence which followed.[4]

The atelier was a far cry from the dull, gentlemanly Academy in Philadelphia, and its atmosphere had a profound effect upon Eakins, shaping his concept of the ideal relationship between teacher and student. Later, like Gérôme, Eakins would dominate his students and would allow them little opportunity to develop their individual talents.

cat. no. 227. Thomas Eakins. *Walt Whitman,* 1887.

Eakins quickly became a part of the atelier. He submitted good naturedly to his introductory hazing and countered with some wild exploits of his own. He learned the French language and manners, but unlike his Pennsylvania Academy classmate Mary Cassatt, who was also studying with Gérôme in Paris, Eakins always planned to return to Philadelphia. He stored up his experiences for his friends back home. He sent reports on Parisian fashions to his mother and sisters and descriptions of Gérôme and the Ecole to his father and his friends William Sartain and Charles Fussell; to Emily Sartain, also an artist, he sent intimate letters in Italian. All of his correspondence reflects his eagerness to learn, despite draughty rooms, erratic classes, and the diversions of Paris.

Under Gérôme, Eakins found the same academic insistence on the study of the antique cast which he had endured in Philadelphia. But in Paris he was able to skip the antique classes and visit the Louvre or practice painting instead. In the spring of 1867 Gérôme apparently passed him into the painting class, and there Eakins found he had much to learn. Color was his greatest difficulty, as Gérôme paid little attention to it either in his own work or in his teaching. On the whole, Eakins got along well with Gérôme, although he occasionally lost his temper when his teacher autocratically repainted his studies. Eakins's debt to his master is apparent in much of his early work, especially his genre painting.[5] Many of the characteristics of Gérôme's *The Guardian* (cat. no. 233)—its small size, the carefully researched costume and setting, and its detailed finish—are evident in Eakins's historical scenes from the 1870s and 1880s. Gérôme may also have introduced Eakins to the uses of photographs for composing pictures. Gérôme had purchased photographs for such purposes in 1861, and in 1867 he took photographic equipment along on a trip to the Near East.[6]

Eakins studied with Gérôme for almost three years, developing his painting skills as well as his confidence. In 1869 he was sure enough of himself to plan a career "painting faces," and he entered the independent atelier of Léon Bonnat to learn more about that specialized and profitable field. Departing from traditional American academic practice, which did not include modeling classes for painters, Eakins also studied with the sculptor Augustin Dumont. At Dumont's he worked in clay or wax from the live model, producing bas-reliefs and three-dimensional studies. Eakins may have studied at Bonnat's and Dumont's at the suggestion of Gérôme. From the continuing interest Gérôme evinced in his pupil's work, it is apparent that the French master felt that he had an outstanding student. Eakins absorbed everything that his teachers offered and eagerly searched for more.

In the winter of 1869 Eakins left Paris for Spain. Accompanied by William Sartain, he divided his time between sketching trips in the Spanish countryside and visiting the Prado museum. At the Prado he discovered the work of Velázquez—"big painting" as he called it. Eakins learned much from Velázquez's use of light, color, and glazes, but the Spaniard's penetrating studies of mood and character impressed him most. It was this aspect of Velázquez's work which Eakins would emulate in his later portraits.

Exposure to the work of Velázquez, so different from that of Gérôme, seems to have convinced Eakins that he was still not ready for a career. Discouraged with his first major painting, *Street Singers in Seville* (Collection of Mrs. John Randolph Garrett), he returned home in the summer of 1870 and applied himself to painting portraits of his sisters and close family friends. The death of Eakins's mother in 1872 coincided with the end of this period of solitary study.[7] That year he resumed his anatomical work at Jefferson Medical College, and he painted outdoor scenes of the oarsmen on the Schuylkill River. These early paintings reveal his command of perspective, anatomy, and the construction of the human figure. Although he continued to admire Gérôme, Eakins began to develop his own kind of painting, which, unlike Gérôme's, relied on observation of nature rather than on anecdotal content for its impact.

Eakins had exhibited his work publicly for the first time in 1871, and its penetrating realism was soon noticed in Philadelphia. He was invited to teach the life class at the Philadelphia Sketch Club, and he also received a few portrait commissions. In 1875 the students of Jefferson Medical College asked him to paint a portrait of Dr. Samuel Gross, and he embarked on the most ambitious and most successful effort of his long career. The painting, showing Dr. Gross lecturing to his students during an operation on a young man's leg, was finished in time for exhibition at the Centennial Exposition. The hanging committee sequestered it in the Medical Department, where it nevertheless attracted a great deal of attention, as much for its subject matter as for its qualities as a painting.

During the years that Eakins was in Europe and teaching at the Sketch Club, the Pennsylvania Academy began to develop a professional art school based on the schools of contemporary European academies. Most of the important new policies were suggested in student petitions to the Board of Directors. In response to one such petition, Christian Schussele was hired in 1868 to teach drawing and painting to the students in the antique and life classes. Further petitions resulted in the following developments: students were allowed to paint as well as to draw from the live model; more life classes were added to the curriculum; these life classes met during the day as well as in the evening; and women students received much more encouragement than they had in the past.[8] These improvements, particularly the new life classes, were instrumental in changing the Academy school from a facility to augment the training of professional artists to a modern institution oriented to the needs of students. They also had a beneficial effect on the school's enrollment, which rose steadily. The cost of running the school increased as well. Before 1865 the school's annual budget had never exceeded one hundred dollars, but from 1868 to 1870 it was six times as great.[9]

In part because of the overcrowded school studios in the building at Tenth and Chestnut streets, the Board of Directors, in 1870, decided to erect the present building on the corner of Broad and Cherry streets. An examination of the design of the school floor of the new building shows how carefully the building committee considered the needs of the Academy school and planned for its growth and development. The school studios were designed, principally by John Sartain,[10] to have ample light for the painting classes. The life class studios were large and provisions were made for models' dressing rooms. A modeling room was included, as was an auditorium for lectures.

By the time the building was ready for use in 1876, the school was well on its way to professionalization under the liberal guidance of John Sartain and Fairman Rogers of the Committee on Instruction. The new classes already established under Schussele, especially painting by daylight, were accommodated in the new building and plans for further expansion of the curriculum and faculty had been made. These plans called for a professor of drawing and painting, an instructor for the evening life classes, a professor of anatomy, and a lecturer on perspective; a professor of sculpture was to be hired should the need arise.[11] The student body now consisted primarily of young art students expecting to receive a complete art education at the Academy; a number of them were women, who found that their professional ambitions were treated seriously. The administration of the school and most of the teaching were the responsibility of the professor of drawing and painting, Christian Schussele. In 1876 Schussele was asked to appoint an assistant to teach the evening classes, and he selected his friend Thomas Eakins, who had volunteered for the job.

Eakins's offer may have resulted from affection for his old school or from the realization that many of his Sketch Club students planned to attend the new school. His job required little time, only three evenings a week, but he threw himself into it with enthusiasm. Soon after he began teaching, he wrote to the board, requesting that respectable females, rather than prostitutes, be hired as models for the life classes. Eakins claimed that the Academy's regular models were "coarse, flabby, ill formed & unfit in every way for the

cat. no. 228. Thomas Eakins. *The Cello Player,* 1896.

requirements of a school" and that there was not a "sufficient change of models for the successful study of form."[12] The suggestion did not seem reasonable to the directors, who felt that prostitutes were acceptable for the disreputable work of modeling for artists and that genteel women should pose only for portraits. Consequently, the request, which also naively proposed that John Sartain advertise for respectable women in the newspapers, was turned down.

Eakins was more successful in the anatomy department. In January 1877 he offered to serve the professor of anatomy, Dr. W. W. Keen, as his prosector, the assistant who prepared the cadaver for the doctor's weekly lectures. Keen accepted Eakins's offer and within three months Eakins was not only preparing the corpses but was also instructing the advanced life class students in dissection.

In May 1877 the directors asked Christian Schussele, for reasons unknown, to take over the life classes which Eakins had been teaching. Eakins left the Academy that month and soon began teaching at the Philadelphia Art Union, where he remained until January 1878. While Eakins was away, Christian Schussele commended the work he had done in the anatomy department and suggested that dissection become a permanent part of the Academy's curriculum.[13] Schussele also continued to urge the expansion of the life school by the addition of more classes.

In the fall of 1877 Eakins returned to the Academy to work for Dr. Keen as an unpaid assistant. He resumed his duties as prosector and continued to teach dissection to the life class students. The dissecting class was so well attended that Fairman Rogers began to look for a larger room; in December 1877 he ordered the pump room to be fitted up for instruction. In January the directors finally recognized Eakins's contributions to the class and thanked him for his voluntary services. They authorized Dr. Keen to appoint a chief demonstrator of anatomy whose job would be to instruct the life class students. Keen gave the job to Eakins.

Under Eakins's supervision, the dissecting class expanded to include most of the life class students, including the women. As Eakins remarked in 1879, "We had one student who abstained a year ago, but this year finding his fellows are getting along faster than himself, he changed his mind and is now dissecting diligently."[14] Later, horses, dogs, cats, and a lion as well as humans were studied in the dissecting class. Plaster casts were made from dissected cadavers and hung in the life class studios. The anatomy department was soon as well organized and as rigorous as that of a medical school.

Eakins's changes at the Academy would probably have been restricted to the anatomy department had not Christian Schussele been suffering from palsy. In the fall of 1878 it became clear that Schussele was too ill to teach all of the life classes, and Eakins was asked to assist him. Eakins resumed teaching the men's evening life class and agreed to oversee the modeling class, which had run into difficulties in 1878. These new responsibilities offered Eakins more opportunities for modifying the curriculum.

Eakins almost immediately suggested another change in the life class policies. This time he requested admission for a student who had not, and who could not, produce the cast drawing required for promotion to the life class. "Being of the opinion . . . that the study of the living model should not be based on the study of the antique, or at least should not be required to be based thereon,"[15] Eakins took the problem to the Board of Directors, who promptly turned down the request. This seems to have convinced him that the directors would not tolerate additional alterations in a class which they and the Committee on Instruction already deemed sufficiently advanced. Because he was not permitted to modify the life classes or to abolish the antique classes, Eakins was forced to apply his ideas to other parts of the curriculum.

cat. no. 217. Walter M. Dunk. *Men's Life Class,* 1879.

The modeling class was the first class which Eakins changed to suit his own concepts of an ideal art education. Between 1876 and 1878 the Academy sculpture students had worked in clay from the antique, under the instruction of Joseph Bailly. In 1878 the instruction committee could not afford to rehire Bailly, and the poorly attended class would have been discontinued if Eakins had not volunteered to supervise it. Because he disliked antique study, Eakins instituted the practice of modeling from life. In this way he hoped to teach his painting students as well as the sculpture students about the problems of three-dimensional form. The students worked from human models and later from animal models, particularly the horse. The radicalism of the new class drew criticism from conservative local artists, but these complaints were silenced by Fairman Rogers's defense of the importance of the study of the live model.

The year 1879 was an important one for the Academy school. The different policies of its two professors, Schussele and Eakins, were temporarily balanced, offering the students alternative courses of study. The school's growing reputation and the unusual character of its assistant professor of drawing and painting, Thomas Eakins, even brought a reporter down from New York to visit the classes and to interview him. William Brownell's article, which was published in 1879 in *Scribner's,*[16] compared the Academy school with that of the National Academy of Design in New York. Brownell called Eakins a "radical," and, compared to the teachers at the National Academy, he certainly was. Brownell also discussed Eakins's ideas at length but failed to credit Schussele and the Academy directors for the design of the school's basic curriculum.

In spite of the attention Eakins was receiving, Schussele was still an important figure in the Academy school. Although he seems to have been a blandly traditional teacher, that very quality made him the ideal sponsor of new developments before an equally conservative board. His reputation as a traditionalist lent respectability to some of the school's more unusual programs. He had begun the painting classes which his students requested, he had championed Eakins's dissecting class, and he had been the first to pay serious attention to women students. Above all, he was willing to accept and encourage new methods in the teaching at the school.

Christian Schussele's death in October 1879 ended the harmony which he had created among students, faculty, and board. Unlike Schussele, Thomas Eakins, who was appointed the next professor of drawing and painting, was not a very tolerant teacher, and he did not care much for respectability. He could not easily win the confidence of the Board of Directors, which was necessary if he was to continue to modify the school's curriculum. Fortunately, he found a supporter in the chairman of the Committee on Instruction, the influential Fairman Rogers. With the help of Rogers, Eakins continued to impose his ideas on art education on the school.

The antique classes suffered almost immediately. Soon after his appointment, it became apparent that Eakins was unable to judge student antique drawings because he was totally unfamiliar with the work.[17] Consequently, he was permitted to delegate the antique class responsibilities to his student Thomas Anshutz, and thereafter he visited these classes only to urge students to begin painting.

However, Eakins continued to develop those aspects of the curriculum which interested him. The staff of the anatomy department was increased to eight, then to eleven members in 1880. Two of the new demonstrators were women, since Eakins insisted that women participate in all areas of study. He made it clear that he was teaching professional artists, not "china painters." Portraiture and perspective, minor parts of the curriculum in Schussele's time, were given important places in the schedule during Eakins's first year in charge. A portrait class had been taught informally since the 1860s, but Eakins and Rogers made arrangements for the class to meet regularly. That year Eakins also gave the first lectures on perspective that had been given at the Academy since 1876.

To become formally part of the school's curriculum, Eakins's innovations had to be approved by the Board of Directors, and here the assistance of Fairman Rogers was crucial for success. His influence in the Academy boardroom won approval for most of Eakins's ideas. However, although Rogers could often persuade the directors to do what he and Eakins wanted, he was powerless to prevent them from instituting policies which he and Eakins disliked. This was especially true when large sums of money were involved. For example, in 1878, 1879, and 1881 the board established endowed prizes for student work, despite the objections of Eakins and Rogers, who felt that prizes encouraged excessive competition among students and distracted them from more serious work.[18] Once the prizes were established, however, Eakins did use them to reward promising students. Thus, the first Mary Smith Prize was awarded to Susan Macdowell in 1879 for her *Portrait of a Gentleman and Dog* (cat. no. 218), painted very much in Eakins's style. Subsequently, the prize was repeatedly awarded to women with the professional ambitions which Eakins admired; the winners included Emily Sartain and Cecilia Beaux.

Not only did Eakins modify courses to suit his ideas, he also introduced new techniques which were not used in other American academies. Photography was probably the most radical technique he suggested to his students. Schussele had previously bought photographs of paintings by old masters to use as teaching aids, but Eakins exhibited at the Academy photographs of human figures and animals and encouraged his students to use them as

cat. no. 218. Susan Macdowell Eakins. *Portrait of a Gentleman and a Dog,* 1878.
COLLECTION OF MARY MACDOWELL WALTERS.

cat. no. 221. Thomas Eakins. *The Fairman Rogers Four-in-Hand,* 1879. THE PHILADELPHIA MUSEUM OF ART.

cat. no. 241. Eadweard Muybridge. *Smith with Rider,* 1887. PRIVATE COLLECTION.

an aid to painting. Eakins was using photographs for his compositions by 1879, and he acquired his own camera a year later. The board and the conservative members of the exhibitions committee, however, did not encourage his interest in the new medium. In 1880 the exhibitions committee resolved that drawings from photographs would not be accepted for the annual exhibition.[19] Furthermore, when Eakins showed Eadweard Muybridge's photographs of a galloping horse at the Academy later that year in an informal exhibition, the directors were displeased.[20]

Because of the directors' disapproval of the medium, photography became an extracurricular study for Eakins's students, as dissection had been for Eakins fifteen years earlier. His student Susan Macdowell was apparently a capable photographer before 1879. Her sister Elizabeth, also an Academy student, used Eakins's photograph of his sister Caroline[21] for her composition *Daydreams* (cat. no. 237), exhibited at the Academy in 1882. Many students posed for Eakins's photographs and almost all of them used a camera at some point in their careers. Henry O. Tanner considered becoming a portrait photographer when he could not earn a living from painting; Thomas Anshutz used photographs for *Ironworkers: Noontime* (Collection of John D. Rockefeller, Jr.) ; and Charles Fussell, who usually painted in a mid-century style, combined exposures of a landscape and a portrait to create a self-portrait (Pennsylvania Academy of the Fine Arts). Thus, photography was an integral part of the students' education although it was never established in the curriculum.

By 1882 Eakins had modified the curriculum as much as the directors would allow, and the school was doing extremely well. Classes were meeting from seven in the morning until nine o'clock at night, and the enrollment had climbed to over two hundred students. The Committee on Instruction was forced to limit the size of the men's life class and to forbid students to study at the Academy for more than four years. The directors were pleased with the success but worried by the expenditures, which created a serious deficit. At one point, in 1879, they had seriously considered closing the school in order to save money.

cat. no. 242. Eadweard Muybridge. *Man Performing Forward Handspring,* 1887.
THE PHILADELPHIA MUSEUM OF ART.

Therefore, when John G. Johnson wrote the Committee on Instruction suggesting that the Academy charge admission like any other art school,[22] the idea was readily accepted. The plan which Fairman Rogers drew up included not only a proposed tuition charge but also an outline for the reorganization of the school's faculty and curriculum. Eakins contributed to the plan a list of salaries that other art teachers in Philadelphia and New York were receiving and suggested that two of the life classes be extended into the summer; he also made a statement to the effect that charging tuition must not alter the professional aims of the school.[23] Rogers presented the plan to the board in February 1882, and it was approved. With the reorganization, Rogers finally completed the task of making the Academy a professional art school.

Rogers's plan projected an annual profit of about one thousand dollars, and this quickly became a reality. In the 1884 annual report, the Committee on Instruction announced that "from a heavy tax upon the resources of the Academy [the school] has become largely self supporting . . . its thorough success is a very gratifying announcement to make.[24] After the first profitable year—1882-83—the directors were determined to maintain the status quo. They would view future alterations suspiciously as deviations from a successful formula, especially after Fairman Rogers, who had supported Eakins's policies for four years, resigned from the Academy board in 1883.

Like his teaching, Eakins's painting from 1876 to 1886 was characterized by modifications of well-established academic formulas. Often the innovations in the paintings anticipated or reflected changes he attempted to make in the Academy's curriculum. For example, *William Rush Carving His Allegorical Statue of the Schuylkill River* (1876; Philadelphia Museum of Art), showing a Philadelphia debutant posing for the sculptor, coincided with Eakins's request for respectable models for the life classes. Moreover, Eakins's preparations for *The Fairman Rogers Four-in-Hand* (cat. no. 221) included a number of the techniques

cat. no. 226. Thomas Eakins. *The Swimming Hole,* 1883. The Fort Worth Art Museum.

he was advocating at the Academy. Eakins based the drawing of the horses upon the recently published Muybridge photographs taken in California, and he made three-dimensional clay models of the horses and rough oil portraits from life of the passengers in the coach. He also spent hours watching the coach and horses in motion, recording his observations in oil sketches. In his final representation of the turnout, the realistic depiction of the horses' gaits is somewhat inconsistent with the illusionistic spin of the coach wheels. But, as the earliest known photographically accurate depiction of animal motion, it represented a breakthrough in nineteenth-century art.[25]

Between 1881 and 1883 Eakins's interest in photography led him to execute several watercolors and oils based on photographs. Some, like *Drawing the Seine* (Philadelphia Museum of Art), were direct copies from single photographs, while others combined several in one composition. In *Mending the Net* (cat. no. 223), for example, the realistic poses of the figures suggest that they, like the figures of the geese in the foreground,[26] were derived from photographs. These compositions of figures in landscapes led to another group of works, the Arcadian paintings, for which Eakins utilized photographs as well as studies of the nude model. These paintings also showed figures in landscapes, but the figures are nude or classically draped. The last composition in this series, *The Swimming Hole* (cat. no. 226), was one of the most important paintings of Eakins's Academy years.

For *The Swimming Hole* Eakins drew upon a number of the visual sources he had introduced at the Academy—photographs, life class studies, and the Muybridge work (cat. no. 242)—to produce a work which summarizes the ideals of his teaching there. Both in this painting and in his classes he was using such techniques as aids in the study of the construction of the human figure, which was the focus of his ideal art education. By emphasizing the study of the nude, Eakins felt that he was emulating the ancient Greek sculptors, who did not have antiques to imitate.[27] Phidias, he thought, must have worked from nature. *The Swimming Hole* was to Eakins a modern equivalent of the achievements of the classical sculptors. At the Academy, Eakins wanted to teach his students his methods of observation, so that they too could emulate the classical ideals which he embodied in this painting.[28]

After 1880, with his curriculum firmly established, Eakins spent less time at the school and more on his own projects, causing his students to accuse him of neglect. He was teaching twice a week at the Brooklyn Art Guild, and he turned his less interesting classes over to assistants. In 1884 and 1885 he served on the advisory committee supervising Eadweard Muybridge's experimental photographs of human and animal locomotion. At the same time, independently of Muybridge, he made his own photographic motion studies, using his students as models. He stopped teaching dissection, delegating that responsibility to the student demonstrators of anatomy. His chief demonstrators included James Kelly in 1881, Thomas Anshutz in 1882, and J. Laurie Wallace in 1883. In 1885 Thomas Anshutz was appointed assistant professor of drawing and painting, finally relieving Eakins of all responsibility for the drawing and antique classes. Anshutz soon became an influential member of the Committee on Instruction.

Eakins's neglect of his students might have been tolerated in chaotic ateliers like Gérôme's, but, unlike their French counterparts, the Academy students were paying tuition and were justifiably disappointed with Eakins's teaching. The dissatisfaction caused by his absences was matched by unhappiness with his curriculum. Schussele's flexibility, which had permitted Eakins's innovations in 1877 and 1878, was replaced by Eakins's insistence on a specific, almost rigid, course of study. He expected his pupils to do much more than he had been expected to accomplish as an Academy student. They had none of the free time which had permitted their predecessors in the 1860s and 1870s to study with other painters or to experiment on their own. In this respect Eakins's program diverged from French and American academic models, both of which allowed for independent work. Eakins was trying to impart to his students in a few years time the knowledge he had gained from almost eight years of study. His teaching at the Academy, intense and narrowly directed, was aimed at students with his kind of intellect, his interests, and his strengths. It was not effective for the students who did not share his interests, nor did it offer them opportunities for the development of their own talents and ideas. This was a serious fault in Eakins's teaching.

The directors would probably have ignored the complaints about the curriculum if the school had continued to do well financially. However, the enrollment of the paying students began to drop in 1884. In the school year 1882-83, the first year that tuition was charged, the student body numbered 203. In 1883-84 the number dropped to 174. The next year the students numbered 224, but the figure was inflated by the admission of "free" students. In 1885-86 the number had fallen to 172, and the Academy lost over six thousand dollars that year on the operation of the school.[29]

Another problem which the directors were unable to ignore was the public and private criticism directed at Eakins's conduct in the women's life class. This was an extremely delicate matter, for women constituted almost fifty percent of the tuition-paying student body, and the directors feared they might leave the Academy if their respectability was threatened by attendance at a life class. On the other hand, the professionalism of the women's classes was one of the school's strong points, and too much consideration of feminine sensibilities would destroy that reputation. The directors were primarily concerned with the financial problem and Eakins, of course, with the latter. In 1882 an anonymous Philadelphia woman sent a letter to the Board of Directors charging that the life classes corrupted the morals of young art students and created "unbelievers, even infidels," while "the study of the beautiful in landscapes and draped figures, and the exquisitely beautiful in the flowers that the Heavenly Father has decked and beautified the world with is ignored."[30] The letter was turned over to Fairman Rogers, who took no action on it. In 1884 the directors received a more serious complaint from one of the women students, Diana Franklin, about Eakins's use of the male students as models for the women's life class.[31] This complaint prompted the directors to make a new rule forbidding students to pose for the life classes. However, Eakins apparently continued to disregard life class rules, for Charles Bregler reported that in 1885 there were "rumors and whisperings about Eakins because he was having male and female models pose for some of the life classes."[32] These and other rumors may have been spread by some of Eakins's students and assistants, including Thomas Anshutz,[33] who were perhaps motivated by personal dislike of Eakins or by ambitions to replace him on the faculty. In 1886 Eakins defiantly removed the loincloth from a male model in the women's life class, an action that led to the end of his career at the Academy. The removal of the loincloth was cited as the reason for the directors' request for his resignation. Eakins was told that he would have to change his policies or resign, and he chose the latter alternative.

The controversy was magnified when a number of students resigned from the Academy in sympathy with Eakins. The protesters publicly accused the Academy directors of prudery and ingratitude, causing the scandal which has since made the resignation so notable. Neither Eakins nor the directors were especially pleased by the crusade, and Eakins seems to have been hurt as much by the gossip rising from his students' overspirited defense of his policies, as by the original rumors. Realizing that accusations of immoral conduct could damage his career, Eakins moved to correct the rumors circulating in Philadelphia newspapers. On March 25, 1886, he sent an explanatory statement to Emily Sartain, which he authorized her to publish if she thought it was appropriate. Emily, an art teacher and his long-time friend, was an able and sympathetic judge of the situation. She did not publish the bitter statement in which Eakins had written:

> In pursuance of my business and professional studies, I use the naked model.
>
> A number of my women pupils have for economy studied from each others figures, and some have obtained from time to time my criticism on their work.

I have frequently used as models for myself my male pupils; very rarely female pupils and then only with the knowledge and consent of their mothers.

One of the women pupils, some years ago gave to her lover who gave to Mr. Frank Stephens a list of those pupils as far as she knew them, and since that time Mr. Frank Stephens has boasted to witnesses of the power which this knowledge gave him to turn me out of the Academy, the Philadelphia Sketch Club, & the Academy Art Club, and of his intention to drive me from the city.[34]

No single factor actually caused Eakins's resignation. His emphatic, sometimes improper, use of the nude model, the Academy's financial difficulties, and the lack of sympathetic directors on the Committee on Instruction all contributed to the event. Perhaps the greatest problem was one rarely mentioned at the time—a growing disagreement between Eakins and the directors about the aims and functions of the Academy school. In creating his ideal curriculum, Eakins felt that he was adhering to the principles developed by the great Greek sculptors. To him these principles were the proper basis of all academic study. Eakins's emphasis on the observation of nature, however, began to detract from the Academy's stated purpose of teaching art students how to draw and paint. His teaching became too specific, becoming an almost scientific investigation of the structure and appearance of the human figure. Such a narrow approach could not survive in the face of a developing idea of the art school as the source of all artistic training.

The 1880s saw immense growth and variations in the curriculums of other institutions, especially at the National Academy of Design. Sketch classes, drapery classes, and landscape classes became the order of the day in New York and elsewhere.[35] These classes had no relationship to Eakins's concept of an ideal art education, and he did not encourage them at the Academy. In this he opposed the wishes of the Academy directors and students, who were naturally interested in keeping up with the latest ideas on art theory and education.

The directors' explanation of the resignation in their annual report for 1886 suggests that general dissatisfaction with Eakins's inflexible curriculum was one of their reasons for requesting his resignation. In the report, Edward Coates stated:

For some time prior to the year just closed, the Committee on Instruction were of the opinion that better results would be obtained, and a broader teaching follow, from the influence of several minds in the school rather than from the influence of one.[36]

By restoring the antique and life classes to their proper roles in the student's education, and by adding new courses, the directors hoped to compete with other rising art institutions and to restore the school's financial equilibrium. The loss of Eakins, who was beginning to demand his unpaid back salary and who was, at the same time, alienating paying students, was not difficult for the directors to justify to themselves or to the Academy's stockholders.

After the resignation the ideological split between the teaching of the school and of its ex-director widened. Under the brief guidance of Thomas Hovenden and then more firmly under Thomas Anshutz, the school followed a conventional pattern of art education which included the developments which Eakins deplored. A number of new courses were added in the 1890s, and cast drawing was reinstated as a respectable part of the curriculum. Anshutz discontinued the use of photography as a teaching aid and phased out the dissecting class by 1895. The class was replaced with Anshutz's lectures on anatomy in the tradition of Dr. Keen. In 1896 William Merritt Chase was invited down from New York to teach the sketch and portrait classes. A skilled painter in the Munich manner, he taught very differently from Eakins. He did not care so much about observing as he did about painting. *Lady with the White Shawl* (cat. no. 215) shows Chase as concerned with the abstract disposition of colors and shapes as with the details of his subject's appearance. Chase's approach empha-

cat. no. 215. William Merritt Chase. *Lady with the White Shawl,* 1893.

cat. no. 214. Margaret Lesley Bush-Brown. *Self-Portrait,* 1914.

sized technical proficiency but gave his students many opportunities to develop their own styles, while Eakins's students had been limited by their instructor's very narrow teaching. By 1906 the school had changed so much that Eakins wrote to an inquiring art student:

> If you care to study in Philadelphia, you could enter the life classes at the Pennsylvania Academy of the Fine Arts and I could give you advice as to your work and studies, or you might go to Paris and enter some life classes there. Nearly all the schools are bad here and abroad.
>
> . . . I am not connected with the Pennsylvania Academy and my advice would be contrary to nearly all the teaching there.[37]

In 1892 the Academy's new managing director Harrison Morris had attempted to lure Eakins back into Academy circles. Deciding that Eakins was the best painter in Philadelphia, he tried unsuccessfully to persuade Eakins to return to the faculty; but, under his influence, Eakins once again submitted his work to the Academy's annual shows. Most of his important paintings after 1886, including *Walt Whitman* (cat. no. 227), *The Agnew Clinic* (Collection of the University of Pennsylvania), and *The Concert Singer* (Philadelphia Museum of Art), were shown at annual exhibitions. In 1897 the Academy purchased *The Cello Player* (cat. no. 228) and in 1904 awarded him the Temple Gold Medal, probably at the instigation of Morris. The relationship between the two men ended in 1905, when Morris resigned from the Academy's Board of Directors. Eakins's growing reputation in the early years of the twentieth century, especially in New York, ensured that he would not be entirely forgotten in Philadelphia. However, the Academy directors and curators tolerated rather than accepted him, an attitude which would persist until his death.

An evaluation of Eakins's abilities as a teacher rests, in large part, on the success of his students' work. Eakins's Academy students fall roughly into two groups: those who worked in his tradition and those who did not. The pupils who followed his manner understood and applied his techniques to their work. Several of them gave promise of developing his ideas further until halted by the limits of their talent or ambition. Although some of his students comprehended his ideas, they were unable to match his achievements.

Thomas Anshutz studied with Eakins from 1875 to 1880. His early paintings, such as *In a Garret* (cat. no. 211) and *Ironworkers: Noontime,* show an interest in the ideas Eakins was developing at the Academy. For the latter painting, he utilized photographs and life studies and applied an aesthetic learned from Eakins to a modern industrial genre subject, thus foreshadowing the art of the Ashcan School. Anshutz continued his association with Eakins until 1886, assisting at the Academy and participating in Eakins's photographic experiments at the University of Pennsylvania. Anshutz's involvement in the rumors leading to Eakins's resignation ended their friendship, but Anshutz continued to apply many of Eakins's principles to his painting until 1893.

In 1892-93 Anshutz re-educated himself by studying for a year at the Académie Julian and learning of contemporary developments in French art. As a result of this experience and of his contacts with William Merritt Chase, Anshutz's style became flatter and more decorative in paintings like *The Incense Burner* (cat. no. 212).

Like Thomas Anshutz, Susan Macdowell was a devoted Eakins student whose art is worthy of recognition. She had been impressed by Eakins's *Portrait of Dr. Gross* when it was exhibited at the Centennial, and she was attracted by his teaching at the Academy. She soon became one of his best students. Her *Portrait of a Gentleman and Dog* and *The Chaperone* (cat. no. 219) show that she understood his teaching and could apply it to her own painting. Beside learning from Eakins, she also seems to have been one of the few students who contributed to his art. Her early interest in photography encouraged his own when he began taking photographs in 1880. The *Portrait of a Gentleman and Dog* probably introduced

Eakins to her father, William Macdowell, who became one of his favorite subjects for portraits and photographs. Susan Macdowell married Eakins in 1884 and painted only sporadically thereafter. Eakins encouraged her to continue painting, but she spent much of her time advancing his career.

Susan Macdowell's sister Elizabeth also admired Eakins's work. She began studying with him in 1878 and accepted his teaching enthusiastically. She adopted at least one of his techniques, using a photograph for the composition of *Daydreams*. This was one of the few pictures she exhibited at the Academy, for her professional career was restricted after her marriage to Louis Kenton.

The majority of Eakins's Academy students did not know him as well as Anshutz and the Macdowells did. As a result, they did not fully understand the reasoning behind his teaching, and consequently they had great difficulty adapting the principles of his ideal education to their own talents.

Henry O. Tanner, for example, studied at the Academy in 1884 and 1885, having been admitted to the school by Eakins's special request. From 1886 to 1891 he struggled to make a living painting portraits and genre scenes in the realistic style he had learned from Eakins, and he was ready to abandon his vocation when a Chicago patron gave him money for a trip to France. After three years of study with Benjamin Constant in Paris, Tanner developed his own very successful style characterized by Biblical subject matter, muted colors, and hazy outlines, as in *Nicodemus* (cat. no. 246).

Although Eakins had few students who became highly succesful artists, most of them benefited from some aspect of his instruction. Margaret Lesley Bush-Brown acquired a thorough knowledge of the human figure, which, in her *Self-Portrait* (cat. no. 214), is evident in the drawing of the hands and in the modeling of the caryatids below the fireplace mantel. She did not, however, use details of physical construction to suggest character, as Eakins and Anshutz had done; and her interest in color and brushwork led her away from the Eakins tradition.

Charles Fussell, primarily a landscape painter, returned to the Academy in 1879 to study under Eakins. He worked in the life class and the dissecting room, painting one of the grisaille studies (cat. no. 65) for the *Scribner's* article published in that year. His later interest in grisaille and the occasional intrusion of a human figure into his minutely rendered landscapes (cat. no. 232) may be the result of Eakins's influence.

For Eakins's Academy students who later became sculptors, his teaching made only a limited contribution to their development. Their studies at the Academy consisted of a brief stint in the antique class and longer hours in the dissecting room and modeling classes. It was understood that the sculpture students would learn advanced techniques and styles in Europe. The mature works of most of Eakins's sculpture students, in spite of the various styles and media they employed, have in common a thorough understanding of human anatomy. All of the sculptors were interested in the physical details which gave the subject character and individuality. Although Sergeant Kendall's *Quest* (cat. no. 236), a wooden polychromed figure, represents an ideal rather than a person, the artist has also created a strong likeness of the model which belies the generalized title. Equally the product of anatomical study and careful observation is Charles Grafly's *Oarsman* (cat. no. 234). Grafly modeled the figure as a demonstration for his own students in 1910. In spite of the generally didactic nature of the work, he portrayed the model carefully, including his insignificant moustaches.

In view of Eakins's high ideals for the education of the artist, the results of his teaching are generally disappointing. He was unable to transmit his ideas to his students without the benefit of close personal friendship. The eventual success of some of his students

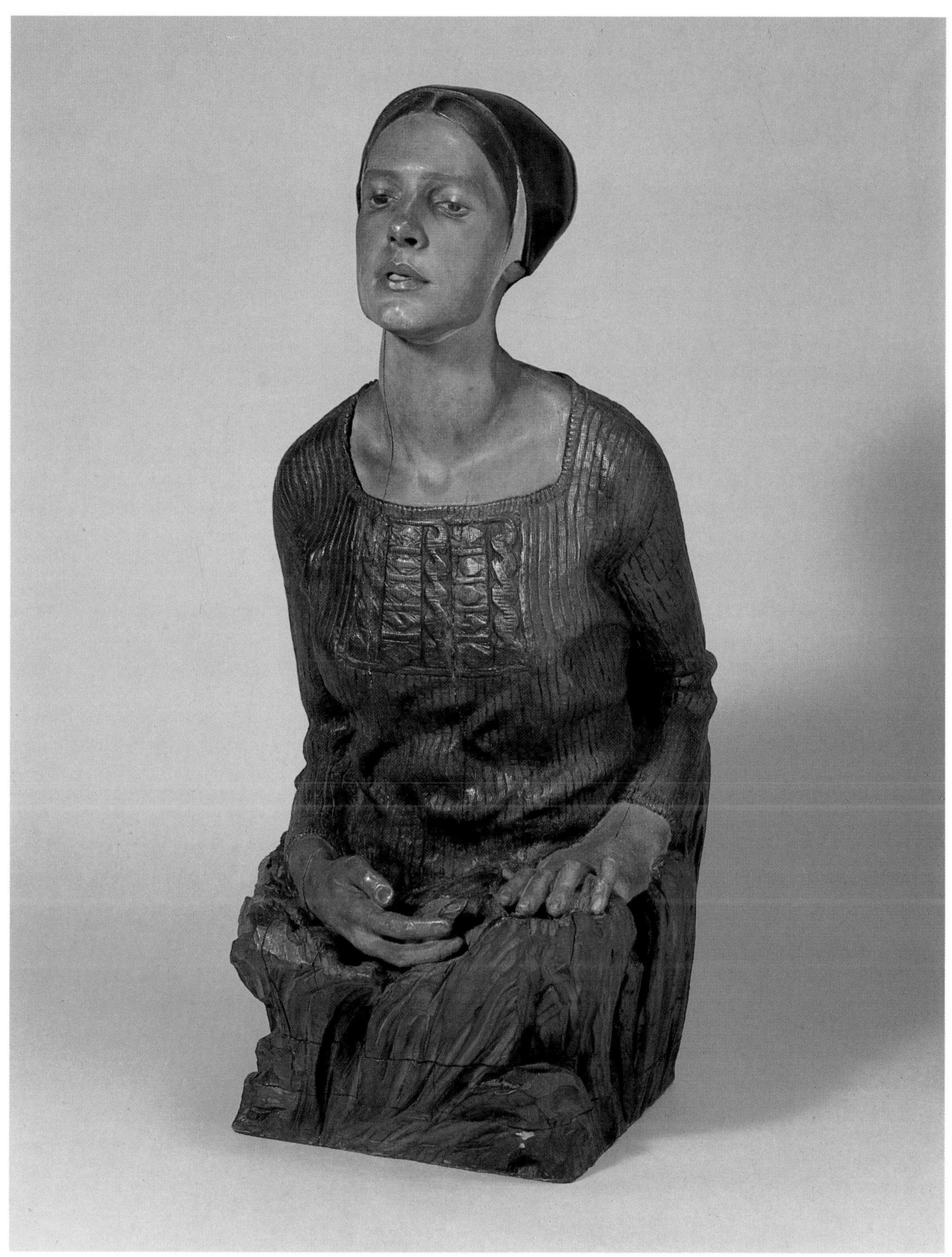

cat. no. 236. William Sergeant Kendall. *Quest,* 1910.

can be ascribed as much to the training they received after they left the Academy as to Eakins's instruction. Although Eakins made an impression on most of his pupils, he did not develop a lasting tradition.

As an independent teacher after 1886, Eakins could safely ignore new developments in art education. He continued to teach those subjects which interested him, lecturing on anatomy at the National Academy of Design in 1887 and at the New York Art Students League until 1895. At the Philadelphia Art Students' League, established by his former Academy students, Eakins taught his ideal curriculum until about 1892, but produced only one notable pupil, the sculptor Samuel Murray. Murray became Eakins's closest friend; his work shows that he understood his mentor's theories well. His small statues of Susan Eakins (cat. no. 239) and Thomas Eakins (cat. no. 240) were modeled in the nude and then the clothes were added, producing both anatomical correctness and realistic portraiture. Murray, more than any other pupil, had an opportunity to understand the aims behind Eakins's teaching, as these aims became increasingly visible in Eakins's art.

Eakins's resignation from the Academy forced him to reevaluate his conceptions of academic art and to examine the relationship between the academic principles he had learned and his basic committment to realism. His disillusionment with academicism must have made him view many of his earlier pictures, such as *William Rush, The Fairman Rogers Four-in-Hand,* and *The Swimming Hole,* as compromises, essentially conventional compositions with a few innovative elements. After 1886 Eakins's painting began to lose its didactic character, for he stopped trying to impose his techniques on others and began to integrate them into his own work. The portrait was an ideal format for this purpose. In this genre, Eakins could be truthful without offending contemporary morality. All of the interest which he had exhibited in the human body he now concentrated on the human face. His portraits exhibit the fascination with bone and flesh and texture seen in his earlier work, but working within the limited format of a person's head, hands, and clothing, Eakins was able to probe much deeper into individual moods and characters. His subjects were mainly professional people and personal friends—doctors, musicians, poets, artists, and students—people who usually did not sit for portraits and rarely paid for them. One of Eakins's earliest portraits after his resignation from the Academy was that of Walt Whitman, painted in 1887. In Whitman, already well known for *Leaves of Grass,* Eakins recognized a kindred spirit who had endured a public scandal over the allegedly immoral content of two of his poems published in that book. The portrait expresses all of the humor and warmth of the poet, revealing, as well, a degree of self-consciousness. Eakins's later portraits are even stronger than his earlier ones, for he had learned to subordinate the various "scientific" techniques he had previously used to capture an image to his own personal vision. In *The Cello Player,* for example, Eakins's techniques are entirely unobtrusive, so that the viewer of the painting seems to confront the cellist himself, without the intervention of the artist. But when Eakins was not in perfect sympathy with his sitters, his work became stiffer and somewhat satiric. Charles Edmund Dana, the stuffy president of the Academy Fellowship, is shown staring out at a seemingly bleak future, fortified with his cigarette holder and his coat of arms (cat. no. 229).

Eakins's late portraits, in their integration of the scientific and the aesthetic, most completely develop the principles and techniques he tried to teach at the Pennsylvania Academy. Although he was only partially successful in instituting these ideas into the curriculum and less successful in transmitting them to his students, Eakins must be considered a unique and highly innovative educator in terms of the concepts he wanted to communicate. He was one of the first American artists to comprehend the importance of the scientific advances of his age—in photography, in medicine, even in physics—and one of the very few to incorporate this knowledge into his art and teaching. His confrontation of social problems such as the roles of women and the rigid morality of Victorian Philadelphia also placed him well before his time.

cat. no. 232. Charles L. Fussell. *Young Girl by a Forest Spring,* 1903.

cat. no. 229. Thomas Eakins. *Charles Edmund Dana,* ca.1902.

cat. no. 240. Samuel Murray.
Thomas Eakins, 1894.

An art school dedicated to teaching young students how to draw and paint was not the ideal place for a man of Eakins's aims and intellectual interests, which were bound to be frustrated by the conventional expectations and practical ambitions of his students and colleagues. On the other hand, Eakins was not the ideal man for the Academy, which required a teacher receptive to changes in theories of art education and willing to encourage the independent development of his students. The conflict between the ideals of Eakins's teaching and the purposes of the Academy school created the bitter misunderstandings which characterized his career there.

Frank H. Goodyear, Jr.

THE EIGHT

The name "The Eight" is not of our making nor do we desire that or any other name. We are not a society and are not organized for any other purpose nor for a longer time than the duration of this exhibition. . . . We have made no plans for continuation as a body. If it should happen that the same men reunite for an exhibition in the future it must be entirely a new affair. There has therefore never been an organization of a society called "The Eight." Nor has there been any idea of opposition to any other body or institution.

Robert Henri to John E. D. Trask,
March 1, 1908 PAFA Archives

The revolution in American art associated with the work of The Eight, or the Ashcan School, began in the studios of the Pennsylvania Academy of the Fine Arts. Robert Henri, John Sloan, William Glackens, George Luks, and Everett Shinn were all Academy students. The training they received there made a vital imprint on their careers; their mature ideas of what constituted good painting were conditioned, in large part, by their early Academy education. Later, the Academy continued to support Henri and his friends despite the challenges they mounted against the academic system at the beginning of the twentieth century. Each artist, in varying degrees, continued his ties with the Academy. Each acknowledged his own special debt to the Academy.

During their often rowdy, fun-loving, but serious, student years, the Henri gang brought excitement, vibrancy, and purpose to the Academy. Later, they also brought change to the hierarchical structure of American art. From among their ranks came the proponents of radical ideas about the traditional jury system governing art exhibitions in America. They advocated non-juried exhibitions open to all serious artists. They did away with prizes in their own exhibitions. They epitomized the spirit of artistic independence.

The work of The Eight is, in the history of American art, a revolution less in style than in subject matter.[1] In fact, when one considers fully the city life and industrial genre paintings of American artists like John George Brown, Joseph Decker, or John Ferguson

Weir, even their subject matter scarcely seems revolutionary. The Eight were not the first American artists to paint the look of urban America. They were the first American artists to concentrate on painting city life.

Intellectually, the basis of the Ashcan aesthetic can be traced from the ideas of Thomas Eakins to the teaching of Thomas Anshutz at the Academy. Eakins was held in the highest esteem by both Henri and Sloan. Henri wrote of Eakins:

> Thomas Eakins was a man of great character. He was a man of iron will and his will was to paint and to carry out his life as he thought it should go. This he did. It cost him heavily but in his works we have the precious result of his independence, his generous heart and his big mind. Eakins was a deep student of life, and with a great love he studied humanity frankly. He was not afraid of what his study revealed to him.[2]

Eakins's practice of painting with honesty the world that he saw around him served as an inspiration to the younger realists. His insistence that no subject matter was below the dignity of the painter provided countless channels for exploration. Combined with Eakins's example was the popular teaching method of Anshutz, the Academy's principal instructor in the 1890s. Emphasizing some of Eakins's precepts,[3] Anshutz advocated a basic program to give the student the necessary knowledge to pursue his own abilities and interests. Although he believed that art was "based on knowledge and knowledge on facts,"[4] he recognized that such knowledge was only the first requirement of an artist. To create great art, one had to transcend mere facts to attain a higher truth. To give both the small fact and the higher truth was beyond the power of ordinary artists. Anshutz recognized that the role of the mature artist was to "put such facts aside as interfere with the full rendering of the new truth, using only those which translate it."[5]

Anshutz's dedication to teaching young art students won him the lifelong respect and friendship of scores of students who passed through the Academy. More than anything else, Anshutz sought to arouse in each of his students "an individual interest in the world about him"[6] and the confidence to pursue his own course in the creation of art. George Luks, in acknowledging Anshutz as "the best art instructor I have ever had the 'good' fortune to encounter"[7] not only expressed the sentiments of Henri, Sloan, Glackens, and Shinn but those of countless other Academy students.

Anshutz's tolerance for individuality among his students helps to explain the diversity of styles among them. Henri, Sloan, Glackens, Luks, and Shinn, all students of Anshutz at the Academy, manifest this diversity. While all were inveterate quick sketchers, carrying out Anshutz's dictum of observing the world about them, their similar drawing styles did not translate into similar painting styles. Later, with the addition of Maurice Prendergast, Ernest Lawson, and Arthur B. Davies into The Eight, three radically different painting styles were added. Clearly, Henri's purpose in forming the group was not to present a united front, but simply to organize a modern exhibition. In its efforts to identify similarities in the work of The Eight, at the expense of each of the artists' individuality, modern criticism has partially confused the meaning of this temporary association.[8]

As a group, The Eight shared a common desire to promote modern painting, not just what might have then been called academic realism.[9] Henri, the most vociferous in defense of his own students whose work was regularly rejected at the conservative National Academy of Design exhibitions, saw the need for non-juried shows. It was his pioneer crusading that eventually led to the non-juried Independents show in New York City in 1910 and the Armory show of 1913. The latter, under the leadership of Arthur B. Davies, in its promotion of a legitimate modernism, went a long way toward eclipsing the modernism label formerly linked in the critical mind with the work of The Eight. Certainly, even limited historical perspective quickly and justifiably discounted the label of modernism associated with the work of The Eight.

cat. no. 252. Robert Henri. *Ruth St. Denis in the Peacock Dance,* 1919.

The work of The Eight is best seen as a link between the traditions of the late nineteenth century and early modernism in America. In this connection, the ideas of The Eight were more modern than their painting styles. Sloan expressed specific feelings of admiration for Hogarth and Constable,[10] and Luks frequently blustered about the greatness of Hals, Goya, and Velázquez. Such a respect for the past was partially a legacy of academic training[11] and partially the influence of Robert Henri. Although Henri's immediate influence may have come from Eakins and Anshutz, he looked closely at past art traditions; in *The Art Spirit,* he summarized this attitude:

> Know what the old masters did. Know how they composed their pictures, but do not fall into the conventions they established. These conventions were right for them, and they are wonderful. They made their language. You make yours. They can help you. All the past can help you.[12]

Henri was the natural leader of the group. Possessed of tremendous energy, determination, and wit, he inspired the men who gathered around him. A born teacher, he urged his students never to undervalue their own emotions and encouraged new methods of expression. His own style of painting reflected his quick mind and eye. He was never satisfied to stay with the same problem for long, and, consequently, the range of his work encompasses portraiture in the manner of Eakins, dark impressionistic cityscapes, impressionistic landscapes and seascapes painted in America and Ireland, and portrait studies of ethnic types and children.

Henri was always intent on capturing an effect. Nowhere does he achieve his goal better than in his full-length portrait of *Ruth St. Denis in the Peacock Dance* (cat. no. 252), painted in 1919. Sensuous in line and color, the portrait of the slender dancer, shimmering in a jewel-like peacock costume, epitomizes Henri's concern for massing essential forms and colors. The light surfaces are painted thinly, with little sense of underlying structure, in contrast to the thick impasto of the darks, making the portrait a tour de force in terms of Henri's technical experiments.

Henri advocated painting the facial features toward the completion of a portrait. He emphasized that it was not so much a question of painting the features as it was painting their expression. This expression was to manifest the state of mind of the sitter. In addition, the luscious red lips, tantalizing eyes, and evocative tilt of the head in the portrait of Ruth St. Denis all reveal the attraction the artist himself felt for the sitter.

Henri always urged his students to be genuinely interested in the subject. He advised his students at the Art Students League:

> The processes of painting spring from this interest, this definite thing to be said. Completion does not depend on material representation.[13]

Like Eakins, Henri sought out expressive faces to paint. He was especially attracted to the Spanish and Indian middle and lower classes. His 1923 portrait, *Man from Segovia in Fur-Trimmed Cap* (cat. no. 253), exhibited at the Academy in 1926, expresses that attraction. The man in the portrait, weather-beaten and aged, yet full of the intense spirit of life, exemplifies Henri's basic understanding of human character. The Segovia man reveals the same honesty and expressiveness as Eakins's portrait of Walt Whitman (cat. no. 227).

Henri's versatility in portraiture is further demonstrated in his portraits of little children, the majority of which were painted toward the end of his life. *Wee Maureen* (cat. no. 254), painted in 1926, reflects his love of ordinary, pretty children whose portraits stand not only as individuals but also as symbols of childhood. Henri's love for humanity was his special gift to his friends and his legacy to John Sloan.

cat. no. 253. Robert Henri. *Man From Segovia in Fur-Trimmed Cap,* 1923.
COLLECTION OF MRS. JOHN C. LECLAIR.

Sloan was Henri's closest friend among The Eight. To honor his friend's death in 1929, Sloan etched a portrait of *Robert Henri, Painter* (cat. no. 268) in 1931. Sloan was a skilled graphic artist, employing the medium easily in portraiture and city life genre scenes. As a newspaper illustrator with both the *Philadelphia Inquirer* and the *Philadelphia Press.* he had developed an incisive eye for accurate detail and humorous incidents. Sloan recorded his pleasure with the plate, feeling that it revealed "some of the kindly strength and helpful wisdom which this great artist so freely gave to others."[14]

cat. no. 264. John Sloan.
Turning Out the Light, 1905.
KRAUSHAAR GALLERIES, NEW YORK.

Sloan had been a student at the Pennsylvania Academy in Thomas Anshutz's antique class in 1892 and 1893. He first met Henri in Philadelphia, and it was Henri who finally persuaded Sloan to move permanently to New York in 1904. Sloan, in spite of the difficulty he encountered trying to find work in New York, was stimulated by his new surroundings. In 1905 he began a series of ten etchings inspired by the city. The "New York City Life" series, as they became known, represents Sloan's first serious encounter with the city in its many aspects and moods. Full of light-hearted sarcasm, joyousness, social commentary, and love of the city and its inhabitants, the series was sent by Sloan, at the invitation of the etcher Charles Mielatz, to the American Water Color Society exhibition in 1906. To Sloan's horror, four of the prints—*Roofs, Summer Night* (cat. no. 265), *Man, Wife, and Child, Turning Out the Light* (cat. no. 264), and *The Women's Page*—were returned as being too "vulgar" to exhibit. In their candor and human expression, they rival the narratives of Hogarth, Rowlandson, and Daumier.

cat. no. 265. John Sloan.
Roofs, Summer Night, 1906.
KRAUSHAAR GALLERIES, NEW YORK.

Sloan's social commentary found a release in his oil canvases. He was never afraid to confront what he saw in the city. He painted ordinary scenes of ordinary people—the bustle of street life, festive gatherings at McSorley's bar, carefree girls playing in the parks. Possessing a profound sense of the inequalities of American society, in 1912 he became an editor of the Socialist Party magazine *The Masses,* a position he retained until the advent of World War I.

One of his most severe canvases, *Coffee Line* (cat. no. 263) of 1905, developed these social overtones more than usual in his work. *Coffee Line* is not only a commentary on the tragic condition of man and the cold anonymity of the city but it also expresses Sloan's own frustrations at not achieving early critical recognition. Thus, he was especially pleased that

cat. no. 266. John Sloan. *Easter Eve,* 1907. PRIVATE COLLECTION.

the painting won an Honorable Mention at the Carnegie Institute exhibition in 1905 and that Thomas Eakins had served on the award jury.

Sloan's work most often expressed his own affirmative commitment to life. Like Henri's, its range was great. Sloan responded not only to the urban environment but also to the picturesque scenery around Gloucester, Massachusetts and Santa Fe, New Mexico. *Easter Eve* (cat. no. 266) of 1907, shown at both the Macbeth Galleries and the Pennsylvania Academy landmark exhibition of The Eight in 1908, is one of Sloan's most important early paintings done in New York. It demonstrates Sloan's versatility in opposing areas of pure color painted in impressionistic strokes against darker surfaces rendered in generalized outlines.

William Glackens was a close friend of both Sloan and Henri. He attended night classes at the Pennsylvania Academy with Sloan, who introduced him to Henri. Glackens shared a studio with Henri at 806 Walnut Street in Philadephia, and in 1895 both went off to Paris, where they were constant companions. In the spring of 1896, the two, along with Elmer Schofield, took a bicycling trip through northern France, Holland, and Belgium. When Glackens returned to America later that year, he settled in New York rather than in Philadelphia and shared a studio with George Luks.

Glackens's experience as a reporter-illustrator with the *Philadelphia Record* and the *Philadelphia Inquirer* made it easier for him to find a job in the art department of the *New York Herald* upon his return from Europe. He quickly became one of the *Herald's* best illustrators; his work combined accuracy of detail, humor, and a keen perception of human foibles. Among The Eight, Glackens held the distinction of being the most capable and accomplished illustrator.

Glackens's illustrations carry the conviction of an intuitive sensitivity to line. He seemed at his best, whether at illustration or painting, when he was least self-conscious about style. In painting, Glackens's style was strongly influenced by the work of the French Impressionists, especially Renoir. Glackens's paintings of female nudes and flower still lifes particularly recall Renoir's manner and, like the paintings of Renoir and Degas, retain the imprint of an academic background. In Glackens's figure paintings, forms rarely lose their substance. And yet form is not conceived in terms of substance alone, but of color and light as well. Glackens's high-keyed tones of bright colors are strongly derived from Renoir's later work. In 1912, Glackens, at the direction of his friend Dr. Albert C. Barnes, traveled to Europe to buy modern European paintings for his client. Along with works by Manet, Degas, Cézanne, van Gogh, Gauguin, and Matisse, Glackens purchased a large number of Renoirs for Barnes.

The Soda Fountain (cat. no. 251), painted by Glackens in 1935, only three years before his death, shows the influence of Renoir's palette and brushwork. It is typically American, however, in its emphasis on the details of the scene. It is also reminiscent of Glackens's background as an illustrator by virtue of its narrative quality.

Glackens was a quiet, gentle, lonely man with the security of a wealthy wife. His friend, George Luks, was radically different. Luks was known as a pugilist and heavy drinker. He was constantly impoverished, finding it always difficult to sell his paintings. His natural aesthetic gravitated to the powerful images of the Dutch and Spanish schools, notably those of Hals, Rembrandt, and Velázquez. Unlike Glackens, whose work expressed a happy optimism about life, Luks's work often revealed life's uglier, gloomier side. While he painted clowns and entertainers like the *Polish Dancer* (cat. no. 257) and was a great mimic himself, his repertoire ranged to aged hags and impoverished street children. He recognized the meanness and cruelty of life in his work.

Luks had no patience for modernism. As a student under Anshutz at the Pennsylvania Academy and later at the Düsseldorf Academy, he was reared in the humanistic traditions

cat. no. 257. George Luks. *Polish Dancer.*

cat. no. 251. William J. Glackens. *The Soda Fountain,* 1935.

of art. Like Henri, Sloan, Glackens, and Shinn, Luks's motivation for painting was his own deep belief in humanity. His paintings capture in a rough, at times crude, style the salient features of character types.

The *Polish Dancer* is one of Luks's gayest and most brilliant portraits. Its flamboyance elevates the mood of the painting to a visual excitement that is so often missing in Luks's drabber subjects. Luks seems most comfortable in his paintings of entertainers. Like Shinn and, to a lesser extent, Glackens, Luks found inspiration in the theatrical life of the city.

Luks shared an apartment with Everett Shinn when both worked as staff artists for the *Philadelphia Press*. Shinn, the youngest of The Eight, was a student at the Pennsylvania Academy under Anshutz from 1893 to 1897. In the latter year he moved to New York and soon began doing decorative murals in interior architectural settings for impresarios like David Belasco and decorators like Elsie de Wolfe. He continued as an illustrator, working in pencil, watercolor, and pastel. In the early 1900s he completed a series of monochromatic city vignettes that dealt with both the depravity of New York and its new architectural beauty. The meaning of *The Docks—New York City* (cat. no. 259) of 1901 is cloaked in ambiguity. It may be conceived of either as a statement about the harsh conditions of the working class or as a symbol of the confused dislocation of the newly arrived immigrant in America. In either case, Shinn has cast the subject in a purposefully cold and unpleasant scene.

Shinn's real love was the theater, and the rich, glittering women associated with it. He himself was known for his dapper dress and brilliant conversation. Throughout his career he painted theatrical subjects. Although he often claimed that he studied no one

cat. no. 259. Everett Shinn. *The Docks—New York City,* 1901. MUNSON-WILLIAMS-PROCTOR INSTITUTE, UTICA, N.Y.

cat. no. 260. Everett Shinn. *London Hippodrome,* 1902. ART INSTITUTE OF CHICAGO, FRIENDS OF AMERICAN ART COLLECTION.

but Manet, the influence of Degas, and of Degas's disciple, Jean Louis Forain, is unmistakable in Shinn's theater and cabaret compositions. Shinn's *London Hippodrome* (cat. no. 260) of 1902 seems to be closely derived from Forain's *Tightrope Walker* (Art Institute of Chicago). *London Hippodrome* is quintessentially Shinn. He recognized his difficulty in rendering portraits, and the dark balcony setting allows him to leave the mass of the audience in relative obscurity. A sense of opulence is created through rich coloration and dramatic lighting. Curiously, the audience's attention is on the stage below and not on the trapeze dancer who floats just above their heads. In his use of such a dramatic device as a swinging trapeze artist, Shinn recalls the work of Degas and Forain and anticipates the similar environments of the contemporary sculptor George Segal.

London Hippodrome was one of eight canvases Shinn exhibited at the Macbeth Galleries and subsequently at the Pennsylvania Academy in 1908. Nine years earlier, when Shinn was only twenty-three, the Academy had sponsored an exhibition of his pastels. Such one-man shows at the Academy were not unusual for members of The Eight; in 1897 and again in 1902 Robert Henri's work was shown in one-man shows, and in 1907 an exhibition of the work of Ernest Lawson was held.

The Henri gang shared a similar background, and their work dealt with many of the same images of the city. It was these realistic depictions of the city that prompted hostile critics to label the artists "apostles of ugliness."[15] Ernest Lawson, Maurice Prendergast, and Arthur B. Davies were outside the inner circle of the Henri gang. Conceptually and stylistically, their work bears no affinity to the Ashcan School. Lawson was an Impressionist, Prendergast a Neo-Impressionist, and Davies a visionary lyricist in the American tradition of Ryder and Vedder.

Ernest Lawson was a landscape painter with a unique, heavy, impressionistic style. After working in Mexico City as a draftsman for an engineering firm, he studied at the Art Students League in New York. He worked for a year with John Twachtman and J. Alden Weir in Cos Cob, Connecticut. In 1893 he went to Paris to study at the Académie Julian under John Paul Laurens and Benjamin Constant. His greatest influence at the time was the work of the English Impressionist Alfred Sisley, whom he met near Fontainebleau on his first trip abroad.

Even though Lawson's work sold relatively well, he was continually plagued with financial debts. Not infrequently, the Pennsylvania Academy found buyers for his paintings. In 1907, in acknowledging the honor of receiving the Jennie Sesnan Gold Medal awarded to the best landscape in an Academy annual exhibition, Lawson noted his appreciation: "Whatever success I have had in painting has always been connected in some way with the Pennsylvania Academy of the Fine Arts."[16] In 1920 Lawson's *Ice Bound Falls* was awarded the Temple Gold Medal for the best painting in the annual.

Nevertheless, it was not until 1935, when Lawson was sixty-two, that the Academy first purchased one of his paintings. *Peggy's Cove, Nova Scotia* (cat. no. 256), painted about 1935, is typical of Lawson's landscape vision. Almost always Lawson's compositions are strongly structured and his forms solidly outlined. He rarely allowed his penchant for traditional realism to be negated by the looseness of the Impressionist style. Even in his many winter landscapes, Lawson never lost sight of form and structure.

Lawson considered color the most revealing quality of his painting; he used it to create moods. He seemed to favor the quieter, more introspective moods of nature, developed through subtle tonal variations within a limited range of colors, evident in such canvases as *The Broken Fence; Spring Flood* (cat. no. 255), but was equally capable of bolder color statements. *Peggy's Cove, Nova Scotia* (cat. no. 256) is one of Lawson's most brilliant canvases, full of the vitality obtained by juxtaposing pure colors.

cat. no. 256. Ernest Lawson. *Peggy's Cove, Nova Scotia,* ca.1935.

cat. no. 258. Maurice Prendergast. *Bathers in a Cove,* 1916. THE PHILADELPHIA MUSEUM OF ART, JOHN H. MCFADDEN, JR. FUND.

Maurice Prendergast was equally moved by the joy of color. As a watercolorist, and in his oils and monotypes, Prendergast's exuberance for color was well noted in his day. His earliest work in Paris shows the influence of Whistler and later the Nabis. Unlike the Nabis, however, Prendergast was less interested in color theory than in color.

Prendergast had tentative beginnings as an artist. Until 1891, at the age of thirty-one, he had pursued painting as an avocation. In 1891 he traveled to Paris where he enrolled at Colarossi's and at the Académie Julian. He quickly became a close friend of the Canadian painter, James Morrice, who introduced Prendergast into the artistic life of Paris. Exposed to the diversity of painting styles and theories of art of late nineteenth-century Paris and with a recent academic background, Prendergast, in his early work, showed a multiplicity of influences. The effects of these influences were to remain evident throughout his life. Out of his Parisian experience Prendergast quickly developed a mature style.

Prendergast's Parisian work dealt with the everyday life of the city—the milling crowds along the wide boulevards and in the parks, café life, and market stalls. Following the dictum given thirty years earlier by Charles Baudelaire, the great French poet and critic, he found inspiration for his paintings in "la vie moderne." His work would continue to be a response to the world he observed.

By 1895 Prendergast had returned to Boston. In four short years he had become an accomplished artist. His favorite subjects, most often rendered in watercolor, were beach scenes populated by holiday crowds. In 1898 Prendergast went back to Europe to see Italy. In the long tradition of American artists who had visited Italy, Prendergast was captivated by Venice and his discovery of Italian Renaissance painting. His interest in the early Italian Gothic painters was exceeded only by that in Carpaccio's work. From the Italians, Prendergast learned to structure his paintings with a more rigid geometry, often presenting a frieze of figures in varying attitudes along the foreground against a diminishing level of activity leading horizontally to a landscape background. His figures often show their dependence on classical poses and yet they succeed, unlike the figures of Puvis de Chavannes, whom Prendergast admired, as contemporary statements from the real world. The combination of tradition and newness is resolved into a strong personal style in Prendergast's work.

Bathers in a Cove (cat. no. 258) of 1916 is both joyous and free in its use of color and tightly structured compositionally. Although the scene is interpreted in an impressionistic style, it clearly exists in reality and not in the artist's imagination. In this respect, among The Eight, only the work of Arthur B. Davies, in its flights of fancy, transcends the real world.

Davies's work continues the visionary tradition in American art associated with Albert Pinkham Ryder and Elihu Vedder in the nineteenth century. And like Ryder and Vedder, Davies came out of an academic background, having studied at the Art Institute of Chicago. His model in France, Puvis de Chavannes, had strong academic leanings and was also interested in Italian primitive painting. One can only wonder at Davies's visionary sensibility in light of this background.

Davies's work reveals his own mystical propensities often combined with subtle references to classical mythology as well as overt references to classical art. Into his mysterious surroundings, Arcadian worlds, he introduced nymphlike figures based on his study of human form. As a sculptor, his approach to the human figure was both traditional and experimental. In his drawings of nude models, such as *Reclining Nude* (cat. no. 248), he manifested a real ability to draw the human figure. When he introduced these figures into his paintings, they regularly became symbols of his own introspective world and lost their substance. *Discoveries: Isle of Destiny* (cat. no. 250) is indicative of this metamorphosis. Its horizontal format exists almost as a diptych, with a disturbing void at the center. The figures

cat. no. 250. Arthur B. Davies. *Discoveries: Isle of Destiny.*

clearly relate to his sculptured and drawn forms,[17] but they exist as flat patterns of light color against a darker background. In *Discoveries: Isle of Destiny* the figures may be icons of human vanity in the face of childhood innocence.

Davies seemed to have an intuitive sense about modern art. Unlike other members of The Eight, he spoke positively about the abstract developments of art in Europe of the early twentieth century. Next to Alfred Stieglitz, Davies did more to promote modern art in the United States than any other person. Ironically, as president of the American Association of Painters and Sculptors, which sponsored the 1913 Armory Show in New York, he was the leader of the first important modern art exhibition in America that quickly brought on the decline of Robert Henri as the spokesman for the modern American art scene. After 1913 Henri was never again to gain the same leadership status he had enjoyed in the early twentieth century.

The Armory Show did much to promote modernism in America. It was not, however, the death knell of that brand of realism espoused by The Eight. Not only did each of The Eight continue painting for many years after, but their influence remained strong, especially in academic circles like the Pennsylvania Academy. In the later work of the Fourteenth Street School—in Bellows and Marsh and Soyer—they had creative disciples. Their tradition remains a strong one to this day. In the urban images of contemporary artists, like those of Richard Estes and Robert Cottingham, the legacy of The Eight is at work.

Carolyn Diskant

MODERNISM AT THE PENNSYLVANIA ACADEMY, 1910-1940

Eight years have passed [since the Armory Show]; and now the Pennsylvania Academy of the Fine Arts has opened its finest galleries to the pictures of the modern Americans. . . . The Philadelphia Academy is to be commended for its new vision: it abandoned its traditional judgement [sic] that art should be a representation of material phenomena, and invited to its halls a group of painters who have at least one interest in common, the knowledge that art is based on design and not on natural imitation. . . . The future of American art will certainly repose in a number of men represented at Philadelphia, not in the illustrators, imitators, and literalists of fashionable exploitation.

Thomas J. Craven,
"The Awakening of the Academy,"
The Dial, June 1921

The period 1910-1940 saw the emergence of two diverse artistic tendencies in America: modernism, characterized by a concern for new, abstract styles of expression, and American Scene painting, with its interest in the depiction of American life. Although both existed simultaneously, the decades before the Depression were dominated by modernism, and those after by the American Scene painters. These tendencies found some support in Philadelphia, where the Pennsylvania Academy was the dominant force in the arts.

Modernism, the more radical of the two tendencies, had its origins in the European styles of Cubism, Fauvism, Futurism and Expressionism of the early twentieth century. American artists adapted these new styles for their own use; they never became obsessed with the affirmation of European modernism *per se.* Alfred Stieglitz, who championed modernism in America, in fact, always urged artists to commit themselves to the "expression of subjective feelings"[1] in preference to artistic theory.

Into the early twentieth century, academies retained their popular position as the preliminary training ground for American artists. Traditional in their attitudes to art, schools such as the Pennsylvania Academy trained an extraordinary number of America's future important avant-garde painters. Their tendency toward modernistic styles, however, was clearly not a legacy of the Academy. Nearly all of these painters went on to study in Paris, where there was ample opportunity to associate with European modernist artists.

At the same time, advanced tendencies in art were also being promoted in the United States by Alfred Stieglitz, whose gallery, "291," in New York City became a center for the support of both European and American avant-garde art. In 1908 Stieglitz held the first exhibitions in America of Rodin and Matisse. Between that year and 1917, he exhibited the work of Matisse, Cézanne, Picasso, Braque, Picabia, and Brancusi. Important for the development of American avant-garde painting were the exhibitions Stieglitz held of the work of young American artists, including Alfred Maurer, John Marin, Max Weber, Arthur Dove, Georgia O'Keeffe, and Marsden Hartley.

The most significant event in the history of modernism in America, however, was the 1913 International Exhibition of Modern Art held in New York at the Sixty-ninth Regiment Armory.[2] The Armory Show's presentation of the most radical European and American art was important in introducing modernism to the public and to the many American artists outside of the "291" circle who had not been to Europe. It also stimulated American collectors of modern art, paved the way for a large number of gallery and museum exhibitions, and prompted the formation of avant-garde artistic organizations. These activities helped to accelerate the acceptance of modern art in America.

The Pennsylvania Academy's interest in advanced tendencies in art was demonstrated by its early recognition of photography as a significant art form. From 1898 to 1901 the Academy encouraged serious photographers through its annual photographic salons, which were organized jointly with the Photographic Society of Philadelphia. The purpose of the salons was to exhibit only such photographs "in which there [was] distinct evidence of individual artistic feeling and execution."[3] Alfred Stieglitz, Gertrude Käsebier, F. Holland Day, and Clarence White served as jurors for these salons which were cited as "the recognized presentation of all that is best in the photographic field."[4] In 1906 the Academy again collaborated with Stieglitz in showing "An Exhibition of Photographs Arranged by the Photo-Secession." Most of the photographs in the exhibition came directly from Stieglitz's own gallery, which had opened in New York in 1905. The exhibition was intended to "summarize in a broad way the trend of the international movement of which the Photo-Secession is the organized American exponent, a protest against the conventional conception of what constitutes Pictorial Photography."[5] Well received in Philadelphia, the exhibition was declared to represent the best work produced in the United States, Austria, Germany, France, and England[6] and was considered the finest collection of photographs ever brought together.[7]

The Pennsylvania Academy's commitment to modern photography seems to have ceased after 1906. It was not until the 1920s that the Academy again recognized avant-garde artistic tendencies, this time through a series of painting and sculpture exhibitions relating to modernism. In the spring of 1920 Arthur B. Carles and Carroll S. Tyson, Jr., organized an exhibition entitled "Paintings and Drawings by Representative Modern Masters." It consisted of 256 works by important French artists of the late nineteenth and early twentieth centuries, illustrating the development of modern art in France. Included in the exhibition were works by the Realists Courbet and Daumier; the Impressionists Manet, Degas, Renoir, and Monet; the Post-Impressionists Gauguin, Cézanne, and Seurat; the Fauves Matisse and Derain; and the Cubists Picasso and Braque. A review in the *American Magazine of Art* noted that, although the Academy was reputedly conservative, "in recent years, however, it has been most hospitable to the work of the so-called modernists."[8]

The next year the Academy held the "Exhibition of Paintings Showing the Later Tendencies in Art," the first comprehensive collection of modern American works exhibited in an American museum. Academy officials, however, emphasized that the exhibition would not actually be conducted under the auspices of the Academy, pointing out that it was being organized by a committee of Philadelphia and New York artists and that the Academy was merely extending the modernists the courtesy of space. The committee, composed of seven modernist artists—Thomas Hart Benton, Paul Burlin, Arthur B. Carles, Bernard Gussow, Joseph Stella, Alfred Stieglitz, and William Yarrow—chose two hundred and eighty works by eighty-eight artists, including Arthur B. Carles, Charles Demuth, Arthur G. Dove, Marsden Hartley, Gaston Lachaise, Robert Laurent, John Marin, Alfred Maurer, Georgia O'Keeffe, H. Lyman Saÿen, Morton Schamberg, Charles Sheeler, Joseph Stella, Max Weber, and William Zorach. The show attracted large crowds and some favorable criticism. While the art critic for the *Philadelphia Inquirer* had mixed feeling about the exhibition,[9] critics for the New York based magazines *The Arts* and *American Art News* considered it the best exhibition of modern American art ever held.[10]

In the spring of 1923 the Academy held an exhibition of contemporary European paintings and sculpture from the collection of Albert C. Barnes, who wrote the introduction to the catalogue. Consisting of seventy-five works shown earlier that year at a Paris gallery, the exhibition included paintings by Soutine, Modigliani, Lipchitz, Derain, Matisse, Picasso, De Chirico, and Utrillo. The purpose of the show, Barnes stated, was to give Philadelphians additional exposure to modern art. Barnes hoped that these modern works would be interpreted both in the context of art historical tradition and as valid, original artistic expressions.

Barnes's efforts to educate Philadelphians were not successful. The public response ranged from derision to admiration to bewilderment;[11] critical reviews were unfavorable. In the *Philadelphia Inquirer* the work of Soutine was described as "incomprehensible" and that of Modigliani "very odd."[12] The review in the *Philadelphia Record* was far harsher:

> These pictures are most unpleasant to contemplate. It is debased art in which the attempt for a new form of expression results in the degradation of the old formulas, not in the creation of something new . . . The pictures shown are best described as "nasty," with full realization of the exact meaning of the word. It is a little hard to see why the Academy should sponsor this sort of trash.[13]

The Academy's support of modernism did not carry over strongly into its annual exhibitions. There were, nonetheless, exceptions. In the annual of 1911, a place of honor was given to a group of fifteen watercolors by John Marin, a former student; the hanging committee was subsequently congratulated "for its courage in placing Mr. Marin's work in so favorable a place—defying traditions and doing insidious violence to the timid painters and the commercially inclined."[14] Additionally, the annual of 1929 was described in the *Art News* as containing "modernistic works of various moods and manners," this tendency being "apparent also to some extent in the exhibition of sculpture."[15] In general, however, the Academy annuals contained few modernistic works. The only progressive artists to appear consistently were Henry Breckenridge, Henry McCarter, and Arthur B. Carles, all of whom taught at the Academy.

In spite of important, albeit sporadic, manifestations of support for avant-garde European and American art, the fundamental attitudes about art at the Academy remained conservative. A limited amount of support for advanced tendencies in art was tolerated; more often the Academy acted as the cautious host rather than the fervent sponsor. Fortunately for Philadelphia's avant-garde artists, several small galleries filled the gap. Foremost among these was James McClees's Gallery, known for its avant-garde exhibitions. In 1908 and 1910 respectively, the McClees Gallery gave Charles Sheeler and Morton Schamberg their first

cat. no. 280. Charles Demuth. *Gladiolas.*

one-man shows. In 1916, Schamberg persuaded McClees to hold an exhibition featuring a group of works from the Armory Show, the first presentation of modern art in Philadelphia. The thirty-one examples chosen by Schamberg included works by Matisse, Picasso, Duchamp, Man Ray, Derain, Rouault, Brancusi, Duchamp-Villon, Sheeler, Stella, Saÿen, and Schamberg. Schamberg wrote, in defense of modern art:

> The whole tendency of the modern movement, especially since Cézanne, has been toward a greater and greater insistence upon those qualities in painting which are most directly capable of stimulating pure aesthetic emotion, and a greater and greater elimination of the illustrative, of the photographic, of associated ideas, in other words, of the irrelevant. . . . It should be added that modern paintings are either good or bad for precisely the same reasons that old pictures are either good or bad.[16]

The McClees Gallery held another exhibition of modern art the following year and several exhibitions of the "Thirty-One," an association of Philadelphia modernists who protested against academic restrictions. The "Thirty-One" included such artists as Charles Demuth, Henry Breckenridge, Henry McCarter, Franklin Watkins, Charles Sheeler, and Arthur B. Carles.

These Philadelphia exhibitions filled a need not satisfied by the Pennsylvania Academy, which had provided some support for modernism, but apparently not enough to suit local artists. At an exhibition of the "Thirty-One," Carles commented:

> Don't you think these are the most talented students that came out of the Academy? You, see, one kind of student goes up the Delaware River and the other kind goes to Paris. This is the Paris kind and most of them don't get into the Academy. Don't you think they are doing good work? I think it is a lot more interesting than the dead wood that is admitted.[17]

Instruction in the Academy's school reinforced the prevailing conservative ideas about art in Academy circles. At the beginning of the twentieth century, its curriculum remained traditional. While instructors like Thomas Anshutz encouraged young students to experiment with new painterly modes of expression, avant-garde tendencies in art were inconsistent with an academic point of view. John Marin, Arthur B. Carles, H. Lyman Saÿen, Charles Demuth, Charles Sheeler, Morton Schamberg, John Storrs, Henry McCarter, and Abraham Rattner, all students at the Academy, developed their modernistic modes of expression after they left the Academy. Even with the appointments of Henry Breckenridge, Arthur B. Carles, and Henry McCarter, disciples of modernism, as instructors in the school, the impact of modernism remained limited.

What styles of modernism developed in America? Of the major European styles of the early twentieth century, which appealed to American artists, and how did they adapt them? The most influential style was Cubism, although Futurism was also popular among American artists. Many American artists experimented with Fauvism, but its emotional excesses limited its appeal. Dada's pessimism likewise attracted few followers in America. Unlike Europeans, American artists were little concerned with the intellectual theories related to these styles. Moreover, Americans never went as far as Europeans in the dissection of form; they were always more concerned with maintaining the visual identity of the object. They were equally concerned with developing their own personal styles.

One of the earliest American styles of modern painting based on Cubist precedents was Precisionism. Precisionists were attracted to forms that were adaptable to geometric shapes; they particularly found suitable subjects in modern industrial architecture. Although the Precisionists did not produce pure abstractions, they greatly reduced the number and complexity of the shapes in a marked departure from naturalistic representation. The three

cat. no. 299. Charles Sheeler. *Clapboards,* 1936.

major American practitioners of this style all had been students at the Pennsylvania Academy: Charles Demuth, Charles Sheeler, and Morton Schamberg.

Primarily a watercolorist, Charles Demuth is known for both his Precisionist architectural works and still lifes. Demuth studied at the Academy from 1905 to 1907 and again from 1908 to 1910, traveling to Paris in the interim. His earliest work is devoted to figural compositions and still lifes. *Gladiolas* (cat. no. 280) is an example of a still life rendered in watercolor in the mid-teens, before he had developed his Precisionist style. Demuth made extensive use of the watercolor medium, using it to express the freshness and fragility of his flower pieces. His interest in the careful observations of nature, an interest that recurs in the work of modern American artists, is consistent with a pragmatic American vision. Demuth's realistic still lifes run counter to the tendency of modernism to abstract organic forms, a tendency especially evident in the work of Dove and O'Keeffe.

Charles Sheeler's work is based on Cubist principles, direct observation, and photography. Studies at the Pennsylvania Academy from 1903 to 1906 had provided Sheeler with the skills to become a competent painter in the manner of William M. Chase. However, exposure to the French modernists subsequently convinced him of the importance of disciplined pictorial structure, which he combined with distinctly American subjects to produce his own form of Precisionism. Precision of form and insistence on structure are evident in *Clapboards* of 1936 (cat. no. 299) , and the work is, at the same time, clearly related to photography, a parallel interest of Sheeler's. Sheeler's manner of truncating parts of the build-

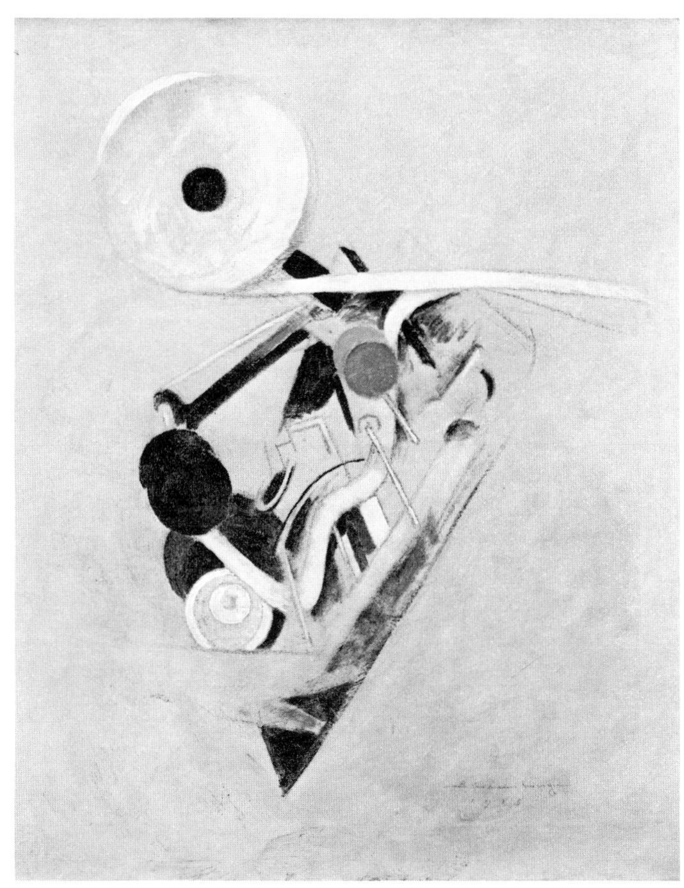

cat. no. 298. Morton Livingston Schamberg. *Camera Flashlight,* 1916. COLLECTION OF DR. AND MRS. IRA LEO SCHAMBERG, JENKINTOWN, PA.

ings, combined with his precise depiction of forms, creates a strong photographic effect. Moreover, his decision to focus on the rooftops of these small-town American buildings serves to abstract them, since the viewer perceives them separately from the buildings themselves.

Machine forms were a favorite subject of Morton Schamberg, who was influenced by the work of Duchamp and Picabia. Like Sheeler, Schamberg studied at the Academy from 1903 to 1906, and, as in Sheeler's case, visits to Paris decisively influenced his career. The two artists were friends and studied the works of the Fauves and Cubists together while in Paris. Both were also interested in photography. *Camera Flashlight* of 1916 (cat. no. 298) reveals Schamberg's combined interest in photography and machines. While the painting does not read precisely as a camera, it is clear that Schamberg combined the flash attachment of a camera with other camera parts, notably the two rollers with the film. The box of the camera is missing, however, and the parts do not resemble the working parts of a real camera; it is thus a Dadaesque assemblage of parts, in the manner of Duchamp. This work is not drawn with the precision of Sheeler's *Clapboards.* The edges of the forms are not sharply outlined; in fact, an examination of the perimeter of the form reveals Schamberg's use of "passage," a favorite device of Analytic Cubism, as he allows the ground to penetrate the borders of the form itself.

cat. no. 292. John Marin. *The Singer Building,* 1921. The Philadelphia Museum of Art, The Alfred Stieglitz Collection.

cat. no. 276. Arthur B. Carles. *Composition No. 6,* 1936.

cat. no. 279. Stuart Davis. *Ultra-Marine,* 1943.

In addition to the Precisionists, other American artists developed styles based on the Cubist idiom. One of the most important of these early modernists in America was John Marin. After his studies at the Pennsylvania Academy with William M. Chase and Thomas Anshutz from 1899 to 1901, Marin spent the years between 1905 and 1911 in Europe. While there, Marin came under the influence of the works of James Whistler, the Fauves, and the Nabis. Upon his return to New York, he developed a style combining Cubist structure with a personal expressionism. He began to explore a favorite, lifelong theme—the architecture of New York City. In these scenes of New York, Marin viewed the city in a far different manner from that of The Eight or the Fourteenth Street School. Whereas John Sloan and Raphael Soyer dealt with the human life of the modern city, Marin concentrated on its architecture. Attracted and frightened by the city and its buildings, he wrote about the buildings as if they had personalities of their own.[18]

In *The Singer Building* of 1921 (cat. no. 292) the forms of the city, though broken and interrupted, remain discernible. The building rises above the complex and threatening level of street life to establish its own forceful presence. To Marin, the skyscraper symbolized both the advanced and destitute condition of modern man. Marin himself sought to escape this condition by turning to an isolated life in Maine.

The early work of Arthur B. Carles shows the influence of Matisse, but Carles did experiment with Cubism at the end of his career. After his initial studies at the Pennsylvania Academy from 1900 to 1907 with Chase and Anshutz, he traveled to Paris. His mature style, much affected by Cubism, may be seen in *Composition No. 6* of 1936 (cat. no. 276). Although Carles has fragmented and simplified the objects in the composition, the general shape of a model posed on a sofa is discernible. Carles's insistence on retaining a semblance of reality while working in a non-realist style of painting is indicative of the American artists' vision; likewise, Abraham Rattner's *The Round Table* (cat. no. 297) expresses the same need for objectivity that ran counter to European Cubist tendencies.

Stuart Davis was another American artist who experimented with Cubism and Futurism before evolving his mature style in the 1930s. His interest in the organization of abstract, fragmented objects is apparent in *Ultra-Marine* of 1943 (cat. no. 279). Davis's version of Cubism differs greatly from that of Carles in *Composition No. 6*. Carles's work remains closer to traditional painting; his forms are still recognizable, and he depicts objects behind one another, creating an illusion of depth. Davis's work, however, is extremely surface-oriented, with the dense detail and restless surface activity forming a totally abstract pattern. This emphasis on a multiplicity of detail is characteristic of Davis's work after 1931 and of his desire to unify his works completely.

Not all American modernists turned to Cubism. Marsden Hartley, after initially experimenting with Cubism, was drawn to the bold, free colors characteristic of Fauvism and German Expressionism. Hartley was particularly influenced by the work of the expressionists Franz Marc and Vasily Kandinsky. *Painting No. 4 (Black Horse)* of 1915 (cat. no. 284) shows this dual influence as it combines decorative quality with bold, unmodulated colors. Hartley painted this work in Berlin in 1914-15, when he was painting his second Berlin series, a montage of visual images of the early war years, comprising fragments of forms. The black horse and the number "8" in this painting seem to relate to the Berlin series; however, the work also appears to reflect Hartley's interest in primitive cultures and their artistic iconography. Nevertheless, the various forms in this work do not appear to possess any disguised meaning, for Hartley denied the existence of any symbolism in these works, referring to them as purely pictorial arrangements of forms.[19]

Apart from those artists who borrowed heavily from specific European styles, there were others in this period who shunned European styles of painting. Artists such as Henry Breckenridge, Arthur Dove, and Georgia O'Keeffe evolved unique, abstract styles based more on their own reactions and personal sensibilities than on the precepts of European modernism. Breckenridge, who was associated with the Academy for fifty years, painted in several styles, ranging from realistic portraiture in the Eakins tradition to pure abstraction. Although in his early years he produced primarily naturalistic and impressionistic works, Breckenridge's work is difficult to group into chronological periods. Believing strongly in the artist's right to choose a style to convey a particular idea, Breckenridge worked variously in realistic, impressionistic, and abstract styles for most of his career. Abstractions such as *Sky Drama* of about 1917 (cat. no. 274) predominated much of his work. In *Sky Drama* Breckenridge reveals his interest in impressionistic color. The juxtaposition of colors, often in pale and subtle tonalities, emerged as the dominant factor in his abstract works, the forms themselves appearing tentative.

The abstractions of Arthur Dove seem, by comparison, much stronger than those of Breckenridge. Dove was among America's first abstractionists, and he created a lyrical personal style based on his love for nature. Although Dove was responding to specific experiences in nature, his images are more abstract than those of Demuth and the Precisionists. While Demuth depicted specific images of flowers, Dove, in *Naples Yellow Morning* of 1934 (cat. no. 281), used organic, non-specific shapes in modulated color arranged across the picture surface. The work is composed in a landscape format, but Dove's interest in sensuous color and elemental forms becomes its predominant feature.

Georgia O'Keeffe is often linked with Arthur Dove, who, together with Arthur Wesley Dow, influenced her early work. During the 1920s and after, O'Keeffe painted a series of close-ups of flowers, of which *Coxcomb* (cat. no. 296) is a striking example. *Coxcomb* deals with recognizable forms of flowers, which are abstracted by enlarging their scale and by removing them from a specific environment. O'Keeffe's brilliant use of color, in the subtle gradation from rose to blue, produces a lush, sensual effect. The sexual overtones and high level of mystery in her work add a strong psychological dimension to the beautiful imagery.

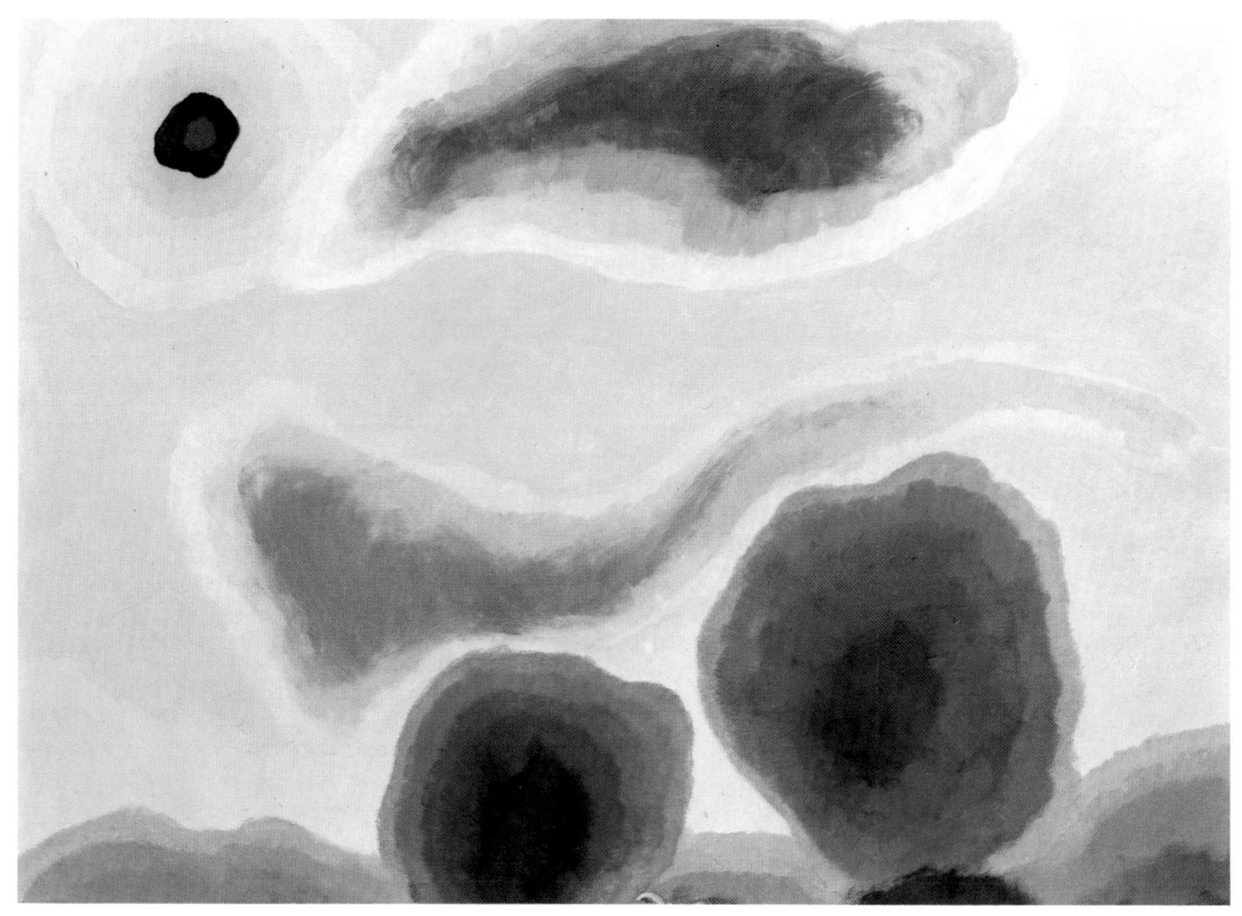

cat. no. 281. Arthur Dove. *Naples Yellow Morning,* 1935. COLLECTION OF MR. AND MRS. MEYER P. POTAMKIN.

The pioneers of avant-garde American painting developed styles which, in varying degrees, were influenced by European modernism. This interest in modernism spread, and by the 1920s many American artists were eagerly experimenting with new styles of painting. However, other artistic styles were evolving, too, and by the time of the stock market crash of 1929, marked changes were occurring in American art.

After World War I, a cynical and conservative element in society had slowly begun to assert itself. The artists' desire to define and describe the American experience began to grow, reaching its peak in the 1930s. The general mood in America became one of isolationism and nationalism. It was a time of self-examination, a time characterized by a wish to cast off European ties. The dream of an American artistic renaissance emerged among certain critics and artists, reflecting a desire to surpass European achievements in art—a desire for America's cultural coming of age. Serious questions began to be raised about the validity of modernism in America. Critics felt that a national art style would never emerge if artists constantly emulated foreign art styles. A definite reaction against French modernism had appeared in America by 1930.[20]

cat. no. 296. Georgia O'Keeffe. *Coxcomb*. COLLECTION OF MRS. JOHN WINTERSTEEN.

There was much debate among critics about what "American" art should be. Critics such as Thomas Craven, Edwin Alden Jewell, and Holger Cahill favored a realistic, simplified style dealing with the common experiences of America.[21] The Midwest was seen as a new source of themes for American artists, in part because it had been less affected by European influences. Obviously in a country as large and diverse as America, no single artistic style could prevail. Nevertheless, by 1932 the "American Wave," as it was termed,[22] was a loose, but coherent artistic movement.

The Regionalists were one of the most important and popular groups in the "American Wave" movement. Including such artists as Thomas Hart Benton, John S. Curry, and Grant Wood, this group painted the rural aspects of America, valuing its down-to-earth qualities. The Fourteenth Street School, a group of New York artists, was more interested in observing and recording the city and its character. These artists did not hesitate to paint the squalor of the city.

Along with this interest in the depiction of the American scene, and as a result of severe political and economic crises, painting came to be used by some artists primarily as an expression of social conscience, either as commentary or protest. Artists like Ben Shahn, Jack Levine, and William Gropper expressed their concern over current issues through an art conveying specifically political messages. The Social Protest school was an alternative for those artists who felt either that the American Scene movement lacked complexity or that the theories of Socialism or Marxism were applicable to America's economic situation.[23]

The change of emphasis during the Depression years pushed modernism out of the mainstream. But modernist artists continued to develop their artistic styles and to produce important works of art during this period, even though they were not supported strongly by the public and critics.

The Pennsylvania Academy gave even less support to the artists of the American Scene than they had to the modernist artists. The Academy did not organize exhibitions during the 1930s comparable to those of modern art of the pre-Depression years. In fact, neither American Scene nor modernist works were presented; instead, various memorial and retrospective exhibitions of such artists as Charles Grafly and Anna H. Huntington, both academic sculptors with strong ties to the nineteenth century, were held. Examples of other exhibitions from this period include the work of Jessie Willcox Smith, an illustrator of children's books, and W. Sergeant Kendall, a conservative painter and sculptor.

Clearly, these exhibitions were far more *retardataire* than those of earlier years. Although probably influenced by the general decline in artistic activity brought on by the Depression, the shift in patronage is most likely related to the absence of active contemporary artists' groups in Philadelphia. The Academy's innovative exhibitions in the earlier part of the century had generally been organized by outsiders, and the modernists had had an outspoken champion on the Academy's faculty in Arthur B. Carles. The Regionalists and other contemporary schools, however, had no spokesman in Philadelphia comparable to Carles. Lacking someone to encourage and help organize an exhibition of contemporary art of the 1930s, the Academy staff made no such effort on its own.

It should be noted, however, that the major artists of the 1930s were consistently included in the Pennsylvania Academy annual exhibitions from the late 1920s until the Second World War. In addition, by the 1930s many more abstract artists were being included in these annuals, but these modernist artists, finally acceptable to the Academy juries, did not represent the major national trends at that time. It is not surprising, then, to find that far more wall space was given to representational artists such as Thomas Hart Benton, Grant Wood, Charles Burchfield, Edward Hopper, Reginald Marsh, Raphael Soyer, Jack Levine, Guy Pène du Bois, and Isabel Bishop.

cat. no. 272. Thomas Hart Benton. *Aaron*, 1941.

cat. no. 287. Walt Kuhn. *Clown with Folded Arms,* 1944.

cat. no. 275. Charles Burchfield. *End of the Day,* 1938.

The logical inference to be drawn is that the artistic styles of the 1930s were ones to which an academy was more naturally attracted. A jury was more likely to approve realistic art than modernist work, which dealt to a greater extent with formal problems. Yet, the fact that an increasing number of abstract artists were being included indicated that the Academy was becoming more open-minded.

One of the most vigorous spokesman for the growing feeling of nationalism was Thomas Hart Benton. Despite his preference for an "American" art in the 1930s, Benton had spent his early years, from 1908 to 1919, experimenting with Pointillism and Synchromism. After his change in attitude, he vehemently attacked his former modernist colleagues as "an intellectually diseased lot."[24] *Aaron* (cat. no. 272) demonstrates Benton's emotional response to an old, destitute, black American. It is not so much a portrait as a narrative: the old man's deeply furrowed brow, downward gaze, and ragged clothes tell an effective story of long years of toil and privation. Benton heightens the effect by an exaggerated realism that adds a high degree of expressiveness to the narrative.

Walt Kuhn, like Benton in *Aaron,* chose a traditional portrait format for his painting of *Clown with Folded Arms* of 1944 (cat. no. 287). Both Benton and Kuhn, in their choice of subject, followed a long tradition of representing the poor, the physically deformed, or the socially rejected. Kuhn's choice of subject matter was more radical, although clowns had been the subject of painters from Velázquez to Watteau to Seurat. *Clown with Folded Arms* is typical of Kuhn's style, depicting a figure who gazes out with intense, brooding eyes, alone, set off against a dark background. Both Benton and Kuhn showed careful attention to the sculptural qualities of the figures, a trait which reflects their academic training.

cat. no. 285. Edward Hopper. *East Wind Over Weehawken,* 1934.

cat. no. 293. Reginald Marsh. *End of the 14th Street Crosstown Line,* 1936.

Also associated with the "American Wave" movement was Charles Burchfield, who developed in the 1920s from a grim fantasist to a sympathetic observer of the boredom and loneliness of rural America. In *End of the Day* of 1938 (cat. no 275), Burchfield conveys the mid-winter bleakness of a small town. The rapid rhythm of the shifting planes of the houses and the strong verticals at the right lead the eye directly down the hill. This movement is countered by the line of men slowly trudging upwards, which, in conjunction with the poverty of the clapboard houses, conveys a sense of loneliness and isolation.

A different treatment of the theme of loneliness is found in the work of Edward Hopper. Hopper also recorded life in modern America, painting both the city and countryside and choosing to depict the least prepossessing visual elements of American life. It is as much Hopper's style of painting as his choice of subject that evokes the sensation of loneliness. In *East Wind Over Weehawken* of 1934 (cat. no. 285), Hopper's contrast of the sharply painted houses with the tiny blurred figures at the left illustrates the disconcerting anonymity of modern America, in which the facade of a house provides the only information one has about the inhabitants within. The "For Sale" sign adds to the sense of desolation.

Another painting that deals with a form of loneliness is Reginald Marsh's *End of the 14th Street Crosstown Line* of 1936 (cat. no. 293). Marsh painted the everyday aspects of city life with unabashed honesty. *End of the 14th Street Crosstown Line* shows his interest in the bustling crowds of the streets of lower New York City. Within the crowd there is a sense of isolation, for the various groups of people seem to be totally unaware of one another. The men working in the street are intent upon their job, the strikers hold their signs, and the shoppers push past the strikers, eager to go about their business. The mannequins in the store windows reinforce this image of isolation and self-involvement within a crowd of bustling activity. This type of depiction of city life is reminiscent of that of The Eight, but there is a fundamental difference in attitude between Marsh and an artist like John Sloan or Robert Henri. The work of the earlier realists was more optimistic, often humorous, while Marsh's work presents the grim reality, and often inhumanity, of the city.

In addition to the "American Wave" movement, schools such as Surrealism and Magic Realism emerged in America in the 1930s. Ivan Albright worked in a style of microscopic realism. Although he studied at the Pennsylvania Academy in 1923-1924, it was his prior experience as a medical draftsman in World War I that seems to have most affected him. Albright developed as a figure painter, concentrating on the phenomenon of deterioration. In *Fleeting Time Thou Hast Left Me Old* of 1929-1930 (cat. no. 269), he presents an image that obsesses him: a man in decay, examined in disquietingly minute detail. Like Benton in *Aaron,* Albright treats the subject of old age rather than concentrating on the representation of a specific individual. The two artists' treatments of their subjects are similar in that both works are examples of forms heightened by an exaggerated realism.

Paintings such as these, popular in the 1930s in America, expressed ideals quite different from those of the early modernists. The major trends in American painting had gone from one extreme to the other in the period from 1910 to 1940. Interest in problems of form, composition, and color came to be subordinated to an interest in the depiction of American people and the American way of life, presented in a realistic style. But what of American sculpture during this time period? Did it follow the same directions, or did it develop independently?

American sculptors tended to lag behind American artists in the development of modernistic styles. The accepted academic style at that time relied upon traditional sources and emphasized beauty, elegance, and craftsmanship.[25] By 1910, various alternatives to this style had begun to emerge. Among these were a style based on the dramatic, roughly finished work of Auguste Rodin, a style derived from the stylized sculpture of Paul Manship, itself based on ancient sources, and a realistic style which depicted the everyday people of America engaged in their normal activities.[26]

While there was no single style of avant-garde sculpture at this time, the predominant technique in use from 1920 to 1940 was that of direct carving, practiced first in this country by Robert Laurent and William Zorach. Under the influence of Constantin Brancusi and African Negro sculpture, the direct carvers advocated respect for materials and emphasized personal expression. The requirements of this technique forced sculptors to think in terms of a few simple masses, as it did not allow them to create the intricate designs permitted by other methods of sculpting.

Other sculptors were experimenting with different techniques and styles, many of which were extremely personal abstractions or stylizations. Gaston Lachaise, for instance, created abstract images of women, and Elie Nadelman experimented with Cubist-inspired figures and folk art. John Storrs and Morton Schamberg created examples of constructed sculpture. Both of these men received their early training at the Pennsylvania Academy, Schamberg from 1903 to 1906 and Storrs from 1910 to 1911. It was only after their Academy training, however, that they began to experiment—Storrs with an abstract style based on Cubism, and Schamberg with constructions inspired by the Dada movement.

Their abstract work was quite different from the sculptural style they had been taught at the Academy. The major instructor of sculpture at the Academy was Charles Grafly, who taught there from 1893 until his death in 1929. Formerly a student of Eakins and Anshutz, Grafly practiced a naturalistic style of portraiture and frequently created allegorical figures in the French academic manner. His teaching methods reflected his own style. A firm believer in the practice of teaching the fundamentals of form and technique, Grafly strongly

cat. no. 307. William Zorach. *Affection,* 1933. MUNSON-WILLIAMS-PROCTOR INSTITUTE, UTICA, N.Y.

cat. no. 286. Paul Jennewein. *The Hackney*, 1942.

disapproved of the instruction of "modern" art. As he said, "It does not require any actual knowledge to produce what is called 'modern art.' "[27] Other instructors of sculpture at the Academy in the 1920s and 1930s were Walker Hancock and Albert Laessle, both of whom had studied with Grafly and continued his academic viewpoint.

The Academy museum, like its school, did not give a great deal of encouragement to avant-garde sculpture. Few special exhibitions of sculpture were held during this period, and none was devoted to the works of young, innovative artists. Exhibitions were organized of the work of Anna Coleman Ladd, Charles Grafly, and Anna H. Huntington, all traditional sculptors. The Academy annuals, however, included some modern sculpture. The work of Paul Manship and his follower Paul Jennewein was frequently exhibited, and works by Jo Davidson, Robert Laurent, William Zorach, and Gaston Lachaise were occasionally shown.

Many sculptors continued to work in less daring styles. Naturalistic portraiture was still popular, and one of the best and most sought-after portraitists at this time was Jo Davidson. Although Davidson had traveled to Paris, he never received any formal training, but worked on his own, slowly establishing a reputation as a portraitist. He was aware of the new art but preferred to develop his own personal, naturalistic style. This style is exemplified in his portrait of Samuel M. Vauclain (cat. no. 278) of 1927, which shows his ability to infuse his work with life and spirit without flattering the subject.

Another popular style was based on the stylized, decorative works of Paul Manship, a former Academy student and teacher. Paul Jennewein, a student of Manship, spent five years in Rome, where he evolved a conservative, decorative style based on classical art. This stylized, curvilinear mode is seen in the graceful forms of *The Hackney* (cat. no. 286) of 1942. Reminiscent of Elie Nadelman's *Horse* of about 1911 in its elegance and fluidity, Jennewein's work, like Nadelman's, shows a great concern with the inherent qualities of materials. The highly polished surfaces and graceful shapes of Jennewein's sculptures caused his work to be in great demand from the 1920s through the 1940s.

Concern for the material—its qualities and textures—was a general characteristic of the period for sculptors. It was an important aspect of the direct carving school, which grew in popularity during the 1920s and 1930s. Robert Laurent was one of the first American artists to utilize direct carving, first in wood and then in stone. Although he worked with many materials, his most successful work was in alabaster. *Seated Nude* (cat. no. 289) of 1940 is a superb example of Laurent's sensitivity to this medium; its simplicity and massive volumes give it a classical dignity in addition to its beauty of sculptural form.

Another of the American sculptors who carved directly in stone was William Zorach. After some years as a painter, Zorach turned to sculpture, developing a style of simplified masses and emphatic planes. *Affection* (cat. no. 307) from the early 1930s shows a young girl embracing a dog and illustrates Zorach's appreciation of the relationship between his material and the sculptural volumes of this form. In that sense, it relates to Laurent's *Seated Nude,* which not only deals with the problem of retaining the texture and qualities of the material, but also shows a similar concern with the relationship of void to mass in a monolithic carved figure.

Of those sculptors who evolved their own abstract styles, Gaston Lachaise serves as an important example. Coming to America from Paris in 1906, Lachaise evolved a style based on a conception of woman as the symbol of fecundity. He introduced into American sculpture the recognition of woman as abundantly sensual and continually developed this idea until his late works became boldly sexual and expressionistic. *Equestrienne* of 1918 (cat. no. 288), which probably refers to his childhood visits to the circus,[28] shows his use of full, voluptuous forms, combined with a sinuous flowing line. A comparison with Laurent's work reveals Lachaise's different conception of woman. Lachaise enlarged and rounded the breasts and hips of the figure and repeated these round forms in the body of the horse. Laurent's nude is stockier and more evenly proportioned; she is not presented here with the sexual overtones of Lachaise's figure. Like Laurent, however, Lachaise revealed his interest in the material, and the smooth, polished bronze serves as a further contrast to the more subdued surface of the nude.

The period of American art from 1910 to 1940 immediately preceded that period in which American art first became internationally influential. Early in the century modern art had made its initial impact in the United States, and new formal idioms were developed. This assimilation and adaptation of the new concepts in art that were developing in Europe temporarily displaced the older tradition of realism that had been established in America. But this realistic school, opposed to the dictums of the formalists, was too strong to disappear. Interest in the depiction of America and its people gained in strength during the 1920s and took the lead during the Depression years, and the modernist movement was reduced to an undercurrent.

The Pennsylvania Academy's involvement with modernism in the early twentieth century was as great or greater than other American museums'. However, its role was, on the one hand, serious and pioneering and, on the other, sporadic and detached. The most active Academy modernists were a handful of its own teachers. By example and by word they championed modernism's cause. The Academy's involvement in American Scene realism of the 1930s and 1940s was almost non-existent. It did exhibit the work of American Scene painters in its annuals, but never in group shows. Nor did the Academy make a serious commitment to purchase either American modernism or American Scene canvases. In its unwillingness or inability to recognize or accept significant new developments in American painting and sculpture of the period 1910-1940, the Pennsylvania Academy was foreshadowing its future position on contemporary American art.

Joan M. Marter

CONTEMPORARY AMERICAN ART AT THE ACADEMY

Knowing what to buy has always been a difficult problem. It was difficult in 1897 when the Academy purchased The Cello Player *by Thomas Eakins from among literally hundreds of works hanging in that year's annual exhibition. The challenge is no greater now than it was eighty years ago. And the old acquisition policy of buying contemporary work is still sound. The direction of the future is a continuation of the record of the past. We must look both backward and forward—backward for perspective, forward for the new Eakins.*

Frank H. Goodyear, Jr.,
Curator of the Pennsylvania Academy
of the Fine Arts March 1975

Throughout its history the Pennsylvania Academy of the Fine Arts has purchased outstanding examples of American painting and sculpture. Originally intended as teaching tools, these works now constitute one of the finest public collections of American art. The preeminence of the collection, however, has not been sustained over the past thirty years. The basic conservatism of the Academy's Committee on Collections and Exhibitions,[1] restricted purchase funds, and inflated prices in the art market have resulted in a collection of contemporary art that has not kept pace with mainstream developments. With a few exceptions, the painting and sculpture acquired during the past thirty years reflect a *retardataire* attitude toward contemporary art.

Inadequate finances have always limited acquisitions by the Academy. Until 1969, when the annual exhibition was discontinued, only three small funds were available for the purchase of contemporary works, and these were restricted by the stipulations of the bequests. The Gilpin Fund,[2] initiated in 1879, was intended for the acquisition of works of art exhibited at the Academy, while both the Temple Fund,[3] established in 1880, and the Lambert Fund,[4] initiated in 1912, were limited to the purchase of works by American artists in annual exhibitions. Since most of the paintings and sculpture in the permanent collection were selected from the annuals, these exhibitions had a special significance in the formation of the collection of contemporary art.

The Academy's former director, Joseph Fraser, was proud of the policy of using artists rather than critics or art historians as jurors for the annual exhibitions. In 1964, he wrote:

> The exhibits in these rooms are the end selection of literally thousands of works seen and considered. The final decisions were not made by the Academy Director, or any local art authority, who might have tempered the inclusions to Philadelphia's taste. They are the choices of an out of town jury who are all men of distinction. They are all practicing artists.[5]

Most of the appointed jurors were conservative painters and sculptors who were no longer part of the mainstream of twentieth-century art. Some served as teachers at other art institutions[6] and represented the "academic tradition" in many respects. Jurors after 1950 included Charles Sheeler, Louis Bouché, Isabel Bishop, George Grosz, Yasuo Kuniyoshi, Charles Burchfield, Peter Blume, and Ivan Albright. These artists were members of a generation of American painters active during the 1920s and 1930s. At times, the juries for annuals were composed of members of the Pennsylvania Academy faculty. Even when the jurors were from other institutions, they consistently espoused traditional approaches to art. Thus, few works by Abstract Expressionist painters or Pop artists were exhibited in the annuals becauses these vanguard styles were not acceptable to the jurors.

In sculpture, traditional techniques and materials such as carving in wood or stone were preferred to kinetic sculpture or plexiglass constructions. This is not surprising when one considers the roster of artists who awarded prizes and served as consultants for the acquision of paintings and sculpture. Robert Laurent, William Zorach, and José de Creeft, who served on sculpture juries during the past twenty-five years, were all direct carvers who were part of the avant-garde in American art during the 1920s.

Although the actual selection of works for purchase was made by the Committee on Collections and Exhibitions, an artist-consultant, who was usually a faculty member of the Academy, made recommendations which were generally accepted by the members.[7] One of the reasons for the existence of the permanent collection was its use as a teaching device for the Academy's art faculty, whose bias was essentially conservative. Could the collection have been truly innovative considering the teaching it was intended to support? Thus, the contemporary collection at the Academy served the needs of the faculty and reflected the conservative taste of Philadelphia's collectors, who refrained from responding to the obsession with novelty for its own sake which characterized the art scene in New York.

The formalist aesthetic of the post-war era[8] is not strongly represented in the contemporary collection of the Pennsylvania Academy. Since World War II, the major developments in American art have included Abstract Expressionism,[9] Minimal Art,[10] Pop Art,[11] and Color-Field Abstraction.[12] In these, form and manner were important and the properties of the painting as object were stressed. Optical Painting,[13] Conceptual Art,[14] and Earthworks and Environmental Art[15] were also products of the 1960s.

New Realism,[16] one of the most significant contemporary developments, emerged in the later years of the 1960s. The return to the figure was a solution to the increasingly limited visual vocabulary of Minimal Art of the preceding decade. Artists involved in New Realism often attempt a more direct relationship to the environment in which they live than did the artists working in the abstract styles of the 1950s and 1960s. Although distinct from traditional realism in their indebtedness to the formalist aesthetic of the 1960s and their utilization of photographic technology, the New Realists express some commitment to the human condition.

It is through more recent developments such as New Realism that the Pennsylvania Academy can regain its contact with the mainstreams of American art. Figurative painting and sculpture have always dominated the Academy's permanent collection. New Realism is not the only artistic development of the 1970s, but it is a major trend which has gained the

cat. no. 341. Andrew Wyeth. *Young America,* 1950.

attention of younger artists. Their new figurative and representational works have already been recognized by the Academy, and both faculty and staff have responded favorably to them.[17] Recent acquisitions have included paintings and sculpture by George Segal, Raymond Saunders, Noel Mahaffey, and John Moore.

Because the present exhibition spans the entire history of the Pennsylvania Academy, only twenty-four of the paintings and sculpture acquired by the Academy during the past thirty years could be included. Works by prominent artists which have been purchased by the Academy or donated to the collection have been combined with recent acquisitions which represent some of the current developments in American art. These have been supplemented by a few works borrowed from other art institutions and private collectors in order to present some of the more innovative developments of the post-war era. In this essay, individual works will be discussed in the order of their purchase to chronicle the collecting history of the Academy.

During the late 1940s and early 1950s, the paintings purchased for the collection were selected from annual exhibitions juried by Social Realists and Regionalists. Since their predilection was primarily for humanism in painting, they selected works by artists who shared their commitment to humanism. For example, in 1951 Andrew Wyeth's *Young America* (cat. no. 341) was purchased from the 146th Annual Exhibition. Wyeth's concern for human experience attracted both the jurors and the Committee on Collections and Exhibitions to his work.

In *Young America,* a tempera panel rendered with minute brushstrokes, Wyeth depicted Allen John Lynch riding a bicycle in the countryside near Chadds Ford, Pennsylvania.[18] The youth with his bicycle decorated with foxtails reminded Wyeth of "a mixture of young boy and General Custer."[19] The subject occupies the foreground of the composition and is placed at an oblique angle to the spectator. The low horizon line and neutral sky emphasize the silhouette of the figure and bicycle as a complex linear and planar configuration against a flat color field. The precision of execution and economy of means enhance the abstraction of the composition.

Wyeth has said of his work: "A lot of people say I've brought realism back—they try to tie me up with Eakins and Winslow Homer. To my mind they are mistaken. I honestly consider myself an abstractionist."[20] Despite the inherent abstraction found in *Young America,* it was more likely the subject which interested the Academy; the adventurousness and independence of youth suggested in this picture must have appealed to the humanists on the jury.

In the same year that *Young America* was purchased, the Academy also acquired Karl Knaths's *Number Nine—Eliphaz* (cat. no. 322), one of a series of pictures devoted to characters from the Old Testament. Like most of Knaths's paintings, this one contains some recognizable imagery, but it is essentially an abstract composition. The figure of Eliphaz on the left side of the painting and the surrounding landscape are transformed into color shapes. Heavy lines define the figures and articulate the larger patterns within the composition. The geometry of design, the orchestration of vivid colors, and the spatial interrelationships of elements are not merely decorative but are intended to contribute to the emotional expression. Knaths chose his theme from the Biblical story of the suffering of Job (Job 42:7-8). Eliphaz and his two companions are witnessing a whirlwind from which the Lord speaks to answer Job's plea for vengeance. The artist derived the title of his painting from Tarot card number nine which shows "The Hermit" and symbolizes "wisdom refracted in the corporeal."[21] Knaths used Eliphaz as a respresentative of this card because he offered Job self-knowledge as a panacea for his plight.[22]

Illimited Sequences (cat. no. 339) by Yves Tanguy was awarded the Jennie Sesnan Gold Medal in the annual exhibition of 1953[23] and was purchased for the permanent collec-

cat. no. 322. Karl Knaths. *Number Nine—Eliphaz,* 1948.

cat. no. 339. Yves Tanguy. *Illimited Sequences,* 1951.

tion. Tanguy's reputation as an artist was already firmly established, for he was a Surrealist who had first come into prominence in the late 1920s. Tanguy was born in Paris in 1900. His childhood summers were spent at the family home in Brittany, where the rugged landscape along the seacoast had a profound effect on him. His meticulous rendering of vaguely biomorphic elements populating an imaginary landscape emerged in the 1930s after several years of a freer, more humorous style of floating forms. In 1939, Tanguy came to the United States, where he lived until his death in 1955. This relocation signaled little modification of the personal surrealist idiom he had developed during the 1930s.

Tanguy is considered the most "academic" of all of the Surrealists because of the precision of his technique. But he lacked the pictorial metaphor and inventive imagery of other members of the group.[24] *Illimited Sequences* is typical of his mature style, which remained unchanged for thirty years. The painting features a variety of carefully delineated forms, some of which cast shadows to suggest their volumetric nature. Shifts in scale and overlapping of bonelike elements suggest their location in a fantastic landscape where there is no distinction between earth and sky. The precision of execution, as well as Tanguy's link with a historically important movement of the twentieth century, explains the suitability of this painting for the Academy's collection.

While the Abstract Expressionists were active in New York during the 1950s, the Academy's Committee on Collections and Exhibitions continued to follow the dictates of its jurors and artist-consultants, who were not impressed by works dependent upon pure form and color for their aesthetic validity. Instead of de Kooning's gestural paintings, for example, they favored more personal visions of the plight of all mankind found in the works of Karl Knaths, Philip Evergood, and Rico Lebrun.

Philip Evergood's paintings deal with common human experiences magnified to fantastic proportions. The artist was born in New York City in 1901 and studied at the Slade School in London and at the Art Students League. Although Evergood began painting in the 1920s and gained recognition for his WPA murals in the 1930s, the Academy did not purchase any of his works until 1958.

Threshold to Success (cat. no. 318), painted in 1955, is typical of Evergood's later style. His satire is less bitter than in his earlier works and is mixed with a critical humor. Evergood began this painting as a demonstration piece for a summer school course he was conducting at Duluth University.[25] The final result was an erotic fantasy based on the daydreams of a young athlete with scholarly pretensions. Dressed in a football uniform and mortarboard, the youth clutches a large book stamped with the names of Old Testament heroes, great writers, scientists, and artists. His awakening sexual fantasies involve scantily dressed women who frolic in the upper regions of the painting. Space is drastically compressed, and the proportions of the youth are exaggerated. The heavy-handed satire found in Evergood's earlier paintings has been tempered here by his acceptance of human weakness and the humor with which he approaches his subject.

Rico Lebrun's *The Listening Dead* (cat. no. 323), painted in 1957 and acquired by the Academy in 1962,[26] is characteristic of the artist's concern with man's suffering, torments, and fears. In 1956 Lebrun began to deal with the atrocities at Buchenwald and Dachau in his paintings. Photographic documentation of the grisly happenings in the German concentration camps provided him with a source for his violent imagery. In the tradition of Goya, Orozco, and Picasso, Lebrun's *Listening Dead* depicts the tragedy of the condemned man awaiting his final execution. The artist's skillful draftmanship combined with a subtle use of color suggests the underlying violence and psychological intensity of Lebrun's personal vision. Throughout his lifetime Lebrun remained an articulate and compassionate humanist.

Conrad Marca-Relli's skill with collage and his ability to create monumental paintings in a personal idiom attracted the attention of the Academy, although no works by other

cat. no. 318. Philip Evergood. *Threshold to Success,* 1955-57.

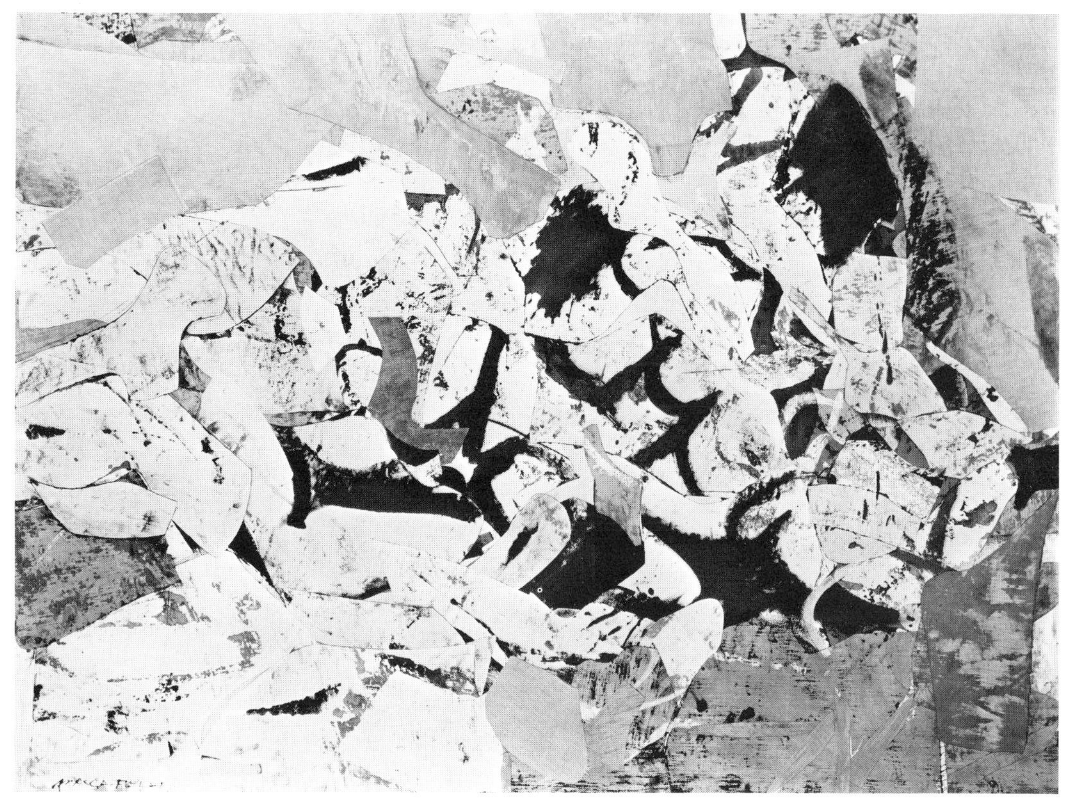

cat. no. 326 Conrad Marca-Relli. *The Hurdle,* 1959.

members of the New York School had yet been purchased for the permanent collection. His collage *The Hurdle* (cat. no. 326) was purchased by the Academy in 1960 and was one of the first works that it acquired by an artist associated with Abstract Expressionism.

Marca-Relli is an American-born painter who has maintained close ties with European art throughout his life. He was born in Boston in 1913 and received his first drawing lessons in Italy. After studying at Cooper Union in 1930, he taught in both the mural and easel divisions of the WPA Federal Arts Project. His paintings of the 1940s featured surrealistic dream spaces dominated by motifs derived from Italian Renaissance architecture in the manner of De Chirico.[27]

In the early 1950s, Marca-Relli's compositions became more abstract, and he began to introduce the collage technique into his work. In 1953 he moved to East Hampton and developed friendships with Willem de Kooning and Jackson Pollock. Some of Marca-Relli's figurative works of that year may have been inspired by de Kooning's *Woman I,* which was created from collage elements.[28]

Marca-Relli's work can be linked to Abstract Expressionism because of his spontaneous shifting and rearranging of collage segments. After a series of pictures in which a single figure was flattened against the picture plane, Marca-Relli's collages became more dynamic. *The Hurdle* represents the last phase of a series of works begun in the mid-1950s, in which biomorphic canvas shapes are interlocked with energetically brushed areas of color. In *The Hurdle,* Marca-Relli established an intricate spatial relationship between the dynamic forms, suggesting figures or animals jumping over a hurdle, and the surrounding space. The static, hieratic arrangements of his earlier studies of single figures are replaced by a dynamic composition involving figures which move diagonally through space. Complex configurations of shapes, textures, and colors are locked in convulsive motion.

At a time when artists were expanding the vocabulary, the scale, and the range of materials utilized in sculpture, the Academy awarded prizes to and purchased much more traditional works. In the annual exhibition of 1960, Lee Bontecou's *Grounded Bird*[29] (cat. no. 312) received the Widener Gold Medal and was purchased for the Academy's collection. Bontecou was born in Providence, Rhode Island, in 1931. From 1952 to 1954 she studied at the Art Students League with William Zorach. *Grounded Bird,* cast in 1957, was produced during her two years of study in Rome under a Fulbright Grant. All of her sculptures from that period involved fantastic birds and animals which were made by attaching terracotta sections to an armature and finishing them in canvas or bronze.[30] In recent years Bontecou has gained international recogition for her constructions of canvas and welded steel.

The direct carver William Zorach was chairman of the sculpture jury for the 1960 annual exhibition; so it is not surprising that both Lee Bontecou and Isamu Noguchi were awarded medals. *Girl Torso* (cat. no. 328), a carving in Greek marble by Noguchi, received the Logan Medal and was purchased for the permanent collection. Noguchi's highly polished marbles were unusual in the 1940s and 1950s, when most sculptors were creating expressionistic surfaces of direct-metal construction or junk sculpture.

Noguchi was born in Los Angeles in 1904 of Japanese-American parentage. His childhood was spent in Japan, where he first became sensitive to natural materials. At a young age, he decided to become a sculptor and studied briefly at the Da Vinci School in New York. The most significant experience of his early years was his work in the studio of Constantin Brancusi in 1927. Under the tutelage of Brancusi, Noguchi increased his facility with wood and stone. During the 1930s he worked for the WPA, creating sculptures, murals, and bronzes. After 1940, Brancusi's carvings were the evident source for most of his work.

Girl Torso was first shown at the Stable Gallery in 1959 in an exhibition which Noguchi considered to be a tribute to Brancusi.[31] Subtle surface modulations suggest the sensuous flesh of a young girl. Partially inspired by fragments of Greek statuary, Noguchi also responded to the shape and texture of the marble itself. Thus, his work is indebted to direct carvers of the twentieth century as well as to Greece and to Japan.

During the 1960s, the Academy's acquisitions reflected limited acceptance of some contemporary developments in American art, although the stipulations of existing purchase funds precluded the acquisition of many works by major artists of the period. The Gilpin Fund did provide money for the purchase in 1962 of *Route Barrée* (cat. no. 313), a mobile by Alexander Calder. Calder was a native of Philadelphia who had many associations with the Pennsylvania Academy; his grandfather, Alexander Milne Calder, and his father, Alexander Stirling Calder, had studied there, and his mother, the former Nanette Lederer, had also been a student.[32] Although the Academy could not claim any direct responsibility for the international success of the creator of the mobile and the stabile, members of the board and the faculty probably thought to honor the memory of Stirling Calder and Milne Calder by acquiring a work by their internationally renowned descendant.

Alexander Calder was born in 1898. He received a degree in engineering before attending the Art Students League in New York. In 1926 Calder went to Paris where he established friendships with some of the leading avant-garde artists, including Piet Mondrian, Jean Arp, Marcel Duchamp, and Joan Miró. Calder created his first kinetic sculpture in 1931, and, soon after, he produced wind-driven mobiles suspended from a single wire. His recent mobiles show few variations from his earliest ones, except for an increase in scale and complexity.

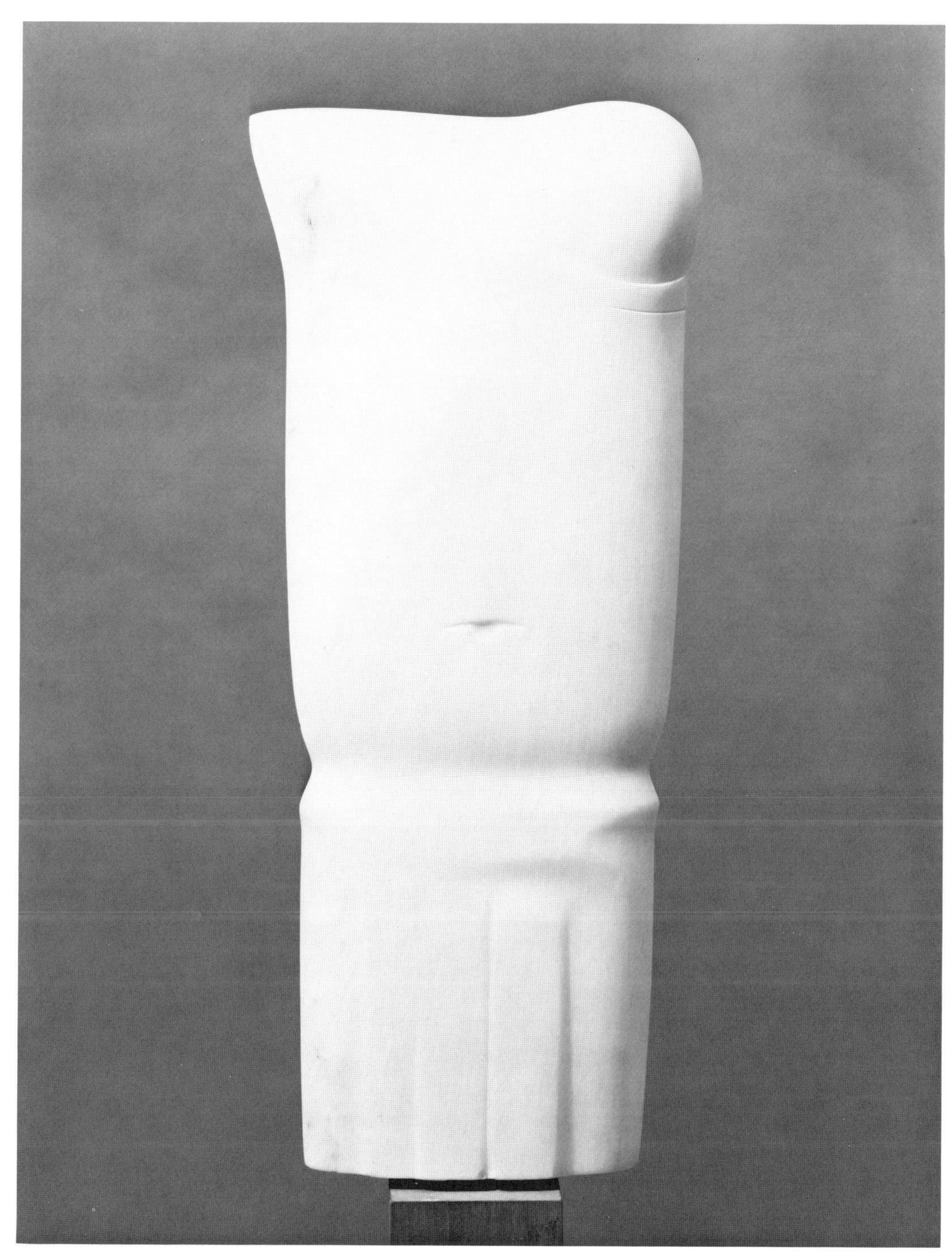

cat. no. 328. Isamu Noguchi. *Girl Torso,* 1958.

Route Barrée is typical of the mobiles constructed by Calder during the past forty years.[33] Organically shaped metal pieces are balanced on the ends of heavy gauge wire rods. Colors, sizes of the metal plates, spatial relationships, and speed of movement vary from element to element, resulting in a complex kinetic configuration. This is one of the few sculptures in the Academy's collection in which the constructivist methods and materials have been utilized.

Like Calder, Stuart Davis was a native Philadelphian whose creative years spanned four decades, but who received little recognition at the Academy until the last years of his life. He received the Temple Gold Medal only five months before his death for *Letter and His Ecol* (cat. no. 314), a major purchase for the Academy's collection.[34]

Stuart Davis was born in 1894. Although he was a student of Robert Henri and a friend of artists of the Ashcan School, Davis considered the Armory Show of 1913 to have been the most profound influence on the future development of his work. During the 1920s, Davis experimented with cityscapes and still-life paintings, combining the vocabulary of Cubism with Fauve color. He painted murals for the WPA during the 1930s. The rhythms of jazz music, which Davis associated with the American landscape, appeared in his works of the 1940s as abstract color harmonies combined with flat patterns and rich textures. In his later years Davis's work became more monumental, but the complex arrangement of elements on a flat surface remained.

About 1963 Davis painted *Letter and His Ecol* which represents his final exploration of word fragments as abstract forms and symbols. The dynamic opposition of precisely defined color areas is the rhythmic counterpart of Davis's view of American life. In other paintings, he utilized popular advertisements and commercial products, providing a link between the American *trompe l'oeil* paintings of the late nineteenth century and American Pop Art of the 1960s.

The acquisition of a painting by Richard Diebenkorn in 1964, the same year that the Stuart Davis was purchased, suggests that the Academy was willing to honor promising younger artists. However, the selection of his *Interior with Doorway* (cat. no. 316) demonstrates the Academy's continuing preference for representational painting.

Richard Diebenkorn was born in Portland, Oregon, in 1922. In the early 1940s he studied at Stanford University and at the University of California. Stationed near Washington, D.C., during the Second World War, he frequented the Phillips Collection where he saw works by Matisse, Bonnard, Picasso, and Braque—artists who were all concerned with the figurative image conceived in abstract terms. In 1946 he enrolled at the California School of Fine Arts in San Francisco, where David Park became his most influential teacher and friend. By the following year he was teaching at the school along with Clyfford Still, Mark Rothko, and Edward Corbett. Contact with these artists caused Diebenkorn to abandon his earlier figurative approach and to adopt a non-objective, expressionistic style.

Diebenkorn's paintings remained abstract until 1955 when he became dissatisfied with the explosive emotionalism of his paintings and returned to a quieter, figurative style. Some critics were disdainful of his new work,[35] but he continued to follow his convictions regarding the need for a recognizable subject in his work. Still, abstraction remained essential to Diebenkorn, even in his representational paintings. Observed motifs were organized into asymmetrical compositions of color areas counterbalanced by the suggestion of pictorial space.[36]

Interior with Doorway is a picture of the studio Diebenkorn built in the hills of Berkeley, California, during the summer of 1956, the time when he made the crucial change in his style.[37] There is a special significance, therefore, to the subject chosen, even though no figures are included in this canvas. Diebenkorn sees his studio, as well as his canvas, as a man-

cat. no. 314. Stuart Davis. *Letter and His Ecol,* ca.1963.

cat. no. 316. Richard Diebenkorn. *Interior with Doorway,* 1962.

made structure within which pictorial events can take place. The observed and the remembered are combined, both from experience and from art.

The darkness of the studio interior contrasts sharply with the rectangular areas of the light formed by the opened door and windows. Geometric forms dominate the painting. Light and dark areas, horizontals, and verticals organize the composition. The predominant grid structure is relieved only by the diagonals of the folding chair and the oblique angle of the transom above the door. An introspective mood is suggested here: personal experiences, the inner life of the artist, and his activities in this studio are implied. Despite its formalist organization, the painting is subjective in approach, exploring the recesses of the artist's mind and the reality outside his door. The artist's presence is implied here. No figures are needed.

Diebenkorn's more recent work, such as the Ocean Park Series,[38] represents the achievement of artistic maturity and the synthesis of his early Abstract Expressionist style with the discipline of his figurative style.

Between 1966 and 1968, several abstract paintings and sculpture were acquired for the collection, including works by Richard Anuskiewicz, Julian Stanczak, Edna Andrade, and Harry Bertoia. The Academy purchased *Interlocking Shadows* (cat. no. 337) by Stanczak, an artist involved in perceptual abstraction, less than a year after five shows devoted to so-called "Optical Art" had been installed in New York.[39] In 1968 Helen Frankenthaler and Seymour Lipton were awarded gold medals in the annual exhibition,[40] further indicating that the Academy was beginning to recognize artists with more innovative, abstract styles. In the same year, the Academy purchased *Systematic Whole* (cat. no. 309) by Richard Anuskiewicz, another artist involved with perceptual abstraction.

Anuskiewicz became the leading American Op artist, but his interest in the interaction of colors in geometric configurations antedates the Op Art movement of the early 1960s. He was born in Erie, Pennsylvania, in 1930. After three years of study at the Cleveland Institute of Art, he went to Yale for instruction with Josef Albers. Under Albers's expert tutelage, Anuskiewicz reevaluated his previous work. A tendency toward precision and symmetry and an interest in the exploration of intricate figure-ground relationships, already apparent in his earlier work, evolved into definitive perceptual studies. Anuskiewicz himself considers Albers's greatest influence on him to have been "making me color sensitive, making me aware of the properties and possibilities of color."[41]

Many of Anuskiewicz's paintings, including the Academy's *Systematic Whole,* are composed of a series of nested squares which produce an optical illusion. These precise linear structures can be viewed as four pyramidal forms or as narrow corridors leading to a distant aperture. Albers favored the square for many of his compositions and explored similar optical effects in his Graphic Tectonics series. *Systematic Whole* is typical of the hard-edged, surgically precise painting which emerged as one of the stylistic alternatives to Abstract Expressionism. The basic illusion, involving variations in luminosity and the kinetic energy of shifting viewpoints, is mostly achieved through line. But the interrelationships of color are orchestrated with a resonance that fortifies the retinal stimulus of line. The picture surface vibrates with linear configurations and color harmonies which are intended to engage the perceptual energies of the beholder.

Edna Andrade, a Philadelphia artist and a graduate of the Pennsylvania Academy, represents a local response to the interest in optical effects in painting. Andrade was born in Portsmouth, Virginia, in 1917. During her years of study at the Academy, she was awarded a Cresson Scholarship for European travel and instruction. In the 1940s and 1950s she worked as a graphic designer and as an instructor in color and design. Presently she is an associate professor at the Philadelphia College of Art.

cat. no. 309. Richard Anuskiewicz. *Systematic Whole,* 1966.

Torsion (cat. no. 308), a painting created by Andrade in 1973, is an example of her personal approach to the formal problems addressed by optical painters. The painting is divided into two opposing rectangular configurations joined by a brilliant yellow strip. Red hemispheres are attached at either end of the yellow band and serve as the points of convergence for a system of lines which radiate at oblique angles from the corners of the rectangles. Diagonal lines change into horizontal lines at points along a curve formed by the conjunction of circular arcs to form the overall configuration of a circle within a square. Although the two rectangular areas suggest movement in space, the yellow strip anchors the composition to the two-dimensional surface.

Harry Bertoia is another local artist who is represented in the Academy's collection. Bertoia served as chairman of the sculpture jury for the 1966 annual, and his metal construction *Tonal* (cat. no. 311) was purchased by the Academy in 1968; it is one of the few non-figurative sculptures in the permanent collection.

Bertoia was born in 1915 in San Lorenzo, Italy. He came to the United States in 1930 and studied at the Detroit Society of Arts and Crafts and the Cranbrook Academy of Art. Before turning to sculpture, Bertoia worked as a furniture designer and graphic artist. He has since created architectural sculpture for public buildings, including a fountain for the Civic Center in Philadelphia.[42]

Tonal is a "musical" sculpture. In this piece, the artist investigated problems of vertical balance and sound. Bertoia has indicated that the work is meant to be touched, "as that is part of the pleasure and is the main reason for its sound-producing form."[43] The artist's experiments with sound in sculpture stem from his lifelong interest in music. He discovered that different tonalities could be produced by using various metals and by varying the length, diameter, and separation of the metal rods. When the tips of the metal rods are touched, vibrations are transmitted through to the metal bases of the sculptures, resulting in a sound.

Bertoia's *Tonal*, an iron and glass work by Italo Scanga, and Rafael Ferrer's *Neon Corner* (cat. no. 319) are the only works in the collection that approximate the non-figurative approach, the economy of means, and the utilization of modern industrial materials found in Minimal sculpture.

The demise of the annual exhibitions was foreshadowed in 1968 by the change to an invitational format. In that year the director chose a jury of three painters and three sculptors who were asked to invite individual artists to exhibit groups of their works. In addition, the deans of Philadelphia's five art institutions were asked to choose thirty works by artists in the Philadelphia area. No provisions were made for unsolicited works. This kind of invitational exhibition was a distinct departure from the Academy's traditional policy of selecting works for the annuals. There had been a certain pride over the years in the fact that any artist could submit his work for consideration by the jury. The purpose of some of the purchase funds, such as the Lambert Fund, was the support of younger, relatively unknown artists. Restructuring of the selection process, therefore, undermined the original intention of the fund donor because the roster of artists was limited to those who had already gained critical attention.

In 1969, the annual exhibitions were discontinued. The increase in operational costs was only one of many factors which resulted in this decision. Before the final annual, thousands of unsolicited works were sent to the jurors; review of these paintings and sculpture was a time-consuming task and an expensive undertaking for the Academy. Moreover, the Academy was also aware that the annual was not adequately representing all of the major developments in contemporary art. In his candid and critical review of the annual exhibition of 1968, John Canaday doubted the alleged impartiality of the artist-jurors:

> Perhaps as painters and sculptors they were victims of defective perception in judging other artists' work, or perhaps they just hadn't been into the galleries recently or perhaps were too loyal to friends.[44]

In the 1970s a resurgence of interest in figurative art gradually began to fuse with other contemporary trends. Artists did not abandon formalist considerations totally, but these concerns were combined with a growing commitment to representational imagery. New Realism has contributed to this revival of the figurative, but even former Pop artists such as Claes Oldenburg and Roy Lichtenstein have favored themes involving human experiences or have returned to more traditional realist imagery. They have joined innovative materials and methods with the representational.

Claes Oldenburg, for example, wants to make works which express his passionate engagement with his environment, but he uses objects of popular culture rather than effigies of humanity to accomplish his intentions. The complexities of life are expressed through the metaphor of commercial products. Oldenburg was originally identified with Pop Art, but his transformation of consumer items is more radical and more intentionally topical than that of most Pop artists. The profound humanism in most of his works sets him apart from other artists using popular icons.

Oldenburg was born in 1929 in Stockholm, Sweden. His childhood was spent in New York City, Oslo, and Chicago. After graduating from Yale in 1950 with a major in art and literature, he became an apprentice reporter in Chicago. From 1952 to 1954 he attended the Art Institute of Chicago. In the late 1950s Oldenburg moved to New York, where he became involved with a group of avant-garde artists initiating a new form of art called "Happenings."[45] In the early 1960s Oldenburg participated in many Happenings which directly involved the audience in the artistic process. After creating stage-props and costumes for these events, he was inspired to plan a major environmental work, *The Store.*[46] In *The Store,* painted replicas of consumer items, food, and familiar household necessities were sold. These items evoked the human being without incorporating his image. Oldenburg continued to produce similar objects throughout the 1960s. He favored soft vinyl or canvas stuffed with kapok for many of his pieces. These large-scale, collapsing objects suggested the weariness of man, the frustration and exhaustion of life itself. Oldenburg wrote:

> Objects are used as characters. They are "handles" I reach for to get my message across. Like the man in *Gulliver's Travels* who speaks through objects, I carry my luggage around. Unlike him, I have museums to transport my load.[47]

Thus Oldenburg's objects serve as surrogates for the human body. Man is evoked through the consumer products, clothes, and food that he uses.

The Soft Baked Potato, Open and Thrown, Scale A (cat. no. 329) would satisfy a Brobdingnagian appetite, but the materials used here distinguish this item from its natural state. The canvas skins of the potato zip open to reveal butter pats which are almost one foot wide. Changes in the materials and the normal scale of his objects are important aspects of Oldenburg's work. His art is involved with change; every time the soft sculptures are moved, their forms are readjusted. Oldenburg views his objects as involving life processes.[48] The fragility of his works suggests the perishable, the transitory nature of life itself. In addition, his objects become more evocative when their scale is increased to colossal dimensions.

Oldenburg's interest in the baked potato dates from the early 1960s. The potato is a soft form which is similar in its natural state to some of the artist's soft sculpture. It carries its own jacket, which can be pulled back or broken, like a banana, to reveal its own insides. *Baked Potato II,* for example, was larger than actual scale and made of burlap soaked in plaster and painted with enamel.[49] The original soft state of the potato was transformed and presented in a "hard" format. Oldenburg wrote about the potato:

> The pleasure of the baked potato, apart from its mass, is in the slitting of the potato—east, west, north, and south—compressing its sides and then laying into the slit a geometric shape of butter and watching it melt.[50]

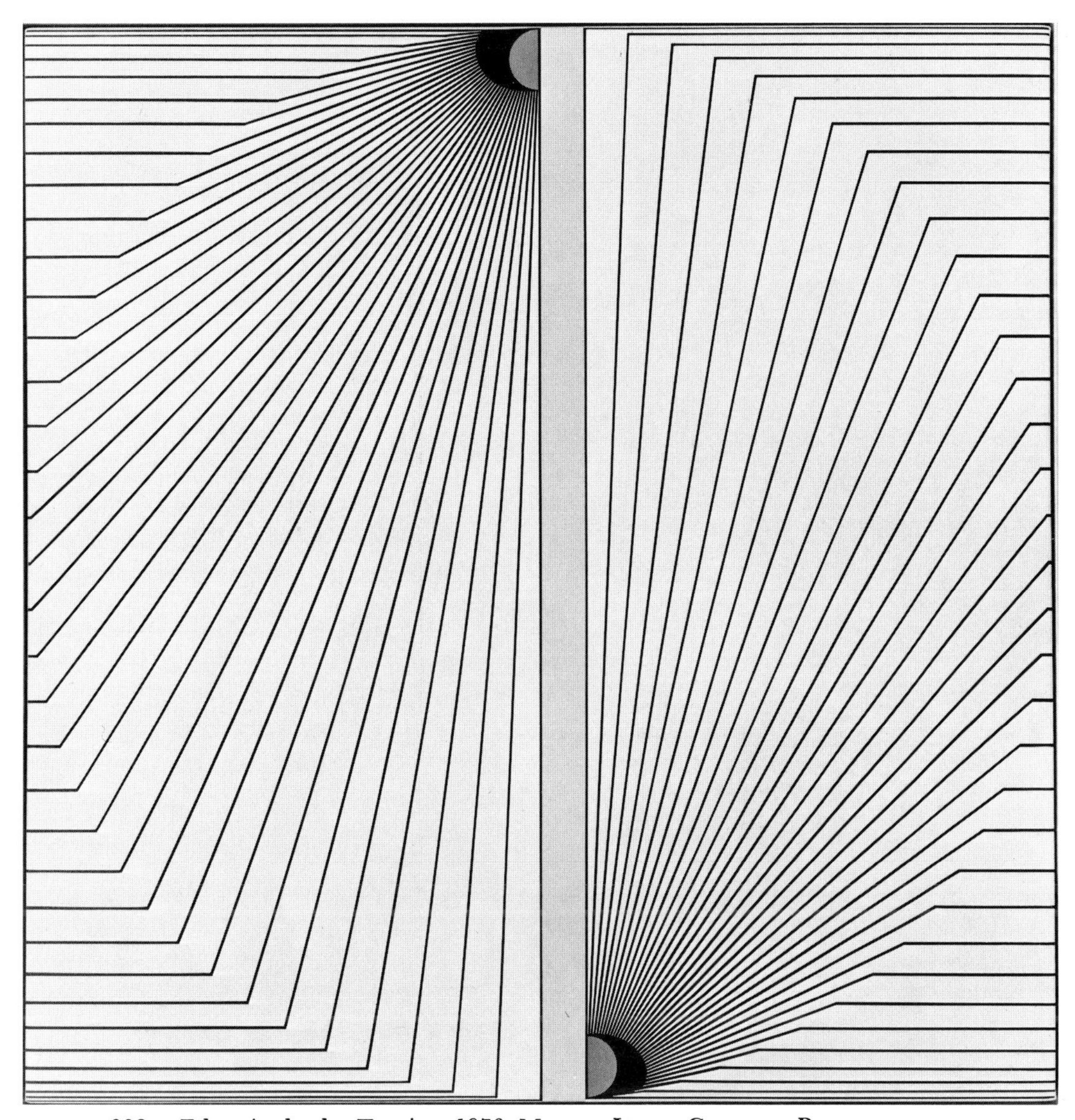

cat. no. 308. Edna Andrade. *Torsion,* 1973. MARIAN LOCKS GALLERY, PHILADELPHIA.

In *Soft Baked Potato, Scale A* the separate pats of butter can be removed so that the sensual experience of slitting open the potato and laying in the butter can be repeated endlessly. The artist has proposed a baked potato as a colossal monument for Grand Army Plaza in New York City.[51] Oldenburg has supplanted the traditional bronze statue of the war hero with a monument representing American dietary delights on a heroic scale.

Although the Academy has yet to acquire a work by Oldenburg, recent acquisitions give evidence that representational art is still the prevailing interest of the Pennsylvania Academy. But it is also evident that representational imagery, especially New Realism, is dominant among contemporary artists on the national scene as well.

New Realism is a very generalized term which encompasses the works of many contemporary artists. Some of these artists are humanistic in their approach, while others represent a continuation of the objective formalist principles of the abstract paintings and sculpture of the 1960s. Of the more humanistic artists working in a figurative style, the Academy has acquired works by George Segal, Tommy Palmore, and Raymond Saunders. These artists use representational imagery but can be linked only indirectly with the New Realists. Their interest in figurative art is not a recent development in their work, nor do they utilize the photographic technology or formalist principles of the New Realists.

George Segal's *Girl Against a Post* (cat. no. 336), a recent acquisition by the Academy, is an example of humanism in contemporary art. Although Segal was identified with Pop Art because he combined plaster figures with actual objects of popular culture, his personal involvement with his subjects and his desire to reveal their inner nature is contrary to the dispassionate approach of most Pop artists. When asked to comment on this sculpture, Segal wrote:

> The *Girl Against a Post* is part of a new series of work in which I'm trying to intensify a merging of matter and spirit. It is important to me that the wood, skin, and clothing have a vividly real texture, that the gesture of the girl ring true to her internal nature as I sense it, that the gesture of the post is locked with the gesture of the girl, that this collection of fragments feels like a whole thing.[52]

Thus, the combination of plaster and wood is not intended simply as a representational image but is meant to suggest the thoughts and feelings of the girl.

Segal was born in 1924 in New York City. He studied at Cooper Union School of Art and Rutgers University. During the early 1950s, Segal produced expressionistic paintings and participated in a number of Happenings which were organized at his New Jersey farm by Allen Kaprow. In 1958 he began experimenting with life-size figures made of wire, plaster, and burlap. By 1960 the artist had given up painting completely and was producing plaster casts made from identifiable human models. His subjects were often members of his own family, artists, and friends. Segal's sculptures also involved locations with which he was familiar: his own home, the local bus depot, gas station, and restaurant.

Segal's sculpture of the 1970s, including *Girl Against a Post,* are often only fragments of human figures and relate only vaguely to the surrounding environment. The sculptures are meant to be hung on a wall like reliefs, rather than placed in an architectural space created by the artist. Segal revitalized the tradition of figurative sculpture in America. Considering the Academy's historical commitment to the figurative, it is highly appropriate for a work by Segal to be included in the permanent collection.

Jack Johnson (cat. no. 335) by Raymond Saunders was also purchased for the Academy's collection in 1974; it was the first in his series of paintings of black culture heroes. A graduate of the Pennsylvania Academy, Saunders adhered to the artistic precepts of his teachers and considered his canvases as vehicles for intensely personal expression. Saunders

cat. no. 329. Claes Oldenburg. *Soft Baked Potato, Open and Thrown, Scale A,* 1970.
THE SIDNEY JANIS GALLERY, NEW YORK.

was born in Pittsburgh, Pennsylvania, in 1934. He studied at the Carnegie Institute of Technology before being awarded a scholarship to the Pennsylvania Academy in 1953. In 1956 he received the Cresson European Travel Fellowship. Saunders received the M. F. A. in 1961 from the California College of Arts and Crafts in Oakland. He has been a visiting artist at the Pennsylvania Academy and the Rhode Island School of Design, and since 1969 he has been professor of painting at California State College.

Although Saunders often exhibits with contemporary black artists who are concerned with racial issues, his interest is in a basic humanism, and he does not require a socio-political message as the *raison d'être* for his paintings.[53] Although Saunders's work has assumed a violent expressionism, his concern with human experience derives from his Academy background. *Jack Johnson* features a truncated figure, brutally cropped and presented among color areas into which his name and dates have been incised.

A sculpture by Duane Hanson would be an appropriate addition to the Academy's collection. Hanson, in the venerable tradition of the Ashcan School, and the Social Realists, prefers democratic, anti-elitist subject matter. The blue-collar worker is Hanson's hero, characterized not just by his appearance but by his activities and the objects which surround him. *Man in Chair with Beer* (cat. no. 321) represents a workman home from a long day on the job. His well-worn shoes and clothing are soiled and sweaty. The man holds a can of beer but appears too exhausted to drink. The discarded evening paper is scattered on the floor.

Hanson's sculptures involve the afflictions which result from life in contemporary America: drug addiction, alcoholism, violence, frustration. In *Man in Chair with Beer* the artist comments on the boring, unrewarding existence of the common laborer. He suggests the futility of an occupation which leaves the worker too tired to enjoy the fruits of his labor.

Hanson was born in 1925 in Alexandria, Minnesota. The artist studied at the Cranbrook Academy of Art and the University of Washington. His early work included experimentation with wood, clay, and metal, and he did not begin working with life-size painted figures until 1967.[54] Hanson's first figures were placed in an environment which the artist created for the works. During the late 1960s his sculptures often involved heavy-handed social commentary, but recently he has stressed the individuality of his sitters. The sculptures invade our space and our lives. Hanson intends the spectator to identify with the figures he creates and, through them, to confront the reality of his own life.

Segal, Saunders, and Hanson are New Humanists. These artists, as well as many others working in a figurative style in the 1970s, are indebted to Abstract Expressionism, Pop Art, and Color-field Abstraction of the preceding decades. The New Humanists are not simply revisionists, although they can be justifiably linked with the Social Realists of the 1930s and 1940s. As Schwartz states in his book, *The New Humanism:*

> Many of the Humanists discussed in this book have roots in the tradition of Social Realism. But unlike the Social Realists, these Humanists offer no view of historical inevitability. Today's Humanist is without dogma, without an encompassing ideology. Because he knows that the future is not predictable or certain, his work incorporates both the confusion and the possibility of our time.[55]

Thus, New Humanism is distinguishable from other humanistic styles because of its freedom from an overriding ideology. Many of the New Realists, however, find it unnecessary and undesirable to impose humanist content on their representational imagery. Their primary concern is the affirmation of visual perception. Although there are individual differences among New Realists, subject matter is a common denominator. All of the artists avoid narrative themes and symbolism. They seek out the banal, the inglorious aspects of

cat. no. 336. George Segal. *Girl Against a Post,* 1973.

cat. no. 335. Raymond Saunders. *Jack Johnson,* 1971.

cat. no. 321. Duane Hanson. *Man in Chair with Beer,* 1973. THE RICHARD BROWN BAKER COLLECTION.

cat. no. 317. Richard Estes. *The Candy Store,* 1969. The Whitney Museum of American Art, New York.

everyday life. Most often, their involvement is with their immediate experiences, indicated by such divergent images as superhighways, store-fronts, studio interiors, and beach scenes. These artists are different from the traditional realists who were also preoccupied with the commonplace. For the New Realist, the boundaries of contemporary American life have been narrowed to the artist's immediate circle of friends and his environment. Technical innovations also separate him from the realist tradition. The utilization of radical and arbitrary cropping, the close-up vantage point, the precision of execution, and the assertion of the flat pictorial surface are the legacy of the reductionist painters of the 1960s. The concern with scale and space intervals and the dispassionate attitude towards subjects can also be linked to television and film of the 1960s and 1970s.

New Realism has helped to destroy the modernist myth that twentieth-century art has been a continuous progression toward pure abstraction. It is to the credit of the Pennsylvania Academy that is has accepted this contemporary development and has purchased works by New Realists soon after they were first exhibited. The Academy owns works by Noel Mahaffey, John Moore (cat. no. 327),[56] and Philip Pearlstein, all of which were acquired during the past five years.

Richard Estes's *Candy Store* (cat. no. 317) is an interesting counterpart to *Atlanta, Georgia* (cat. no. 325) by Noel Mahaffey, a graduate of the Academy. Both paintings involve the urban landscape. Estes includes a close-up of a single shop window in New York City. Mahaffey presents an aerial view of the unremarkable skyline of Atlanta at twilight. Precision of brushwork, cropping of forms, and lack of compositional focus are common to both works.

Estes comes to terms with the realities of everyday experience, but with a dispassionate eye. He wrote:

> Places and things can, if you look at them objectively as forms and colors divorced of their function, or threat, or whatever, provide unexpected possibilities for painting.[57]

This concern with objectivity resulted in such paintings as *Candy Store,* which conveys no special content or narrative suggestion. It incorporates image and reflection of image and transforms both into a flat pictorial pattern. Fluorescent light bars inside the store form a series of chevrons, a representational equivalent of the abstract forms favored by Kenneth Noland and other Post-Painterly Abstractionists. Reflections of buildings, automobiles, and pedestrians compete with the signs pasted on the store window to limit the illusion of spatial recession. Estes uses photographs only as an equivalent of preliminary sketches in the preparation of his paintings. The paintings are constructed after a careful selection of perceptual data.

Noel Mahaffey was born in St. Augustine, Florida, in 1944 and attended art classes at the Dallas Museum of Fine Arts in 1959. He studied at the Pennsylvania Academy from 1962 to 1966 and continues to reside in Philadelphia. As a product of the Academy's art instruction, he demonstrates that the realist tradition can be effectively linked to New Realism.

Mahaffey's paintings resemble large-scale postcards of American cities.[58] *Atlanta, Georgia* is a panoramic view of an urban landscape. The oblique angle of vision and the distant viewpoint prevent direct involvement with the subject. The artist is mindful of the formalist aesthetic. Dark silhouettes form a flat pattern against an unmodulated sky; the buildings are cropped; no compositional focal point disturbs the pictorial surface. The cool, precise brushwork, lacking expressive modulation, is a product of the hard-edged canvases of the 1960s.

It is particularly appropriate that one of the Academy's promised gifts is a painting by Philip Pearlstein, *Two Female Models—on Hammock and Seated on Floor* (cat. no. 332). The selection of his frankly observed, large-scale depiction of nude models sug-

cat. no. 332 Philip Pearlstein. *Two Female Models—On Hammock and Seated on Floor,* 1974. Private Collection.

cat. no. 325. Noel Mahaffey. *Atlanta, Georgia,* 1971.

gests the new maturity of vision at the Pennsylvania Academy. Ninety years ago Thomas Eakins was dismissed from the faculty for advocating the use of the naked male as a class model. Today Pearlstein juxtaposes male and female nudes with about as many prurient overtones as two pieces of fruit in a basket. Pearlstein takes the ultimate risk in his paintings —the use of the human figure as a still-life object. The artist's principal concern is with the problems of painting, and he denies any evocative or expressive intention in his depiction of nudes. The models are shown slouching, sitting, posing with a suggestion of the psychic detachment of the act. Formalist concerns dominate Pearlstein's compositions, and the nudes have as much expressive force as "academies," those dispassionate drawings of uncomfortably posed nude models by generations of art students.

Philip Pearlstein was born in 1924 in Pittsburgh, Pennsylvania. After several years studying painting and design at Carnegie Institute of Technology, he went to New York in the early 1950s. Pearlstein combined painting and design work with study in art history at New York University. The major influence on his paintings up to 1960 was Abstract Expressionism. Aside from a few figurative paintings, his most successful works were expressionistic landscapes. These paintings seem indebted to de Kooning or Soutine in the violence of their brushwork, but the colors are more somber. After studying in Italy on a Fulbright Grant in 1958, Pearlstein began to work in a more realistic style. In 1962 he showed his first group of figurative works.[59] From that year until the present, Pearlstein has continued to paint directly from the model.

Two Female Models—on Hammock and Seated on Floor gives evidence of his use of harsh studio lighting which bleaches out skin tones and casts strong shadows. Radical cropping, close-up vantage point, large scale, and precision of execution link this painting with New Realism. Unlike many of the New Realists, Pearlstein does not use a camera, even for preliminary studies. His painting is created from many separate visual experiences. In this painting he includes a seated woman, a reclining woman, and a pattern of shadows which alludes to the gentle motion of the hammock. The implied motion of the reclining nude is contrasted with the stability of the seated figure. Pearlstein suggests the passage of time here, because the painting was produced over an extended period in which both model and hammock shifted position. Pearlstein reminds us that his paintings are far removed from snapshots. The flat pictorial surface asserted by the immediacy of the models in the foreground of the composition and the pattern of cast shadows opposes the illusion of space suggested by the oblique line of the baseboard and the interior modeling of the figures.

During the 1970s New Realism has continued as a significant aspect of the contemporary art scene. The Academy has recognized that this new representational style has roots in the past. Thus it is very appropriate for the Pennsylvania Academy to unite tradition with modernity by acquiring paintings by the New Realists. The Academy has purchased excellent paintings and sculptures throughout its history. By selecting fine examples of recent American art, the Academy will continue its commitment to artists mindful of the academic tradition and other contemporary styles.

NOTES

A HISTORY OF THE PENNSYLVANIA ACADEMY OF THE FINE ARTS, 1805-1976

1. Rembrandt Peale, "Reminiscences: Exhibitions and Academies," *The Crayon,* 1 (January-June 1855), 290.
2. "Review of the Second Annual Exhibition," *The Port Folio,* 8 (July 1812), 18.
3. Charles Willson Peale to Thomas Jefferson, June 13, 1805, CWP Letterbook VI, Collection of the American Philosophical Society, Philadelphia.
4. Charles Willson Peale to Benjamin H. Latrobe, June 21, 1805, CWP Letterbook VI, Collection of the American Philosophical Society, Philadelphia.
5. The first twelve directors of the Pennsylvania Academy of the Fine Arts (cited hereafter as PAFA) included William Tilghman, William Rawle, John R. Coxe, Joseph McKean, John Dorsey, William Poyntell, Joseph Hopkinson, Thomas James, Charles Willson Peale, Moses Levy, William Meredith, and William Rush.
6. For a list of the antique plaster casts ordered by PAFA, see Anna Wells Rutledge, *Cumulative Record of Exhibition Catalogues. The Pennsylvania Academy of the Fine Arts, 1807-1870* (Philadelphia, 1955), p. 1.
7. A report of the Society of Artists, printed in Rutledge, p. 2, records that "from the nature of the charter of that institution [PAFA], and a variety of other circumstances, it was found impracticable to unite."
8. PAFA Board Minutes, May 20, 1811. All of the PAFA minutebooks are located in the Academy archives.
9. For a complete history of this association, see Frank Goodyear, Jr., *Pennsylvania Academicians* (exhibition catalogue, PAFA, March-April, 1973).
10. For details of the grievances, see "Memorial of the Resident Artists of Philadelphia" (ms.), 1828, PAFA Archives. See also William Dunlap, *A History of the Rise and Progress of the Arts of Design in the United States* (1843; reprint ed., New York, 1969), vol. 1, p. 422.
11. John Neagle to Joseph Hopkinson, March 10, 1829, PAFA Archives.
12. Joseph Hopkinson, *Annual Discourse delivered before the Pennsylvania Academy of the Fine Arts on the 13th of November, 1810* (Philadelphia, 1810), p. 6.
13. PAFA Board Minutes, December 26, 1807.
14. Like Dorsey, William Strickland was a member of the Academy's Board of Directors, serving from 1819 to 1846. It should be noted that Thomas Sully proposed the erection of a west wing in the 1820s, but his plan was never approved.
15. Quoted in Dunlap, vol. 2, p. 176.
16. Henry D. Gilpin, *An Annual Discourse before the Pennsylvania Academy of the Fine Arts on the 29th of November, 1826* (Philadelphia, 1827), unpaged.
17. "Report of the Board of Directors . . . to the Stockholders' Meeting" (ms.), June 2, 1845, PAFA Archives.
18. *Public Ledger and Daily Transcript,* June 13, 1845.
19. *The Illustrated London News,* July 19, 1845, p. 37.
20. A. B. Durand to John F. Lewis, May 3, 1854, PAFA Archives.
21. Henry D. Gilpin to John F. Lewis, July 21, 1854, PAFA Archives.
22. Ibid.
23. "Sketchings: Pennsylvania Academy," *The Crayon,* 3 (July 1856), 217-18.
24. PAFA Board Minutes, May 30, 1849.
25. "Sketchings: Domestic Art Gossip," *The Crayon,* 4 (June 1857), 186.
26. PAFA Board Minutes, December 24, 1867.
27. PAFA, *Report of the Board of President and Directors to the Stockholders, June 2, 1851* (Philadelphia, 1851), pp. 5-15.
28. PAFA, *Proceedings of the Annual Meeting of the Stockholders, June 4, 1855* (Philadelphia, 1855), p. 9.
29. "Special Report to the Directors," bound into the PAFA Board Minutes, January 16, 1865.
30. *Inauguration of the New Building of the Pennsylvania Academy of the Fine Arts, 22 April 1876* (Philadelphia, 1876), p. 16.
31. "Directors Report to the Stockholders," PAFA Board Minutes, February 5, 1877.
32. PAFA Board Minutes, February 9, 1885.
33. See Frank Goodyear, Jr., and Carolyn Diskant, "Harrison Collection," in *The Beneficent Connoisseurs* (exhibition catalogue, PAFA, January-February 1974).
34. PAFA Board Minutes, March 11, 1901.
35. The original version of Craig's *Evening* was lost in the gallery fire of April 8, 1886. The replica was given to the Academy by the artist in 1887.
36. PAFA Board Minutes, January 10, 1887.
37. PAFA Board Minutes, March 12, 1906.
38. "Directors Report to the Stockholders," PAFA Board Minutes, February 5, 1877.
39. See [William C. Brownell], "The Art Schools of Philadelphia," *Scribner's Monthly,* 18 (May-October 1879), 737-50; Fairman Rogers, "The Schools of the Pennsylvania Academy of the Fine Arts," *The Penn Monthly,* 12 (January-December 1881), 453-62.
40. PAFA Board Minutes, January 18, 1879.
41. Quoted in E. V. Lucas, *Edwin Austin Abbey, Royal Academician: The Record of His Life and Work,* (New York, 1921), vol. 1, p. 13.
42. A. Stirling Calder to Joseph Fraser, 1939, PAFA Archives.
43. PAFA Board Minutes, April 8, 1886.
44. PAFA Board Minutes, February 2, 1898.
45. Thomas Anshutz to Edward Coates, May 15, 1893, PAFA Archives.
46. See Milton Brown, *The Story of the Armory Show* (New York, 1963), p. 28.

THE EDUCATION OF THE AMERICAN ARTIST

1. Kenneth C. Lindsay, *The Works of John Vanderlyn* (exhibition catalogue, University Art Gallery, State University of New York, Binghamton, 1970), p. 8.

2. Edward J. Nygren, "Art Instruction in Philadelphia, 1795-1845" (Master's thesis, University of Delaware, 1969), pp. 33-38. Throughout this essay, I am indebted to this exceptional scholarly work for factual and conceptual information.

3. For the history of the American Academy of Fine Arts, see Theodore Sizer, "The American Academy of Fine Arts," in M. B. Cowdrey, *American Academy of Fine Arts and American Art-Union* (New York, 1953), pp. 3-93; Nancy Elizabeth Richards, "The American Academy of Fine Arts, 1802-1816, New York's First Art Academy" (Master's thesis, University of Delaware, 1965).

4. For the history of the National Academy of Design (hereafter cited as NAD), see Thomas S. Cummings, *Historic Annals of the National Academy of Design* (Philadelphia, 1865); Lois Marie Fink and Joshua C. Taylor, *Academy: The Academic Tradition in American Art* (exhibition catalogue, National Collection of Fine Arts, Washington, D.C., 1975).

5. For the history of the Art Students League, see Frank Waller, "School History," in *First Report of the Art Students League of New York* (New York, 1886); Marchal E. Landgren, *Years of Art: The Story of the Art Students League of New York* (New York, 1940).

6. Christian Schussele, "To the Committee on Instruction of the Academy of Fine Arts" (ms.) [June 1877], PAFA Archives.

7. "Programme of Study of the Antique at the Pennsylvania Academy of the Fine Arts" [1877?], PAFA Archives.

8. See, for example, PAFA Committee on Instruction Minutes, December 5, 1868, and NAD Minutes, May 11, 1864, NAD Archives, made available through the generosity of Alice Melrose.

9. "Mr. DeCamp's Report," in Museum of Fine Arts, School of Drawing and Painting (hereafter cited as MFA School), *Tenth Annual Report . . .* (Boston, 1886), p. 12.

10. For a discussion of life drawing in European art academies, see Nikolaus Pevsner, *Art Academies Past and Present* (Cambridge, 1940); Albert Boime, *The Academy and French Painting in the Nineteenth Century* (New York, 1971); and A. Boime, *Strictly Academic: Life Drawing in the Nineteenth Century* (exhibition catalogue, University Art Gallery, State University of New York, Binghamton, 1974). For a discussion of life classes in America during the nineteenth century, see "Talks with Artists (Lemuel Wilmarth)," *The Art Amateur,* 16 (January-March 1887), 30-31, 78.

11. Nygren, pp. 69-74.

12. Cummings, pp. 134, 185, 228; Fink and Taylor, pp. 31-32.

13. Nygren, pp. 139, 141; Cummings, pp. 256-60; PAFA, "Distribution of Studies for each evening through the six months, beginning October 1, and ending with the close of March" [1856], PAFA Archives.

14. The introduction of the female model came quite early to America, since the female model was not common in European schools until the 1850s, a decade after its appearance here (Pevsner, p. 231). The female model was used at the NAD during the 1840s (Fink and Taylor, p. 32) and at PAFA by 1856 (Nygren, pp. 141-42). Christian Schussele suggested a ratio of three male for every female model at PAFA (Schussele, "To the Committee on Instruction"). Eakins encouraged the recruitment and use of female models (Gordon Hendricks, *The Life and Work of Thomas Eakins* [New York, 1974], pp. 104-5).

15. Quoted in [William C. Brownell], "The Art Schools of Philadelphia," *Scribner's Monthly,* 18 (September 1879), 744-45.

16. Nygren, p. 52, quotes Nicholas Biddle's letter to PAFA, November 20, 1805, which discusses the inclusion of the Houdon in Biddle's first shipment of casts to the Academy; Frank H. Goodyear, Jr., *Pennsylvania Academicians* (exhibition catalogue, PAFA, March-April 1973), p. 3.

17. Cummings, pp. 33, 114-16.

18. Cummings, p. 185; PAFA, "Distribution of Studies"; PAFA Committee on Instruction Minutes, October 12, 1857.

19. PAFA Board Minutes, November 12, 1860 and January 14, 1861.

20. "Programme of Anatomical Studies at the Pennsylvania Academy of the Fine Arts," 1868-69, PAFA Archives. Lectures on sexual differences were omitted by 1880 (Hendricks, pp. 129-30).

21. NAD Minutes, January 17, 1865. William Rimmer (1816-79) was a painter and sculptor who practiced medicine between 1855 and 1863. He lectured on anatomy in Boston and Lowell, Massachusetts, from 1864 to 1866, in Providence, Rhode Island, from 1871 to 1873, and at the art school of the Museum of Fine Arts in Boston from 1877 to 1879 (Truman H. Bartlett, *The Art Life of William Rimmer* [Boston, 1882]).

22. NAD Minutes, May 9, 1872.

23. MFA School, *Third Annual Report . . .* (Boston, 1879), pp. 12-13.

24. F. Waller, *Art Students League Report on Art Schools* (New York, 1879), p. 26.

25. Schussele, "To the Committee on Instruction."

26. The city dog pound saved stray dogs for the PAFA students' dissections (Superintendent of the City Pound and Shelter to PAFA, February 3 and 18, 1879, PAFA Archives). The Zoological Society provided a cadaver of a lioness for study purposes (PAFA Committee on Instruction Minutes, November 1885).

27. [Brownell], "Art Schools of Philadelphia," 743; Dr. W. W. Keen, "Report" (ms.), April 7, 1877, PAFA Archives.

28. Hendricks, p. xxvi; Fink and Taylor, pp. 117-18; Sandra Denney Heard, *Thomas P. Anshutz, 1851-1912* (exhibition catalogue, PAFA, 1973), p. 18.

29. The National Academy had great difficulty convincing its members to participate in such a program. See Cummings, pp. 124-25, 127, 195-96, 231, 235; W. Brownell, "The Art-Schools of New York," *Scribner's Monthly,* 16 (October 1878), 766-67; and Sigma, "A Philadelphia Art School," *The Art Amateur,* 10 (January 1884), 32.

30. PAFA Board Minutes, November 12, 1855. The Anglo-American genre painter and sculptor Robert Wylie served as curator of the Pennsylvania Academy until 1863, when he went to France to pursue his artistic studies. He continued to exert a tremendous influence on American artists, many of whom were Philadelphians who would have known him personally or by reputation from his Academy years. For a biographical statement, see A. V. Butler, "Robert Wylie," *The Aldine,* 9, no. 2 (1878), 77-78.

    Thomas S. Cummings was devoted to the National Academy. He served as its treasurer for forty years and as its vice-president for seven years; he also compiled its history. During the 1840s and 1850s, he ran a private art school in New York (Cummings, pp. 194-95; Fink and Taylor, pp. 112-14).

31. Cummings, pp. 256-60; PAFA Committee on Instruction Minutes, January 8 and February 13, 1856; PAFA, "Distribution of Studies."

32. Pevsner, pp. 204-20. For a discussion of Düsseldorf as an educational center for American artists, see Wend von Kalnein and Donelson F. Hoopes, *The Düsseldorf Academy and the Americans* (exhibition catalogue, The High Museum of Art, Atlanta, Georgia, 1972).

33. PAFA Board Minutes, February 10 and May 10, 1868; Nygren, p. 147; NAD Minutes, January 3, 1870. For information on Schussele, see George W. Dewey, "C. Schussele," *Sartain's Magazine,* 10 (June 1852), 462-63; Rev. George H. Johnston, *A Memorial Sermon to Christian Schussele, for Eleven Years Professor of Drawing and Painting in the Pennsylvania Academy of the Fine Arts, Philadelphia* (Philadelphia, 1879).

34. For the course of action taken by the Pennsylvania Academy during this critical period, see PAFA Board Minutes, June 6 and November 14, 1870; January 12 and April 10, 1871; May 13 and July 1872; and December 13, 1875.

35. PAFA Board Minutes, November 13, 1871.

36. For a discussion of these copying activities, see Margaret Bertha Wright, "Copyists at the Louvre," *The Art Amateur,* 2 (May 1880), 116-17.

37. Edward Biddle and Mantle Fielding, *The Life and Works of Thomas Sully (1783-1872)* (Philadelphia, 1921), p. 360, no. 2325.

38. PAFA, "Regulations Relating to Painting in the Galleries of the Pennsylvania Academy of the Fine Arts. From Pictures owned by the Institution" [c. 1868-69], PAFA Archives.

39. A distinction must be made between the theoretical and practical aspects of the painter's education. Theoretical training was certainly offered earlier than 1870. The Society of Artists in Philadelphia planned occasional lectures on painting; it is not known if they were actually given (Nygren, pp. 76-77). As early as 1827, Samuel F. B. Morse was designated professor of painting at the National Academy; his responsibilities seem to have been limited to theoretical lectures (Cummings, p. 175).

40. Pevsner, p. 232; Boime, *The Academy,* p. 4.

41. NAD Minutes, November 12 and 30, 1865. In light of Düsseldorf's preeminence in the development of the master class and painting class, it is interesting that a small painting class for advanced students would have been suggested by Leutze, who spent much of his career working and teaching in that city.

42. PAFA Board Minutes, February 8 and November 8, 1869; PAFA Committee on Instruction Minutes, December 13, 1869.

43. NAD Board Minutes, November 10, 1869.

44. NAD Minutes, February 9, 1870, January 13 and February 3, 1873.

45. PAFA Board Minutes, April 9, 1877.

46. Quoted in [Brownell], "Art Schools of Philadelphia," 740-41.

47. Art Students League of New York, *Circulars of 1885-86* (New York, 1885), pp. 7-8.

48. MFA School, *Third Annual Report,* pp. 6-7.

49. MFA School, *Fourth Annual Report . . .* (Boston, 1881), p. 3.

50. MFA School, *Fifth Annual Report . . .* (Boston, 1882), p. 4.

51. NAD Minutes, May 10, 1882, May 28 and November 26, 1883.

52. Schussele, "To the Committee on Instruction."

53. Unsigned ms. in Eakins's hand, October 8, 1883, PAFA Archives.

54. Brownell, "Art-Schools of New York," 771.

55. NAD Minutes, November 12, 1883 and January 31, 1884.

56. Art Students League of New York, *Circulars of 1885-86,* p. 8; Waller, "School History," pp. 28, 32-33. By the mid-1880s the portrait class at the League was designated the "Head Class" and was one of the most popular of the many painting classes offered there.

57. Schussele, "To the Committee on Instruction"; [Brownell], "Art Schools of Philadelphia," 742; PAFA Board Minutes, October 11, 1886; PAFA Committee on Instruction Minutes, December 26, 1887; "Instructors" (typed list), n.d., PAFA Archives.

58. NAD Minutes, December 20, 1878 and January 17, 1881.

59. PAFA, *Ninety-third Annual Report* (Philadelphia, 1900), p. 16.

60. Fink and Taylor, pp. 30-31, 110. The activities and vague histories of such offshoots of the National Academy as the Sketch Club (founded 1829), the Artists' Sketching Club (1844-c. 1847), and the New York Sketch Club (founded 1847) are discussed in Cummings, pp. 110-13, 175-76, 198, 202. Several examples of sketches made at the meetings of these clubs are preserved in the Karolik Collection at the Museum of Fine Arts in Boston, at the Yale University Art Gallery, and at the Addison Gallery of American Art. Informal studio meetings for the purpose of sketching are discussed in Cummings, p. 267.

61. Boime, *The Academy,* pp. 43-47.

62. Waller, "School History," p. 28.

63. PAFA Board Minutes, October 14, 1878; "Sketch Class" (ms.), 1878, PAFA Archives; MFA School, *Third Annual Report,* p. 15; MFA School, *Fourth Annual Report,* p. 3.

64. Daniel Huntington, "President's Annual Address," NAD Minutes, May 8, 1878.

65. For the history and activities of these clubs, see Florence N. Levy, ed., *American Art Annual 1898* (New York, 1899). For more specific treatments, con-

sult: for the Philadelphia Sketch Club, Henry Russell Wray, "A Bohemian Art Club," *The Quarterly Illustrator,* 1 (April-June 1894), 150-62; for the Salmagundi Club, *Art Digest,* 16 (November 5, 1941), 20; for the Tile Club, Mahonri S. Young, "The Tile Club Revisited," *The American Art Journal,* 2 (Fall 1970), 81-91; for Boston art clubs, Sigma, "The Art Clubs of Boston," *The Art Amateur,* 9 (October 1884), 100-102; for the Kit Kat Club, Nym Crinkle, "Round About the Kit Kat," *The Quarterly Illustrator,* 2 (October-December 1894), 361-71.

66. MFA School, *Seventh Annual Report . . .* (Boston, 1883), p. 11; *Ninth Annual Report . . .* (Boston, 1884), p. 4.

67. Waller, "School History," p. 34; Art Students League of New York, *Circulars of 1885-86,* p. 9.

68. PAFA, *Circular of the Committee on Instruction, 1882-1883* (Philadelphia, 1882), p. 10; *Circular of the Committee on Instruction, 1889-1890* (Philadelphia, 1889), p. 10.

69. *Catalogue of the Sixty-fifth Annual Exhibition* (NAD, New York, 1890), p. 11.

70. NAD Minutes, November 9, 1885.

71. PAFA, *Eighty-eighth Annual Report* (Philadelphia, 1895), p. 11; *Eighty-ninth Annual Report* (Philadelphia, 1896), p. 11; *Ninetieth Annual Report* (Philadelphia, 1897), p. 15.

72. Cummings, p. 159.

73. These purchases began in 1856 and ceased in 1869, since a sufficiently large collection had been amassed (PAFA Committee on Instruction Minutes, September 19, 1856; PAFA Board Minutes, February 8, 1869).

74. PAFA Committee on Instruction Minutes, December 3, 1869.

75. "Costume Classes," *The Art Amateur,* 13 (October 1885), 94.

76. NAD Board Minutes, November 28, 1881 and January 23, 1882; MFA School, *Fourth Annual Report,* p. 5; *Fifth Annual Report,* p. 5; *Sixth Annual Report . . .* (Boston, 1882), pp. 6-7.

77. PAFA, "Rules of the Class for the Study of the Living Model, of the Pennsylvania Academy of the Fine Arts" [1856], PAFA Archives; PAFA Board Minutes, June 13, 1859.

78. MFA School, *Twenty-fifth Annual Report . . .* (Boston, 1901), pp. 10-11; PAFA Board Minutes, February 5, 1877.

79. Schussele, "To the Committee on Instruction"; PAFA Board Minutes, October 8, 1877 and June 9, 1884.

80. PAFA Board Minutes, October 14 and December 8, 1879; Fairman Rogers, *The Schools of the Pennsylvania Academy of the Fine Arts,* reprinted from *The Penn Monthly* for June 1881 (Philadelphia, 1881), p. 7.

81. A. Stirling Calder, "Reminiscences of PAFA, 1886-1889" (ms.) [1939], PAFA Archives. See also [Brownell], "Art Schools of Philadelphia," 742; Sigma, "A Philadelphia Art School," *The Art Amateur,* 10 (January 1884), 34.

82. MFA School, *Third Annual Report,* p. 12; *Twenty-fifth Annual Report,* pp. 10-11.

83. The modeling class was not re-established at the NAD until 1907; the first women's modeling class was held in 1915 (Fink and Taylor, p. 117).

84. MFA School, *Twenty-fifth Annual Report,* pp. 10-11; John C. Van Dyke, "The Art Students League of New York," *Harper's New Monthly Magazine,* 83 (October 1891), 700; Levy, ed., *American Art Annual 1898,* p. 307; Wayne Craven, *Sculpture in America* (New York, 1968), p. 435.

85. PAFA Board Minutes, September 6 and 28, 1892; February 27, 1893; and February 28 and November 28, 1894.

86. The American Barbizon painters are treated in Peter Bermingham, *American Art in the Barbizon Mood* (exhibition catalogue, National Collection of Fine Arts, Washington, D.C., 1975).

87. Theodore C. Grannis, "The Art Schools of America," *The Aldine,* 9, no. 2 (1878), 66-67; "Mr. Crowninshield's Report," in MFA School, *Seventh Annual Report,* p. 11; Frederic Crowninshield, "The American Art Student," *American Architect and Building News,* 9 (June 24, 1882), 300; "Mr. Crowinshield's Report," in MFA School, *Fifth Annual Report,* p. 14.

88. J. Nilsen Laurvik, "The Art Students League Summer School," *International Studio,* 43 (May 1911), lxi-lxiv.

89. W. H. deB. Nelson, "New School on Old Ground at Chester Springs, Pennsylvania," *International Studio,* 62 (July 1917), xiv-xv; PAFA, *Ninety-third Annual Report* (Philadelphia, 1900), p. 16.

90. I am indebted to Ronald G. Pisano, author of the historic essays in *The Students of William Merritt Chase* (exhibition catalogue, Heckscher Museum, Huntington, New York, and The Parrish Art Museum, Southampton, New York, 1973), both for his published ideas and those shared orally with me.

91. "Learning to Draw—Landscape Sketching," *The Art Student,* 4 (May 1894), 11; Marguerite Tracy, "A Foreground Figure," *The Quarterly Illustrator,* 2 (October-December 1894), 407-13; John I. H. Baur, *Theodore Robinson, 1852-1896* (exhibition catalogue, The Brooklyn Museum, New York, 1946), pp. 10, 41-42; William Innes Homer, *Robert Henri and His Circle* (Ithaca and London, 1969), pp. 72-73.

92. Charles M. Skinner, "Art Study Out-of-Doors," in *Illustrated Catalogue with short letters on art topics, Seventieth Annual Exhibition* (NAD, New York, 1895), pp. 32, 37; *Second Annual Exhibition of Works by Members of the Country Sketch Club* (NAD, New York, 1899), unpaged.

93. Pisano, p. 17. DuMond's approach to teaching landscape painting appears to have been rather conservative. He condemned paintings executed outdoors and advocated a complex system of on-the-spot notations which could later be worked into oils back in the studio. "The world's greatest landscapes were not painted out-of-doors," he wrote in "The Lyme Summer School of Art," *The Lamp,* 27 (August 1903), 7-18.

94. Rosalind C. Pratt, "Thoughts and Suggestions from Studio and School," *The Quarterly Illustrator,* 2 (July-September 1894), 342.

95. For a discussion of the impact of expositions on art schools, see W. S. Harwood, "Art Schools of America," *Cosmopolitan,* 18 (November 1894), 27-34. These expositions were also the occasion for the discussion of educational issues ("A Plea for the Liberal Art Education: A Paper Read by J. W. Stimson

before the Educational Conference, World's Fair Auxiliary," *The Art Critic*, 1 [January 1894], 23-26) and for the exhibition of student works from various art schools throughout the country. For PAFA's role in these exhibitions, see PAFA, *Eighty-eighth Annual Report*, p. 12; PAFA Committee on Instruction Minutes, March 27, 1901, March 25, 1903, and October 26, 1904. The spread of art organizations, museums, and schools during the 1880s and 1890s was incredibly broad and rapid; for example, in 1883 the Art Association of Indianapolis and the Minneapolis Society of Fine Arts were organized; in 1887 the Cincinnati Art Museum opened; the following year, the Detroit Museum and the Layton Art Gallery in Milwaukee were opened; and in 1895 the Carnegie Institute opened in Pittsburgh. The histories and activities of these organizations are given in Levy, ed., *American Art Annual 1898*.

96. "Art Study Practically Applied," *The Art Amateur*, 21 (July 1891), 42-43.

97. Levy, ed., *American Art Annual 1898*, pp. 300-304.

98. "Cooper Institute School of Design," *The Art Amateur*, 1 (July 1891), 24; Grannis, "Art Schools of America," 66.

99. Levy, ed., *American Art Annual 1898*, pp. 357-61, 118; L. W. Miller, "The Philadelphia School of Industrial Art," *The Art Amateur*, 16 (April 1887), 114-15.

100. PAFA, *Circular of the Committee on Instruction, 1889-1890*, p. 4.

101. See, for example, PAFA Committee on Instruction Minutes, October 31, 1894, and PAFA Faculty Minutes, September 23, 1897, where newspaper illustrators requested schedule changes and reduced tuition rates. For a discussion of the Society of Fakirs, see Landgren, *Years of Art*, pp. 69-76. In 1893, John Frederick Lewis offered a student prize for caricatures of works in the PAFA annual, a direct take-off on the Fakirs' spoof of NAD and Society of American Artists annual exhibitions (ts., 1894, PAFA Archives).

102. Henry C. Pitz, *The Brandywine Tradition* (Boston, 1969), chapters 8 and 9.

103. PAFA Committee on Instruction Minutes, May 17 and 29, 1895.

104. "Art Notes of Real Interest," *The Quarterly Illustrator*, 1 (April-June 1893), 135-36; *Catalogue, Ninety-seventh Annual Exhibition* (NAD, New York, 1902), p. 17.

105. "Illustration: Introductory Talks by W. Lewis Fraser . . .," 1889, PAFA Archives; PAFA *Eighty-eighth Annual Report*, p. 17; W. Lewis Fraser to PAFA, April 21, 1899; Walter A. Clark to PAFA, April 6 and 15, 1900; PAFA Committee on Instruction Minutes, March 31 and May 25, 1897, May 25 and November 19, 1899, and December 26, 1900.

106. "Mr. Crowninshield's Report," in MFA School, *Sixth Annual Report*, pp. 12-13; *Ninth Annual Report*, pp. 5-6; *Twenty-fifth Annual Report*, pp. 9-10.

107. PAFA, *Ninetieth Annual Report*, pp. 18-19; *Ninety-first Annual Report*, p. 13.

108. Fink and Taylor, p. 64.

CHARLES WILLSON PEALE AND HIS FAMILY OF PAINTERS

1. Reynolds delivered his first discourse to the Royal Academy in 1769, the year Peale left London. Peale does not seem to have been familiar with the discourses until well after they had been published in England.

2. Charles Willson Peale to John Beale Bordley, November 1772, CWP Letterbook I. Charles Willson Peale's letterbooks are located in the collection of the American Philosophical Society in Philadelphia.

3. Charles Willson Peale, "Address to the visitors and directors of the Philadelphia Museum," n.d., Collection of the American Philosophical Society, Philadelphia.

4. See Jean Lambert Brockaway, "The Miniatures of James Peale," *Antiques*, 22 (October 1932), and E. Grosvenor Paine, "Miniaturists in the Peale Family," *The Peale Family* (exhibition catalogue, Detroit Institute of Arts, 1967).

5. Rembrandt Peale, "Reminiscences: The Painter's Eyes," *The Crayon*, 3 (June 1856), 163-65.

6. James's replica is now in the collection of the Independence National Historical Park. James copied the pose and features exactly from Stuart's portrait, while remaining uninfluenced by his style.

7. Charles Willson Peale to Thomas Jefferson, December 18, 1804, CWP Letterbook V.

8. Rembrandt Peale to Gilbert Stuart, March 24, 1806, published in *The Boston Transcript* and reprinted in "Sketchings: Domestic Art Gossip, Boston," *The Crayon*, 7 (January 1860), 24-25. Rembrandt's reference to Sir Joshua Reynolds indicates that he had read the *Discourses*. In the *Fourteenth Discourse* ("Gainsborough"), Reynolds advises painting by candlelight. Stuart's influence is apparent in at least one portrait Rembrandt completed in Washington, *Albert Gallatine* (1805; Collection of the Independence National Historical Park).

9. Charles Willson Peale sketched the installation in a letter to Robert Fulton, November 15, 1807, CWP Letterbook VIII. The bills for the preparation of the galleries, for whitewash, carpentry, etc., authorized by Peale, are in the PAFA Archives.

10. Rembrandt Peale, "Reminiscences: Inventions—Odds and Ends," *The Crayon*, 3 (April 1856), 101-2.

11. Charles Willson Peale to Angelica Robinson, September 8, 1808, CWP Letterbook IX.

12. Charles Willson Peale to Angelica Robinson, October 27, 1808, quoting a letter from Rembrandt Peale, September 13, 1808, CWP Letterbook IX.

13. Charles Willson Peale to Angelica Robinson, August 26, 1810, quoting a letter from Rembrandt Peale, April 1810, CWP Letterbook XI.

14. Charles Willson Peale to Rembrandt Peale, December 17, 1820, CWP Letterbook XVI.

15. Charles Coleman Sellers, *Portraits and Miniatures by Charles Willson Peale, Transactions of the American Philosophical Society*, vol. 42, pt. 1 (Philadelphia, 1952), cat. no. 637, p. 162.

16. Charles Willson to Rembrandt Peale, August 23, 1823, CWP Letterbook XVII.

17. Rembrandt Peale, "Reminiscences: Adolph Ulric Wertmuller," *The Crayon,* 2 (October 3, 1855), 207.

18. Charles Coleman Sellers, "Rembrandt Peale, Instigator," *Pennsylvania Magazine of History and Biography,* 39 (July 1955); Rembrandt Peale, "Reminiscences: The Painter's Eyes," *The Crayon,* 3 (June 1856), 163-65.

19. Unlike the still life in the San Diego Museum of Art, the Pennsylvania Academy's is signed and dated, suggesting that it is the original.

20. Jessie Poesch, *Titian Ramsay Peale, 1799-1885, and His Journals of the Wilkes Expedition, Memoirs of the American Philosophical Society,* vol. 52 (Philadelphia, 1961), pp. 46-47.

21. Mary Jane Peale's student card is in the PAFA Archives. She is the only Peale recorded as a student, although Rembrandt joined the life class as a professional artist near the end of his life.

THE ARTIST AS INTERPRETER OF AMERICAN HISTORY

1. "Benjamin West," *The Port Folio,* 6 (September 1811), 253.

2. Charles Willson Peale to Thomas Jefferson, June 13, 1805, PAFA Archives.

3. Robert Fulton to PAFA, November 21, 1807, PAFA Archives.

4. *The American Daily Advertiser,* November 27, 1807, p. 3.

5. PAFA Board Minutes, May 30, 1849. The category for historical, scriptural, and dramatic works had a first prize of $750, while the category for landscape and marine painting had a first prize of $300.

6. Henry Edwin Brown to Harrison S. Morris, secretary of PAFA, December 11, 1900, PAFA Archives.

7. Quoted in Charles Coleman Sellers, *Charles Willson Peale* (New York, 1969), p. 62.

8. "Twenty-Sixth Annual Exhibition of the National Academy of Design," *Bulletin of the American Art-Union,* May 1, 1851, p. 21.

9. Fairman Rogers to George Corliss, secretary of PAFA, July 20, 1882, PAFA Archives.

10. "Letter to the Editor: Leutze's Washington," *The Crayon,* 1 (January 1855), 67.

11. Quoted in *Catalogue of the Second Annual Exhibition* (Artists' Fund Society, Philadelphia, 1836), p. 5.

12. Bayard, "Anecdotes of American Painters: West," *The Port Folio,* 2 (October 1809), 320.

13. John Sartain, "Benjamin West's Picture," *Eclectic Magazine,* 55 (February 1862), 271. The engraving appears as the frontispiece to the issue.

14. Felicia Hemans, "The Landing of the Pilgrim Fathers in New England," in *The Works of Felicia Hemans, Edited by Her Sister* (New York, 1849), vol. 1, pp. 291-92.

15. PAFA Board Minutes, April 12, 1852.

16. Charles Fairman, *Art and Artists of the Capitol* (Washington, D.C., 1927), p. 138.

17. Eleanore Price Mather, "A Quaker Icon: The Inner Kingdom of Edward Hicks," *The Art Quarterly,* 36 (1973), 84-99.

18. H., "Revolutionary Recollections," *The New York Mirror and Ladies' Literary Gazette,* 7 (January 23, 1830), 227.

19. Henry Steele Commager, "The Search for a Usable Past," *American Heritage,* 16 (February 1965), 4-9, 90-96.

20. Albert G. Remington, "The Influence of Art," *Sartain's Union Magazine of Literature and Art,* 9 (December 1851), 476.

21. Quoted in Betty I. Strauss, "The Memorial Iconography of George Washington" (Master's thesis, University of Delaware, 1966), p. 15.

22. Charles Coleman Sellers, *Portraits and Miniatures by Charles Willson Peale, Transactions of the American Philosophical Society,* vol. 42, pt. 1 (Philadelphia, 1952), p. 227.

23. Marianna Jenkins, *The State Portrait: Its Origins and Evolution,* Monographs on Archaeology and Fine Art, Sponsored by the Archaeological Institute of America and the College Art Association of America, no. 3 (New York, 1947), p. 1.

24. Mason Locke Weems, *The Life of George Washington,* ed. Marcus Cunliffe (Cambridge, 1962), p. 12.

25. Quoted in *Gilbert Stuart, Portraitist of the Young Republic, 1755-1828* (exhibition catalogue, National Gallery of Art, Washington, D.C., and Rhode Island School of Design, Providence, 1967), p. 25.

26. Darrell Garwood, *Artist in Iowa: A Life of Grant Wood* (New York, 1944), p. 227.

27. George Murray, "Review of the Second Annual Exhibition," *The Port Folio,* 8 (August 1812), 144.

28. Francis Grubar, *William Ranney, Painter of the Early West* (exhibition catalogue, The Corcoran Gallery of Art, Washington, D.C., 1962), p. 30.

29. Washington Irving to H. T. Tuckerman, January 8, 1856, published in Pierre Irving, *The Life and Letters of Washington Irving* (New York, 1889), vol. 3, p. 285.

30. John W. McCoubrey discusses the problem of the antagonism between the reportorial and the heroic in L. B. Wright, G. B. Tatum, J. W. McCoubrey, and R. C. Smith, *The Arts in America, The Colonial Period* (New York, 1966), p. 243.

31. Doris J. Creer, "Thomas Birch: A Study of the Condition of Painting and the Artist's Position in Federal America" (Master's thesis, University of Delaware, 1958), p. 27.

32. John Sartain, "James Hamilton," *Sartain's Magazine,* 10 (April 1852), 333.

33. A parallel observation is noted in William Gerdts, *Revealed Masters, Nineteenth Century American Art* (exhibition catalogue, American Federation of Arts, New York, 1974), p. 15.

34. Charles Gayarré, *History of Louisiana, American Dominion* (New York, 1866), p. 620.

35. C. J. Hedenberg, *Explanation of the Picture of Andrew Jackson before Judge Hall at New Orleans, 1815, Sustaining the Laws of His Country, as He Had Defended Her Liberties in the Field* (Philadelphia, n.d.), p. 10.

36. "Sketchings: Exhibitions," *The Crayon,* 5 (December 1858), 355.

37. Quoted from *The Chicago Daily Inter-Ocean,* September 28, 1884, in *The "Last Moments of John Brown"* (Philadelphia, 1885), p. 16.

38. Ibid., p. 7.

39. Ibid.

40. Quoted in Selden Rodman, *Horace Pippin, A Negro Painter in America* (New York, 1947), p. 4.

41. Ibid., p. 18. However, in Selden Rodman and Carole Cleaver, *Horace Pippin, The Artist as a Black American* (New York, 1972), it is stated that the artist's grandmother witnessed the hanging.

42. William Trego to Edward Coates, president of PAFA, January 11, 1891, PAFA Archives.

43. Ibid.

44. Ellwood Parry, *The Image of the Indian and the Black Man in American Art, 1590-1900* (New York, 1974), p. 140.

45. Adelyn Breeskin, *William H. Johnson, 1901-1970* (exhibition catalogue, National Collection of Fine Arts, Washington, D.C., 1971-72), p. 18.

46. Ibid.

AMERICAN LANDSCAPE PAINTING, 1795-1875

1. In the nineteenth century, landscape painting did acquire "an academic rationale and hence an artistic respectability" (Lois Fink and Joshua C. Taylor, *Academy: The Academic Tradition in American Art* [exhibition catalogue, National Collection of Fine Arts, Washington, D.C., 1975], p. 13). In Europe, at academies like the one in Düsseldorf, there was a stronger interest in landscape painting. Many American landscape painters studied at the Düsseldorf Academy in the 1850s and 1860s because similar opportunities to study landscape painting did not exist in American academies. See *The Düsseldorf Academy and the Americans* (exhibition catalogue, The High Museum of Art, Atlanta, Georgia, 1973).

2. PAFA Board Minutes, June 13, 1881.

3. *Lippincott's Monthly Magazine,* March-August 1872.

4. See *Catalogue of Pictures in the Gallery of Joseph Harrison, Jr., Rittenhouse Square, Philadelphia,* n.d., Collection of the Historical Society of Pennsylvania, Philadelphia.

5. In addition to exhibiting important American landscapes, the Academy elected many of the major American landscapists as Honorary Professional Members well before they received public recognition.

6. See J. Hall Pleasants, *Four Late Eighteenth Century Anglo-American Landscape Painters* (reprinted from the *Proceedings of the American Antiquarian Society,* Worcester, Mass., 1943).

7. Joshua Shaw, *Picturesque Views of American Scenery* (Philadelphia, 1820), intro.

8. James Fenimore Cooper, "American and European Scenery Compared," in *The Home Book of the Picturesque* (New York, 1852), p. 52.

9. Roderick Nash, *Wilderness and the American Mind* (New Haven and London, 1967).

10. William Cullen Bryant, *Poems by William Cullen Bryant* (New York, 1856), pp. 27-28.

11. Quoted in Barbara Novak, *American Painting of the Nineteenth Century* (New York, 1969), p. 66.

12. Exceptional patrons like Luman Reed of New York, Thomas Cole's most generous patron, never tried to influence what an artist painted but supported and encouraged all kinds of work.

13. Quoted in Louis Legrand Noble, *The Life and Works of Thomas Cole,* ed. Elliot Vesell (Cambridge, Mass., 1964), p. 63.

14. Ibid., p. 99.

15. Ibid., p. 101.

16. Otto Wittman, "American Artists in Italy, 1830-1895," *American Quarterly,* 4 (Spring, 1952); Barbara Novak, *The Arcadian Landscape: Nineteenth-Century American Painters in Italy* (exhibition catalogue, University of Kansas Museum of Art, Lawrence, 1972).

17. See, for example, Elizabeth Lindquist-Cock, "Stereoscopic Photography and the Western Paintings of Albert Bierstadt," *The Art Quarterly* (Winter, 1970), 361-76. At Olana, Frederic Church's estate, there are close-up photographs of rocks and vines along with panoramic views that probably were taken by Church.

18. See David H. Dickason, *The Daring Young Men: The Story of the American Pre-Raphaelites* (Bloomington, Indiana, 1953); Roger Stein, *John Ruskin and Aesthetic Thought in America, 1840-1900* (Cambridge, Mass., 1967).

19. See Linda Ferber, *William Trost Richards, American Landscape and Marine Painter, 1833-1905* (exhibition catalogue, The Brooklyn Museum, New York, 1973). Richards was the only nineteenth-century American realist landscape painter to be awarded the Academy's Gold Medal of Honor.

20. Quoted in Nicolai Cikovsky, Jr., *Sanford Robinson Gifford, 1823-1880* (exhibition catalogue, The University of Texas at Austin, 1970-71), p. 28.

21. For the most complete discussion of this school, see Peter Bermingham, *American Art in the Barbizon Mood* (exhibition catalogue, National Collection of Fine Arts, Washington, D.C., 1975).

AMERICAN IMPRESSIONISM

1. The discovery of new pigments by the chemical industry from the beginning of the nineteenth century onwards played an important but largely overlooked role in the development of Impressionism. In a letter of June 3, 1905, to his dealer Durand-Ruel, Claude Monet described the colors he used. These were cobalt blue, cadmium yellow, vermilion, deep madder, emerald green, and white. With the exception of vermilion and white, the colors he mentions were introduced to artists in the nineteenth century. For further discussion of the influence of technology on Impressionist painting, see Richard J. Boyle, *American Impressionism* (Boston, 1974), chapters I and II.

2. For a more thorough study of these significant collections, see Frank H. Goodyear, Jr. and Carolyn Diskant, *The Beneficent Connoisseurs* (exhibition catalogue, PAFA, 1974).

3. For criticism and comment on the art section of the Philadelphia Centennial, see Edward Strahan, "The Fine Art of the International Exposition," in *Illus-*

trated Catalogue, The Masterpieces of the Centennial Exposition, vol. 1 (Philadelphia, 1876).

4. Quoted in George Inness, Jr., *The Life, Art, and Letters of George Inness* (New York, 1917), p. 169.

5. Lawrence Park, *Gilbert Stuart: An Illustrated Descriptive List of His Works* (New York, 1926), vol. 1, p. 69.

6. Harrison S. Morris, *Confessions in Art* (New York, 1930), pp. 85, 88.

7. "Poetic" also was the critical description of the work of Alexander Harrison's brother Birge Harrison (1854-1929), who became known for his paintings of winter landscapes. Birge founded The Woodstock School in New York State, which is still the summer school of the Art Students League of New York, and he was probably responsible for the growth of Woodstock as an art colony. The father of the two painters was a Philadelphia intellectual who had the delightful name of Apollos Harrison.

8. This phrase was derived from the title of an exhibition which explored the influences of the Barbizon School on American landscape painting, organized by the National Collection of Fine Arts. See Peter Bermingham, *American Art in The Barbizon Mood* (exhibition catalogue, National Collection of Fine Arts, Washington, D.C., 1975).

9. Lloyd Goodrich, *Winslow Homer* (exhibition catalogue, Whitney Museum of American Art, New York, 1973), p. 28.

10. E. P. Richardson, "The Dinner Horn by Winslow Homer," *Art Quarterly,* 2 (1948), 153-57. The format in the Detroit picture is horizontal, and the figure more monumental. The same porch in the Detroit picture appears in Homer's painting, *Shelling Peas* (Cooper-Hewitt Museum, New York). At the time, Dr. Richardson did not know of the version exhibited here.

11. Morris, p. 49. The Academy Gold Medal was awarded to Whistler for his painting, *Arrangement in Black: Lady in the Yellow Buskin, Lady Archibald Campbell,* now in the Philadelphia Museum of Art, W. P. Wilstach Collection.

12. Morris, p. 45.

13. Quoted from Christian Brinton, *A Glance in Retrospect: Mary Cassatt* (exhibition catalogue, Haverford College, Haverford, Pennsylvania, 1939), p. 5.

14. Mary Cassatt to Harrison S. Morris, March 2, 1904, PAFA Archives.

15. Mary Cassatt to John Frederick Lewis, March 22, 1912, PAFA Archives.

16. John I. H. Baur, *Theodore Robinson* (exhibition catalogue, The Brooklyn Museum, New York, 1946), p. 51.

17. Morris, p. 173.

18. Quoted in Donelson F. Hoopes, *The American Impressionists* (New York, 1972), p. 50.

19. Morris, p. 174.

20. Ibid.

21. Ibid., p. 145.

22. Ibid., pp. 69-70.

23. Childe Hassam to Harrison Morris, November 17, 1894, PAFA Archives.

24. Quoted in Morris, p. 131.

25. Ibid., p. 66.

26. Harrison S. Morris to Robert Vonnoh, July 25, 1901, PAFA Archives.

27. For the most part Impressionism in California was more idiosyncratic than it was in the East and not as widespread. Ritschel's style tends to be more European than that of other California Impressionists, who used a bright palette more for expressionist, than for impressionist ends. Further, California painters seem to have made a stylistic jump from the tonalism of William Keith (1838-1911), who was the best known nineteenth-century California painter outside California, to a flat-patterned style derived from the Japanese (via the French Nabis group) through the strong influence of the San Francisco muralist Arthur Mathews (1860-1945). This was probably in part due to the distance from the East Coast, where an Anglo-European influence predominated, and in part due to the influence of Mathews himself. San Francisco was the art world of California and Mathews and his wife were the dominant figures in it. See Harvey L. Jones, *The Mathews: Masterpieces of the California Decorative Style* (exhibition catalogue, The Oakland Museum, California, 1971).

28. Guy Pène du Bois, "Ernest Lawson, Optimist," *Arts and Decoration* (September 1916), 505.

29. Morris, p. 66.

THOMAS EAKINS AND THE ACADEMY

1. For biographical information and complete bibliographies on Eakins, see Lloyd Goodrich, *Thomas Eakins: His Life and Work* (New York, 1933) and Gordon Hendricks, *The Life and Work of Thomas Eakins* (New York, 1974).

2. PAFA, "Rules of the Class for the Study of the Living Model, of the Pennsylvania Academy of the Fine Arts" [1856], PAFA Archives; PAFA Board Minutes June 13, 1859.

3. There is no record of the date of Eakins's admission to the life class. One assumes he was admitted shortly after his twenty-first birthday in 1865. See Hendricks, *The Life and Work of Thomas Eakins,* p. xxv.

4. Letter from John H. Niemeyer in "Open Letters on Gérôme," *The Century Magazine,* 37 (February 1889), 634-36.

5. Gerald M. Ackerman, "Thomas Eakins and His Parisian Masters Gérôme and Bonnat," *Gazette des Beaux Arts,* series 6, 73 (April 1969), 235-56.

6. Bruce H. Evans, Gerald M. Ackerman, and Richard Ettinghausen, *Jean-Léon Gérôme (1824-1904)* (exhibition catalogue, The Dayton Art Institute, Dayton, Ohio, The Minneapolis Institute of Arts, and the Walters Art Gallery, Baltimore, 1972), p. 60.

7. Rebecca Fussell to Molly, April 2, 1870 or 1871, PAFA Archives. The letter states that as a result of his mother's illness, Eakins had been confined to the house since his return from Europe.

8. PAFA Committee on Instruction Minutes, 1860-1870. Budgets and attendance figures are listed by the year or by the month.

9. PAFA Board Minutes, 1868-1870.

10. Minutes of a "Meeting of the Building Committee," January 4, 1872, PAFA Archives.

11. "Schools," a report by John Sartain, Fairman Rogers, and Joseph W. Bates (Committee on Instruction) bound into the PAFA Board Minutes, December 13, 1875.

12. Thomas Eakins to the Board of Directors, January 8, 1877, PAFA Archives. Quoted in full in Hendricks, *The Life and Work of Thomas Eakins,* pp. 104-5.

13. Christian Schussele, "To the Committee on Instruction of the Academy of Fine Arts" (ms.) [June 1877], PAFA, Archives.

14. [William C. Brownell], "The Art Schools of Philadelphia," *Scribner's Monthly,* 18 (September 1879), 744.

15. PAFA Board Minutes, September 9, 1878.

16. See [William C. Brownell], "The Art Schools of Philadelphia," described above. The article is an important source for Eakins's pedagogical theories. However, Brownell overemphasized the impact of Eakins's "radicalism" on the school; several of the ideas which Eakins expressed in the article were never so fully developed at the Academy. He also did not credit Schussele and Fairman Rogers for several of their accomplishments, including the development of the basic curriculum and the institution of the practice of painting from life.

17. PAFA Committee on Instruction Minutes, October 15, 1879.

18. Fairman Rogers, "The Schools of the Pennsylvania Academy of the Fine Arts," *The Penn Monthly,* June 1881, pp. 4-5.

19. PAFA Committee on Exhibitions Minutes, March 22, 1880.

20. W. M. R. French of the Chicago Academy of Fine Arts to George Corliss, December 15, 1880, PAFA Archives.

21. For complete discussions of Eakins's photographic work, see Gordon Hendricks, *The Photography of Thomas Eakins* (New York, 1972) and Gordon Hendricks, *Thomas Eakins: His Photographic Works* (exhibition catalogue, PAFA, 1970). The identification of the photographic source is in Hendricks, *The Life and Works of Thomas Eakins,* p. 206, although the painting is there attributed to Susan Macdowell.

22. PAFA Committee on Instruction Minutes, January 6, 1881.

23. There are two plans for the reorganization of the schools in the PAFA Archives. The most complete is in Fairman Rogers's hand.

24. *Seventy-seventh Annual Report* (ms.), June 1882-February 1884, PAFA Archives.

25. Gordon Hendricks, "A May Morning in the Park," *Philadelphia Museum Bulletin,* April 1969.

26. Hendricks, *The Life and Works of Thomas Eakins,* p. 148-49.

27. [Brownell], p. 742.

28. Eakins brought his canvases into his classes to use in demonstrating his ideas. *The Swimming Hole* may have been one such work. Exhibited at the Academy in 1885, it would have certainly influenced Eakins's students then.

29. *The Eightieth Annual Report of the Pennsylvania Academy of the Fine Arts* (ms.), February 1887, PAFA Archives.

30. R. S. to James Claghorn, April 11, 1882, PAFA Archives. Quoted in full in Sylvan Schendler, *Eakins* (Boston, 1966), pp. 90-92.

31. PAFA Committee on Instruction Minutes, March 24, 1884.

32. Charles Bregler, "Thomas Eakins as a Teacher," *The Arts,* 17 (March 1931), 380.

33. Thomas Anshutz, along with Colin Campbell Cooper, Frank Stephens, Charles Stephens, and James Kelly, wrote a letter to the Board of Directors on March 12, 1886, soon after Eakins's resignation. The signers asked the board to discourage rumors that Eakins's "personal or professional enemies" had contributed to the events leading to the resignation. In the letter they did not deny the fact that they had spread the rumors. The letter is located in the PAFA Archives.

34. Statement by Thomas Eakins enclosed in a letter to Emily Sartain, March 25, 1886, PAFA Archives.

35. Goodrich, *Thomas Eakins: His Life and Work,* pp. 85-86.

36. Report of the Committee on Instruction written by Edward Coates, *The Eightieth Annual Report of the Pennsylvania Academy of the Fine Arts.*

37. Thomas Eakins to George Barker, February 24, 1906. Quoted in full in Hendricks, *The Life and Works of Thomas Eakins,* pp. 260-61.

THE EIGHT

1. This remark is intended to apply to the work of Henri, Sloan, Glackens, Luks, and Shinn more than to Prendergast, Lawson, and Davies. Critically, the idea of revolution has been limited to the former group.

2. Quoted in William Innes Homer, *Robert Henri and His Circle* (Ithaca and London, 1969), p. 177.

3. Anshutz never emphasized the study of anatomy to the same degree that Eakins did. This came as a relief to most Academy students. For further discussion of the differences between Eakins's teaching and Anshutz's, see Sandra Denney Heard, *Thomas P. Anshutz, 1851-1912* (exhibition catalogue, PAFA, 1973), p. 9.

4. Thomas P. Anshutz to Edward H. Coates, May 15, 1893, PAFA Archives.

5. Ibid.

6. Quoted in Heard, p. 10.

7. George Luks to John A. Myers, June 28, 1918, PAFA Archives.

8. The strategy in prior publications on The Eight has been to isolate the work of Prendergast, Lawson, and Davies from that of the other five artists and to see Henri, Sloan, Glackens, Luks, and Shinn as forming an inner circle. However, there is such diversity in the work of all eight of the artists that they should not be thought of primarily in terms of similarities.

9. However, as William Innes Homer points out in *Avant-Garde Painting and Sculpture in America 1910-25* (exhibition catalogue, Delaware Art Museum, 1975), p. 12, "none of the artists linked with Stieglitz was asked to exhibit" in the 1910 Independents show, organized primarily by Henri and Sloan. This re-

flects their narrow-mindedness toward European avant-garde art, which strongly influenced the artists of the Stieglitz circle.

10. John Sloan, *Gist of Art* (New York, 1939), p. 2.

11. Henri, Sloan, Glackens, Luks, and Shinn studied at the Pennsylvania Academy, Davies at the Art Institute of Chicago, Lawson at the Académie Julian, and Prendergast at Colarossi's and the Académie Julian.

12. Robert Henri, *The Art Spirit* (Philadelphia, 1923), p. 6.

13. Ibid., p. 10.

14. Quoted in Peter Morse, *John Sloan's Prints: A Catalogue Raisonné of the Etchings, Lithographs, and Posters* (New Haven, 1969), p. 272.

15. The term "Ashcan School" was not coined until 1934, when it appeared in Holger Cahill and Alfred Barr's book *Art in America.*

16. Ernest Lawson to the Directors of the Pennsylvania Academy, February 19, 1907, PAFA Archives.

17. The stooping figure of the man on the right of the canvas is also similar to the figure at the upper right in his *Flower Destiny* (Cleveland Museum of Art). See Walter Pach, *Arthur B. Davies, 1862-1928* (exhibition catalogue, Memorial Art Gallery, University of Rochester, Rochester, New York, 1962), fig. 72.

MODERNISM AT THE PENNSYLVANIA ACADEMY, 1910-1940

1. William Innes Homer, "Alfred Stieglitz and '291'" in *Avant-Garde Painting and Sculpture in America 1910-25* (exhibition catalogue, Delaware Art Museum, Wilmington, 1975), p. 14.

2. For discussion of the Armory Show and the period immediately following, see Milton W. Brown, *American Painting from the Armory Show to the Depression* (Princeton, 1955), and *Avant-Garde Painting and Sculpture in America 1910-25* (exhibition catalogue, Delaware Art Museum, Wilmington, 1975).

3. *Philadelphia Photographic Salon* (exhibition catalogue, PAFA, 1898), intro.

4. "Two New Exhibitions for the Art World," *Philadelphia Inquirer,* November 17, 1901, section 2, p. 5.

5. *An Exhibition of Photographs Arranged by the Photo-Secession* (exhibition catalogue, PAFA, 1906), intro.

6. Francis J. Ziegler, "News of the Art World," *Philadelphia Record,* April 29, 1906, p. 4.

7. "Pictorial Photography at the Academy of Fine Arts," *Philadelphia Inquirer,* April 29, 1906, section 4, p. 5.

8. "Notes: Exhibition of Work by Modern Artists," *American Magazine of Art,* 11 (June 1920), 300.

9. B. Diamond, "Boredom Banished by the Modernists," *Philadelphia Inquirer,* April 17, 1921, news section, p. 2.

10. "Comment on the Arts," *The Arts,* 1 (May 1921), 34; "Philadelphia Sees Best in New Art," *American Art News,* April 23, 1921, p. 6.

11. "Academy Opens Notable Exhibit," *Public Ledger,* April 12, 1923, p. 3.

12. C. H. Bonte, "Art: Peales, Moderns, and Japanese," *Philadelphia Inquirer,* April 15, 1923, section 1, p. 7.

13. Francis J. Ziegler, "Many Paintings of Many Different Kinds," *Philadelphia Record,* April 15, 1923, society section, p. 4.

14. "Philadelphia," *American Art News,* November 25, 1911, p. 7.

15. "Modernism in Pennsylvania Show," *Art News,* February 9, 1929, p. 3.

16. "Art and Artists Pass in Review," *Philadelphia Inquirer,* May 21, 1916, p. 4.

17. Edith W. Powell, "What Our Artists and Musicians Are Doing," *Public Ledger,* April 18, 1923, p. 11.

18. Sheldon Reich, *John Marin: A Stylistic Analysis and Catalogue Raisonné* (Tucson, 1970), vol. 1, p. 46.

19. Elizabeth McCausland, *Marsden Hartley* (Minneapolis, 1952), p. 26.

20. Matthew Baigell, "The Beginnings of 'The American Wave' and the Depression," *Art Journal,* 27 (Summer 1968), 391.

21. Ibid., 391-92.

22. Ibid., 387. The term "American Wave" was coined during the 1931-32 exhibition season to describe a "state of mind, type of subject, and, hopefully, a style."

23. David Shapiro, "Social Realism Reconsidered," in *Social Realism: Art as a Weapon,* ed. David Shapiro (New York, 1973), p. 6.

24. Henry Geldzahler, *American Painting in the Twentieth Century* (New York, 1965), p. 93.

25. Roberta K. Tarbell, "Advanced Tendencies in American Sculpture, 1910-1925," in *Avant-Garde Painting and Sculpture in America 1910-25* (exhibition catalogue, Delaware Art Museum, Wilmington, 1975), p. 26.

26. Ibid.

27. "Dr. Barnes Assails Philadelphia Art," *Art News,* May 31, 1924, p. 1. Grafly's statement was prompted by the University of Pennsylvania's hiring of Thomas Munro, a colleague of Albert C. Barnes, to teach three courses in modern art.

28. Gerald Nordland, *Gaston Lachaise: The Man and His Work* (New York, 1974), p. 127.

CONTEMPORARY ART AT THE ACADEMY

1. The Committee on Collections and Exhibitions was appointed by the Board of Directors from within their own ranks. A faculty member of the Academy often served as an advisor to the committee. Members of the board were not favorably disposed toward the most avant-garde tendencies in art. Faculty members, such as Franklin Watkins, who served on the committee during the 1960s, shared the conservatism of the board.

2. The Gilpin Fund was given in 1860 under the will of Henry Gilpin, but the first work was not purchased until 1879.

3. The Temple Purchase Fund was established by Joseph E. Temple. According to the minutes of the Academy's exhibition committee of May 12, 1884:

   "The Temple Trust Fund now yields each year $1800.00 for the purchase of works of art and the issue of medals to artists. Its application is limited to works by American artists in the annual exhibitions. All American artists exhibiting are eligible, but no work will be purchased or medalled if none be submitted of sufficient merit in the opinion of the Board of Directors of the Academy."

4. Under the will of John Lambert, a former pupil of the Academy, the sum of $50,000 was bequeathed "for the establishment of a fund, the income of which shall be used to purchase pictures from its Annual Oil Exhibitions by American Artists" (published in the catalogue of the 108th annual exhibition, PAFA, 1913, p. 6).

5. Joseph Fraser, "A Professional Statement," in *159th Annual Exhibition* (exhibition catalogue, PAFA, 1964).

6. Many of the artists who served as jurors for the annual exhibitions since 1945 were also teachers at the Art Students League in New York. This list includes Robert Laurent, Louis Bouché, Vaclav Vytlacil, William Zorach, George Grosz, José de Creeft, Will Barnet, Julian Levi, Morris Kantor, Yasuo Kuniyoshi, Peppino Mangravite, Stuart Davis, and Isabel Bishop.

7. Interview with Joseph Fraser, Philadelphia, March 31, 1975. Fraser, who was the director of the Academy from 1934 to 1968, recalled that the director and members of the faculty served in an advisory capacity on the Committee on Collections and Exhibitions. The faculty made the preliminary selection of works from which the final decision on purchases was made by the committee.

8. For a complete survey of American art after 1945, see Sam Hunter and John Jacobus, *American Art of the 20th Century* (New York, 1973); Barbara Rose, *American Art Since 1900* (New York, 1967); and Edward Lucie-Smith, *Late Modern: The Visual Arts Since 1945* (New York, 1969).

9. There are three monographs on Abstract Expressionism: Dore Ashton, *The New York School* (New York, 1973); Irving Sandler, *The Triumph of American Painting* (New York, 1970); Maurice Tuchman, ed., *New York School, First Generation* (Greenwich, Conn., 1965).

10. See Gregory Battock, ed., *Minimal Art* (New York, 1968).

11. Monographs on Pop Art include Mario Amaya, *Pop Art and After* (New York, 1965); Lucy Lippard, ed., *Pop Art* (New York, 1967); and John Russell and Suzi Gablik, *Pop Art Redefined* (New York, 1969).

12. See Udo Kultermann, *The New Painting* (New York, 1969); and John Coplans, *Serial Imagery* (exhibition catalogue, Pasadena Art Museum, 1968).

13. See Cyril Barrett, *Optical Art* (London, 1971); and Frank Popper, *Origins and Development of Kinetic Art* (Greenwich, Conn., 1968).

14. For a survey of some of the projects conceived by Conceptual Artists, see Lucy Lippard, ed., *The dematerialization of the art object from 1966 to 1972* (New York, 1973); Ursula Meyer, ed., *Conceptual Art* (New York, 1972); and Gerald Woods, Philip Thompson, and John Williams, *Art Without Boundaries* (New York, 1972).

15. For a discussion of Earthworks, Environmental Art, and Happenings, see Jack Burnham, *Great Western Salt Works* (New York, 1974); Germano Celant, *Art Povera* (New York, 1969); and Adrian Henri, *Total Art* (New York, 1974).

16. See Udo Kultermann, *New Realism* (Greenwich, Conn., 1972); *Aspects of New Realism* (exhibition catalogue, Milwaukee Art Center, 1969); and Gregory Battock, ed., *Super Realism: A Critical Anthology* (New York, 1975).

17. Since the 1960s Tony Greenwood, instructor in sculpture at the Academy, has worked on life-like figures which parallel works by New Realists. An exhibition of his work was held at the Peale House in April of 1975. In January and February of 1975, paintings by Sidney Goodman and Raymond Saunders were shown at the Peale House.

18. The registrar's files at the Academy include Wyeth's own description of the subject.

19. Quoted from an interview with Andrew Wyeth conducted by Richard Meryman published in Wanda Corn, *The Art of Andrew Wyeth* (exhibition catalogue, Fine Arts Museum of San Francisco, 1974), p. 45.

20. *Andrew Wyeth* (exhibition catalogue, PAFA, 1966-67), cat. no. 35.

21. Knaths's personal description of this painting can be found in the registrar's files at the Academy.

22. Charles Eaton and Isabel Eaton, *Karl Knaths* (exhibition catalogue, International Exhibitions Foundation, Washington, D.C., 1973-74), p. 65.

23. *148th Annual Exhibition* (exhibition catalogue, PAFA, 1953).

24. William Rubin, *Dada and Surrealist Art* (New York, 1968), p. 194.

25. John I. H. Baur, *Philip Evergood* (New York, 1960), p. 104.

26. *The Listening Dead* is reproduced in the catalogue of the 157th annual exhibition, PAFA, 1962.

27. See, for example, Marca-Relli's *Ochre Buildings* (1952), reproduced in Lee Nordness, ed., and Allen Weller, *Art U.S.A. Now* (New York, 1963), vol. 2, p. 274.

28. William Agee, *Marca-Relli* (exhibition catalogue, Whitney Museum of American Art, New York, 1967), p. 13.

29. *Grounded Bird* is illustrated in *155th Annual Exhibition* (exhibition catalogue, PAFA and Detroit Institute of Arts, 1959-60).

30. Donald Judd, "Lee Bontecou," *Arts Magazine,* 39 (April 1965), 17.

31. Isamu Noguchi, *A Sculptor's World* (New York, 1968).

32. For Calder's own reminiscences of his parents and grandfather, see Alexander Calder, *An Autobiography with Pictures* (New York, 1966).

33. Monographs on Calder include James Johnson Sweeney, *Alexander Calder* (exhibition catalogue, Museum of Modern Art, New York, 1943); and H. H. Arnason, *Calder* (New York, 1966).

34. *Letter and His Ecol* received the Temple Gold Medal. See *159th Annual Exhibition* (exhibition catalogue, PAFA, 1965), cat. no. 67, illus.

35. Hilton Kramer, "Pure and Impure Diebenkorn," *Arts Magazine,* 38 (December 1963), 46-53. Kramer writes: "To turn to the latter—to what might be called the impure Diebenkorn—first, one is dismayed to note that wherever the artist has made his subjects more explicit, wherever he has sought to effect a greater congruence between realistic observation and pictorial design, the result is either bland or brilliantly old-fashioned."

36. For other works, see *Richard Diebenkorn* (exhibition catalogue, Washington Gallery of Modern Art, Washington, D.C., November-December 1964).

37. Diebenkorn's personal description of this painting can be found in the registrar's files at the Academy.

38. *Richard Diebenkorn, The Ocean Park Series, Recent Work* (exhibition catalogue, Marlborough Galleries, New York, 1971).

39. The major exhibition devoted to Optical Painting was "The Responsive Eye" at the Museum of Modern Art. Other "Op Art" exhibitions also held in 1965 included "Color Dynamism, Then and Now" at the East Hampton Gallery, "Vibrations II" at Martha Jackson Gallery, "Impact" at Green Gallery, and "Abstract Trompe l'Oeil" at the Sidney Janis Gallery.

    Stanczak's *Interlocking Shadows,* a tempera painting created in 1965, was purchased by the Academy from the annual exhibition in 1966.

40. Helen Frankenthaler was awarded the Temple Gold Medal for *Tobacco Landscape,* and Seymour Lipton received the George Widener Gold Medal for *Gateway.* See *163rd Annual Exhibition* (exhibition catalogue, PAFA, 1968).

41. Quoted in Jay Jacobs, "Richard Anuskiewicz," *Art Gallery Magazine,* 14 (March 1971), 31.

42. June Kompass Nelson, *Harry Bertoia* (Detroit, 1970), plate 45.

43. Harry Bertoia to Joseph Fraser, January 26, 1968, PAFA lregistrar's files.

44. John Canaday, "The Annual Exhibition, Pennsylvania Academy of the Fine Arts," *New York Times,* January 21, 1968.

45. For a survey of Happenings during the 1960s, see Michael Kirby, *Happenings* (New York, 1966).

46. Barbara Rose, *Oldenburg* (exhibition catalogue, Museum of Modern Art, New York, 1970), illus. p. 66.

47. Quoted in *Claes Oldenburg* (exhibition catalogue, Arts Council of Great Britain, Tate Gallery, London, 1970), p. 8.

48. Barbara Haskell, *Claes Oldenburg, Object into Monument* (exhibition catalogue, Pasadena Art Museum, 1971), p. 9.

49. Tate Gallery, *Oldenburg,* illus. p. 49.

50. Quoted in Haskell, p. 15.

51. Ibid.

52. George Segal to Frank Goodyear, July 26, 1974, PAFA registrar's files.

53. Robert Doty, *Contemporary Black Artists in America* (exhibition catalogue, Whitney Museum of American Art, New York, 1971), p. 11.

54. Kirk Varnedoe, "Duane Hanson, Retrospective and Recent Work," *Arts Magazine,* 49 (January 1975), 66.

55. Barry Schwartz, *The New Humanism* (New York, 1974), p. 20.

56. *Summer* by John Moore is illustrated in "Reviews," *Arts Magazine,* 47 (November 1972), 70.

57. Quoted in Linda Nochlin, *Realism Now* (exhibition catalogue, Vasser College Art Gallery, Poughkeepsie, New York, 1968), p. 24.

58. For other works by Noel Mahaffey, see Udo Kultermann, *New Realism,* plates 145-49.

59. *Philip Pearlstein* (exhibition catalogue, Georgia Museum of Art, Athens, 1970), plates 1-6.

PENNSYLVANIA ACADEMY GOLD MEDAL OF HONOR

ESTABLISHED IN 1893 BY JOHN H. CONVERSE, A MEMBER OF THE BOARD OF DIRECTORS, THE MEDAL IS AWARDED BY THE BOARD TO AMERICAN PAINTERS AND SCULPTORS EXHIBITING IN THE ACADEMY OR REPRESENTED IN THE PERMANENT COLLECTION. IT IS ALSO AWARDED FOR EMINENT SERVICES IN THE CAUSE OF ART OR TO THE ACADEMY.

1893. D. Ridgway Knight
1894. Alexander Harrison
1895. William M. Chase
1896. Winslow Homer
1897. Edwin A. Abbey
1898. Cecilia Beaux
1899. Charles Grafly
1901. Henry J. Thouron
1902. James A. McN. Whistler
1903. John S. Sargent
1904. John W. Alexander
1905. William T. Richards
1905. Violet Oakley
1906. Horatio Walker
1907. Edward W. Redfield
1908. Edmund C. Tarbell
1909. Thomas P. Anshutz
1911. Willard L. Metcalf
1914. Mary Cassatt
1915. Edward H. Coates*
1916. J. Alden Weir
1918. John McLure Hamilton
1919. Hugh H. Breckenridge
1920. Childe Hassam
1926. Frank W. Benson
1929. Daniel Garber
1939. C. Paul Jennewein
1949. Alfred G. B. Steel*
1949. Franklin C. Watkins
1953. Walker Hancock
1953. George Harding
1955. Joseph T. Fraser, Jr.*
1955. William Clarke Mason*
1959. John F. Lewis, Jr.*
1961. Francis Speight
1966. Andrew Wyeth
1975. Henry S. McNeil*

* *Awarded for eminent services to the Academy.*

CATALOGUE OF THE EXHIBITION

Catalogue entries, following the order of the ten chapter headings, are arranged alphabetically by the artist's last name. Dimensions are given in inches, height preceding width. In cases where extensive reference literature exists on an artist, references have been limited to the three most important sources of information, both to the artist's work in general and specifically to the object in the exhibition.

A HISTORY OF THE PENNSYLVANIA ACADEMY OF THE FINE ARTS, 1805-1976

WASHINGTON ALLSTON (1779-1843)

1 THE DEAD MAN RESTORED TO LIFE BY TOUCHING THE BONES OF THE PROPHET ELISHA
Oil on canvas, 156 x 120 inches
Unsigned; painted 1811-13
PAFA, Academy Purchase, 1816

References: Jared B. Flagg, *The Life and Letters of Washington Allston* (London, 1893); Edgar P. Richardson, *Washington Allston: A Study of the Romantic Artist in America* (Chicago, 1948); Kenyon C. Bolton III and Elizabeth Johns, *The Paintings of Washington Allston* (exhibition catalogue, Lowe Art Museum, Coral Gables, Florida, 1975).

THOMAS POLLOCK ANSHUTZ (1851-1912)

2 HELEN HENDERSON
Pastel on canvas, 30¼ x 24 inches
Signed u.l.: Thos. Anshutz; painted ca. 1910
PAFA, Bequest of Helen Henderson, 1956

References: Sandra Denney Heard, *Thomas P. Anshutz, 1851-1912* (exhibition catalogue, PAFA, 1973).

JOSEPH A. BAILLY (1825-1883)

3 WILLIAM E. CRESSON
Plaster relief, 22 x 17 inches (oval)
Signed l.l.: JA Bailly 1866
PAFA, Bequest of Priscilla P. Cresson, 1902

References: Nicholas B. Wainwright, ed., *Sculpture of a City: Philadelphia's Treasures in Bronze and Stone* (New York, 1974), pp. 40, 42-43, 63, 68, 73-74.

CECILIA BEAUX (1855-1942)

4 MOTHER AND DAUGHTER (Mrs. Clement A. Griscom and daughter Frances)
Oil on canvas, 83 x 44 inches
Signed l.l.: Cecilia Beaux; painted 1898
PAFA, Gift of Frances C. Griscom, 1950

References: Frank H. Goodyear, Jr., and Elizabeth Bailey, *Cecilia Beaux: Portrait of an Artist* (exhibition catalogue, PAFA, 1974-75), p. 93.

ALEXANDER CABANEL (1823-1889)

5 THE BIRTH OF VENUS
Oil on canvas, 33½ x 53 inches
Signed l.l.: Alex. Cabanel; painted 1863
PAFA, Bequest of Henry C. Gibson, 1892

References: Edward Strahan, *The Art Treasures of America* (Philadelphia, ca. 1879-80), vol. 1, pp. 65-80; Donelson F. Hoopes, *Triumph of Realism* (exhibition catalogue, Brooklyn Museum, New York, 1967), illus.; Joseph C. Sloan, *French Paintings Between the Past and the Present* (Princeton, 1973), illus.

HUGH CANNON (ca. 1814-1881)

6 NICHOLAS BIDDLE
Marble bust, 23½ x 16½ x 8 inches
Unsigned
PAFA, Gift of D. W. Coxe, 1850

References: Nicholas B. Wainwright, "Nicholas Biddle in Portraiture," *Antiques*, 108 (November 1975), illus. 962.

SHOBAL VAIL CLEVENGER (1812-1843)

7 WASHINGTON ALLSTON
Plaster bust, 21½ x 15¾ inches
Unsigned
PAFA, Provenance unknown

References: Thomas Brumbaugh, "Shobal Clevenger: An Ohio Stonecutter in Search of Fame," *Art Quarterly,* 29 (1966), 29-45; William H. Gerdts, Jr., *American Neo-Classic Sculpture: The Marble Resurrection* (New York, 1973), pp. 106-7.

SHOBAL VAIL CLEVENGER (1812-1843)

8 JOSEPH HOPKINSON
Plaster bust, 26 x 15 x 8 inches
Unsigned
PAFA, Provenance unknown

References: Thomas Brumbaugh, "Shobal Clevenger: An Ohio Stonecutter in Search of Fame," *Art Quarterly,* 29 (1966), 29-45.

JOHN DORSEY (n.d.)

9 SKETCH OF A PLAN FOR PENNSYLVANIA ACADEMY
Ink on paper, 9¾ x 7¾ inches
Included in a letter from John Dorsey to Colonel Jonathan Williams, August 1, 1805
PAFA Archives

THOMAS EAKINS (1844-1916)

10 HARRISON S. MORRIS
Oil on canvas, 54 x 36 inches
Signed l.r.: To his friend/Harrison Morris/Thomas Eakins/1896
Collection of Mr. and Mrs. Harrison Wright

References: Harrison S. Morris, *Confessions in Art* (New York, 1930); Lloyd Goodrich, *Thomas Eakins: His Life and Work* (New York, 1933), p. 187.

CHARLES LORING ELLIOT (1812-1868)

11 SELF-PORTRAIT
Oil on canvas, 24½ x 19⅝ inches
Unsigned; painted ca. 1845
PAFA, John F. Lewis Memorial Collection, 1933

References: Ann C. Van Devanter and Alfred Frankenstein, *American Self-Portraits, 1670-1973* (exhibition catalogue, National Portrait Gallery, Smithsonian Institution, Washington, D.C., 1974), pp. 70-71.

HENRI FANTIN-LATOUR (1836-1904)

12 VASE OF FLOWERS
Oil on canvas, 17¾ x 19½ inches
Signed l.r.: Fantin — 72
PAFA, Bequest of Henry C. Gibson, 1892

References: Henri Fantin-Latour, 1836-1904 (exhibition catalogue, Smith College Museum of Art, Northampton, Mass., 1966); Victoria Fantin-Latour, *Catalogue de l'oeuvre complète de Fantin-Latour* (reprint ed., New York, 1969).

FRANK FURNESS (1839-1912) and GEORGE W. HEWITT (1841-1916)

13 ELEVATION ON BROAD STREET, PENNSYLVANIA ACADEMY OF THE FINE ARTS
Ink and wash on paper, 25½ x 34½ inches
Inscribed u.r. (for exterior stonework contractors): Atkinson & Myhlerts; executed ca. 1873
PAFA, Gift of the architects, 1876

References: James F. O'Gorman, *The Architecture of Frank Furness* (exhibition catalogue, Philadelphia Museum of Art, 1973), pp. 80-85.

FRANK FURNESS (1839-1912) and GEORGE W. HEWITT (1841-1916)

14 ELEVATION ON CHERRY STREET, PENNSYLVANIA ACADEMY OF THE FINE ARTS
Ink and wash on paper, 25⅛ x 72¾ inches
Inscribed u.r. (for exterior stonework contractors): Atkinson & Myhlerts; executed ca. 1873
PAFA, Gift of the architects, 1876

References: James F. O'Gorman, *The Architecture of Frank Furness* (exhibition catalogue, Philadelphia Museum of Art, 1973), pp. 80-85.

FRANK FURNESS (1839-1912) and GEORGE W. HEWITT (1841-1916)

15 LONGITUDINAL SECTION THROUGH CENTER, PENNSYLVANIA ACADEMY OF THE FINE ARTS
Ink and wash on paper, 26¼ x 38¼ inches
Unsigned; executed ca. 1873
PAFA, Gift of the architects, 1876

References: James F. O'Gorman, *The Architecture of Frank Furness* (exhibition catalogue, Philadelphia Museum of Art, 1973), pp. 80-85.

CHARLES GRAFLY (1863-1929)

16 EDWARD HORNER COATES
Bronze bust, 35 x 9 x 11 inches
Signed on back: Charles Grafly — May 1903
PAFA, Gift of Mrs. E. H. Coates in memory of Edward Coates, 1923

References: Pamela H. Simpson, "The Sculpture of Charles Grafly: A Catalogue Raisonné" (Ph.D. dissertation, University of Delaware, 1974).

CHARLES GRAFLY (1863-1929)

17 THOMAS POLLOCK ANSHUTZ
Bronze bust, 17½ x 14 x 9½ inches
Signed on back: Grafly
PAFA, Gift of the Friends and Admirers of Thomas Pollock Anshutz, 1913

References: Pamela H. Simpson, "The Sculpture of Charles Grafly: A Catalogue Raisonné" (Ph.D. dissertation, University of Delaware, 1974).

GEORGE PETER ALEXANDER HEALY (1813-1894)

18 SELF-PORTRAIT
Oil on canvas, 20 x 17½ inches
Signed l.c.: G.P.A. Healy/1881; inscribed on back: To Mr. and Mrs. A. C. Harrison with kind regards of George P. A. Healy, New York Oct. 10th 1881
PAFA, Gift of John F. Lewis, 1928

References: George Peter Alexander Healy, *Reminiscences of a Portrait Painter* (Chicago, 1894); Marie de Mare, *G.P.A. Healy, American Artist: An Intimate Chronicle of the Nineteenth Century* (New York, 1954).

WINSLOW HOMER (1836-1910)

19 THE FOX HUNT
Oil on canvas, 38 x 69½ inches
Signed l.l.: Homer/1893
PAFA, Temple Fund Purchase, 1894

References: Lloyd Goodrich, *Winslow Homer* (exhibition catalogue, Whitney Museum of American Art, New York, 1973), p. 107.

HENRY INMAN (1801-1846)

20 HENRY D. GILPIN
Oil on canvas, 36¾ x 30½ inches
Unsigned; painted ca. 1834
PAFA, Gift of Miss Gilpin, 1876

References: C. Edwards Lester, *The Artists of America* (reprint ed., New York, 1970), pp. 35-67.

HENRY INMAN (1801-1846)

21 THOMAS SULLY
Oil on millboard, 25 x 21½ inches
Unsigned; painted ca. 1837
PAFA, Gift of Blanche Sully, 1891

References: C. Edwards Lester, *The Artists of America* (reprint ed., New York, 1970), pp. 35-67.

HENRY INMAN (1801-1846)

22 MUMBLE THE PEG
Oil on canvas, 24 x 19½ inches
Signed l.r.: Inman 1842
PAFA, Bequest of Henry C. Carey, 1879

References: C. Edwards Lester, *The Artists of America* (reprint ed., New York, 1970), pp. 35-67; Patricia Hills, *The Painter's America: Rural and Urban Life, 1810-1910* (exhibition catalogue, Whitney Museum of American Art, New York, 1974), p. 148.

EASTMAN JOHNSON (1824-1906)

23 SANFORD ROBINSON GIFFORD
Oil on wood, 25 x 20 inches
Signed l.r.: E.J.; painted ca. 1880
PAFA, Gift of John F. Lewis, 1920

References: Patricia Hills, *Eastman Johnson* (exhibition catalogue, Whitney Museum of American Art, New York, 1972), see illus. p. 112.

JOHN LEWIS KRIMMEL (1789-1821)

24 FOURTH OF JULY IN CENTRE SQUARE
Oil on canvas, 23 x 28¾ inches
Unsigned; painted ca. 1810-12
PAFA, Academy Purchase, 1845

References: Hermann Warner Williams, Jr., *Mirror to the American Past: A Survey of American Genre Painting, 1750-1900* (Greenwich, Conn., 1973), pp. 40-46; Patricia Hills, *The Painter's America: Rural and Urban Life, 1810-1910* (exhibition catalogue, Whitney Museum of American Art, New York, 1974), pp. 2-5.

CHARLES ROBERT LESLIE (1784-1859)

25 MURDER OF RUTLAND BY LORD CLIFFORD
Oil on canvas, 96¾ x 79½ inches
Signed l.r.: C. R. Leslie 1815
PAFA, Gift of the Leslie Family, 1831

References: Charles Robert Leslie, *Autobiographical Recollections* (Boston, 1860).

CHARLES ROBERT LESLIE (1784-1859)

26 HENRY C. CAREY
Oil on wood, 9½ x 6⅞ inches
Unsigned
PAFA, Bequest of Henry C. Carey, 1879

References: Charles Robert Leslie, *Autobiographical Recollections* (Boston, 1860).

EMANUEL GOTTLIEB LEUTZE (1816-1868)

27 SELF-PORTRAIT
Oil on canvas, $28\frac{7}{8}$ x $23\frac{5}{8}$ inches
Signed on back: Self-Portrait / E. Leutze
PAFA, Gift of John F. Lewis, 1928

References: Henry T. Tuckerman, *Book of the Artists* (New York, 1867), pp. 333-45; Donelson F. Hoopes, *American Narrative Painting* (exhibition catalogue, Los Angeles County Museum of Art, 1974), pp. 96-99; Ann C. Van Devanter and Alfred Frankenstein, *American Self-Portraits, 1670-1973* (exhibition catalogue, National Portrait Gallery, Smithsonian Institution, Washington, D.C., 1974), pp. 68-69.

WILLIAM SIDNEY MOUNT (1807-1868)

28 SELF-PORTRAIT
Oil on canvas, 24 x $20\frac{1}{8}$ inches
Signed on back: Portrait of Wm. S. Mount No. A/Painted by Himself-/Sept. 1854
PAFA, Gift of John F. Lewis, 1920

References: Alfred Frankenstein, *Painter of Rural America: William Sidney Mount, 1807-1868* (exhibition catalogue, International Exhibitions Foundation, Washington, D.C., 1969).

WILLIAM RUDOLF O'DONOVAN (1844-1920)

29 WINSLOW HOMER
Bronze bust, 12 x 4 x $5\frac{3}{4}$ inches
Signed on back: O'Donovan 1876
PAFA, Cast by the Academy in bronze from the original plaster owned by Thomas Eakins, 1911

MAXFIELD PARRISH (1870-1966)

30 POSTER SHOW: PENNSYLVANIA ACADEMY OF THE FINE ARTS PHILADELPHIA
Silk screen on paper, $37\frac{1}{2}$ x $27\frac{7}{8}$ inches
Inscribed in plate l.l.: Maxfield Parrish; l.r.: LEDGER SHOW PRINT PHILA; in pencil l.r.: Maxfield Parrish; executed 1896
PAFA, Asbell Fund Purchase and Gift of Dr. Edgar P. Richardson, 1972

References: Coy Ludwig, *Maxfield Parrish* (New York, 1973), p. 121; *Maxfield Parrish: Master of Make-Believe* (exhibition catalogue, Brandywine River Museum, Chadds Ford, Pennsylvania, 1974).

CHARLES WILLSON PEALE (1741-1827)

31 GEORGE CLYMER
Oil on canvas, $27\frac{1}{4}$ x $22\frac{1}{2}$ inches
Unsigned; painted ca. 1807-9
PAFA, Gift of Charles Willson Peale, 1809

References: Charles Coleman Sellers, *Portraits and Miniatures by Charles Willson Peale, Transactions of the American Philosophical Society,* vol. 42, pt. 1 (Philadelphia, 1952), pp. 55-56.

CHARLES WILLSON PEALE (1741-1827)

32 SELF-PORTRAIT ("in the character of a painter")
Oil on canvas, 26 x 22 inches
Unsigned; painted 1824
PAFA, Provenance unknown, 1845

References: Charles Coleman Sellers, *Portraits and Miniatures by Charles Willson Peale, Transactions of the American Philosophical Society,* vol. 42, pt. 1 (Philadelphia, 1952), p. 162.

REMBRANDT PEALE (1778-1860)

33 SELF-PORTRAIT
Oil on paper on canvas, $20\frac{3}{4}$ x $16\frac{1}{2}$ inches
Unsigned; painted ca. 1845
PAFA, Gift of Mrs. Rembrandt Peale, 1869

References: C. Edwards Lester, *The Artists of America* (reprint ed., New York, 1970), pp. 199-231; Ann C. Van Devanter and Alfred Frankenstein, *American Self-Portraits, 1670-1973* (exhibition catalogue, National Portrait Gallery, Smithsonian Institution, Washington, D.C., 1974), pp. 62-63.

WILLIAM RUSH (1756-1833)

34 SELF-PORTRAIT
Terracotta bust, 20 x $18\frac{1}{2}$ x $11\frac{1}{2}$ inches
Unsigned; executed ca. 1822
PAFA, Provenance unknown, 1849

References: Henri Marceau, *William Rush, 1756-1833, The First Native American Sculptor* (exhibition catalogue, Pennsylvania Museum of Art, Philadelphia, 1937), pp. 53-54.

WILLIAM RUSH (1756-1833)

35 MARQUIS DE LAFAYETTE
Terracotta bust, 24 x 19 x $10\frac{1}{2}$ inches
Unsigned; executed 1824
PAFA, Gift of Dr. William Rush Dunton, 1911

References: Henri Marceau, *William Rush, 1756-1833, The First Native American Sculptor* (exhibition catalogue, Pennsylvania Museum of Art, Philadelphia, 1937), p. 55.

JOHN SINGER SARGENT (1856-1925)

36 Mr. and Mrs. John W. Field
Oil on canvas, 44 x 32½ inches
Signed u.r.: John S. Sargent Paris 1882
PAFA, John W. and Eliza W. Field Collection, 1891

References: David McKibbin, *Sargent's Boston* (exhibition catalogue, Museum of Fine Arts, Boston, 1956).

JOHN SARTAIN (1808-1897)

36a The Pennsylvania Academy of the Fine Arts — Second Building
Engraving and etching, 5⅞ x 9 inches
Signed: Picture by J. Hamilton Engraving by J. Sartain
PAFA, Provenance unknown

References: David McNeely Stauffer, *American Engravers on Copper and Steel* (New York, 1907), vol. 1, pp. 234-36.

D. B. SHEAHAN (n.d.)

37 Joseph Harrison, Jr.
Marble bust, 22½ x 21 x 13¼ inches
Signed: D. B. Sheahan Sculpt. New York, 1874
PAFA, Joseph and Sarah Harrison Collection, 1912

References: Frank H. Goodyear, Jr., "Harrison Collection," in *The Beneficent Connoisseurs* (exhibition catalogue, PAFA, 1974).

THOMAS SULLY (1783-1872)

38 Edward L. Carey
Oil on canvas, 30 x 25½ inches
Signed on back: TS 1859 / March Copy no. 3
PAFA, Gift of Miss Carey, 1859

References: Edward Biddle and Mantle Fielding, *The Life and Works of Thomas Sully (1783-1872)* (Philadelphia, 1921), p. 117.

BENJAMIN TANNER (1775-1848)

39 The Pennsylvania Academy of the Fine Arts — First Building
Engraving, 5 x 6⅞ inches
Signed: J. J. Barralet del — B. Tanner Sc.; executed 1809
PAFA, The John S. Phillips Collection, 1876

References: David McNeely Stauffer, *American Engravers on Copper and Steel* (New York, 1907), vol. 1, pp. 263-65.

JAMES JACQUES JOSEPH TISSOT (1836-1902)

40 The Reverie
Oil on canvas, 12¾ x 20 inches
Signed u.r.: J. J. Tissot; dated u.l.: 1889
PAFA, Bequest of Henry C. Gibson, 1892

References: Henri Zerner, David S. Brooke, and Michael Wentworth, *James Jacques Joseph Tissot, 1836-1902: A Retrospective Exhibition* (exhibition catalogue, Museum of Art, Rhode Island School of Design, Providence, 1968).

ALBERT BERNHARD UHLE (1847-1930)

41 Joseph E. Temple
Oil on canvas on wood, 30 x 25¼ inches
Unsigned; painted ca. 1885
PAFA, Joseph E. Temple Collection, 1886

References: Mantle Fielding, *Dictionary of American Painters, Sculptors, and Engravers* (New York, 1965), pp. 377-78.

ALBERT BERNHARD UHLE (1847-1930)

42 Henry C. Gibson
Oil on canvas, 34¼ x 27 inches
Signed l.r.: B. Uhle, 1891
PAFA, Bequest of Henry C. Gibson, 1892

References: Frank H. Goodyear, Jr., "Gibson Collection," in *The Beneficent Connoisseurs* (exhibition catalogue, PAFA, 1974).

CLAUDE JOSEPH VERNET (1714-1789)

43 Shipwreck
Oil on canvas, 60 x 122 inches
Signed l.r.: Joseph Vernet 1782
PAFA, Academy Purchase, 1846

References: F. Ingersoll-Smouse, *Joseph Vernet, peintre de marine, 1714-1789. Etude critique suivie d'un catalogue raisonné de son oeuvre peint*, 2 vols. (Paris, 1926).

FRANKLIN C. WATKINS (1894-1972)

44 JOSEPH T. FRASER

Oil on canvas, 29½ x 23¾ inches

Signed l.l.: Watkins, 1970

PAFA, Commissioned by the Academy, 1970

References: Henry Clifford, *Franklin C. Watkins* (exhibition catalogue, Philadelphia Museum of Art, 1964); Ben Wolf, *Franklin C. Watkins: Portrait of a Painter* (Philadelphia, 1966).

BENJAMIN WEST (1738-1820)

45 CHRIST REJECTED

Oil on canvas, 200 x 260 inches

Unsigned; painted ca. 1814

PAFA, Joseph and Sarah Harrison Collection, 1878

References: John Galt, *The Life, Studies and Works of Benjamin West* (London, 1820); Grose Evans, *Benjamin West and the Taste of His Times* (Carbondale, Illinois, 1959), pp. 96-102.

THE EDUCATION OF THE AMERICAN ARTIST

THOMAS POLLOCK ANSHUTZ (1851-1912)

46 DISSECTING ROOM

Oil on composition board, 10 x 12½ inches

Unsigned; painted 1879

PAFA, Acquired from the artist, 1879

References: [William C. Brownell], "The Art Schools of Philadelphia," *Scribner's Monthly,* 18 (September 1879), 747; Sandra Denney Heard, *Thomas P. Anshutz, 1851-1912* (exhibition catalogue, PAFA, 1973), pp. 5, 24; Ellwood C. Parry III and Maria Chamberlin-Hellman, "Thomas Eakins as an Illustrator," *The American Art Journal,* 5 (May 1973), 37.

THOMAS POLLOCK ANSHUTZ (1851-1912)

47 MILO OF CROTAN

Charcoal on paper, 24½ x 18⅝ inches

Unsigned

PAFA, Gift of Mrs. Edward Anshutz, 1971

References: Sandra Denney Heard, *Thomas P. Anshutz, 1851-1912* (exhibition catalogue, PAFA, 1973), cat. no. 30.

THOMAS POLLOCK ANSHUTZ (1851-1912)

48 STUDY OF A MODEL

Oil on canvas, 19⅞ x 13¾ inches

Unsigned

PAFA, Gift of Mrs. Edward Anshutz, 1971

ALICE BARBER (1858-1932)

49 FEMALE LIFE CLASS

Oil on board, 12 x 14 inches

Signed l.l.: Alice Barber/'79

PAFA, Acquired from the artist, 1879

References: [William C. Brownell], "The Art Schools of Philadelphia," *Scribner's Monthly,* 18 (September 1879), 743; Christine Jones Huber, *The Pennsylvania Academy and Its Women, 1850-1920* (exhibition catalogue, PAFA, 1973), illus. p. 17, cat. no. 30; Ellwood C. Parry III and Maria Chamberlin-Hellman, "Thomas Eakins as an Illustrator," *The American Art Journal,* 5 (May 1973), 36-37.

CECILIA BEAUX (1855-1942)

50 SUPPER AT EMMAUS

Oil on cardboard, 9½ x 11⅜ inches

Signed l.r.: Beaux; inscribed l.l.: a monsieur Julian/souvenir respecteuse/de son élève — Cecilia Beaux.; painted ca. 1888-89

PAFA, Gift of Henry S. Drinker, 1950

References: Cecilia Beaux, *Background with Figures* (Cambridge, 1930), pp. 122-23; Henry S. Drinker, *The Paintings and Drawings of Cecilia Beaux* (Philadelphia, 1955), p. 100; Frank H. Goodyear, Jr. and Elizabeth Bailey, *Cecilia Beaux: Portrait of an Artist* (exhibition catalogue, PAFA, 1974-75), pp. 26, 68, cat. no. 35.

CECILIA BEAUX (1855-1942)

51 A COUNTRY WOMAN

Oil on canvas, 14 x 8¾ inches

Unsigned; painted 1888

PAFA, Gift of Henry S. Drinker, 1950

References: Frank H. Goodyear, Jr. and Elizabeth Bailey, *Cecilia Beaux: Portrait of an Artist* (exhibition catalogue, PAFA, 1974-75), p. 64, cat. no. 29.

ARTHUR B. CARLES (1882-1952)

52 WHITE CALLAS

Oil on canvas, 50½ x 38 inches

Signed l.r.: Carles; painted 1925
PAFA, Gift of Harry G. Sundheim, Jr., 1958

References: Memorial Exhibition: Arthur B. Carles, 1882-1952 (exhibition catalogue, PAFA and Philadelphia Museum of Art, 1953), cat. no. 12.

MARY CASSATT (1844-1926)

53 COPY AFTER FRANS HALS
Oil on canvas, 18¼ x 28½ inches
Unsigned; painted ca. 1873
Collection of Mrs. Percy C. Madiera, Jr.

References: Frederick A. Sweet, *Miss Mary Cassatt, Impressionist from Pennsylvania* (Norman, Oklahoma, 1966), pp. 27, 195; Adelyn Dohme Breeskin, *Mary Cassatt: A Catalogue Raisonné of Oils, Pastels, Watercolors, and Drawings* (Washington, D.C., 1970), p. 36, cat. no. 25.

JEFFERSON DAVID CHALFANT (1856-1931)

54 STUDY FOR BOUGUEREAU'S ATELIER AT THE JULIAN ACADEMY, PARIS
Pencil on paper, 10½ x 14 inches
Inscription indistinct; executed 1891
Private Collection

References: American Paintings and Historical Prints from the Middendorf Collection (exhibition catalogue, Baltimore Museum of Art and Metropolitan Museum of Art, 1967), cat. no. 48b.

JEFFERSON DAVID CHALFANT (1856-1931)

55 BOUGUEREAU'S ATELIER AT THE JULIAN ACADEMY, PARIS
Oil on wood panel, 11 x 14½ inches
Signed l.l.: J. D. Chalfant/1891; inscribed on back: Atelier de Bouguereau/a l'Academie Julian /J. D. Chalfant/Paris/1891
Private Collection

References: Jefferson D. Chalfant, 1856-1931 (exhibition catalogue, The Wilmington Society of the Fine Arts, Delaware Art Museum, 1959), cat. no. 4; *American Paintings and Historical Prints from the Middendorf Collection* (exhibition catalogue, The Baltimore Museum of Art and The Metropolitan Museum of Art, 1967), cat. no. 48a.

JOHN GADSBY CHAPMAN (1808-1889)

56 THE TRYING HOUR
Pen, brown and white wash on buff paper, 10½ x 15¼ inches
Signed u.r.: Trying Hour/Chapman/for Cole; executed ca. 1844-46
Museum of Fine Arts, Boston, M. and M. Karolik Collection of American Water Colors & Drawings

References: Museum of Fine Arts, Boston, *M. & M. Karolik Collection of American Water Colors & Drawings* (Boston, 1962), vol. 1, p. 274, no. 653.

WILLIAM MERRITT CHASE (1849-1916)

57 STILL LIFE
Oil on canvas, 36 x 36 inches
Signed: 3 Hour Sketch/By Wm. M. Chase
PAFA, Gift of the artist, 1909

References: Ronald G. Pisano, Catalogue raisonné of the artist's work, in preparation.

JANE COOPER SULLY DARLEY (1807-1877)

58 MADONNA (After Raphael's "Madonna Della Sedia")
Oil on canvas, 19 x 15⅛ inches
Signed l.r.: Jane Sully after TS 1826
PAFA, Bequest of Harriet P. Smith, 1905

References: Mantle Fielding, *Dictionary of American Painters, Sculptors, and Engravers* (New York, 1965), p. 87.

EDGAR DEGAS (1834-1917)

59 AU LOUVRE: LA PEINTURE (MARY CASSATT)
Etching and aquatint, 12 x 5 inches
Unsigned; executed 1879-80
Indianapolis Museum of Art, Carl H. Lieber Memorial Fund

References: Loys Delteil, *Le peintre-graveur illustré: Degas* (reprint ed., New York, 1969), vol. 9, cat. no. 29.

ASHER B. DURAND (1796-1886) after John Vanderlyn

60 ARIADNE ASLEEP ON THE ISLAND OF NAXOS
Etching and engraving (intermediate state), 14¼ x 17⅞ inches
Signed in plate l.r.: A. B. Durand Sc.; executed 1835

Museum of Fine Arts, Boston, Gift of John Durand

References: Grolier Club, *Catalogue of the Engraved Work of Asher B. Durand* (New York, 1895), pp. 9-10, 101-3, no. 237; David Lawall, *A. B. Durand, 1796-1886* (exhibition catalogue, Montclair Art Museum, New Jersey, 1971), p. 50, cat. no. 3, p. 78; Wayne Craven, "Asher B. Durand's Career as an Engraver," *The American Art Journal,* 3 (Spring 1971), 55-57.

FRANK DUVENECK (1848-1919)

61 Turkish Page
Oil on canvas, 42 x 56 inches
Signed c.l.: F. Duveneck. Munich, 1876
PAFA, Temple Fund Purchase, 1894

References: "Art," *Atlantic Monthly,* 38 (May 1877), 641-42; Josephine W. Duveneck, *Frank Duveneck, Painter-Teacher* (San Francisco, 1970), p. 63; Francis W. Bilodeau, *Frank Duveneck, 1848-1919* (exhibition catalogue, Chapellier Galleries, New York, 1972), fig. 14.

THOMAS EAKINS (1844-1916)

62 Ecorche Horse and Detail of Neck
Plaster relief, 22½ x 29½ x 2½ inches
Signed l.c.: Eakins/1882
PAFA, Gift of the Moore Institute through Paulette Van Roekens, 1960

References: Moussa M. Domit, *The Sculpture of Thomas Eakins* (exhibition catalogue, Corcoran Gallery of Art, Washington, D.C., 1969), p. 20, cat. no. 6, plate 39; Gordon Hendricks, *The Life and Work of Thomas Eakins* (New York, 1974), p. 337, no. 216.

THOMAS EAKINS (1844-1916)

63 Male Ventral Torso
Plaster, 32 x 19 x 8 inches
Unsigned; inscribed with names of principal muscles
PAFA, Gift of the Moore Institute through Paulette van Roekens, 1960

References: Lloyd Goodrich, *Thomas Eakins: His Life and Work* (New York, 1933), p. 77; Moussa M. Domit, *The Sculpture of Thomas Eakins* (exhibition catalogue, Corcoran Gallery of Art, Washington, D.C., 1969), cat. no. 21 f, illus. p. 56; Gordon Hendricks, *The Life and Work of Thomas Eakins* (New York, 1974), pp. 130-31, 337, cat. no. 215.

ROBERT FEKE (1707-1752)

64 Mary McCall
Oil on canvas, 50 x 40 inches
Unsigned; painted ca. 1746
PAFA, Bequest of Helen Ross Scheetz, 1891

References: Henry Wilder Foote, *Robert Feke, Colonial Portrait Painter* (Cambridge, 1930) pp. 70-71, 91-93, 167-68, 210; R. Peter Mooz, "Robert Feke: The Philadelphia Story," in *American Painting to 1776: A Reappraisal,* Winterthur Conference Report (Charlottesville, Virginia, 1971), pp. 181-216; R. Peter Mooz, "New Clues to the Art of Robert Feke," *Antiques,* 94 (November 1968), 706-7.

CHARLES LEWIS FUSSELL (ca. 1840-1909)

65 Academy Students Dissecting a Horse
Oil on cardboard, 7⅜ x 10¼ inches
Unsigned; painted 1879
PAFA, Acquired from the artist, 1879

References: [William C. Brownell], "The Art Schools of Philadelphia," *Scribner's Monthly,* 18 (September 1879), 746; Felix Regamey, *L'enseignment du dessin aux Etats-Unis (Notes et documents)* (Paris, 1881), p. 87; Elwood C. Parry III and Maria Chamberlin-Hellman, "Thomas Eakins as an Illustrator," *The American Art Journal,* 5 (May 1973), 37.

DANIEL GARBER (1880-1958)

66 Students of Painting
Oil on board, 18 x 21¾ inches
Signed l.l.: Daniel Garber; inscribed on reverse: Students of Painting/by Daniel Garber; Record Book Page 26-Line 19; painted 1923
PAFA, Gift of John Garber and Mrs. Tanis Page, 1974

References: Daniel Garber, "Record of Paintings" (ms. in the collection of John Garber, copy in PAFA Archives), p. 26; *Daniel Garber Retrospective Exhibition: Paintings, Drawings, Etchings* (exhibition catalogue, PAFA, 1945), cat. no. 100.

CHARLES GRAFLY (1863-1929)

67 Hugh Henry Breckenridge
Bronze bust, 19¾ x 8¾ x 10 inches
Signed on back: To my friend Breckenridge/ Chas. Grafly; cast in 1938
PAFA, Academy Purchase, 1938

References: Lorado Taft, "Charles Grafly, Sculptor," *Brush and Pencil,* 3 (March 1899), 343; Wayne Craven, *Sculpture in America* (New York, 1968), pp. 441, 462, fig. 12.13; Pamela H. Simpson, "The Sculpture of Charles Grafly: A Catalogue Raisonné" (Ph.D. dissertation, University of Delaware, 1974), pp. 218-19, cat. no. 72.

WILLIAM MICHAEL HARNETT (1848-1892)

68 The Borghese Warrior
(After a cast of the antique statue in the Louvre)
Black and white chalks and body color on tan paper, 39½ x 34 inches
Signed l.r.: WMHarnett 1873
PAFA, Gift of Mr. and Mrs. David J. Grossman, 1960

References: Alfred Frankenstein, *After the Hunt: William Harnett and Other American Still-Life Painters, 1870-1900* (1953; rev. ed., Berkeley and Los Angeles, 1969), pp. 33, 35, 45, 164, no. 4.

ELLA SOPHONISBA HERGESHEIMER (1873-1943)

69 In Competition, Shinnecock Hills
Oil on canvas, 16 x 20⅛ inches
Signed l.l.: E. HERGESHEIMER/1900
Collection of Dr. and Mrs. Ralph Carron

References: Ronald G. Pisano, *The Students of William Merritt Chase* (exhibition catalogue, Heckscher Museum, Huntington, New York and The Parrish Art Museum, Southampton, New York, 1973), p. 18, cat. no. 24.

JEAN ANTOINE HOUDON (1741-1828)

70 L'Ecorché
(Cast after 1767 original; Louvre)
Plaster, 69 inches high
Unsigned
PAFA, Academy Purchase through Nicholas Biddle, 1807

References: Charles Henry Hart and Edward Biddle, *Memoirs of the Life and Works of Jean Antoine Houdon, the Sculptor of Voltaire and of Washington* (Philadelphia, 1911), pp. 10, 13, 307, Appendix F; Louis Réau, *Houdon, sa vie et son oeuvre* (Paris, 1964), part I, pp. 39-40, part II, pp. 207-9, part III, p. 24, no. 69, part IV, 16A/69, 16B; H. H. Arnason, *Sculpture by Houdon* (exhibition catalogue, Worcester Art Museum, Mass., 1964), pp. 13, 15, 18, 20.

JAMES P. KELLY (1854-1893)

71 The Modeling Class
Oil on cardboard, 10⅛ x 12¾ inches
Unsigned; painted 1879
PAFA, Acquired from the artist, 1879

References: [William C. Brownell], "The Art Schools of Philadelphia," *Scribner's Monthly,* 18 (September 1879), 744; Felix Regamey, *L'enseignement du dessin aux Etats-Unis (Notes et documents)* (Paris, 1881), p. 81; Ellwood C. Parry III and Maria Chamberlin-Hellman, "Thomas Eakins as an Illustrator," *The American Art Journal,* 5 (May 1973), 37.

WILLIAM SIDNEY MOUNT (1807-1868)

72 The Painter's Triumph
Oil on wood, 19½ x 23½ inches
Signed l.l.: Wm S. Mount/1838
PAFA, Bequest of Henry C. Carey, 1879

References: The Gift: A Christmas and New Year's Present for 1840 (Philadelphia, 1839), illus. opp. p. 208, pp. 216-218; Bartlett Cowdrey and Hermann Warner Williams, *William Sidney Mount 1807-1868, An American Painter* (exhibition catalogue, Metropolitan Museum of Art, New York, 1944), p. 18, no. 28, pp. 39-40, fig. 29; Alfred Frankenstein, *Painter of Rural America: William Sidney Mount* (exhibition catalogue, International Exhibitions Foundation, Washington, D.C., 1969), p. 25, no. 15.

MAXFIELD PARRISH (1870-1966)

73 Male Nude
Pencil on paper, 25 x 19 inches
Signed u.r.: Parrish; executed ca. 1895
Collection of Mr. and Mrs. Herbert P. Reed, Windsor, Vermont

References: Maxfield Parrish: Master of Make-Believe (exhibition catalogue, Brandywine River Museum, Chadds Ford, Pennsylvania, 1974), p. 41, cat. no. 103.

REMBRANDT PEALE (1778-1860)

74 William Raborg
Oil on canvas, 36 x 27 inches
Signed l.r.: Rembrandt/Peale/Pinxt/1797; inscribed on paper: William Raborg/Merchant/Baltimore

PAFA, Gift of Brigadier General and Mrs. Edgar R. Owen, 1973

References: C. Edwards Lester, *The Artists of America* (reprint ed., New York, 1970), pp. 199-231; Karen M. Jones, "Museum Accessions," *Antiques*, 106 (November 1974), 762.

RICHARD S. RANCK (b. 1946)

75 NOT A SOCIAL COMMENT
Oil on cotton, 54¼ x 48¼ inches
Unsigned; painted 1975
Lent by the artist

WILLIAM TROST RICHARDS (1833-1905)

76 SKETCHBOOK, EUROPEAN SUBJECTS, 1855-1856
(Cast study of Venus de Milo in the Louvre)
Pencil on heavy white paper, 6⁵⁄₁₆ x 4⁹⁄₁₆ inches
Inscribed u.r.: Louvre/Aug 29th 1855/Venus Victrix
Collection of Nelson C. White, Waterford, Connecticut

References: Linda Ferber, "William Trost Richards: American Landscape and Marine Painter 1833-1905" (Ph.D. dissertation in preparation, Columbia University).

WILLIAM TROST RICHARDS (1833-1905)

77 SKETCHBOOK, AMERICAN AND EUROPEAN SUBJECTS, 1855-1856
(Sketch made during [October] 1855 trip to the Apennines)
Pencil on white paper, 4¹⁄₁₆ x 6⅝ inches
Unsigned
The Brooklyn Museum, Gift of Edith Ballinger Price

References: Linda Ferber, *William Trost Richards: American Landscape and Marine Painter 1833-1905* (exhibition catalogue, Brooklyn Museum, New York and PAFA, 1973), p. 51; Linda Ferber, "William Trost Richards: American Landscape and Marine Painter 1833-1905" (Ph.D. dissertation in preparation, Columbia University).

WILLIAM TROST RICHARDS (1833-1905)

78 A MOUNTAIN LAKE
Oil on canvas, 12 x 17¾ inches
Signed l.r.: Wm T. Richards, painted ca. 1856-57
PAFA, Gift of Mr. and Mrs. Evan Randolph, 1974

References: Linda Ferber, "William Trost Richards: American Landscape and Marine Painter 1833-1905" (Ph.D. dissertation in preparation, Columbia University).

JOHN SLOAN (1871-1951)

79 ANSHUTZ ON ANATOMY
Etching, 7½ x 9 inches
Unsigned; executed 1912
PAFA, Gift of Helen Farr Sloan, 1972

References: Albert E. Gallatin, *Certain Contemporaries: A Set of Notes in Art Criticism* (New York, 1916), p. 29, no. 79; Bruce St. John, ed., *John Sloan's New York Scene* (New York, 1965), pp. 604-5; Peter Morse, *John Sloan's Prints: A Catalogue Raisonné of the Etchings, Lithographs, and Posters* (New Haven and London, 1969), pp. 179-80, cat. no. 155.

JOHN SMITH (1652-1742) after Sir Godfrey Kneller

80 HER ROYAL HIGHNESS PRINCESS ANN OF DENMARK
Mezzotint, 12⅜ x 9⅞ inches
Inscribed in plate l.l.: G. Kneller Eques. pinx.; l.r.: J. Smith fec. et excudit.; executed 1692
The Library of Congress, Washington, D.C.

References: Waldron Phoenix Belknap, Jr., *American Colonial Painting: Materials for a History* (Cambridge, Mass., 1959), p. 294, no. 18, plate XXI.

THOMAS SULLY (1783-1872)

81 CHILD WITH DOG AND FLOWERS
Oil on canvas, 32¼ x 38¼ inches
Signed l.c.: TS 1828
PAFA, Bequest of Mrs. Aspinwall, 1842

References: PAFA Board Minutes, November 9, 1842; Edward Biddle and Mantle Fielding, *The Life and Works of Thomas Sully (1783-1872)* (Philadelphia, 1921), p. 343, no. 2162.

UNKNOWN

82 CAST AFTER VENUS DE MILO
(from Andros Aphrodite, ca. 150-120 B.C.; Louvre)

Plaster, 84 inches high
Stamped on center of base: 132
PAFA, Gift of Dr. Francis W. Lewis, 1856

References: Catalogue of the Statues, Busts, Studies, etc. forming the collection of the Antique School of the National Academy of Design (New York, 1846), pp. 14-15, no. 173; *Catalogue of Plaster Reproductions from antique, medieval, and modern sculpture . . . made and for sale by P. P. Caproni and Brother* (Boston, 1913), p. 10, no. 501.

UNKNOWN

83 CAST AFTER BORGHESE WARRIOR
(from Roman copy after the original, ca. 100 B.C.; Louvre)
Plaster, 63 inches high
PAFA, Provenance unknown, 1905

References: Catalogue of the Statues, Busts, Studies, etc. forming the collection of the Antique School of the National Academy of Design (New York, 1846), pp. 7-8, no. 141; "Some Masterpieces of Art," *The Art Amateur,* 2 (December 1879), 6; *Catalogue of Plaster Reproductions from antique, medieval, and modern sculpture . . . made and for sale by P. P. Caproni and Brother* (Boston, 1913), p. 13, nos. 517, 790-93.

UNKNOWN

84 THOMAS SULLY'S COLLECTION OF CASTS
a. child's mask; b. child's hand; c. child's hand; d. child's leg
Plaster, each under 9 inches
Unsigned
PAFA, Gift of Rebecca N. Van Trump, 1909

JOHN VANDERLYN (1775-1852)

85 ARIADNE ASLEEP ON THE ISLAND OF NAXOS
Oil on canvas, 68 x 87 inches
Signed l.l.: J. Vanderlyn fect/Parisiis 1814
PAFA, Joseph and Sarah Harrison Collection, 1878

References: Marius Schoonmaker, *John Vanderlyn Artist, 1775-1852, Biography* (Kingston, New York, 1950), pp. 25-27; Kenneth C. Lindsay, *The Works of John Vanderlyn,* (exhibition catalogue, University Art Gallery, State University of New York, Binghamton, 1970), cat. no. 57, illus. pp. 82-83; William H. Gerdts, *The Great American Nude* (New York and Washington, 1974), frontispiece, pp. 52-53, 57-60.

FRANKLIN WATKINS (1894-1972)

86 STILL LIFE WITH BIRD CAGE
Oil on canvas, 36 x 54 inches
Signed l.l.: Watkins; painted 1955
PAFA, Gift of James P. and Ruth Magill, 1957

References: Henry Clifford, *Franklin C. Watkins* (exhibition catalogue, Philadelphia Museum of Art, 1964), p. 63.

MAX WEBER (1881-1961)

87 THE APOLLO IN MATISSE'S STUDIO
Oil on canvas, 23 x 18 inches
Signed l.r.: MAX WEBER '08
Forum Gallery, New York

References: Max Weber: The Years 1906-1916 (exhibition catalogue, Bernard Danenberg Galleries, New York, et al., 1972), p. 15, no. 14.

BENJAMIN WEST (1738-1820)

88 ELIZABETH PEEL
Oil on canvas, 47 x 34¼ inches
Unsigned; painted ca. 1757-58
PAFA, Gift of John F. Lewis, 1923

References: William Sawitzky, "The American Work of Benjamin West," *Pennsylvania Magazine of History and Biography,* 62 (October 1938), 443-44, 455-56, cat. no. 18; *Philadelphia Painting and Printing to 1776* (exhibition catalogue, PAFA and the Historical Society of Pennsylvania in conjunction with the Seventeenth Annual Winterthur Conference, 1971), p. 39, cat. no. 32; Wayne Craven, "Painting in New York City, 1750-1775," in *American Painting to 1776: A Reappraisal,* Winterthur Conference Report (Charlottesville, Virginia, 1971), pp. 274-75.

BENJAMIN WEST (1738-1820)

89 SELF-PORTRAIT
Oil on canvas, 36 x 28 inches
Signed u.r.: B.West 1806
PAFA, Gift of Mr. and Mrs. Henry R. Hallowell, 1964

References: William Dunlap, *History of the Rise and Progress of the Arts of Design in the United States* (New York, 1834), vol. 1, p. 231; *Benjamin West, 1738-1820* (exhibition catalogue, Pennsylvania Museum of Art, Philadelphia, 1938), pp. 50-51, cat. no. 59; Grose Evans, *Benjamin West and the Taste of his Times* (Carbondale, Illinois, 1959), p. 12, plate 12.

CHARLES WILLSON PEALE AND HIS FAMILY OF PAINTERS

ANNA CLAYPOOLE PEALE (1791-1878)

90 MADAME L'ALLEMAND
Ivory, 1⅞ x 1½ inches (oval)
Signed l.r.: Anna C./Peale 18 . . .; inscribed on back of locket: Madame Lallemand/Anna C. Peale/Pinxit; painted ca. 1818
PAFA, Gift of Charles Hare Hutchinson, 1898

References: Anne Hollingsworth Wharton, *Heirlooms in Miniatures* (Philadelphia and London, 1898) illus. p. 190; Harry B. Wehle, *Catalogue of an Exhibition of Miniatures Painted in America* (Metropolitan Museum of Art, New York, 1927), p. 38.

CHARLES WILLSON PEALE (1741-1827)

91 WORTHY OF LIBERTY, MR. PITT SCORNS TO INVADE THE LIBERTIES OF OTHER PEOPLE
Mezzotint, 23 x 14¾ inches
Inscribed l.r.: Chas. Willson Peale pinxt. et fecit.; executed 1768
PAFA, John S. Phillips Collection, 1876

References: Horace Wells Sellers, "Engravings by Charles Willson Peale, Limner," *Pennsylvania Magazine of History and Biography,* 57 (1934), 153-74, 284-85, cat. no. 1; Charles Coleman Sellers, *Portraits and Miniatures by Charles Willson Peale, Transactions of the American Philosophical Society,* vol. 42, pt. 1 (Philadelphia, 1952), cat. no. 695; Charles Coleman Sellers, *Charles Willson Peale* (New York, 1969), pp. 67-70, illus. p. 68.

CHARLES WILLSON PEALE (1741-1827)

92 BARON FREDERICK WILLIAM VON STEUBEN
Oil on canvas, 30 x 24¾ inches
Unsigned; painted 1780
PAFA, Gift of Mrs. M. L. M. Peters, 1881

References: Charles Willson Peale, *Historical Catalogue of the Paintings in the Philadelphia Museum . . .* (exhibition catalogue, Philadelphia, 1813), cat. no. 24, pp. 16-17; *Exhibition of Portraits by Charles Willson Peale and James Peale and Rembrandt Peale* (exhibition catalogue, PAFA, 1923), cat no. 31; Charles Coleman Sellers, *Portraits and Miniatures by Charles Willson Peale* (Philadelphia, 1952), cat. no. 825, illus. no. 105.

CHARLES WILLSON PEALE (1741-1827)

93 GOUVERNEUR AND ROBERT MORRIS
Oil on canvas, 43¼ x 51½ inches
Signed l.l.: C W Peale Pinxt 1783
Inscribed c.l.: A plan of Finance to / restore public credit & for / establishing a national / Bank
PAFA, Bequest of Richard Ashhurst, 1969

References: Charles Coleman Sellers, *Portraits and Miniatures by Charles Willson Peale* (Philadelphia, 1952), cat. no. 572, illus. 131; Charles Coleman Sellers, "Charles Willson Peale's Portrait of Gouverneur and Robert Morris, a convergence of politics and art," *Antiques,* 99 (March 1971), 404-6.

CHARLES WILLSON PEALE (1741-1827)

94 BENJAMIN FRANKLIN
Oil on canvas, 23 x 19 inches
Unsigned; painted ca. 1785
PAFA, Joseph and Sarah Harrison Collection, 1912

References: Charles Willson Peale, *Historical Catalogue of the Paintings in the Philadelphia Museum . . .* (exhibition catalogue, Philadelphia, 1813), cat. no. 1, pp. 3-4; Charles Coleman Sellers, "Peale Portraits of Benjamin Franklin," *Proceedings of the American Philosophical Society,* 94, no. 3 (June 1950), 251-57; Charles Coleman Sellers, *Portraits and Miniatures by Charles Willson Peale,* (Philadelphia, 1952), cat. no. 279, illus. 172.

CHARLES WILLSON PEALE (1741-1827)

95 GEORGE WASHINGTON
Oil on canvas, 23½ x 19 inches
Unsigned; painted 1787
PAFA, Joseph and Sarah Harrison Collection, 1912

References: Charles Willson Peale, *Historical Catalogue of the Paintings in the Philadelphia Museum . . .* (exhibition catalogue, Philadelphia, 1813), cat. no. 17, pp. 10-12; Charles Coleman Sellers, *Portraits and Miniatures by Charles Willson Peale* (Philadelphia, 1952), cat. no. 939, illus. no. 371; Charles Coleman Sellers, "Charles Willson Peale's Portraits of Washington," *Metropolitan Museum Bulletin,* 9 (February 1951), 47-55, illus. p. 152.

CHARLES WILLSON PEALE (1741-1827)

96 JAMES LATIMER

Oil on canvas, 36 x 27¼ inches

Unsigned; painted 1789-90

PAFA, Bequest of Robert C. Latimer, 1974

References: Charles Coleman Sellers, *Portraits and Miniatures by Charles Willson Peale* (Philadelphia, 1952), cat. no. 459, illus. no. 205; Edward H. Dwight, *Paintings by the Peale Family* (exhibition catalogue, Cincinnati Art Museum, 1954), cat. no. 20.

CHARLES WILLSON PEALE (1741-1827)

97 SARAH GEDDES LATIMER

Oil on canvas, 36 x 27¼ inches

Unsigned; painted 1789-90

PAFA, Bequest of Robert C. Latimer, 1974

References: Charles Coleman Sellers, *Portraits and Miniatures by Charles Willson Peale* (Philadelphia, 1952), cat no. 460, illus. no. 204; Edward H. Dwight, *Paintings by the Peale Family* (exhibition catalogue, Cincinnati Art Museum, 1954), cat. no. 21.

CHARLES WILLSON PEALE (1741-1827)

98 SELF-PORTRAIT WITH SPECTACLES

Oil on canvas, 26 x 22 inches

Unsigned; painted ca. 1804

PAFA, Gilpin Fund Purchase, 1937

References: Exhibition of Portraits by Charles Willson Peale and James Peale and Rembrandt Peale (exhibition catalogue, PAFA, 1923), cat. no. 61; Charles Coleman Sellers, *Portraits and Miniatures by Charles Willson Peale* (Philadelphia 1952), cat. no. 630, illus. 379; Charles Coleman Sellers, *Charles Willson Peale* (New York, 1969), illus. frontispiece.

CHARLES WILLSON PEALE (1741-1827)

99 NOAH AND HIS ARK

Oil on canvas, 40¾ x 50¼ inches

Unsigned; painted 1819

PAFA, Collections Fund Purchase, 1951

References: Peale's Museum Gallery of Oil Paintings. Thomas and Sons, Auctioneers . . . (Philadelphia, 1854), cat. no. 127; Charles Coleman Sellers, *Charles Willson Peale with Patron and Populace, Transactions of the American Philosophical Society,* vol. 59, pt. 3 (Philadelphia, 1969), cat. no. S118, illus. no. 46.

CHARLES WILLSON PEALE (1741-1827)

100 THE ARTIST IN HIS MUSEUM

Oil on canvas, 103½ x 80 inches

Unsigned; inscribed l.l.: With this article the Museum commenced, June 1784. Presented by Mr. Patterson; painted 1822

PAFA, Joseph and Sarah Harrison Collection, 1878

References: Peale's Museum Gallery of Oil Paintings. Thomas and Sons, Auctioneers . . . (Philadelphia, 1854), cat. no. 258; Charles Coleman Sellers, *Portraits and Miniatures by Charles Willson Peale,* (Philadelphia, 1952), cat. no. 636, illus. no. 383; Charles H. Elam, ed., *The Peale Family* (exhibition catalogue, Detroit Institute of Arts, 1967), cat. no. 2, illus. frontispiece and p. 41.

CHARLES WILLSON PEALE (1741-1827)

101 JAMES PEALE

("The Lamplight Portrait")

Oil on canvas, 27 x 36 inches

Unsigned; painted 1822

The Detroit Institute of Arts

References: Peale's Museum Gallery of Oil Paintings. Thomas and Sons, Auctioneers . . . (Philadelphia, 1854), cat. no. 88; Edgar P. Richardson, "The Lamplight Portrait," *Detroit Institute Bulletin,* 30, no. 1 (1950-1951); Charles Coleman Sellers, *Portraits and Miniatures by Charles Willson Peale* (Philadelphia, 1952), cat. no. 659, illus. no. 336.

JAMES PEALE (1749-1831)

102 PEALE'S MUSEUM

Oil on wood panel, 5¼ x 7½ inches

Unsigned; painted ca. 1782

The American Philosophical Society, Philadelphia

References: Charles H. Elam, ed., *The Peale Family* (exhibition catalogue, Detroit Institute of Arts, 1967), cat. no. 100, illus. p. 21.

JAMES PEALE (1749-1831)

103 FRANCES GRATZ ETTING

Oil on ivory, 2½ x 2 inches (oval)

Signed u.r.: J. P./1794

PAFA, Gift of Frank Marx Etting, 1886

References: Frederick Fairchild Sherman, "James Peale Portrait Miniatures," *Art in America,* 19

(August 1931), 208-21, illus. p. 215; Jean Lambert Brockaway, "The Miniatures of James Peale," *Antiques,* 22 (October 1932), 130-34; E. Grosvenor Paine, "Miniaturists in the Peale Family," in Charles H. Elam, ed., *The Peale Family* (exhibition catalogue, Detroit Institute of Arts, 1967).

JAMES PEALE (1749-1831)

104 REUBEN ETTING

Oil on ivory, 2¼ x 1⅞ inches (oval)

Signed u.l.: J.P./1794

PAFA, Gift of Frank Marx Etting, 1886

References: Loan Exhibition of Historical Portraits (exhibition catalogue, PAFA, 1887), cat. no. 149; Frederick Fairchild Sherman, "James Peale Portrait Miniatures," *Art in America,* 19 (August 1931) 208-21, cat. no. 19; Harry B. Wehle, *American Miniatures, 1730-1850* (New York, 1927), Chapter V.

JAMES PEALE (1749-1831)

105 THE ARTIST AND HIS FAMILY

Oil on canvas 31¼ x 32¾ inches

Signed l.r.: Jas Peale 1795

PAFA, Gift of John F. Lewis, 1922

References: Exhibition of Portraits by Charles Willson Peale and James Peale and Rembrandt Peale (exhibition catalogue, PAFA, 1923), cat. no. 108, illus. p. 100; *Paintings and Watercolors by James Peale and His Family 1749-1891* (exhibition catalogue, Walker Gallery, New York, 1939), illus.; Charles H. Elam, ed., *The Peale Family* (exhibition catalogue, Detroit Institute of Arts, 1967), cat. no. 72, illus. p. 28.

JAMES PEALE (1749-1831)

106 SELF-PORTRAIT

Oil on canvas, 28 x 23¾ inches

Unsigned; painted ca. 1801

PAFA, Gilpin Fund Purchase, 1915

References: Exhibition of Portraits by Charles Willson Peale and James Peale and Rembrandt Peale (exhibition catalogue, PAFA, 1923), cat. no. 116, illus. p. 107; *Four Generations of Commissions: The Peale Collection* (exhibition catalogue, Maryland Historical Society, Baltimore, 1975), cat. no. II, illus. p. 28.

JAMES PEALE (1749-1831)

107 ANNA AND MARGARETTA PEALE

Oil on canvas, 29 x 23½ inches

Unsigned; painted ca. 1805

PAFA, Academy Purchase, 1902

References: The Peale Heritage, 1763-1963 (exhibition catalogue, Washington County Museum of Fine Arts, Hagerstown, Maryland, 1963), cat. no. 14, illus. p. 37; Charles H. Elam, ed., *The Peale Family* (exhibition catalogue, Detroit Institute of Arts, 1967), cat. no. 74, illus. p. 75; *Four Generations of Commissions: The Peale Collection* (exhibition catalogue, Maryland Historical Society, Baltimore, 1975), cat. no. VI, illus. p. 87.

JAMES PEALE (1749-1831)

108 STILL LIFE NO. 2

Oil on wood, 18 x 26½ inches

Signed l.l.: Jas Peale 1821

PAFA, Gilpin Fund Purchase, 1915

References: Edward H. Dwight, "Still-Life Paintings by the Peale Family," in Charles H. Elam, ed., *The Peale Family* (exhibition catalogue, Detroit Institute of Arts, 1967).

MARGARETTA ANGELICA PEALE (1795-1882)

109 STRAWBERRIES AND CHERRIES

Oil on canvas, 10 x 12 inches

Unsigned

PAFA, Deposited by Miss Mildred Carter, 1924

References: Wolfgang Born, "The Female Peales, Their Art and Its Tradition," *American Collector,* 15 (August 1946), 12-14; Edward H. Dwight, *Paintings by the Peale Family* (exhibition catalogue, Cincinnati Art Museum, 1954), cat. no. 107, illus. p. 14; Charles H. Elam, ed., *The Peale Family* (exhibition catalogue, Detroit Institute of Arts, 1967), cat. no. 197, illus. p. 129.

MARY JANE PEALE (1827-1902)

110 RUBENS PEALE

Oil on canvas, 24½ x 20⅞ inches

Inscribed on back: Rubens Peale, painted by Mary J. Peale, Woodland, April 1855, aged 71

Collection of Mr. and Mrs. James Titelman

References: "The Fabulous Peale Family," *Ken-*

nedy Quarterly, 1 (June 1960) cat. no. 92; Charles Elam, ed., *The Peale Family* (exhibition catalogue, Detroit Institute of Arts, 1967), cat. no. 223; Christine Jones Huber, *The Pennsylvania Academy and Its Women, 1850-1920* (exhibition catalogue, PAFA, 1973), cat. no. 4.

RAPHAELLE PEALE (1774-1825)

111 APPLES AND FOX GRAPES
Oil on wood, 9¾ x 11⅜ inches
Signed lower edge: Apples and Fox
Grapes by Raphael Peale/Phild Sept. 7, 1815.
PAFA, Provenance unknown

References: John I. H. Baur, "The Peales and the Development of American Still Life," *The Art Quarterly,* 3 (Winter 1940), 81-92; Charles Coleman Sellers, *Raphaelle Peale, 1774-1825: Still Lifes and Portraits* (exhibition catalogue, Milwaukee Art Center, 1959); William H. Gerdts and Russell Burke, *American Still-Life Painting* (New York, 1971), illus. p. 27.

RAPHAELLE PEALE (1774-1825)

112 FOX GRAPES AND PEACHES
Oil on wood, 9¾ x 11⅜ inches
Signed l.r.: Raphaelle Peale/August 181[5];
l.l.: Fox Grapes and Peaches
PAFA, Provenance unknown

References: The Peale Heritage, 1763-1963 (exhibition catalogue, Washington County Museum of Fine Arts, Hagerstown, Maryland, 1963), cat. no. 23, illus. p. 55; Charles H. Elam, ed., *The Peale Family* (exhibition catalogue, Detroit Institute of Arts, 1967), cat. no. 128, illus. p. 98; William H. Gerdts and Russell Burke, *American Still-Life Painting* (New York, 1971), illus. p. 27.

REMBRANDT PEALE (1778-1860)

113 DOMINIQUE VIVANT DENON
Oil on canvas, 28½ x 23¼ inches
Unsigned; painted 1808
PAFA, General Fund Purchase, 1854

References: Charles Willson Peale, *Historical Catalogue of the Paintings in the Philadelphia Museum . . .* (exhibition catalogue, Philadelphia, 1813), cat. no. 107, p. 50; *Exhibition of Portraits by Charles Willson Peale and James Peale and Rembrandt Peale* (exhibition catalogue, PAFA, 1923), cat. no. 236; Macgill James, *An Exhibition of Paintings by Rembrandt Peale* (exhibition catalogue, Municipal Museum of Baltimore, 1938), cat. no. 12.

REMBRANDT PEALE (1778-1860)

114 JEAN ANTOINE HOUDON
Oil on canvas, 28¼ x 23 inches
Unsigned; painted 1808
PAFA, General Fund Purchase, 1854

References: Charles Willson Peale, *Historical Catalogue of the Paintings in the Philadelphia Museum . . .* (exhibition catalogue, Philadelphia, 1813), cat. no. 108, p. 50; Charles Henry Hart, "Portrait of Jean Antoine Houdon Painted by Rembrandt Peale," *Art in America,* 3 (February 1915), 78-81, illus. p. 74; Helen C. Frick, "Houdon and Rembrandt Peale," *Antiques,* 26 (July 1934), 8-9.

REMBRANDT PEALE (1778-1860)

115 GEORGE WASHINGTON (PATRIAE PATER)
Oil on canvas, 72¼ x 54¼ inches
Signed l.l.: Rembrandt Peale
Inscribed on back: Copy by Rembrandt Peale
from his original portrait of Washington—
in the U.S. Senate Chamber; painted ca. 1824
PAFA, Joseph and Sarah Harrison Collection, 1912

References: John Hill Morgan, "Rembrandt Peale's Life Portraits of Washington," *Antiques,* 33 (February 1938), 70-72; *Exhibition of Portraits by Charles Willson Peale and James Peale and Rembrandt Peale* (exhibition catalogue, PAFA, 1923), cat. no. 129, illus. p. 119; John A. Mahey, "The Studio of Rembrandt Peale," *The American Art Journal,* 2 (Fall 1969), fig. 1, p. 21.

REMBRANDT PEALE (1778-1860)

116 BENJAMIN FRANKLIN PEALE
Oil on canvas, 21 x 17¼ inches
Signed c.l.: R.P.; painted ca. 1850
PAFA, Gift of the Baldwin Locomotive Works, 1925

References: Macgill James, *An Exhibition of Paintings by Rembrandt Peale* (exhibition catalogue, Municipal Museum of Baltimore, 1938), cat. no. 45; Oliver Jensen, "The Peales," *American Heritage,* 6 (April 1955), 40-51, illus. p. 42.

RUBENS PEALE (1784-1865)

117 The Old Museum
Oil on tin, 14 x 20 inches
Unsigned; painted 1858-60
Collection of Charles Coleman Sellers

References: Edward H. Dwight, *Paintings by the Peale Family* (exhibition catalogue, Cincinnati Art Museum, 1954), cat. no. 83, illus. p. 7; Charles H. Elam, ed., *The Peale Family* (exhibition catalogue, Detroit Institute of Arts, 1967), cat. no. 173, illus. p. 21; Charles Coleman Sellers, *Charles Willson Peale* (New York, 1969), illus. p. 186.

SARAH MIRIAM PEALE (1800-1885)

118 Anna Maria Smyth
Oil on canvas, 36 x 27½ inches
Signed l.r.: Sarah M. Peale/1821
PAFA, John F. Lewis Memorial Collection, 1933

References: The Peale Heritage, 1763-1963 (exhibition catalogue, Washington County Museum of Fine Arts, Hagerstown, Maryland, 1963), cat. no. 38, illus. p. 85; Charles H. Elam, ed., *The Peale Family* (exhibition catalogue, Detroit Institute of Arts, 1967), cat. no. 216, illus. p. 136; Wilbur H. Hunter and John A. Mahey, *Miss Sarah Miriam Peale, 1800-1885: Portraits and Still Life* (exhibition catalogue, The Peale Museum, Baltimore, 1967).

TITIAN RAMSAY PEALE II (1799-1885)

119 Missouri Bears
Watercolor on paper, 7⅜ x 9⅝ inches
Signed l.l.: TRPeale; painted ca. 1820
The American Philosophical Society, Philadelphia

References: Eleventh Annual Exhibition (exhibition catalogue, PAFA, 1822), cat. no. 117; Jessie Poesch, *Titian Ramsay Peale 1799-1885 and His Journals of the Wilkes Expedition, Memoirs of the American Philosophical Society,* vol. 52 (Philadelphia, 1961), p. 60, fig. 31, Charles Coleman Sellers, *Charles Willson Peale with Patron and Populace, Transactions of the American Philosophical Society,* vol. 59, pt. 3 (Philadelphia, 1969), cat. no. 542, illus. no. 16.

TITIAN RAMSAY PEALE II (1799-1885)

120 Buffaloes
Watercolor on paper, 7½ x 9¹⁄₁₆ inches
Inscribed l.l.: Bulls Feby 1820
The American Philosophical Society, Philadelphia

References: Eleventh Annual Exhibition (exhibition catalogue, PAFA, 1822), cat. no. 111; Jessie Poesch, *Titian Ramsay Peale 1799-1885 and His Journals of the Wilkes Expedition, Memoirs of the American Philosophical Society,* vol. 52 (Philadelphia, 1961), fig. 20.

TITIAN RAMSAY PEALE II (1799-1885)

121 Striped Squirrels
Watercolor on paper, 7⅜ x 9⅝ inches
Signed l.l.: TRPeale delin:
caption below: Sc quadra vittatus/Natural size/Specimen obtained at the Rocky mountains/by TRP; executed ca. 1820
The American Philosophical Society, Philadelphia

References: Eleventh Annual Exhibition (exhibition catalogue, PAFA, 1822), cat. no. 113; Jessie Poesch, *Titian Ramsay Peale 1799-1885 and His Journals of the Wilkes Expendition, Memoirs of the American Philosophical Society,* vol. 52 (Philadelphia, 1961), p. 44, fig. 18.

TITIAN RAMSAY PEALE (1799-1885)

122 Wild Turkeys — plate 9 from *American Ornithology*
Engraving with watercolor, 15¼ x 11½ inches
Inscribed in plate l.l.: Drawn from Nature by Titian R. Peale.; l.c.: Wild Turkey, Male and Female./Meleagris Gallopavo./9; l.r.: Engraved by Alexander Lawson.; published 1825
The Pennsylvania Horticultural Society, Philadelphia

References: C. L. Bonaparte, *American Ornithology; or The Natural History of Birds Inhabiting the United States, not given by Wilson.,* vol. 1 (Philadelphia, 1825), plate 9; Jessie Poesch, *Titian Ramsey Peale 1799-1885 and His Journals of the Wilkes Expedition, Memoirs of the American Philosophical Society,* vol. 52 (Philadelphia, 1961), p. 44, fig. 18.

MATHEW PILKINGTON

123 The Gentleman's and Connoisseur's Dictionary of Painters
Printed book with manuscript additions, 11¼ x 8½ inches

London, 1771
The American Philosophical Society, Philadelphia

References: Charles Coleman Sellers, *Charles Willson Peale* (New York, 1969), p. 88.

THE ARTIST AS INTERPRETER OF AMERICAN HISTORY

JOSEPH ANDREWS (1805-1873)
after Peter Frederick Rothermel

124 THE LANDING OF THE PILGRIMS
Engraving, 17 x 24¾ inches
Inscribed l.l.: P. F. Rothermel Paintr;
l.r.: J. Andrews Engravr;
Signed l.r.: Jos. Andrews; executed 1869
Private Collection

References: W. S. Baker, *American Engravers and Their Works* (Philadelphia, 1875), pp. 13-14; David McNeely Stauffer, *American Engravers Upon Copper and Steel* (New York, 1907), vol. 1, p. 11; Francis Russell, "The Pilgrims and the Rock," *American Heritage,* 13 (October 1962), 48-55, illus. 48-49.

THOMAS BIRCH (1779-1851)

125 PERRY'S VICTORY ON LAKE ERIE
Oil on canvas, 66 x 96½ inches
Unsigned; painted 1814
PAFA, Gift of Mrs. C. H. A. Esling, 1912

References: Doris L. Creer, "Thomas Birch: A Study of the Condition of Painting and the Artist's Position in Federal America," (Master's thesis, University of Delaware, 1958), p. 52; William H. Gerdts, *Thomas Birch, 1779-1851, Paintings and Drawings* (exhibition catalogue, Philadelphia Maritime Museum, 1966), illus. 23.

EDWIN DICKINSON (b. 1891)

126 SHILOH
Oil on canvas, 36 x 32 inches
Signed l.l.: Edwin Dickinson 1940
Commerce Bancshares, Inc., Kansas City, Missouri

References: Elaine de Kooning, "Edwin Dickinson Paints a Picture," *Art News,* 48 (September 1949), 26-28, 50-51; Lloyd Goodrich, *Edwin Dickinson* (exhibition catalogue, Whitney Museum of American Art, New York, 1965), p. 11, illus. 32; Norman A. Geske, *Venice 34: The Figurative Tradition in Recent American Art* (exhibition catalogue, National Collection of Fine Arts, Smithsonian Institution, Washington, D.C., 1968), pp. 43-70, illus. 62.

THOMAS EAKINS (1844-1916)

127 THE ARMY OF WASHINGTON CROSSING THE DELAWARE
Photograph of plaster model, 5 x 9¼ inches
Inscribed at bottom: Low Relief. The Army of Washington Crossing the Delaware. Trenton Battle Monument. Eakins.; executed 1893
PAFA Archives

References: Lloyd Goodrich, *Thomas Eakins: His Life and Work* (New York, 1933), p. 209; Moussa M. Domit, *The Sculpture of Thomas Eakins* (exhibition catalogue, Corcoran Gallery of Art, Washington, D.C., 1969), pp. 10-11, 14-15, illus. 55; Zoltan Buki and Suzanne Corlette, eds., *The Trenton Battle Monument: Eakins Bronzes,* New Jersey State Museum Bulletin no. 14 (Trenton, 1973), pp. 57-76, illus. 65.

THOMAS EAKINS (1844-1916)

128 THE ARMY OF WASHINGTON CROSSING THE DELAWARE (detail)
Photograph of plaster model, 9½ x 6¼ inches
Inscribed at bottom: Col. Washington of Georgia. Alex. Hamilton afterwards Sec. Treasury. Lieut. Monroe afterwards President of U.S. Group of Officers in bow of Durham boat. Low Relief. Trenton Battle Monument at Trenton. Eakins [torn]; executed 1893
PAFA Archives

References: Lloyd Goodrich, *Thomas Eakins: His Life and Work* (New York, 1933), p. 209; Moussa M. Domit, *The Sculpture of Thomas Eakins* (exhibition catalogue, Corcoran Gallery of Art, Washington, D.C., 1969), pp. 10-11, 14-15, illus. 55; Zoltan Buki and Suzanne Corlette, eds., *The Trenton Battle Monument: Eakins Bronzes,* New Jersey State Museum Bulletin no. 14 (Trenton, 1973), pp. 57-76, illus. 65.

THOMAS EAKINS (1844-1916)

129 THE OPENING OF THE BATTLE
Photograph of plaster model, 5½ x 8¾ inches
Inscribed at bottom: Low Relief. The Opening of the Battle. Trenton Battle Monument. Eakins; executed 1893
PAFA Archives

References: Lloyd Goodrich, *Thomas Eakins: His*

Life and Work (New York, 1933), p. 209; Moussa M. Domit, *The Sculpture of Thomas Eakins* (exhibition catalogue, Corcoran Gallery of Art, Washington, D.C., 1969), pp. 10-11, 14-15, illus. 55; Zoltan Buki and Suzanne Corlette, eds., *The Trenton Battle Monument: Eakins Bronzes,* New Jersey State Museum Bulletin no. 14 (Trenton, 1973), pp. 57-76, illus. 65.

DAVID EDWIN (1776-1841) after design by James Warrell and drawing by John J. Barralet

130 PETER FRANCISCO'S GALLANT ACTION
Stipple engraving, 21¾ x 29 inches
Inscribed: Designed by J. Warrell, drawn by J. Barralet, engraved by D. Edwin; This Representation of Peter Franciscos Gallant Action with Nine of Tarletons Cavalry in Sight of a Troop of Four Hundred Men Took Place in Amelia County Virginia 1781 Is respectfully inscribed to Him by James Webster and James Warrell.; published 1814
PAFA, John S. Phillips Collection, 1876

References: David McNeely Stauffer, *American Engravers Upon Copper and Steel* (New York, 1907), vol. 2, pp. 154-155; *An Album of American Battle Art, 1755-1918* (Washington, 1947), pp. 42-45, illus. 65.

JAMES HAMILTON (1819-1878)

131 OLD IRONSIDES
Oil on canvas, 60½ x 48 inches
Inscribed on reverse: Old Ironsides/Jas Hamilton/Philada, 1863

'O' better that her shattered hulk,
Should sink beneath the wave;
Her thunders shook the mighty deep,
And there should be her grave;
Nail to the mast her holy flag
Set every threadbare sail,
And give her to the god of storms—
The lightning and the gale

O. W. HOLMES

PAFA, Gift of Caroline Gibson Taitt, 1885

References: John I. H. Baur, "A Romantic Impressionist: James Hamilton," *Brooklyn Museum Bulletin,* 12 (Spring 1951), 1-9; Arlene Jacobowitz, *James Hamilton, 1819-1878: American Marine Painter* (exhibition catalogue, The Brooklyn Museum, New York 1966), p. 49.

GEORGE PETER ALEXANDER HEALY (1813-1894)

132 FRANKLIN URGING THE CLAIMS OF THE AMERICAN COLONIES BEFORE LOUIS XVI
Oil on canvas, 26½ x 36½ inches
Unsigned; painted ca. 1847
The American Philosophical Society, Philadelphia

References: George Peter Alexander Healy, *Reminiscences of a Portrait Painter* (Chicago, 1894), p. 53; *A Catalogue of Portraits and Other Works of Art in the Possession of the American Philosophical Society* (Philadelphia, 1961), pp. 29-30; Marchal E. Landgren, *American Pupils of Thomas Couture* (exhibition catalogue, University of Maryland Art Gallery, College Park, 1970), p. 36, illus. 37.

EDWARD HICKS (1780-1849)

133 PEACEABLE KINGDOM
Oil on canvas, 29 x 35¾ inches
Unsigned; painted ca. 1837
Collection of Robert L. Montgomery, Sydney, Austrailia

References: Alice Ford, *Edward Hicks: Painter of the Peaceable Kingdom* (Philadelphia, 1952); Leon Anthony Arkus, *Hicks, Kane, Pippin: 3 Self-Taught Pennsylvania Artists* (exhibition catalogue, Museum of Art, Carnegie Institute, Pittsburgh and Corcoran Gallery of Art, Washington, D.C., 1966-1967); *Edward Hicks, A Gentle Spirit* (exhibition catalogue, Andrew Crispo Gallery, New York, 1975), illus.

WINSLOW HOMER (1836-1910)

134 PRISONERS FROM THE FRONT
Oil on canvas, 24 x 38 inches
Signed l.r.: Homer, 1866
The Metropolitan Museum of Art, Gift of Mrs. Frank B. Porter, 1922

References: Lloyd Goodrich, *Winslow Homer* (New York, 1944), pp. 21-22; John Wilmerding, *Winslow Homer* (New York, 1972), pp. 43-44, illus. 24; Julian Grossman, *Echo of a Distant Drum: Winslow Homer and the Civil War* (New York, 1974), pp. 114-119, illus.

WINSLOW HOMER (1836-1910)

135 A TROOPER MEDITATING BESIDE A GRAVE
Oil on canvas, 16 x 8 inches
Signed l.r.: Homer; painted ca. 1865

Joslyn Art Museum, Omaha, Nebraska

References: Lloyd Goodrich, *Winslow Homer* (New York, 1944); Hermann Warner Williams, Jr., *The Civil War: The Artists' Record* (exhibition catalogue, Corcoran Gallery of Art, Washington, D.C. and Museum of Fine Arts, Boston, 1961), p. 203; Julian Grossman, *Echo of a Distant Drum: Winslow Homer and the Civil War* (New York, 1974), p. 100.

THOMAS HOVENDEN (1840-1895)

136 LAST MOMENTS OF JOHN BROWN

Copper plate, 31½ x 25¾ inches

Signed l.r.: Hovenden NA 1885/Painter and etcher

Inscribed at bottom:

John Brown of Ossawattomie spake on his dying day:
I will not have to shrive my soul a priest in slavery's pay.
But let some poor slave's mother whom I have striven to free,
With her children from the gallows stair put up a prayer for me
John Brown of Ossawattomie, they led him out to die:
And lo! A Poor slave mother with her child pressed nigh:
Then the broad blue eye grew tender and the old harsh face grew mild
As he stooped between the crowding ranks and kissed the Negro's child

I. C. WHITTIER

PAFA, Gift of John F. Lewis, 1920

References: The "Last Moments of John Brown" (Philadelphia, 1885); *Thomas Hovenden, In Memoriam* (Philadelphia, n.d.), p. 8.

WILLIAM H. JOHNSON (1901-1970)

137 LINCOLN AT GETTYSBURG III

Gouache, pen and ink on paper, 17⅜ x 16³⁄₁₆ inches

Unsigned; painted ca. 1939-42

National Collection of Fine Arts, Smithsonian Institution

References: Adelyn D. Breeskin, *William H. Johnson, 1901-1970* (exhibition catalogue, National Collection of Fine Arts, Smithsonian Institution, Washington, D.C., 1971-72), p. 18, illus. 150.

FREDERICK KEMMELMEYER (active 1788-1805)

138 THE FIRST LANDING OF COLUMBUS

Oil on canvas, 27⅝ x 36½ inches

Inscribed l.l.: [Kemmelm]eyer Pin[xi]t th[. . .] January 180[. . .]; and l.r.: First Landing of/CR COLUMBUS at the/IslandSt SALVADOR South/AMERICA the 11th Octo[ber].

The National Gallery of Art, Gift of Edgar William and Bernice Chrysler Garbisch, 1966

References: National Gallery of Art, *American Paintings and Sculpture: An Illustrated Catalogue* (Washington, D.C., 1970), illus. p. 77.

WALT KUHN (1877-1949)

139 WILD WEST NO. 1

Oil on canvas, 12⅝ x 15 inches

Unsigned; painted 1919

Colorado Springs Fine Arts Center, Gift of Vera and Brenda Kuhn

References: Walt Kuhn, 1877-1949, A Memorial Exhibition (exhibition catalogue, Cincinnati Art Museum, 1960); Walt Kuhn, *An Imaginary History of the West* (Colorado Springs, 1964).

CHARLES WILLSON PEALE (1741-1827)

140 GEORGE WASHINGTON AT PRINCETON

Oil on canvas, 93 x 58½ inches

Signed: CW Peale 1779 (no longer discernible)

PAFA, Gift of the Estate of Elizabeth Wharton McKean, 1943

References: John Hill Morgan and Mantle Fielding, *The Life Portraits of Washington and Their Replicas* (Philadelphia, 1931), pp. 14-16, 27, illus. frontispiece; Charles Coleman Sellers, *Portraits and Miniatures by Charles Willson Peale, Transactions of the American Philosophical Society,* vol. 42, pt. 1 (Philadelphia, 1952), pp. 226-28, illus, 355; Charles Coleman Sellers, *Charles Willson Peale* (New York, 1969), pp. 168-69.

HORACE PIPPIN (1888-1946)

141 JOHN BROWN GOING TO HIS HANGING

Oil on canvas, 24 x 30 inches

Signed l.r.: H. Pippin; painted 1942

PAFA, Lambert Fund, 1943

References: Selden Rodman, *Horace Pippin, A Negro Painter in America* (New York, 1947), pp. 17-18, illus. 50; Leon Anthony Arkus, *Hicks, Kane, Pippin: 3 Self-Taught Pennsylvania Artists* (exhibition catalogue, Museum of Art, Carnegie Institute, Pittsburgh and Corcoran Gallery of Art, Washington, D.C., 1966-67), illus. 98.

WILLIAM T. RANNEY (1813-1857)

142 PRAIRIE BURIAL
Oil on canvas, 28½ x 41 inches
Signed l.c. on dirt pile: Ranney, 1848
Collection of Mr. and Mrs. J. Maxwell Moran, Paoli, Pennsylvania

References: Francis Grubar, *William Ranney, Painter of the Early West* (exhibition catalogue, Corcoran Gallery of Art, Washington, D.C., 1962), p. 30, illus.

WILLIAM T. RANNEY (1813-1857)

143 RETURN OF REVOLUTIONARY VETERANS
Oil on canvas, 30 x 45 inches
Signed l.l.: W. Ranney, 1848
Collection of Mrs. William H. S. Wells, Philadelphia

References: Francis Grubar, *William Ranney, Painter of the Early West* (exhibition catalogue, Corcoran Gallery of Art, Washington, D.C., 1962), p. 30.

PETER FREDERICK ROTHERMEL (1817-1895)

144 STATE HOUSE, DAY OF THE BATTLE OF GERMANTOWN
Oil on canvas, 35 x 48 inches
Signed l.r.: P. F. Rothermel, 1862
PAFA, Bequest of Henry C. Gibson, 1896

References: Thomas Dunn English, "Peter F. Rothermel," *Sartain's Union Magazine of Literature and Art,* 10 (January 1852), 13-16; "A Venerable Artist," *The Public Ledger,* March 19, 1890, p. 3; P. C. Croll, "Famous Pennsylvania-Germans — Peter F. Rothermel," *The Pennsylvania-German,* 5 (July 1904), 99-108.

JOHN SARTAIN (1808-1897) after John Blake White

145 GENERAL MARION IN HIS SWAMP ENCAMPMENT INVITING A BRITISH OFFICER TO DINNER
Mezzotint, 16¾ x 20⅜ inches
Inscribed l.r.: Engraved by John Sartain; executed 1840
PAFA, Dr. Paul J. Sartain Bequest, 1948

References: An Album of American Battle Art 1755-1918 (Washington, D.C., 1947), pp. 40-42, illus. 64; Paul W. Partridge, Jr., "John Blake White, Southern Romantic Painter and Playwright" (Ph.D. dissertation, University of Pennsylvania, 1951), pp. 191-92; Jay Cantor, "Prints and the American Art-Union," in *Prints in and of America to 1850,* ed. John D. Morse, Winterthur Conference Report (Charlottesville, 1970), pp. 297-326.

JOHN SARTAIN (1808-1897) after Benjamin West

146 DEATH OF GENERAL WOLFE, AT QUEBEC, 1759
Mezzotint and stipple engraving, 7 x 10⅛ inches
Inscribed l. to r.: On steel by John Sartain, Phil[a] . . . for the Eclectic . . . the original by Benjn. West; executed 1862
PAFA, Dr. Paul J. Sartain Bequest, 1948

References: John Sartain, "Benjamin West's Picture," *Eclectic Magazine,* 55 (February 1862), 271-73.

CARL HEINRICH SCHMOLZE (1823-1861)

147 GEORGE WASHINGTON SITTING FOR HIS PORTRAIT TO GILBERT STUART
Oil on canvas, 50¾ x 41 inches
Signed l.r.: C. H. Schmolze/Phila./1858
PAFA, John F. Lewis Memorial Collection, 1933

References: Ferdinand Moras, *Carl Heinrich Schmolze, Eine Lebens-Skizze* (Philadelphia, 1885); Kay Mott, "Forgotten Painter," *The Philadelphia Inquirer Magazine,* May 5, 1957, pp. 12-13.

CHRISTIAN SCHUSSELE (1824-1879)

148 GENERAL ANDREW JACKSON BEFORE JUDGE HALL, 1815
Oil on canvas, 20½ x 29¾ inches
Unsigned
PAFA, Collections Fund Purchase, 1957

References: George W. Dewey, "C. Schussele," *Sartain's Union Magazine of Literature and Art,* 10 (June 1852), 462-63; C. J. Hedenberg, *Explanation of the Picture of Andrew Jackson before Judge Hall at New Orleans, 1815. Sus-*

taining the Laws of His Country, As He had Defended Her Liberties in the Field (Philadelphia, 1919); Bernard E. Michel, "Christian Schussele: Portrayer of America," *Transactions of the Moravian Historical Society,* 20 (1965), 249-67.

XANTHUS SMITH (1839-1929)

149 FINAL ASSAULT UPON FORT FISHER, N.C.

Oil on canvas, 56 x 123½ inches
Signed l.r.: Xanthus Smith, 1873; inscribed on reverse: Final Assault on Fort Fisher N.C. painted for Joseph Harrison, Jr., Esq., by Xanthus Smith 1872-3.
PAFA, Joseph and Sarah Harrison Collection, 1878

References: Hermann Warner Williams, Jr., *The Civil War: The Artists' Record* (exhibition catalogue, Corcoran Gallery of Art, Washington, D.C. and Museum of Fine Arts, Boston, 1961), illus. pp. 184-85.

JUNIUS BRUTUS STEARNS (1810-1885)

150 WASHINGTON AS FARMER, AT MOUNT VERNON

Oil on canvas, 37½ x 54 inches
Signed l.r. center: J. B. Stearns, 1851
Virginia Museum of Fine Arts

References: Robert Harley, "George Washington Lived Here, Some Early Prints of Mount Vernon, Part II," *Antiques,* 47 (March 1945), 166-67, illus. 166; "A Life of George Washington Series," *Old Print Shop Portfolio,* 5 (February 1946), 123-25; Millard Rogers, "Fishing Subjects by Junius Brutus Stearns," *Antiques,* 98 (August 1970), 246-50.

JUNIUS BRUTUS STEARNS (1810-1885)

151 WASHINGTON AS STATESMAN, AT THE CONSTITUTIONAL CONVENTION

Oil on canvas, 37½ x 54 inches
Signed l.r.: Stearns; painted 1856
Virginia Museum of Fine Arts

References: Centennial Celebration of the Inauguration of George Washington (exhibition catalogue, Metropolitan Opera, New York, April 17-May 8, 1889), p. 61; "Commemorating the Immortal Signers," *The Art Digest,* 12 (December 15, 1937), 14, illus.; "A Life of George Washington Series," *Old Print Shop Portfolio,* 5 (February 1946), 123-25.

GILBERT STUART (1755-1828)

152 GEORGE WASHINGTON (The "Lansdowne" Portrait)

Oil on canvas mounted on wood, 96 x 60½ inches
Signed l.l.: G. Stuart 1796
PAFA, Bequest of William Bingham, 1811

References: Lawrence Park, *Gilbert Stuart: An Illustrated Descriptive List of His Works* (New York, 1926), vol. 2, p. 854, illus. vol. 4, no. 18; John Hill Morgan and Mantle Fielding, *The Life Portraits of Washington and Their Replicas* (Philadelphia, 1931), pp. 238, 260, 355-61, illus.; *Gilbert Stuart, Portraitist of the Young Republic, 1755-1828* (exhibition catalogue, National Gallery of Art, Washington, D.C. and Rhode Island School of Design, Providence, 1967), pp. 28, 77, illus. 77.

CORNELIUS TIEBOUT (1777-1832)
after Elkanah Tisdale

153 THE BATTLE OF LEXINGTON

Line engraving, 12½ x 16½ inches
Inscribed: E. Tisdale delt. — C. Tiebout Sculpt/ Battle of Lexington; executed 1798
PAFA, John S. Phillips Collection, 1876

References: David McNeely Stauffer, *American Engravers Upon Copper and Steel* (New York, 1907), vol. 2, p. 529; Ian M. G. Quimby, "The Doolittle Engravings of the Battle of Lexington and Concord," in *Winterthur Portfolio 4* (Charlottesville, 1968), p. 106, illus. 107.

WILLIAM BROOKE THOMAS TREGO (1859-1909)

154 BATTERY OF LIGHT ARTILLERY EN ROUTE

Oil on canvas, 30 x 64 inches
Signed l.r.: W. T. Trego, Philada 1882
PAFA, Gift of Fairman Rogers, 1883

References: A. Trego Shertzer, *A Historical Account of the Trego Family* (Baltimore, 1884); Helen H. Gemmill, "William T. Trego," *Bucks County Historical Society Journal,* 1 (Fall 1973), 1-19.

GRANT WOOD (1891-1942)

155 PARSON WEEMS' FABLE

Oil on canvas on masonite, 38⅜ x 50⅛ inches
Signed l.r.: Grant Wood/1939; artist's inscription on frame l.c.: Parson Weems' Fable

The Amon Carter Museum of Western Art, Fort Worth, Texas

References: Darrell Garwood, *Artist in Iowa: A Life of Grant Wood* (New York, 1944), pp. 222-29; Matthew Baigell, *The American Scene, American Painting of the 1930's* (New York, 1974), p. 110, illus. 120.

AMERICAN LANDSCAPE PAINTING, 1795-1875

ALBERT BIERSTADT (1830-1902)

156 Niagara Falls
Oil on board, 19 x 27½ inches
Signed l.r.: ABierstadt; painted ca. 1869
Collection of Sewell C. Biggs, Middletown, Del.

References: Gordon Hendricks, *A. Bierstadt* (exhibition catalogue, Amon Carter Museum, Fort Worth, Texas, 1972-1973), p. 46, cat. no. 52; Gordon Hendricks, *Albert Bierstadt, Painter of the American West* (New York, 1975).

ALBERT BIERSTADT (1830-1902)

157 Storm in the Mountains
Oil on canvas, 38 x 60 inches
Signed l.r.: A. Bierstadt; painted ca. 1870-80
The Museum of Fine Arts, Boston, M. and M. Karolik Collection

References: American Paintings in the Museum of Fine Arts, Boston, (Boston, 1969), vol. 1, p. 28; Gordon Hendricks, *Albert Bierstadt, Painter of the American West* (New York, 1975), pp. 186-87.

THOMAS BIRCH (1779-1851)

158 Fairmount Water Works
Oil on canvas, 20¼ x 30¼ inches
Signed l.l.: T. Birch 1821
PAFA, Charles Graff Estate Bequest, 1845

References: Doris L. Creer, "Thomas Birch: A Study of the Condition of Painting and the Artist's Position in Federal America" (Master's thesis, University of Delaware, 1958); William H. Gerdts, *Thomas Birch, 1779-1851* (exhibition catalogue, Philadelphia Maritime Museum, 1966), p. 39.

WILLIAM BIRCH (1755-1834)

159 Falls of Niagara
Enamel on copper, 2½ x 2½ inches
Signed l.l.: W.B.; painted ca. 1827; inscribed on back: This wild oblique sketch from the corner of the falls of Niagara, taken by Ranagal from the spot and Painted by me Wm. Birch gives in my opinion a greater idea of its magnitude than the front view where the distance necessary loses its immensity.
PAFA, Bequest of Eliza Howard Burd, 1860

References: William Birch, "The Life of William Russell Birch, Enamel Painter, Written by Himself" (ts.), Historical Society of Pennsylvania, Philadelphia; David McNeely Stauffer, *American Engravers Upon Copper and Steel* (New York, 1907), vol. 1, pp. 22-23.

GEORGE LORING BROWN (1814-1889)

160 St. John the Baptist in the Wilderness
Oil on canvas, 58¾ x 81 inches
Signed l.r.: G. L. Brown Florence 1845-6
Inscribed on back: Painted by G. L. Brown/ Florence 1845-6/ For J. L. Schoolcraft, Esq/ Albany, N.Y.
PAFA, Gilpin Fund Purchase, 1969

References: Thomas W. Leavitt, *George Loring Brown, Landscapes of Europe and America, 1834-1880* (exhibition catalogue, The Robert Hull Fleming Museum, Burlington, Vermont, 1973).

FREDERIC E. CHURCH (1826-1900)

161 Mountains of Ecuador
Oil on canvas, 24⅜ x 36¾ inches
Signed l.l.: F. Church '55
The Wadsworth Atheneum, Hartford, Conn., Bequest of Mrs. Clara Hinton Gould

References: David C. Huntington, *The Landscapes of Frederic Edwin Church: Vision of an American Era* (New York, 1966).

THOMAS COLE (1801-1848)

162 On the Arno
Oil on canvas, 32 x 51 inches
Signed l.r.: T. Cole; painted 1837
Collection of Dr. Elliot S. Vesell

References: Louis Legrand Noble, *The Life and Works of Thomas Cole,* ed. Elliot S. Vessell (Cambridge, 1964); Howard S. Merritt, *Thomas Cole* (exhibition catalogue, Memorial Art Gallery, University of Rochester, New York, 1969).

JASPER F. CROPSEY (1823-1900)

163 LANDSCAPE WITH FIGURES, NEAR ROME
Oil on canvas, 29¼ x 42¼ inches
Signed l.l.: J. F. Cropsey/Roma/1847
PAFA, Gift of John F. Lewis, Jr., 1954

References: Peter Bermingham, *Jasper F. Cropsey, 1823-1900: A Retrospective View of America's Painter of Autumn* (exhibition catalogue, University of Maryland Art Gallery, College Park, 1968).

THOMAS DOUGHTY (1793-1856)

164 VIEW NEAR HARTFORD, CONNECTICUT
Oil on canvas, 16¾ x 24 inches
Inscribed on reverse: View near Hartford, Ct. painted by T. Doughty, 1828
PAFA, Gift of Cephas G. Childs, 1828

References: Frank H. Goodyear, Jr., *Thomas Doughty, 1793-1856: An American Pioneer in Landscape Painting* (exhibition catalogue, PAFA, 1973-74), p. 24.

THOMAS DOUGHTY (1793-1856)

165 SUMMER DUCK — plate 22 from *The Cabinet of Natural History and American Rural Sports* (Vol. 1)
Hand-colored lithograph, 6⅝ x 8½ inches
Inscribed l.l.: from Nature and on stone by T. Doughty; l.r.: From Childs and Inman's Press
PAFA, Gift of Theodore T. Newbold, 1973

References: Frank H. Goodyear, Jr., *Thomas Doughty, 1793-1856: An American Pioneer in Landscape Painting* (exhibition catalogue, PAFA, 1973-74).

ASHER B. DURAND (1796-1886)

166 LANDSCAPE
Oil on canvas, 17 x 26 inches
Unsigned; painted ca. 1850
PAFA, Gift of Charles Henry Hart, 1915

References: Barbara Novak, *American Painting of the Nineteenth Century* (New York, 1969), pp. 80-91; John Durand, *The Life and Times of A. B. Durand* (reprint ed., New York, 1970); David B. Lawall, *A. B. Durand, 1796-1886* (exhibition catalogue, Montclair Art Museum, New Jersey, 1971).

JACOB EICHHOLTZ (1776-1842)

167 CONESTOGA CREEK AND LANCASTER
Oil on canvas, 20 x 30 inches
Signed l.r.: J. Eichholtz/1833
PAFA, Gift of Mrs. James H. Beal, 1961

References: Rebecca J. Beal, *Jacob Eichholtz, 1776-1842, Portrait Painter of Pennsylvania* (Philadelphia, 1969); Edgar P. Richardson, *Jacob Eichholtz* (exhibition catalogue, PAFA, 1969), cat. no. 38.

CHARLES LEWIS FUSSELL (ca. 1840-1909)

168 LANDSCAPE
Oil on canvas, 36 x 29 inches
Signed l.l.: C. L. Fussell/1897
PAFA, Gift of Mrs. Morris Fussell, 1973

SANFORD ROBINSON GIFFORD (1823-1880)

169 THE FALLS OF TIVOLI
Oil on canvas, 7 x 13 inches
Signed l.r.: S. R. Gifford 69
Private Collection

References: *A Memorial Catalogue of the Painting of Sanford Robinson Gifford, N.A.* (Metropolitan Museum of Art, New York, 1881), p. 38, cat. no. 550; Nicolai Cikovsky, Jr., *Sanford Robinson Gifford, 1823-1880* (exhibition catalogue, The University of Texas Art Museum, Austin, 1970), p. 28.

WILLIAM GROOMBRIDGE (1748-1811)

170 VIEW ON THE SCHUYLKILL RIVER
Oil on canvas, 25 x 36 inches
Signed l.l.: W. Groombridge, Pinx.t 1800
Private Collection

References: J. Hall Pleasants, *Four Late Eighteenth Century Anglo-American Landscape Painters* (reprinted from the *Proceedings of the American Antiquarian Society, Worcester, Mass.,* 1943), pp. 31-54.

MARTIN JOHNSON HEADE (1819-1904)

171 SALT MARSHES, NEWPORT, RHODE ISLAND
Oil on canvas, 15½ x 30¼ inches
Signed l.l.: M. J. Heade; painted ca. 1865-70
Museum of Fine Arts, Boston, M. and M. Karolik Collection

References: Theodore E. Stebbins, Jr., *The Life*

and Works of Martin Johnson Heade (New Haven and London, 1975), p. 235, no. 117.

GEORGE INNESS (1825-1894)

172 WOODLAND

Oil on canvas, 30 x 45 inches

Signed l.r.: G. Inness 1891

PAFA, Gift of John F. Lewis, Jr., 1954

References: LeRoy Ireland, *The Works of George Inness: An Illustrated Catalogue Raisonné* (Austin, Texas, 1965), p. 349, cat. no. 1368; Nicolai Cikovsky, Jr., "The Life and Work of George Inness" (Ph.D. dissertation, Harvard University, 1965); Nicholai Cikovsky, Jr., *George Inness* (New York, 1971).

JOHN F. KENSETT (1816-1872)

173 HILL VALLEY, SUNRISE

Oil on canvas, 18 x 22¼ inches (oval)

Signed l.l.: JF K/51

PAFA, Gift of John F. Lewis, Jr., 1954

References: John K. Howat, *John Frederick Kensett, 1816-1872* (exhibition catalogue, Metropolitan Museum of Art, New York, 1968), cat. no. 12.

WILLIAM SIDNEY MOUNT (1807-1868)

174 LANDSCAPE WITH FIGURES

Oil on canvas, 19 x 28½ inches

Signed l.r.: Wm. S. Mount/Nov. 26, 1851

PAFA, Provenance unknown

References: Bartlett Cowdrey and Hermann W. Williams, Jr., *William Sidney Mount* (New York, 1944), fig. 51; Alfred Frankenstein, *Painter of Rural America: William Sidney Mount, 1807-1868* (exhibition catalogue, International Exhibitions Foundation, Washington, D.C., 1968-1969).

WILLIAM TROST RICHARDS (1833-1905)

175 PASCHALL HOMESTEAD AT GIBSON'S POINT, PHILADELPHIA

Oil on canvas, 18⅛ x 24¼ inches

Signed l.l.: Wm. T. Richards; dated l.r.: PHIL 1857

PAFA, Gift of Ann Paschall, 1931

References: Linda S. Ferber, *William Trost Richards: American Landscape & Marine Painter 1833-1905* (exhibition catalogue, The Brooklyn Museum, New York, 1973), p. 53.

WILLIAM TROST RICHARDS (1833-1905)

176 PLANT STUDY

Pencil and watercolor on gray-green paper, 8⅛ x 5⅛ inches

Dated: July 9th 1860; l.c.: July 14th

The Brooklyn Museum, Gift of Edith Ballinger Price

References: Linda S. Ferber, *William Trost Richards: American Landscape & Marine Painter 1833-1905* (exhibition catalogue, The Brooklyn Museum, New York, 1973), p. 60.

WILLIAM TROST RICHARDS (1833-1905)

177 FEBRUARY

Oil on canvas laid on wood, 46¼ x 72 inches

Signed l.l.: Wm. T. Richards. 1887

PAFA, Edward H. Coates Memorial Collection, 1923

References: Linda S. Ferber, *William Trost Richards: American Landscape & Marine Painter 1833-1905* (exhibition catalogue, The Brooklyn Museum, New York, 1973), p. 96.

JOSHUA SHAW (ca. 1776-1860)

178 LANDSCAPE WITH WATERMILL

Oil on canvas, 15¼ x 21½ inches

Unsigned

PAFA, Bequest of Henry C. Carey, 1879

References: Maurice H. Grant, *A Chronological History of the Old English Landscape Painters* (London, n.d.), vol. 2, p. 230.

JOSHUA SHAW (ca. 1776-1860)

179 LANDSCAPE WITH FARMHOUSE

Oil on canvas, 15¼ x 21½ inches

Unsigned

PAFA, Bequest of Henry C. Carey, 1879

References: Maurice H. Grant, *A Chronological History of the Old English Landscape Painters* (London, n.d.), vol. 2, p. 230.

RUSSELL SMITH (1812-1896)

180 CHEW HOUSE, GERMANTOWN

Oil on wood, 17 x 24 inches

Signed l.l.: Russell Smith 1843

PAFA, Gift of the Ladies' Bazaar, 1845

DWIGHT WILLIAM TRYON (1849-1925)

181 EVENING

Oil on canvas, 16 x 24 inches
Signed l.l.: D. W. Tryon 1886
PAFA, Gilpin Fund Purchase, 1899

References: Henry C. White, *The Life and Art of Dwight William Tryon* (Boston, 1930); Paul F. Rovetti and Nelson C. White, *Dwight W. Tryon: A Retrospective Exhibition* (exhibition catalogue, Museum of Art, The University of Connecticut, Storrs, 1971); Peter Bermingham, *American Art in the Barbizon Mood* (exhibition catalogue, National Collection of Fine Arts, Smithsonian Institution, Washington, D.C., 1975).

AMERICAN IMPRESSIONISM

FRANK WESTON BENSON (1862-1951)

182 GREAT WHITE HERONS

Oil on canvas, 44 x 36¼ inches
Signed l.l.: F. W. Benson/'33
PAFA, Temple Fund Purchase, 1934

References: W. H. Downes, "Frank W. Benson and His Work," *Brush and Pencil,* 6 (1900), 145-57; Minna Smith, "The Work of Frank W. Benson," *International Studio,* 35 (1908), 99-106; William H. Downes, "The Spontaneous Gaity of Frank Benson's Work," *Arts and Decoration,* March 1911.

SOREN EMIL CARLSEN (1853-1932)

183 SUMMER CLOUDS

Oil on canvas, 39 x 45 inches
Signed l.r.: Emil Carlsen; painted 1913
PAFA, Temple Fund Purchase, 1913

References: Eliot Clark, "Emil Carlsen," *Scribner's Magazine,* 66 (December 1919), 767-70; F. Newlin Price, "Emil Carlsen — Painter and Teacher," *International Studio,* 75 (1922), 300-308; John Steele, "The Lyricism of Emil Carlsen," *International Studio,* 88 (October 1927), 53-60.

MARY STEVENSON CASSATT (1844-1926)

184 YOUNG THOMAS AND HIS MOTHER

Pastel on cardboard, 24 x 20 inches
Signed l.l.: Mary Cassatt; executed 1893
PAFA, Gift of Mrs. Clement Newbold, 1904

References: Frederick A. Sweet, *Miss Mary Cassatt, Impressionist from Pennsylvania* (Norman, Oklahoma, 1966); Adelyn D. Breeskin, *Mary Cassatt: A Catalogue Raisonné of the Oils, Pastels, Watercolors, and Drawings* (Washington, D.C., 1970); Richard J. Boyle, *American Impressionism* (Boston, 1974), illus. p. 104.

JOSEPH RODEFER DE CAMP (1858-1923)

185 THE LITTLE HOTEL

Oil on canvas, 20 x 24 inches
Signed l.l.: Joseph-De-Camp-1903
PAFA, Temple Fund Purchase, 1904

References: William H. Downes, "Joseph DeCamp and His Work," *Art and Progress,* 4 (April 1913), 919-25; Donelson F. Hoopes, *The American Impressionists* (New York, 1972), p. 98, illus. p. 99; Richard J. Boyle, *American Impressionism* (Boston, 1974), p. 180, illus. p. 181.

THOMAS WILMER DEWING (1851-1938)

186 SPRING

Oil on canvas, 20 x 30 inches
Signed l.r.: T W Dewing; painted 1912-14
Davis and Long Company, New York

References: Ezra Thorpe, "Thomas W. Dewing," *Art and Progress,* 4 (March 1914), 156-61; Catherine B. Ely, "Thomas W. Dewing," *Art in America,* 10 (August 1922), 225-29; Richard J. Boyle, *American Impressionism* (Boston, 1974).

FREDERICK CARL FRIESEKE (1874-1939)

187 SEATED NUDE

Oil on canvas, 39½ x 52 inches
Signed l.l.: F. C. Frieseke 1920
PAFA, Temple Fund Purchase, 1937

References: Albert E. Gallatin, "The Paintings of Frederick C. Frieseke," *Art and Progress,* 3 (October 1912), 747-49; E. A. Taylor, "The Paintings of Frederick C. Frieseke," *International Studio,* 53 (October 1914), 259-68; A. S. Weller, *Frederick Frieseke* (exhibition catalogue, Hirschl and Adler Galleries, New York, 1966).

DANIEL GARBER (1880-1958)

188 BATTERSEA BRIDGE

Oil on cardboard, 9¾ x 13¼ inches
Inscribed in pencil on label on back: Battersby Bridge, New . . ./no 136 in the Record/ . . . Painted September 1905/Size 9½ x 13
PAFA, Gift of Vera White, 1956

References: Bayard Breck, "Daniel Garber, A Modern American Master," *Art and Life,* 11 (1919-1920), 493-97; *Daniel Garber Retrospective Exhibition: Paintings, Drawings, and Etchings* (exhibition catalogue, PAFA, 1945); Donelson F. Hoopes, *The American Impressionists* (New York, 1972).

WILLIAM J. GLACKENS (1870-1938)

189 AT THE BEACH
Oil on canvas, 17¾ x 23¾ inches
Signed l.l.: W. Glackens; signed l.r.: To the American + 1917 [American Red Cross]
PAFA, Coates Fund Purchase, 1952

References: Guy Pène Du Bois, *William J. Glackens* (exhibition catalogue, Whitney Museum of American Art, New York, 1931); Ira Glackens, *William Glackens and the Ash Can Group* (New York, 1957); Leslie Katz, *William Glackens in Retrospect* (exhibition catalogue, City Art Museum of St. Louis, 1966).

PHILIP LESLIE HALE (1865-1931)

190 THE CRIMSON RAMBLER
Oil on canvas, 25 x 30 inches
Unsigned; painted ca. 1908
PAFA, Temple Fund Purchase, 1909

References: Catalogue of the One Hundred and Fourth Annual Exhibition (PAFA, 1909), cat. no. 436.

THOMAS ALEXANDER HARRISON (1853-1930)

191 THE WAVE
Oil on canvas, 39¼ x 118 inches
Signed l.l.: Alex Harrison.
PAFA, Temple Fund Purchase, 1891

References: Charles Louis Borgmeyer, "Alexander Harrison, 1853-1930," *Fine Arts Journal,* September 1913; Richard J. Boyle, *American Impressionism* (Boston, 1974).

FREDERICK CHILDE HASSAM (1859-1935)

192 CAT BOATS: NEWPORT
Oil on canvas, 27 x 29 inches
Signed l.r.: Childe Hassam 1901
PAFA, Temple Fund Purchase, 1902

References: Adeline Adams, *Childe Hassam* (New York, 1938); *Impressionism and Its Influences in American Art* (exhibition catalogue, Santa Barbara Museum of Art, 1954), illus. no. 17; C. E. Buckley and Donelson Hoopes, *Childe Hassam* (exhibition catalogue, Corcoran Gallery of Art, Washington, D.C. 1965).

WINSLOW HOMER (1836-1910)

193 MORNING CALL
Oil on canvas, 19 x 13½ inches
Signed l.l.: Winslow Homer 1870
Private Collection

References: Edgar P. Richardson, "The Dinner Horn by Winslow Homer," *Art Quarterly,* 11 (Spring 1948), 153-57; Albert Ten Eyck Gardner, *Winslow Homer, American Artist: His World and His Work* (New York, 1961); Lloyd Goodrich, *Winslow Homer* (exhibition catalogue, Whitney Museum of Art, New York, 1973).

DANIEL RIDGWAY KNIGHT (1840-1924)

194 HAILING THE FERRY
Oil on canvas, 64½ x 83 inches
Signed l.r.: Ridgway Knight/Paris 1888
PAFA, Gift of John H. Converse, 1891

References: Sixty-first Annual Exhibition (exhibition catalogue, PAFA, 1891), p. 24, cat. no. 174; *Dictionary of American Biography,* s.v. Knight, Daniel Ridgway.

ERNEST LAWSON (1873-1939)

195 FORT GEORGE HILL: MORNING
Oil on canvas, 25½ x 30 inches
Signed l.l.: E. Lawson; painted ca. 1911
PAFA, Gift of Bertha Schwacke, 1937

References: F. N. Price, "Lawson of the Crushed Jewels," *International Studio,* 78 (February 1924); Barbara O'Neal, *Ernest Lawson* (exhibition catalogue, The National Gallery of Canada, Montreal, 1967); Richard J. Boyle, *American Impressionism* (Boston, 1974), illus. p. 196.

WILLARD LEROY METCALF (1858-1925)

196 TWIN BIRCHES

Oil on canvas, 40 x 39 inches
Signed l.r.: W. L. Metcalf 1908
PAFA, Temple Fund Purchase, 1909

References: Royal Cortissoz, *Willard L. Metcalf* (exhibition catalogue, American Academy of Arts and Letters, New York, 1927), pp. 1-8; Donelson F. Hoopes, *The American Impressionists* (New York, 1972); Richard J. Boyle, *American Impressionism* (Boston, 1974), p. 171, illus. p. 172.

RICHARD EDWARD MILLER (1875-1943)

197 THE BOUDOIR

Oil on canvas, 34¼ x 36⅛ inches
Signed l.r.: Miller
PAFA, Gift of Mrs. Alfred G. B. Steel, 1937

References: Richard E. Miller, N.A.: An Impression and Appreciation (The Longmire Fund, St. Louis, Missouri, 1968); Richard J. Boyle, *American Impressionism* (New York, 1974), illus. p. 199.

WILLIAM LAMB PICKNELL (1854-1897)

198 ROAD TO NICE

Oil on canvas, 59 x 83¾ inches
Signed l.r.: Wm L Picknell; painted 1896
PAFA, Bequest of Gertrude Flagg, 1906

References: Marquis de Chennevieres, "Le Salon de 1880," *Gazette des Beaux-Arts,* series 2, 22 (July 1880), 41-80; Edward Waldo Emerson, "An American Landscape Painter: William L. Picknell," *Century Magazine,* 40 (September 1901), 710-13; Richard J. Boyle, *American Impressionism* (Boston, 1974).

HENRY WARD RANGER (1858-1916)

199 SHEEP PASTURE

Oil on canvas, 28 x 36 inches
Signed l.l.: H. W. Ranger 1900
PAFA, Temple Fund Purchase, 1901

References: R. H. Bell, *Art Talks with Ranger* (New York and London), 1914; Elliot Daingerfield, "Henry Ward Ranger, Painter," *The Century,* 97 (November 1918), 82-89; Peter Bermingham, *American Art in the Barbizon Mood* (exhibition catalogue, National Collection of Fine Arts, Smithsonian Institution, Washington, D.C., 1975).

EDWARD WILLIS REDFIELD (1869-1965)

200 NEW HOPE

Oil on canvas, 50 x 56 inches
Signed l.l.: E. W. Redfield; painted ca. 1926
PAFA, Temple Fund Purchase, 1927

References: J. Nilsen Laurvik, "Edward W. Redfield, Landscape Painter," *International Studio,* 41 (August 1910), 29-34; F. Newlin Price, "Redfield, Painter of Days," *International Studio,* 75 (1922), 402-10; Richard J. Boyle, *American Impressionism* (Boston, 1974), illus. p. 186.

ROBERT REID (1862-1929)

201 THE MIRROR

Oil on canvas, 37 x 30 inches
Signed l.l.: Robert Reid; painted ca. 1910
The National Collection of Fine Arts, Smithsonian Institution, Washington, D.C.

References: Henry W. Goodrich, "Robert Reid and His Work," *International Studio,* 36 (1909), 112-22; *Inaugural Exhibition, Main Currents in the Development of American Painting* (exhibition catalogue, The Virginia Museum of Fine Arts, Richmond, 1939), illus. p. 38, no. 102.

WILLIAM RITSCHEL (1864-1949)

202 ROCKS AND BREAKERS

Oil on canvas, 60 x 50 inches
Signed l.r.: W. Ritschel/1913
PAFA, Temple Fund Purchase, 1914

References: Mantle Fielding, *Dictionary of American Painters, Sculptors, and Engravers* (New York, 1965), p. 303; *Monterey Peninsula Herald,* October 29, 1965.

THEODORE ROBINSON (1852-1896)

203 PORT BEN, DELAWARE AND HUDSON CANAL

Oil on canvas, 28¼ x 32 inches
Signed l.r.: Th. Robinson '93
PAFA, Gift of the Society of American Artists, 1900

References: John I. H. Baur, *Theodore Robinson* (exhibition catalogue, Brooklyn Institute of Arts and Sciences, New York, 1946), p. 37, plate 31; Sona Johnston, *Theodore Robinson, 1852-1896* (exhibition catalogue, Baltimore Museum of Art, 1973), illus. p. 50; Richard J. Boyle, *American Impressionism* (Boston, 1974), illus. p. 34.

WALTER ELMER SCHOFIELD
(1867-1944)

204 WINTER
Oil on canvas, 29½ x 36 inches
Signed l.l.: Schofield; painted ca. 1899
PAFA, Gilpin Fund Purchase, 1899

References: Arthur Hoeber, "Walter Elmer Schofield, A Painter in the Open," *Arts and Decoration,* October 1911, p. 473; Donelson F. Hoopes, *The American Impressionists* (New York, 1972); Richard J. Boyle, *American Impressionism* (Boston, 1974), illus. p. 95.

EDMUND C. TARBELL (1862-1938)

205 BREAKFAST IN THE STUDIO
Oil on canvas, 25 x 30 inches
Signed l.l.: Tarbell; painted 1896
PAFA, Gift of Clement B. Newbold, 1973

References: Frederick W. Coburn, "Edmund C. Tarbell," *International Studio,* 32 (September 1907), 75-88, illus. p. 74; Philip L. Hale, "Edmund C. Tarbell, Painter," *Arts and Decoration,* 2 (1912), 129-31; John E. D. Trask, "About Tarbell," *American Magazine of Art,* 9 (April 1918).

JOHN HENRY TWACHTMAN
(1853-1902)

206 SAILING IN THE MIST
Oil on canvas, 30½ x 30½ inches
Signed l.l.: J. H. Twachtman; painted ca. 1895
PAFA, Temple Fund Purchase, 1906

References: Richard J. Boyle, *John H. Twachtman Retrospective Exhibition* (exhibition catalogue, Cincinnati Art Musuem, 1966); Donelson F. Hoopes, *The American Impressionists* (New York, 1972), p. 94, illus. p. 95; Richard J. Boyle, *American Impressionism* (Boston, 1974), pp. 167-68, illus. p. 169.

CARROLL SARGENT TYSON
(1878-1956)

207 WESTERN MOUNTAIN, MT. DESERT
Oil on canvas, 30 x 36 inches
Signed l.r.: Carroll Tyson — 1944
PAFA, Temple Fund Purchase, 1945

ROBERT WILLIAM VONNOH
(1858-1933)

208 NOVEMBER
Oil on canvas, 31¾ x 39¼ inches
Signed l.l.: R. W. Vonnoh 1890
PAFA, Temple Fund Purchase, 1894

References: Harold Donaldson Eberlin, "Robert W. Vonnoh: Painter of Men," *Arts and Decoration,* (September 1912); "Vonnoh's Half Century," *International Studio,* 77 (June 1923); Richard J. Boyle, *American Impressionism* (Boston, 1974) pp. 74, 134, 137, illus. p. 75.

JULIAN ALDEN WEIR (1852-1919)

209 MIDDAY REST IN NEW ENGLAND
Oil on canvas, 39½ x 50¼ inches
Signed l.r.: J. Alden Weir-1897/Branchville, Conn.
PAFA, Gift of J. G. Rosengarten, Isaac H. Clothier, Robert C. Ogden, Dr. Francis W. Lewis and Edward H. Coates, 1898

References: J. Alden Weir: An Appreciation of His Life and Works (exhibition catalogue, Phillips Memorial Art Gallery, Washington, D.C., 1922); Dorothy Weir Young, *The Life and Letters of J. Alden Weir* (New Haven, 1960); Richard J. Boyle, *American Impressionism* (Boston, 1974) p. 162, illus. p. 102.

JAMES ABBOTT McNEILL WHISTLER
(1834-1903)

210 HONFLEUR
Oil on canvas, 7⅛ x 13¾ inches
Unsigned; inscribed on back: Honfleur, par Whistler/Drouet & Z.; painted in 1880s or 1890s
PAFA, Bequest of J. Mitchell Elliot, 1952

References: E. R. and J. Pennell, *The Life of James McNeill Whistler,* 2 vols. (London, 1908); Andrew McLaren Young, *James McNeill Whistler* (exhibition catalogue, The Arts Council of Great Britain and the English Speaking Union of the United States, London, 1960); Donald Holden, *Whistler Landscapes and Seascapes* (New York, 1969).

THOMAS EAKINS AND THE ACADEMY

THOMAS POLLOCK ANSHUTZ
(1851-1912)

211 IN A GARRET
Oil on canvas, 10 x 16 inches
Signed l.l.: Thos. Anshutz
PAFA, Gift of the Artist's Pupils, 1897

References: Thomas Pollock Anshutz, 1851-1912 (exhibition catalogue, Graham Gallery, New York, 1963), cat. no. 32; Ruth Bowman, "Thomas

Pollock Anshutz (1851-1912)," *American Art Journal,* 3 (Winter 1971-1972), illus.; Sandra Denney Heard, *Thomas P. Anshutz, 1851-1912* (exhibition catalogue, PAFA, 1973), cat. no. 13.

THOMAS POLLOCK ANSHUTZ (1851-1912)

212 THE INCENSE BURNER
Oil on canvas, 64 x 40 inches
Signed l.l.: Thomas Anshutz; painted ca. 1905
PAFA, Temple Fund Purchase, 1906

References: Thomas Anshutz, 1851-1912 (exhibition catalogue, Graham Gallery, New York, 1963), cat. no. 38; Ruth Bowman. "Thomas Pollock Anshutz (1851-1912)," *American Art Journal,* 3 (Winter 1971-72), illus.

CECILIA BEAUX (1855-1942)

213 SEATED GIRL IN A LONG BLACK DRESS
Oil on cardboard, 19⅝ x 12¼ inches
Unsigned; painted ca. 1885
PAFA, Gift of Henry S. Drinker, 1950

References: Frank H. Goodyear, Jr. and Elizabeth Bailey, *Cecilia Beaux: Portrait of an Artist* (exhibition catalogue, PAFA, 1974), cat. no. 17, illus. p. 53.

MARGARET LESLEY BUSH-BROWN (1857-1944)

214 SELF-PORTRAIT
Oil on canvas, 56½ x 42½ inches
Signed l.l.: M. Leslie Bush-Brown 1914
PAFA, Gift of the artist, 1927

References: Christine Jones Huber, *The Pennsylvania Academy and Its Women, 1850-1920* (exhibition catalogue, PAFA, 1973), cat. no. 29, illus. p. 26.

WILLIAM MERRITT CHASE (1849-1916)

215 LADY WITH THE WHITE SHAWL
Oil on canvas, 75 x 52 inches
Signed l.l.: Wm M Chase; painted 1893
PAFA, Temple Fund Purchase, 1895

References: Catalogue of the Sixty-Fourth Annual Exhibition (PAFA, 1894), cat. no. 68, illus.; Katherine Metcalf Roof, *The Life and Art of William Merritt Chase* (New York, 1917), illus. p. 32; Wilbur D. Peat, *Chase Centennial Exhibition* (exhibition catalogue, John Herron Art Museum, Indianapolis, 1949), cat. no. 32, illus.

CHARLES EDMUND DANA (1843-1914)

216 THE CARPET BAZAAR: CAIRO
Watercolor on paper, 20 x 13 inches
Unsigned
PAFA, Bequest of the Artist, 1915

References: Annual Watercolor and Miniature Exhibition (exhibition catalogue, PAFA, 1914), cat. no. 724, illus. opp. p. 8; "Charles Edmund Dana, Vice President of the Association [Fairmount Park Art Association]," 1914, PAFA Archives.

WALTER M. DUNK (n.d.)

217 MEN'S LIFE CLASS
Oil on cardboard, 10¼ x 12¾ inches
Unsigned; painted 1879
PAFA, Acquired from the artist, 1879

References: [William C. Brownell], "The Art Schools of Philadelphia," *Scribner's Monthly,* 18 (September 1879), illus. p. 741; Gordon Hendricks, *The Life and Work of Thomas Eakins* (New York, 1974), illus. p. 126.

SUSAN MACDOWELL EAKINS (1851-1938)

218 PORTRAIT OF A GENTLEMAN AND DOG
Oil on canvas, 22 x 18 inches
Unsigned; painted 1878
Collection of Mary Macdowell Walters

References: [William C. Brownell], "The Art Schools of Philadelphia," *Scribner's Monthly,* 18 (September 1879), illus. p. 745; Seymour Adelman and Susan P. Casteras, *Susan Macdowell Eakins, 1851-1938* (exhibition catalogue, PAFA, 1973), cat. no. 1, illus. p. 9.

SUSAN MACDOWELL EAKINS (1851-1938)

219 CHAPERONE
Watercolor on paper, 10 x 8½ inches
Signed l.r.: S. Macdowell/1879
Collection of Mr. R. Lee Mastin

References: Seymour Adelman and Susan P. Casteras, *Susan Macdowell Eakins, 1851-1938* (exhibition catalogue, PAFA, 1973), cat. no. 3, illus. p. 17.

THOMAS EAKINS (1844-1916)

220 PERSPECTIVE DRAWING FOR THE SCHREIBER BROTHERS

Pencil and colored ink on paper, 28 x 48 inches
Signed l.r.: EAKINS 1874
PAFA, Gift of Charles Bregler, 1948

References: Gordon Hendricks, *The Life and Work of Thomas Eakins* (New York, 1974), cat. no. 209, illus. p. 73.

THOMAS EAKINS (1844-1916)

221 THE FAIRMAN ROGERS FOUR-IN-HAND (A MAY MORNING IN THE PARK)
Oil on canvas, 24 x 36 inches
Signed l.l.: Eakins 79
The Philadelphia Museum of Art

References: Gilbert S. Parker, *Memorial Exhibition of the Works of the Late Thomas Eakins* (exhibition catalogue, PAFA, 1917), cat. no. 61, illus. p. 162; Lloyd Goodrich, *Thomas Eakins: His Life and Work* (New York, 1933), cat. no. 133, illus. no. 20; Gordon Hendricks, "A May Morning in the Park," *The Philadelphia Museum Bulletin,* 60 (May 1965).

THOMAS EAKINS (1844-1916)

222 FEMALE NUDE
Watercolor on paper, 17 x 9 inches
Signed at bottom in Susan Eakins's hand:
Unfinished Watercolor
T. Eakins; painted ca. 1884
The Philadelphia Museum of Art,
Given by Louis E. Stern

References: Lloyd Goodrich, *Thomas Eakins: His Life and Work* (New York, 1933), cat. no. 205; Donelson F. Hoopes, *Eakins Watercolors* (New York, 1971), pp. 50-53; Gordon Hendricks, *The Life and Work of Thomas Eakins* (New York, 1974), cat. no. 276.

THOMAS EAKINS (1844-1916)

223 MENDING THE NET
Oil on canvas, 32½ x 45¼ inches
Signed on lumber, near center: EAKINS 81
The Philadelphia Museum of Art

References: Gilbert S. Parker, *Memorial Exhibition of the Works of the Late Thomas Eakins* (exhibition catalogue, PAFA, 1917), cat. no. 94, illus p. 176; Lloyd Goodrich, *Thomas Eakins: His Life and Work* (New York, 1933), cat. no. 155, illus. no. 26; Gordon Hendricks, *The Life and Work of Thomas Eakins* (New York, 1974), cat. no. 266, illus. p. 149 and plate 28.

THOMAS EAKINS (1844-1916)

224 KNITTING
Bronze relief, 18 x 15 x 5 inches (oval)
Unsigned; executed ca. 1883
PAFA, Gift of Edward H. Coates, 1887

References: Fifty-fourth Annual Exhibition (exhibition catalogue, PAFA, 1883), cat. no. 415; Lloyd Goodrich, *Thomas Eakins: His Life and Work* (New York, 1933), cat. no. 505; Gordon Hendricks, *The Life and Work of Thomas Eakins* (New York, 1974), cat. no. 218, illus. p. 165.

THOMAS EAKINS (1844-1916)

225 SPINNING
Bronze relief, 18 x 15 x 5 inches (oval)
Unsigned; executed ca. 1883
PAFA, Gift of Edward H. Coates, 1887

References: Lloyd Goodrich, *Thomas Eakins: His Life and Work* (New York, 1933), cat. no. 504; Moussa M. Domit, *The Sculpture of Thomas Eakins* (exhibition catalogue, Corcoran Gallery of Art, Washington, D.C., 1969), cat. no. 10, illus. p. 43; Gordon Hendricks, *The Life and Work of Thomas Eakins* (New York, 1974), cat. no. 217, illus. p. 165.

THOMAS EAKINS (1844-1916)

226 THE SWIMMING HOLE
Oil on canvas, 27 x 36 inches
Signed on rock at end of pier: Eakins, 1883
The Fort Worth Art Museum

References: Gilbert S. Parker, *Memorial Exhibition of the Works of the Late Thomas Eakins* (exhibition catalogue, PAFA, 1917), cat. no. 76, illus. p. 162; Lloyd Goodrich, *Thomas Eakins: His Life and Work* (New York, 1933), cat. no. 190, illus. no. 28; Gordon Hendricks, *The Life and Work of Thomas Eakins* (New York, 1974), cat. no. 322, plate 29.

THOMAS EAKINS (1844-1916)

227 WALT WHITMAN
Oil on canvas, 30 x 24 inches
Signed u.r.: Eakins/1887
PAFA, General Fund Purchase, 1917

References: Annie Nathan Meyer, "Two Portraits of Walt Whitman," *Putnam's Monthly,* 4 (September 1908), 707-10, illus.; Lloyd Goodrich, *Thomas Eakins: His Life and Work* (New York,

1933), cat. no. 220, illus. no. 32; Gordon Hendricks, *The Life and Work of Thomas Eakins* (New York, 1974), cat. no. 219, pp. 96-100, illus. p. 101.

THOMAS EAKINS (1844-1916)

228 THE CELLO PLAYER
Oil on canvas, 64½ x 48 inches
Signed l.r.: Eakins/96
PAFA, Temple Fund Purchase, 1897

References: Gilbert S. Parker, *Memorial Exhibition of the Works of the Late Thomas Eakins* (exhibition catalogue, PAFA, 1917), cat. no. 21, illus. p. 154; Lloyd Goodrich, *Thomas Eakins: His Life and Work* (New York, 1933), cat. no. 291, illus. no. 47; Gordon Hendricks, *The Life and Work of Thomas Eakins* (New York, 1974), cat. no. 220.

THOMAS EAKINS (1844-1916)

229 CHARLES EDMUND DANA
Oil on canvas, 50 x 30 inches
Unsigned; painted ca. 1902
PAFA, Gift of Charles E. Dana, 1913

References: Lloyd Goodrich, *Thomas Eakins: His Life and Work* (New York, 1933), cat. no. 367; Gordon Hendricks, *The Life and Work of Thomas Eakins* (New York, 1974), cat. no. 221.

THOMAS EAKINS (1844-1916)

230 DELAWARE RIVER STUDY
Oil on board, 4¼ x 7½ inches
Initialed l.l.: T. E.
PAFA, Gift of Mrs. Charles Bregler, 1966

References: Gordon Hendricks, *The Life and Work of Thomas Eakins* (New York, 1974), cat. no. 222.

CHARLES LEWIS FUSSELL
(ca. 1840-1909)

231 THE YOUNG ART STUDENT
Oil on canvas, 15 x 12¾ inches
Unsigned; painted ca. 1865
The Philadelphia Museum of Art

References: Gordon Hendricks, *The Life and Work of Thomas Eakins* (New York, 1974), illus. p. 29.

CHARLES LEWIS FUSSELL
(ca. 1840-1909)

232 YOUNG GIRL BY A FOREST SPRING
Watercolor on paper, 14 x 23¾ inches
Signed l.l.: C. L. Fussell/1903
PAFA, Gift of Mrs. Henry M. Fussell, 1974

JEAN-LÉON GÉRÔME (1824-1904)

233 THE GUARDIAN
Oil on canvas, 28¾ x 23½ inches
Signed l.l.: J. L. Gerome; painted ca. 1880
PAFA, Bequest of Henry C. Gibson, 1892

References: Edward Strahan, *Gérôme, A Collection of the Works of J. L. Gérôme in One Hundred Photogravures* (New York, 1881), vol. 1, plate 46; Fanny Field Hering, *The Life and Works of Jean-Léon Gérôme* (New York, 1892), illus, p. 121; Bruce H. Evans, Gerald M. Ackerman, and Richard Ettinghausen, *Jean-Léon Gérôme (1824-1904)* (exhibition catalogue, Dayton Art Institute, Ohio, et. al., 1972).

CHARLES GRAFLY (1862-1929)

234 OARSMAN
Bronze, 38¼ x 12 x 9⅜ inches
Signed on base: Grafly/1910
PAFA, Gift of Dorothy Grafly, 1969

References: Memorial Exhibition of Work by Charles Grafly (exhibition catalogue, PAFA, 1930), cat. no. 67, illus.; Pamela H. Simpson, "The Sculpture of Charles Grafly: A Catalogue Raisonné" (Ph.D. dissertation, University of Delaware, 1974), cat. no. 152.

PHILIP B. HAHS (1853-1882)

235 STUDY OF AN OLD MAN
Oil on canvas, 16 x 12 inches
Signed l.l.: Philip B. Hahs 1881
PAFA, Gift of Mrs. Charles B. Hahs, 1895

References: One Hundredth Anniversary Exhibition (exhibition catalogue, PAFA, 1905), cat. no. 108; Mantle Fielding, *Dictionary of American Painters, Sculptors, and Engravers* (New York, 1965), p. 151.

WILLIAM SERGEANT KENDALL
(1869-1938)

236 QUEST
Painted wood, 34⅛ x 14 x 16 inches
Unsigned; executed 1910

PAFA, Gift of Mrs. Wm. Sergeant Kendall, 1956

References: Memorial Exhibition of the Work of Sergeant Kendall (exhibition catalogue, PAFA, 1939), cat. no. 42.

ELIZABETH MACDOWELL KENTON (1858-1953)

237 LADY IN AN ARM CHAIR (DAYDREAMS)
Oil on canvas, 19 x 15 inches
Signed l.l.: Elizabeth Macdowell;
painted ca. 1880
Collection of Mary Macdowell Walters

References: Gordon Hendricks, *The Life and Work of Thomas Eakins* (New York, 1974), illus. p. 206.

WILLIAM HENRY LIPPINCOTT (1849-1920)

238 INFANTRY IN ARMS
Oil on canvas, 32 x 53 inches
Signed l.r.: Wm. H. Lippincott 1887
PAFA, Gift of Homer F. Emens and
Francis C. Jones, 1922

References: Sixty-second Annual Exhibition (exhibition catalogue, National Academy of Design, New York, 1898), cat. no. 434; Patricia Hills, *The Painter's America: Rural and Urban Life 1810-1910* (exhibition catalogue, Whitney Museum of American Art, New York, 1974), cat. no. 126, illus. p. 104.

SAMUEL MURRAY (1870-1941)

239 MRS. THOMAS EAKINS
(Susan Macdowell)
Bronze, 21¼ inches high
Signed on back of base: Murray '94
PAFA, Gift of Samuel Murray, 1942

References: "Samuel Murray Dies," *Art Digest,* 16 (January 1942), 12.

SAMUEL MURRAY (1870-1941)

240 THOMAS EAKINS
Bronze, 21¼ inches high
Inscribed on base: To my/dear master/Samuel Murray/1894
PAFA, Gift of the artist, 1941

References: Moussa M. Domit, *The Sculpture of Thomas Eakins* (exhibition catalogue, Corcoran Gallery of Art, Washington, D.C., 1969), cat. no. 24, illus. p. 59.

EADWEARD MUYBRIDGE (1830-1904)

241 SMITH WITH RIDER (.043 second)—
plate 602 from *Animal Locomotion*
Collotype photograph on linen paper,
19 x 24 inches
Inscribed and stamped: ANIMAL LOCOMOTION, PLATE 602/Copyright 1887, by Eadweard Muybridge. All rights reserved.
Private Collection

References: Eadweard Muybridge, *Animal Locomotion; An Electro-Photographic Investigation of Consecutive Phases of Animal Movement* (Philadelphia, 1887), plate 602; Eadweard Muybridge, *Animals in Motion,* ed. Lewis S. Brown (reprint ed., New York, 1957), p. 37; William I. Homer and J. Talbot, "Eakins, Muybridge, and the Motion Picture Process," *Art Quarterly,* 26 (Summer 1963), 194-216.

EADWEARD MUYBRIDGE (1830-1904)

242 MAN PERFORMING FORWARD HANDSPRING—
plate 365 from *Animal Locomotion*
Collotype photograph on linen paper,
19 x 24 inches
Inscribed and stamped: ANIMAL LOCOMOTION, PLATE 365/Copyright 1887, by Eadweard Muybridge. All rights reserved.
The Philadelphia Museum of Art

References: Eadweard Muybridge, *Animal Locomotion: An Electro-Photographic Investigation of Consecutive Phases of Animal Movement* (Philadelphia, 1887), plate 365; William D. Marks, Harrison Allen, and Francis X. Dercum, *Animal Locomotion: The Muybridge Work at the University of Pennsylvania. The Method and the Result* (Philadelphia, 1888); Gordon Hendricks, *Eadweard Muybridge: The Father of the Motion Picture* (New York, 1975).

EMILY SARTAIN (1841-1927)

243 FREDERICK FRALEY
Oil on canvas, 33½ x 28 inches
Signed l.l. (partially illegible): Emily Sartain/Philadelphia, 188 . . .
Collection of Mr. Frederick Fraley

References: Fifty-sixth Annual Exhibition (exhibition catalogue, PAFA, 1885), cat. no. 285; *The National Cyclopedia of American Biography,* s.v. Sartain, Emily.

WILLIAM SARTAIN (1843-1924)

244 SOLITUDE

Oil on canvas, 20 x 23¾ inches
Signed l.r.: W. Sartain
PAFA, Gift of Mrs. James Mapes Dodge, 1931

References: Arthur Hoeber, "William Sartain, Painter," *New England Magazine,* 28 (March 1903), 51-61, illus. p. 53; *Dictionary of American Biography,* s.v. Sartain, William.

CHRISTIAN SCHUSSELE (1824-1879)

245 OLD MAN

Oil on compoboard, 10 x 8 inches
Unsigned
PAFA, Gift of John F. Lewis, 1922

References: George H. Johnston, *A Sermon Memorial to Christian Schussele* (Philadelphia, 1879); *Dictionary of American Biography,* s.v. Schussele, Christian.

HENRY OSSAWA TANNER (1859-1937)

246 NICODEMUS

Oil on canvas, 34 x 40 inches
Signed l.l.: H. O. Tanner/Jerusalem 1899
PAFA, Temple Fund Purchase, 1900

References: Sixty-Ninth Annual Exhibition (exhibition catalogue, PAFA, 1900), cat. no. 212; Carroll Greene, *The Art of Henry O. Tanner, 1859-1937* (exhibition catalogue, The Frederick Douglass Institute and National Collection of Fine Arts, Washington, D.C., 1969), cat. no. 27, illus. p. 31; Maria M. Mathews, *Henry Ossawa Tanner, American Artist* (Chicago and London, 1969), plate 4.

THE EIGHT

ALEXANDER STIRLING CALDER (1870-1945)

247 ROBERT HENRI

Bronze bust, 30½ x 24 x 15½ inches
Signed on base: Calder
PAFA, Gift of Mrs. A. Stirling Calder, 1947

References: Nicholas B. Wainwright, ed., *Sculpture of a City: Philadelphia's Treasures in Bronze and Stone* (New York, 1974).

ARTHUR B. DAVIES (1862-1928)

248 RECLINING NUDE

Pastel drawing on paper, 10½ x 16 inches
Unsigned
PAFA, Gift of Robert McIntyre, 1950

References: Walter Pach and Harris K. Prior, *Arthur B. Davies, 1862-1928* (exhibition catalogue, Memorial Art Gallery, University of Rochester, Rochester, New York, 1962).

ARTHUR B. DAVIES (1862-1928)

249 FOUR O'CLOCK LADIES

Oil on canvas, 18¼ x 30 inches
Signed l.l.: A. B. Davies
Wadsworth Atheneum, Hartford, Conn.,
The Ella Gallup Sumner and Mary Catlin Sumner Collection

References: Walter Pach and Harris K. Prior, *Arthur B. Davies, 1862-1928* (exhibition catalogue, Memorial Art Gallery, University of Rochester, Rochester, New York, 1962).

ARTHUR B. DAVIES (1862-1928)

250 DISCOVERIES: ISLE OF DESTINY

Oil on canvas mounted on panel,
18½ x 40¼ inches
Signed l.l.: A. B. Davies
PAFA, Gift of Mr. and Mrs. Alfred B. Steel, 1943

References: Walter Pach and Harris K. Prior, *Arthur B. Davies, 1862-1928* (exhibition catalogue, Memorial Art Gallery, University of Rochester, Rochester, New York, 1962).

WILLIAM J. GLACKENS (1870-1938)

251 THE SODA FOUNTAIN

Oil on canvas, 48 x 36 inches
Signed l.r.: W. Glackens '35
PAFA, Temple and Gilpin Funds Purchase, 1955

References: Ira Glackens, *William Glackens and the Ashcan Group* (New York, 1957).

ROBERT HENRI (1865-1929)

252 RUTH ST. DENIS IN THE PEACOCK DANCE

Oil on canvas, 85 x 49 inches
Signed l. l.: ROBERT HENRI; painted March 1919
PAFA, Gift of the Sameric Corporation in memory of Eric Shapiro, 1976.

References: William Innes Homer, *Robert Henri and His Circle* (Ithaca and London, 1969), p. 257.

ROBERT HENRI (1865-1929)

253 MAN FROM SEGOVIA IN FUR-TRIMMED CAP
Oil on canvas, 41 x 33 inches
Signed l.l.: Robert Henri; painted 1923
Collection of Mrs. John C. LeClair
References: William Innes Homer, *Robert Henri and His Circle* (Ithaca and London, 1969).

ROBERT HENRI (1865-1929)

254 WEE MAUREEN
Oil on canvas, 24 x 20 inches
Signed l.r.: Robert Henri; painted 1926
PAFA, Gift of Mrs. Herbert C. Morris, 1962
References: William Innes Homer, *Robert Henri and His Circle* (Ithaca and London, 1969).

ERNEST LAWSON (1873-1939)

255 THE BROKEN FENCE; SPRING FLOOD
Oil on canvas, 30 x 24 inches
Signed l.l.: E. Lawson
PAFA, Gift of Bertha Schwacke, 1937
References: Henry Berry-Hill and Sidney Berry-Hill, *Ernest Lawson, N.A.: American Expressionist* (Leigh-on-Sea, England, 1968).

ERNEST LAWSON (1873-1939)

256 PEGGY'S COVE, NOVA SCOTIA
Oil on canvas, 25 x 30 inches
Signed l.r.: E. Lawson; painted ca. 1935
PAFA, Temple Fund Purchase, 1937
References: Henry Berry-Hill and Sidney Berry-Hill, *Ernest Lawson, N.A.: American Expressionist* (Leigh-on-Sea, England, 1968).

GEORGE LUKS (1866-1933)

257 POLISH DANCER
Oil on canvas, 66½ x 48 inches
Unsigned
PAFA, Gift of the Locust Club, 1955
References: Joseph S. Trovato, *George Luks, 1866-1933* (exhibition catalogue, Munson-Williams-Proctor Institute, Utica, New York, 1973).

MAURICE PRENDERGAST (1859-1924)

258 BATHERS IN A COVE
Oil on canvas, 19½ x 26 inches
Signed l.l.: Prendergast; painted 1916
The Philadelphia Museum of Art, Purchased: John H. McFadden, Jr. Fund
References: Hedley H. Rhys, *Maurice Prendergast* (Cambridge, 1960).

EVERETT SHINN (1873-1953)

259 THE DOCKS—NEW YORK CITY
Pastel on paper, 15½ x 22 inches
Signed l.l.: E. SHinn/1901
Munson-Williams-Proctor Institute, Utica, N.Y.
References: Edith DeShazo, *Everett Shinn, 1873-1953* (exhibition catalogue, New Jersey State Museum, Trenton, 1973), p. 30.

EVERETT SHINN (1873-1953)

260 LONDON HIPPODROME
Oil on canvas, 26⅜ x 35¼ inches
Signed l.r.: E. Shinn; painted 1902
The Art Institute of Chicago, Friends of American Art Collection
References: Edith DeShazo, *Everett Shinn, 1873-1953* (exhibition catalogue, New Jersey State Museum, Trenton, 1973), p. 32.

EVERETT SHINN (1873-1953)

261 PARIS CABARET
Pastel on paper, 11⅞ x 15¹³⁄₁₆ inches
Signed l.r.: Everett Shinn/1917
Munson-Williams-Proctor Institute, Utica, N.Y.
References: Edith DeShazo, *Everett Shinn, 1873-1953* (exhibition catalogue, New Jersey State Museum, Trenton, 1973), p. 43.

EVERETT SHINN (1873-1953)

262 STRONG MAN, CLOWN AND DANCER
Oil on canvas, 10 x 8 inches
Signed l.l.: E. Shinn
PAFA, Collections Fund Purchase, 1956
References: Edith DeShazo, *Everett Shinn, 1873-1953* (exhibition catalogue, New Jersey State Museum, Trenton, 1973).

JOHN SLOAN (1871-1951)

263 COFFEE LINE
Oil on canvas 21½ x 31½ inches
Signed l.r.: J^{ohn}_{loan} 1905
Kraushaar Galleries, New York

References: David W. Scott and E. John Bullard, *John Sloan, 1871-1951* (exhibition catalogue, National Gallery of Art, Washington, D.C., 1971), p. 71.

JOHN SLOAN (1871-1951)

264 TURNING OUT THE LIGHT

Etching, 5 x 7 inches

Signed l.r.: John Sloan/1905

Kraushaar Galleries, New York

References: Peter Morse, *John Sloan's Prints: A Catalogue Raisonné of the Etchings, Lithographs, and Posters* (New Haven, 1969), p. 143.

JOHN SLOAN (1871-1951)

265 ROOFS, SUMMER NIGHT

Etching, 5¼ x 7 inches

Signed l.r.: John Sloan 1906

Kraushaar Galleries, New York

References: Peter Morse, *John Sloan's Prints: A Catalogue Raisonné of the Etchings, Lithographs, and Posters* (New Haven, 1969), p. 148.

JOHN SLOAN (1871-1951)

266 EASTER EVE

Oil on canvas, 32 x 26 inches

Signed l.l.: John Sloan '07

Private Collection

References: David W. Scott and E. John Bullard, *John Sloan, 1871-1951* (exhibition catalogue, National Gallery of Art, Washington, D.C., 1971). p. 94.

JOHN SLOAN (1871-1951)

267 JEFFERSON MARKET

Oil on canvas, 32 x 26 inches

Signed l.l.: John Sloan; painted 1917 and 1922

PAFA, Gilpin Fund Purchase, 1944

References: David W. Scott and E. John Bullard, *John Sloan, 1871-1951* (exhibition catalogue, National Gallery of Art, Washington, D.C., 1971), p. 151.

JOHN SLOAN (1871-1951)

268 ROBERT HENRI, PAINTER

Etching, 14 x 11 inches

Signed l.r.: John Sloan, 1931

Kraushaar Galleries, New York

References: Peter Morse, *John Sloan's Prints: A Catalogue Raisonné of the Etchings, Lithographs, and Posters* (New Haven, 1969), p. 272.

MODERNISM AT THE PENNSYLVANIA ACADEMY, 1910-1940

IVAN L. ALBRIGHT (b. 1897)

269 FLEETING TIME THOU HAST LEFT ME OLD

Oil on canvas, 30¼ x 20¼ inches

Signed l.l.: IVAN LE LORRAINE ALBRIGHT; painted 1929-30

The Metropolitan Museum of Art, New York, George A. Hearn Fund, 1950

References: Frederick A. Sweet, *Ivan Albright* (exhibition catalogue, Art Institute of Chicago, 1964), illus. no. 9; Joseph Kind, "Albright: Humanist of Decay," *Art News,* 63 (November 1964), 43-45, 68-70.

MILTON AVERY (1893-1965)

270 OXCART — BLUE SEA

Oil on canvas, 32 x 44 inches

Signed l.r.: Milton Avery 1943

PAFA, Gift of Mrs. Herbert Morris, 1952

References: Hilton Kramer, *Milton Avery: Paintings 1930-60* (New York, 1962); Adelyn D. Breeskin, *Milton Avery* (exhibition catalogue, National Collection of Fine Arts, Washington, D.C., 1969); Harry H. Lunn, Jr., *Milton Avery: Prints, 1933-1955* (Washington, D.C., 1973).

GEORGE BELLOWS (1882-1925)

271 NORTH RIVER

Oil on canvas, 32¾ x 43 inches

Signed l.l.: G. Bellows; painted 1908

PAFA, Temple Fund Purchase, 1909

References: Charles H. Morgan, *George Bellows: Painter of America* (New York, 1965), pp. 81-82, illus. p. 313; C. H. Morgan, *George Bellows: Paintings, Drawings, Lithographs* (exhibition catalogue, Gallery of Modern Art, New York, 1966), illus. p. 16; Mahonri S. Young, *The Paintings of George Bellows* (New York, 1973), illus. p. 34.

THOMAS HART BENTON (1889-1975)

272 AARON

Oil tempera on canvas, laid on wood, 30¼ x 24¼ inches

Signed l.l.: Benton; painted 1941

PAFA, Temple Fund Purchase, 1943

References: Thomas H. Benton, *An American in Art* (Lawrence, Kansas, 1969); *Thomas Hart Benton: A Retrospective of His Early Years, 1907-1929* (exhibition catalogue, Rutgers University Art Gallery, New Brunswick, New Jersey, 1972); Matthew Baigell, *Thomas Hart Benton* (New York, 1974), plate 147.

PETER BLUME (b. 1906)

273 NEW ENGLAND BARN
Oil on canvas, 24 x 36 inches
Signed l.l.: Peter Blume; painted 1926
The Whitney Museum of American Art, New York, Gift of Leonard Spiegelglass

HUGH HENRY BRECKENRIDGE (1870-1937)

274 SKY DRAMA
Oil on panel, 12¾ x 10 inches
Signed u.l.: Hugh H. Breckenridge; painted ca. 1917
Collection of Mr. and Mrs. Meyer P. Potamkin

References: Margaret Vogel, *The Paintings of Hugh H. Breckenridge* (exhibition catalogue, Valley House Gallery, Dallas, 1967), illus. p. 58.

CHARLES BURCHFIELD (1893-1967)

275 END OF THE DAY
Watercolor on paper, 28 x 48 inches
Monogram l.r.: CEB/1938
PAFA, Temple Fund Purchase, 1940

References: John I. H. Baur, *Charles Burchfield* (New York, 1956), illus. no. 33; *Charles Burchfield: His Golden Years* (exhibition catalogue, University of Arizona Art Gallery, Tucson, 1965), illus. p. 49; *Charles Burchfield: Catalogue of Paintings in Public and Private Collections* (exhibition catalogue, Munson-Williams-Proctor Institute, Utica, New York, 1970), illus. p. 181.

ARTHUR B. CARLES (1882-1952)

276 COMPOSITION NO. 6
Oil on canvas, 41 x 51 inches
Unsigned; painted 1936
PAFA, Gift of Joseph Wood, 1957

References: John Marin, "On My Friend Carles," *Art News,* 52 (April 1953), 20, 67; Henry G. Gardiner, *Arthur B. Carles* (exhibition catalogue, The Philadelphia Museum of Art, 1970).

JOHN STEUART CURRY (1897-1946)

277 SANCTUARY
Oil on board, 24½ x 30½ inches
Signed l.l.: John Steuart Curry/1935
PAFA, Collection Fund Purchase, 1954

References: Laurence Schmeckebier, *A Retrospective Exhibition of Work by John Steuart Curry* (exhibition catalogue, Syracuse University, 1956); Laurence Schmeckebier, "John Steuart Curry: A Retrospective Exhibition," *College Art Journal,* 17 (Fall 1957), 55-58.

JO DAVIDSON (1883-1952)

278 SAMUEL M. VAUCLAIN
Stone bust, 24½ x 14 x 28 inches
Signed on back: Jo Davidson
PAFA, Deposited by Mr. Samuel M. Vauclain, 1927

References: Guy Pène du Bois, "Jo Davidson," *International Studio,* 76 (November 1922), 180-87; Jo Davidson, *Between Sittings* (New York, 1951).

STUART DAVIS (1894-1964)

279 ULTRA-MARINE
Oil on canvas, 20 x 40 inches
Signed u.r.: Stuart Davis; painted 1943
PAFA, Temple Fund Purchase, 1952

References: James J. Sweeney, *Stuart Davis* (exhibition catalogue, Museum of Modern Art, New York, 1945); H. H. Arnason, *Stuart Davis Memorial Exhibition* (exhibition catalogue, National Collection of Fine Arts, Washington, D. C., 1965), p. 77, illus. no. 80; Diane Kelder, *Stuart Davis* (New York, 1971), plate 7.

CHARLES DEMUTH (1883-1935)

280 GLADIOLAS
Watercolor on paper, 17½ x 11½ inches
Unsigned
PAFA, Gift of John F. Lewis, Jr., 1955

References: Andrew C. Ritchie, *Charles Demuth* (exhibition catalogue, Museum of Modern Art, New York, 1950); Emily Farnham, *Charles Demuth: Behind a Laughing Mask* (Norman, Oklahoma, 1971); David Gebhard and Phyllis Plous, *Charles Demuth: The Mechanical En-*

crusted on the Living (exhibition catalogue, The Art Galleries, University of California, Los Angeles, 1971).

ARTHUR DOVE (1880-1946)

281 NAPLES YELLOW MORNING
Oil on canvas,25 x 35 inches
Signed l.c.: dove; painted 1935
Collection of Mr. and Mrs. Meyer P. Potamkin

References: Frederick S. Wight, *Arthur G. Dove* (exhibition catalogue, University of California Art Gallery, Los Angeles, 1958); Dorothy R. Johnson, *Arthur Dove: The Years of Collage* (exhibition catalogue, University of Maryland Art Gallery, College Park, 1967); Barbara Haskell, *Arthur Dove* (exhibition catalogue, San Francisco Museum of Art, 1974).

GUY PÈNE DU BOIS (1884-1958)

282 CLUB MEETING
Oil on canvas, 24 x 20 inches
Signed l.r.: Guy Pene du Bois '36
PAFA, Gilpin Fund Purchase, 1939

References: Royal Cortissoz, *Guy Pène du Bois* (New York, 1931); Guy Pène du Bois, *Artists Say the Silliest Things* (New York, 1940).

LYONEL FEININGER (1871-1956)

283 POSSENDORF I
Oil on canvas, 30¼ x 38½ inches
Signed l.r.: Feininger '29
PAFA, Gilpin Fund Purchase, 1951

References: Hans Hess, *Lyonel Feininger* (New York, 1961), illus. no. 309; Leona E. Prasse, *Lyonel Feininger: A Definitive Catalogue of his Graphic Work* (Cleveland, 1972); June L. Ness, *Lyonel Feininger* (New York, 1974).

MARSDEN HARTLEY (1877-1943)

284 PAINTING NO. 4 (BLACK HORSE)
Oil on canvas, 39½ x 32 inches
Unsigned; painted 1915
The Philadelphia Museum of Art, Alfred Stieglitz Collection

References: Marsden Hartley, *Adventures in the Arts* (New York, 1921); Elizabeth McCausland, *Marsden Hartley* (Minneapolis, 1952); Gorham P. Munson, "Homage to Marsden Hartley," *Arts,* 35 (February 1961), 32-45.

EDWARD HOPPER (1882-1967)

285 EAST WIND OVER WEEHAWKEN
Oil on canvas, 34¼ x 50¼ inches
Signed l.r.: E. Hopper; painted 1934
PAFA, Collections Fund Purchase, 1952

References: Alfred H. Barr, Jr., *Edward Hopper Retrospective Exhibition* (exhibition catalogue, Museum of Modern Art, New York, 1933); Lloyd Goodrich, *Edward Hopper* (exhibition catalogue, Whitney Museum of American Art, New York, 1964), illus. p. 33; Lloyd Goodrich, *Edward Hopper* (New York, 1971), pp. 99, 142, illus. p. 100.

PAUL JENNEWEIN (b. 1890)

286 THE HACKNEY
Bronze, 11½ x 11¼ x 3⅜ inches
Signed on base: C. P. Jennewein SC/19 0 42
PAFA, Gilpin Fund Purchase, 1947

References: Kineton Parkes, "Plastic Form and Color: Work of Paul Jennewein," *Apollo,* 17 (April 1933), 130-34.

WALT KUHN (1877-1949)

287 CLOWN WITH FOLDED ARMS
Oil on canvas, 30 x 25¼ inches
Signed l.l.: Walt Kuhn/1944
PAFA, Temple Fund Purchase, 1945

References: Philip R. Adams, *Walt Kuhn, 1877-1949* (exhibition catalogue, Cincinnati Art Museum, 1960); Frank Getlein, *Walt Kuhn, 1877-1949* (exhibition catalogue, Kennedy Gallery, New York, 1967).

GASTON LACHAISE (1882-1935)

288 EQUESTRIENNE
Bronze, 11 x 10¼ x 4¼ inches
Signed on base: G. Lachaise/1918
Collection of Mr. and Mrs. Meyer P. Potamkin

References: Lincoln Kirstein, *Gaston Lachaise* (exhibition catalogue, Museum of Modern Art, 1935); Hilton Kramer, *The Sculpture of Gaston Lachaise* (New York, 1967); Gerald Nordland, *Gaston Lachaise: The Man and His Work* (New York, 1974).

ROBERT LAURENT (1890-1970)

289 SEATED NUDE
Alabaster on black marble base, 16 x 14½ x 10½ inches

Signed on base: Laurent; sculpted 1940
PAFA, Gilpin Fund Purchase, 1947

References: *Laurent: Fifty Years of Sculpture* (exhibition catalogue, Indiana University, Bloomington, 1961); *The Robert Laurent Memorial Exhibition* (exhibition catalogue, University of New Hampshire, Durham, 1972); Roberta K. Tarbell, *Robert Laurent, Memorial Exhibition* (exhibition catalogue, Kraushaar Galleries, New York, 1972).

JACK LEVINE (b. 1915)

290 MEDICINE SHOW
Oil on canvas, 40¼ x 45½ inches
Signed l.l.: J. Levine; painted 1955
PAFA, Gilpin and Lambert Fund Purchase, 1956

References: Frederick S. Wight, "Levine Profile," *Art Digest,* 26 (Summer 1952), 10-11; Frederick S. Wight, *Jack Levine* (exhibition catalogue, Whitney Museum of American Art, New York, 1955); Frank Getlein, *Jack Levine* (New York, 1966).

JOHN MARIN (1870-1953)

291 SUNSET, MAINE COAST
Watercolor on paper, 16¼ x 19¼ inches
Unsigned; painted 1919
The Columbus Gallery of Fine Arts, Ohio, Ferdinand Howald Collection

References: Dorothy Norman, *John Marin: Selected Writings* (New York, 1949); Larry Curry, *John Marin: 1870-1953* (exhibition catalogue, Los Angeles County Museum of Art, 1970); Shelden Reich, *John Marin: A Stylistic Analysis and Catalogue Raisonné* (Tucson, 1970), vol. 2, illus. p. 474.

JOHN MARIN (1870-1953)

292 THE SINGER BUILDING
Watercolor on paper, 26½ x 21⅝ inches
Signed l.r.: Marin 21
The Philadelphia Museum of Art, Alfred Stieglitz Collection

References: Dorothy Norman, *John Marin: Selected Writings* (New York, 1949); Larry Curry, *John Marin: 1870-1953* (exhibition catalogue, Los Angeles County Museum of Art, 1970); Sheldon Reich, *John Marin: A Stylistic Analysis and Catalogue Raisonné* (Tucson, 1970), vol. 1, illus. fig. 103, vol. 2, p. 490.

REGINALD MARSH (1898-1954)

293 END OF THE 14TH STREET CROSSTOWN LINE
Oil and tempera on board, 23¾ x 35⅞ inches
Signed l.r.: Reginald/Marsh/'36
PAFA, Gilpin Fund Purchase, 1942

References: Lloyd Goodrich, *Reginald Marsh* (New York, 1955), illus. no. 21; Lloyd Goodrich, *Reginald Marsh* (New York, 1972), illus. p. 73; Edward Laning, *The Sketchbooks of Reginald Marsh* (Greenwich, 1973).

HENRY B. McCARTER (1864-1942)

294 THE ATTIC WINDOW: MORGANTOWN
Pastel on paper, 22¾ x 18¾ inches
Signed l.l.: Henry/McCarter/Morgantown
PAFA, Gift of the Academy Fellowship, 1941

References: R. Sturgis Ingersoll, *Henry McCarter* (Cambridge, 1944).

GEORGE L. K. MORRIS (b. 1905)

295 RSVP
Oil on canvas, 20 x 16 inches
Signed l.r.: Morris; painted 1946
Collection of Alberta A. Kelly

References: George L. K. Morris, "What Abstract Art Means to Me," *Bulletin of the Museum of Modern Art,* 18, no. 3 (1951), pp. 2-4; Donelson F. Hoopes, *George L. K. Morris: Retrospective Exhibition of Paintings and Sculpture, 1930-1964* (exhibition catalogue, Corcoran Gallery of Art, Washington, D.C., 1965); Ward Jackson, "George L. K. Morris: 40 Years of Abstract Art," *Art Journal,* 32 (Winter 1972-73), 150-56.

GEORGIA O'KEEFFE (b. 1887)

296 COXCOMB
Oil on canvas, 20½ x 17½ inches
Unsigned
Collection of Mrs. John Wintersteen, Haverford, Pa.

References: Daniel C. Rich, *Georgia O'Keeffe* (Chicago, 1943); Mitchell Wilder, ed., *Georgia O'Keeffe, an Exhibition of the Work of the Artist from 1915 to 1966* (exhibition catalogue, Amon Carter Museum of Western Art, Fort Worth, Texas, 1966); Lloyd Goodrich and Doris Bry, *Georgia O'Keeffe* (exhibition catalogue, Whitney Museum of American Art, New York, 1970).

ABRAHAM RATTNER (b. 1895)

297 THE ROUND TABLE
Oil on canvas, 32 x 25¾ inches
Signed l.l.: Rattner; painted 1945
PAFA, Temple Fund Purchase, 1946
References: Suzanne Burrey, "Rattner Portfolio," *Arts,* no. 31 (May 1957), 39-40; Allen Leepa, *Abraham Rattner* (New York, 1973).

MORTON LIVINGSTON SCHAMBERG (1881-1918)

298 CAMERA FLASHLIGHT
Oil on canvas, 24 x 20 inches
Signed l.r.: Schamberg, 1916
Collection of Dr. and Mrs. Ira Leo Schamberg, Jenkintown, Pa.
References: Ben Wolf, *Morton Livingston Schamberg* (Philadelphia, 1963), illus. no. 49; Ben Wolf, "Morton Livingston Schamberg," *Art in America,* 52 (February 1964), 76-80.

CHARLES SHEELER (1883-1965)

299 CLAPBOARDS
Oil on canvas, 21 x 19 inches
Signed l.r.: Sheeler 1936
PAFA, Subscription Purchase, 1939
References: Lillian Dochterman, *The Quest of Charles Sheeler* (exhibition catalogue, The University of Iowa, Iowa City, 1963); Martin Friedman, *Charles Sheeler* (exhibition catalogue, National Collection of Fine Arts, Smithsonian Institution, Washington, D.C., 1968); John P. Driscoll, *Charles Sheeler: The Works on Paper* (exhibition catalogue, The Pennslyvania State University Museum of Art, University Park, 1974).

RAPHAEL SOYER (b. 1899)

300 DISORDER
Oil on canvas, 36 x 25 inches
Signed l.r.: Raphael Soyer; painted 1947
PAFA, Gilpin Fund Purchase, 1948
References: Walter Gutman, *Raphael Soyer: Paintings and Drawings* (New York, 1961); Lloyd Goodrich, *Raphael Soyer* (New York, 1972).

JOSEPH STELLA (1877-1946)

301 SKETCH FOR BROOKLYN BRIDGE
Pastel on paper, 21 x 17½ inches
Signed l.r. of center: J. Stella; l.r.: J. Stella
The Whitney Museum of American Art, New York, Gift of Miss Rose Fried
References: Irma B. Jaffe, "Joseph Stella and Hart Crane: The Brooklyn Bridge," *American Art Journal,* 1 (Fall 1969), 98-107; Irma B. Jaffe, *Joseph Stella* (Cambridge, 1970); John I. H. Baur, *Joseph Stella* (New York, 1971), illus. no. 56.

FLORINE STETTHEIMER (1871-1944)

302 PICNIC AT BEDFORD HILLS
Oil on canvas, 40 x 50 inches
Signed l.l.: FS; painted 1918
PAFA, Gift of Ettie Stettheimer, 1950
References: Henry McBride, *Florine Stettheimer* (New York, 1946), illus. p. 15; Parker Tyler, *Florine Stettheimer: A Life in Art* (New York, 1963), pp. 20, 138, 152, illus. p. 34; *Florine Stettheimer: Exhibition of Paintings, Watercolors, Drawings* (exhibition catalogue, Columbia University, New York, 1973).

WALTER STUEMPFIG (1914-1970)

303 RETURN AT SIX
Oil on canvas, 29½ x 36¼ inches
Signed l.r.: W. Stuempfig
PAFA, Lambert Fund Purchase, 1935
References: Rosamund Frost, "Stuempfig Remakes Nature," *Art News,* 44 (December 15, 1945), illus. p. 20; R. S. Ingersoll and James Fosburgh, *Walter Stuempfig, 1914-1970* (exhibition catalogue, PAFA, 1972), illus. no. 1.

FRANKLIN C. WATKINS (1894-1972)

304 R. STURGIS INGERSOLL
Oil on canvas, 23 x 24 inches
Signed l.l.: F.W./38
PAFA, Bequest of R. Sturgis Ingersoll, 1973
References: Andrew C. Ritchie, *Franklin C. Watkins* (New York, 1950), illus. p. 21; Henry Clifford, *Franklin C. Watkins* (exhibition catalogue, The Philadelphia Museum of Art, 1964), p. 10, illus. no. 20; Ben Wolf, *Franklin C. Watkins: Portrait of a Painter* (Philadelphia, 1966), p. 79, illus. no. 20.

MAX WEBER (1881-1961)

305 THE TWO MUSICIANS
Oil on canvas, 40⅛ x 30⅛ inches
Signed l.r.: Max Weber; painted 1917

The Museum of Modern Art, New York, Acquired through the Richard D. Brixey Bequest, 1944

References: Lloyd Goodrich, *Max Weber* (exhibition catalogue, Whitney Museum of American Art, New York, 1949); William H. Gerdts, Jr., *Max Weber, Retrospective Exhibition* (exhibition catalogue, Newark Museum, New Jersey, 1959), illus. no. 23; Ala Story, *First Comprehensive Exhibition in the West, Max Weber* (exhibition catalogue, University of California at Santa Barbara, 1968), illus. on cover.

GRANT WOOD (1892-1942)

306 THE GOOD INFLUENCE

Pencil and watercolor on masonite, 20¼ x 16 inches

Signed l.l.: Grant Wood 1936

PAFA, Collections Fund Purchase, 1952

References: H. W. Janson, "The International Aspects of Regionalism," *College Art Journal,* 2 (May 1943), 110-15; H. W. Janson, "Benton and Wood, Champions of Regionalism," *Magazine of Art,* 39 (May 1946), 184-86, 198-200; Matthew Baigell, "Grant Wood Reinstated," *Art Journal,* 26 (Winter 1966-67), 116-22.

WILLIAM ZORACH (1889-1966)

307 AFFECTION

York fossil marble, 31½ x 10½ x 20 inches

Signed right side of base: Zorach 1933

Munson-Williams-Proctor Institute, Utica, N.Y.

References: Paul S. Wingert, *The Sculpture of William Zorach* (New York, 1959), p. 28, plate 36; William Zorach, *Art is My Life* (Cleveland and New York, 1967), pp. 165, 171.

CONTEMPORARY ART AT THE ACADEMY

EDNA ANDRADE (b. 1917)

308 TORSION

Acrylic on canvas, 40¼ x 40¼ inches

Unsigned; painted 1973

Marian Locks Gallery, Philadelphia

RICHARD ANUSKIEWICZ (b. 1930)

309 SYSTEMATIC WHOLE

Acrylic on canvas, 60¼ x 60¼ inches

Inscribed on back: © 1966/143/Richard Anuskiewicz/1966

PAFA, Lambert Fund Purchase, 1968

References: New Paintings by Anuskiewicz (exhibition catalogue, Sidney Janis Gallery, New York, 1965).

LEONARD BASKIN (b. 1922)

310 SEATED WOMAN

Oak, 54 x 20 x 25 inches

Unsigned; carved 1961

PAFA, Gilpin and Temple Fund Purchase, 1966

References: Leonard Baskin (exhibition catalogue, Bowdoin College Museum of Art, Brunswick, Maine, 1962), cat. no. 29, illus.; *Baskin, Sculpture, Drawings, Prints* (New York, 1970), plate 20; *Sculpture, Drawings, Prints by Leonard Baskin* (exhibition catalogue, National Collection of Fine Arts, Washington, D.C., 1970), fig. 13.

HARRY BERTOIA (b. 1915)

311 TONAL

Copper, nickel, and brass, 72 inches high

Unsigned; constructed 1967

PAFA, Gilpin Fund Purchase, 1968

References: June Kompass Nelson, *Harry Bertoia, Sculptor* (Detroit, 1970).

LEE BONTECOU (b. 1931)

312 GROUNDED BIRD

Bronze, 20 x 62 x 16 inches

Unsigned; cast 1957

PAFA, Temple Fund Purchase, 1960

References: 155th Annual Exhibition of American Painting and Sculpture (exhibition catalogue, Detroit Institute of Arts and PAFA, 1960), illus., cat. no. 30; *Lee Bontecou, Sculpturen* (exhibition catalogue, Museum Boymans-Van Beuningen, Rotterdam, 1968); *Lee Bontecou* (exhibition catalogue, Haus am Waldsee, Berlin, and Städtisches Museum, Berlin, 1968).

ALEXANDER CALDER (b. 1898)

313 ROUTE BARRÉE

Sheet metal and steel wire, 24 x 130 inches

Signed: AC; constructed 1962

PAFA, Gilpin Fund Purchase, 1962

References: James Johnson Sweeney, *Alexander Calder* (exhibition catalogue, Museum of Modern Art, New York, 1943); H. H. Arnason,

Calder (New York, 1966); *Calder: An Autobiography with Pictures* (Boston, 1966).

STUART DAVIS (1894-1964)

314 LETTER AND HIS ECOL
Oil on canvas, 24 x 30¼ inches
Signed u.l.: Stuart Davis; painted ca. 1963
PAFA, Lambert Fund Purchase, 1964

References: E. C. Goossen, *Stuart Davis* (New York, 1959); *Stuart Davis Memorial Exhibition* (exhibition catalogue, National Collection of Fine Arts, et al., 1965), illus. p. 84; Diane Kelder, *Stuart Davis* (New York, 1971), plate 49.

WILLEM DE KOONING (b. 1904)

315 BOUDOIR
Oil on composition board, 27½ x 33¼ inches
Signed l.r.: de Kooning; painted 1951
The William Rockhill Nelson Gallery of Art, Atkins Museum of Fine Arts, Kansas City, Missouri

References: Thomas Hess, *Willem de Kooning* (New York, 1959); *Nelson Gallery-Atkins Museum Handbook,* vol. 1 (1973), illus. p. 209; Harold Rosenberg, *De Kooning* (New York, 1974).

RICHARD DIEBENKORN (b. 1922)

316 INTERIOR WITH DOORWAY
Oil on canvas, 70¼ x 59½ inches
Signed l.l.: R. D. '62; inscribed on back: R. Diebenkorn/Interior — With Doorway/1962
PAFA, Gilpin Fund Purchase, 1964

References: *Richard Diebenkorn* (exhibition catalogue, Pasadena Art Museum, 1960); *Richard Diebenkorn, a Retrospective Exhibition* (exhibition catalogue, Washington Gallery of Modern Art, Jewish Museum, New York, and Pavilion Gallery, Newport Beach, California, 1965); *Richard Diebenkorn: Ocean Park Series* (exhibition catalogue, Marlborough Gallery, New York, 1971).

RICHARD ESTES (b. 1936)

317 THE CANDY STORE
Oil and flourescent paint on canvas, 47¾ x 68¾ inches
Signed l.l.: Painted in 1969 by Richard Estes
The Whitney Museum of American Art, New York

References: James K. Monte, *22 Realists* (exhibition catalogue, Whitney Museum of American Art, New York, 1970), illus. p. 30; *Three Realists: Close, Estes, Raffael* (exhibition catalogue, Worcester Art Museum, Mass., 1974), illus.

PHILIP EVERGOOD (1901-1974)

318 THRESHOLD TO SUCCESS
Oil on panel, 68 x 36 inches
Signed l.r.: Philip Evergood; painted 1955/57
PAFA, Temple Fund Purchase, 1958

References: *Twenty Years of Evergood,* ACA Gallery publication, (New York, 1946); John I. H. Baur, *Philip Evergood* (New York, 1960), plate 80; Lucy Lippard, *The Graphic Work of Philip Evergood* (New York, 1966).

RAFAEL FERRER (b. 1933)

319 NEON CORNER
Galvanized steel and neon tubing, 84 inches high
Signed on paper on transformer: Rafael Ferrer 35/50; constructed 1970
PAFA, Gift of Dr. and Mrs. Paul Todd Makler, 1972

References: *Rafael Ferrer Enclosures* (exhibition catalogue, Institute of Contemporary Art, University of Pennsylvania, Philadelphia, 1971); Rafael Ferrer, *Deseo: an adventure* (exhibition catalogue, Contemporary Arts Center, Cincinnati, 1973).

HELEN FRANKENTHALER (b. 1928)

320 UNTITLED
Gouache on paper, 21½ x 30 inches
Signed u.r.: Frankenthaler 1974
André Emmerich Gallery, New York

References: E. C. Goossen, *Helen Frankenthaler* (exhibition catalogue, Whitney Museum of American Art, New York, 1969); Barbara Rose, *Helen Frankenthaler* (New York, 1971); *Helen Frankenthaler* (exhibition catalogue, Corcoran Gallery of Art, Washington, D.C., 1975).

DUANE HANSON (b. 1925)

321 MAN IN CHAIR WITH BEER
Polyester and fiberglass, 37 x 42 x 65 inches
Unsigned; constructed 1973
The Richard Brown Baker Collection

References: *Duane Hanson, Erste Retrospektive* (exhibition catalogue, Württembergischer Kunstverein, Stuttgart, Neue Galerie, Aachen, and Akademie der Künste, Berlin, 1974), illus.

KARL KNATHS (1891-1971)

322 NUMBER NINE — ELIPHAZ
Oil on canvas, 36 x 60 inches
Signed c.r.: Karl Knaths; painted 1948
PAFA, Temple Fund Purchase, 1951

References: Paintings by Karl Knaths (exhibition catalogue, Art Institute of Chicago, 1942); Paul Mocsanyi, *Karl Knaths* (exhibition catalogue, Phillips Gallery, Washington, D.C., 1957), illus.; *Karl Knaths: Five Decades of Painting* (exhibition catalogue, International Exhibitions Foundation, 1973-74), plate 12.

RICO LEBRUN (1900-1964)

323 THE LISTENING DEAD
Oil on board, 96 x 48 inches
Signed l.l.: Lebrun '57
PAFA, Gift of the Ford Foundation, 1962

References: 157th Annual Exhibition of American Painting and Sculpture (exhibition catalogue, PAFA, 1962), cat. no. 46, illus.; *Rico Lebrun Memorial Exhibition* (exhibition catalogue, Art Gallery of the American Academy of Arts and Letters, New York, 1965-1966); *Rico Lebrun* (exhibition catalogue, Los Angeles County Museum of Art, et al., 1967-69), cat. no. 32.

ROY LICHTENSTEIN (b. 1923)

324 STILL LIFE WITH STRETCHER, MIRROR, AND BOWL OF FRUIT
Oil and magna on canvas, 96 x 54 inches
Signed on reverse: R. Lichtenstein '72
Collection of Sydney and Frances Lewis, Richmond, Virginia

References: Diane Waldman, *Roy Lichtenstein* (exhibition catalogue, Solomon R. Guggenheim Museum, New York, 1969); Diane Waldman, *Roy Lichtenstein* (New York, 1971); *Twelve American Painters* (exhibition catalogue, Virginia Museum of Fine Arts, Richmond, 1974), illus. p. 43.

NOEL MAHAFFEY (b. 1944)

325 ATLANTA, GEORGIA
Acrylic on canvas, 42 x 54 inches
Unsigned; painted 1971
PAFA, Gift of Sydney and Frances Lewis, 1971

References: Udo Kultermann, *New Realism* (Greenwich, 1972).

CONRAD MARCA-RELLI (b. 1913)

326 THE HURDLE
Oil on canvas collage, 56 x 77 inches
Signed l.l.: Marca-Relli; painted 1959
PAFA, Lambert Fund Purchase, 1960

References: Parker Tyler, *Marca-Relli* (Paris, 1960); H. H. Arnason, *Marca-Relli* (New York, 1963); William Agee, *Marca-Relli Retrospective* (exhibition catalogue, Whitney Museum of American Art, New York, 1967).

JOHN MOORE (b. 1941)

327 SUMMER
Oil on canvas, 90 x 75 inches
Unsigned; painted 1972
PAFA, Gift of the Childe Hassam Fund, 1973

References: Udo Kultermann, *New Realism* (Greenwich, 1972).

ISAMU NOGUCHI (b. 1904)

328 GIRL TORSO
Greek marble, 21 x 10 inches
Signed on undersurface: N; carved 1958
PAFA, Gilpin Fund Purchase, 1960

References: Shuzo Takiguchi, *Noguchi* (Tokyo, 1953); John Gordon, *Isamu Noguchi* (New York, 1968); Isamu Noguchi, *A Sculptor's World* (New York, 1968).

CLAES OLDENBURG (b. 1929)

329 SOFT BAKED POTATO, OPEN AND THROWN, SCALE A
Vinyl, canvas, wood, paint, 24 x 40 x 28 inches
Unsigned; constructed 1970
The Sidney Janis Gallery, New York

References: Barbara Rose, *Oldenburg* (exhibition catalogue, Museum of Modern Art, New York, 1970); Ellen Johnson, *Claes Oldenburg* (Baltimore, 1971); Barbara Haskell, *Claes Oldenburg, Object into Monument* (exhibition catalogue, Pasadena Art Museum et al., 1973), illus. p. 14.

ELIZABETH OSBORNE (b. 1936)

330 WEST END POND

Acrylic on canvas, 57 x 65 inches
Inscribed on back: Osborne '73
PAFA, Purchased through the aid of funds from the National Endowment for the Arts, PAFA Women's Committee, and an anonymous donor, 1974

TOMMY DALE PALMORE (b. 1945)

331 I THINK WE'RE ALONE NOW
Acrylic on canvas, 96½ x 72½ inches
Unsigned; painted 1971
PAFA, Gift of Gaye Cooper, 1973
References: New Acquisitions (exhibition catalogue, PAFA, 1973), illus.

PHILIP PEARLSTEIN (b. 1924)

332 TWO FEMALE MODELS—ON HAMMOCK AND SEATED ON FLOOR
Oil on canvas, 72 x 72 inches
Signed l.l.: Pearlstein 74 ©
Private Collection
References: Philip Pearlstein (exhibition catalogue, Georgia Museum of Art, Athens, Wichita Art Museum, and Vassar College Art Gallery, 1970-71); *Philip Pearlstein* (exhibition catalogue, Statliche Museum, Berlin-Dahlem, 1972); McCorquodale, "London Review," *Art International,* 19 (March 20, 1975), illus. p. 30.

ROBERT RAUSCHENBERG (b. 1925)

333 KIESLER POSTER
Offset lithograph, 33¾ x 21⅞ inches
Signed c.r.: Rauschenberg '66
PAFA, Lambert Fund Purchase, 1966
References: Andrew Forge, *Robert Rauschenberg* (New York, 1969); *Rauschenberg Prints, 1948/1970* (exhibition catalogue, Minneapolis Institute of Art, 1970); *Rauschenberg Graphic Art* (exhibition catalogue, Institute of Contemporary Art, University of Pennsylvania, Philadelphia, et al., 1970), illus. p. 20.

THEODORE ROSZAK (b. 1907)

334 ARIADNE
Nickel-silver, steel, 58½ x 32 x 30 inches
Unsigned; constructed 1959
PAFA, Gilpin Fund Purchase, 1968
References: Theodore Roszak: In Pursuit of an Image (exhibition catalogue, Art Institute of Chicago, 1955); H. H. Arnason, *Theodore Roszak* (exhibition catalogue, Walker Art Center, Minneapolis, 1956); *Theodore Roszak Sculpture* (exhibition catalogue, Pierre Matisse Gallery, New York, 1962), cat. no. 17, illus.

RAYMOND SAUNDERS (b. 1934)

335 JACK JOHNSON
Oil on canvas, 81¾ x 63½ inches
Signed l.r.: Saunders; painted 1971
PAFA, Purchased through the aid of funds from the National Endowment for the Arts, PAFA Women's Committee, and an anonymous donor, 1974
References: Blacks, U.S.A. (exhibition catalogue, New York Cultural Center, 1973), illus.

GEORGE SEGAL (b. 1924)

336 GIRL AGAINST A POST
Plaster and wood, 60 x 21 x 20 inches
Unsigned; executed 1974
PAFA, Purchased through the aid of funds from the National Endowment for the Arts, PAFA Women's Committee, and an anonymous donor, 1974
References: William Seitz, *George Segal* (New York, 1972); *Segal* (exhibition catalogue, Centre national d'art contemporain, Paris, 1972); *The Private World of George Segal* (exhibition catalogue, Milwaukee Art History Galleries, University of Wisconsin, 1973).

JULIAN STANCZAK (b. 1928)

337 INTERLOCKING SHADOWS
Liquitex on canvas, 53 x 72 inches
Unsigned; painted 1965
PAFA, Lambert Fund Purchase, 1966
References: Serigraphs and Drawings by Julian Stanczak (exhibition catalogue, Corcoran Gallery of Art, Washington, D.C., 1972).

FRANK STELLA (b. 1935)

338 NAROWLA
Drawing on paper, 32⅜ x 29¾ inches
Signed l.r.; executed 1972
Lawrence Rubin, Knoedler Contemporary Art
References: William Rubin, *Frank Stella* (New York, 1970); *Frank Stella* (exhibition catalogue, Stedelijk Museum, Amsterdam, 1970); Robert Rosenblum, *Frank Stella* (Baltimore, 1971).

YVES TANGUY (1900-1955)

339 ILLIMITED SEQUENCES

Oil on canvas, 39 x 32 inches

Signed l.r.: Yves Tanguy '51

PAFA, Gilpin Fund Purchase, 1953

References: Yves Tanguy, Kay Sage (exhibition catalogue, Wadsworth Atheneum, Hartford, Conn., 1954), illus. no. 26; Pierre Matisse, *Yves Tanguy, a Summary of His Work* (New York, 1963), illus.; *Yves Tanguy* (exhibition catalogue, Acquavella Galleries, New York, 1974), illus.

MARK TOBEY (b. 1890)

340 UNTITLED

Monotype, 39½ x 20¼ inches

Signed l.r.: Tobey 67

PAFA, Lambert Fund Purchase, 1967

References: William Seitz, *Mark Tobey* (exhibition catalogue, Museum of Modern Art, New York, Cleveland Museum of Art, and Art Institute of Chicago, 1962); Wieland Schmeid, *Mark Tobey* (New York, 1966); *Tribute to Mark Tobey* (exhibition catalogue, National Collection of Fine Arts, Washington, D.C., 1974).

ANDREW WYETH (b. 1917)

341 YOUNG AMERICA

Egg tempera on gesso panel, 32½ x 46 inches

Signed l.l.: Andrew Wyeth; painted 1950

PAFA, Temple Fund Purchase, 1951

References: Andrew Wyeth (exhibition catalogue, PAFA et al., 1966), p. 32, illus. p. 33; Richard Meryman, *Andrew Wyeth* (Boston, 1968); Wanda Corn, *Art of Andrew Wyeth* (exhibition catalogue, Fine Arts Museum of San Francisco, 1973).

INDEX OF ARTISTS AND WORKS IN THE EXHIBITION

NOTE: *Page numbers set in italics refer to illustrations*